D1567671

PROJECT MANAGEMENT
The Complete Guide for Every Manager

Clifford Gray

Erik Larson

McGraw-Hill

New York   Chicago   San Francisco
Lisbon   London   Madrid   Mexico City
Milan   New Delhi   San Juan   Seoul
Singapore   Sydney   Toronto

Library of Congress Cataloging-in-Publication Data
Gray, Clifford P.
    Project management : the complete guide for every manager / Clifford Gray and Erik Larson.
        p. cm.
    ISBN 0-07-137601-1
        1. Project management.   I. Larson, Erik W.   II. Title.

HD65.P75 G73 2002
658.4′04—dc21

2001044891

McGraw-Hill

A Division of The McGraw·Hill Companies

1 2 3 4 5 6 7 8 9 0 DOC/DOC 0 9 8 7 6 5 4 3 2

ISBN 0-07-137601-1

This book was set in Times Roman by Matrix Publishing Services.

Printed and bound by R. R. Donnelley & Sons Company.

McGraw-Hill books are available at special quantity discounts to use as premiums and
sales promotions, or for use in corporate training programs. For more information, please
write to the Director of Special Sales, Professional Publishing, McGraw-Hill, Two Penn
Plaza, New York, NY 10121-2298. Or contact your local bookstore.

 This book is printed on recycled, acid-free paper containing a
minimum of 50% recycled, de-inked fiber.

We must not cease from exploration and the end of all exploring will be to arrive where we begin and to know the place for the first time.

T.S. Elliot

To our fellow explorers:
Mary and Ann

CONTENTS

PREFACE

This is an exciting time to be reading a book on project management. Business leaders and experts have proclaimed that project management is the wave of the future. Thomas Stewart, in *Fortune* magazine, asserts that the corporate jungle has a new species: The project manager who will fill the void created by the extinction of middle management.

> If the old middle managers are dinosaurs, a new class of manager mammal is evolving to fill the niche they once ruled: project managers. Unlike his biological counterpart, the project manager is more agile and adaptable than the beast he's displacing, more likely to live by his wits than throwing his weight around.[1]

Similarly, *The Wall Street Journal* reports that more and more of the work in America is project oriented with a beginning, a middle, and an end.[2] This phenomenon is not limited to the United States; it is global. They go on to describe the emergence of project junkies, a growing band of professional gypsies whose careers consist of a series of independent projects.

The demand for project management has created pressure to codify best practices in project management so that wisdom and experience can be passed on to the next wave of project managers. We have written this book to address this need. The book is based on our best-selling textbook *Project Management: The Managerial Process,* which is used in graduate and undergraduate courses around the world. This book is adapted for a professional audience. We have written this book with the practitioner in mind, providing useful tools, concepts, and models to help them successfully complete their projects. At the same time we have not compromised rigor and focused not only on how project management works, but more importantly on why it works. The book is designed as a complete guide and reference. The focus throughout is on basics and the practical best practices. Our objective has been to present the basics so they can be used by the average manager or team member. One criterion for selection of content was whether we "have seen it (the skill, tool, concept) practiced successfully and well."

This book is built around a holistic, integrative view of project management. A holistic view of project management focuses on how projects contribute to the strategic goals of the organization. The linkages for integration include the process of selection of projects which best support organization strategy and all the technical and managerial processes to complete those projects. The goals for prospective project professionals are to clearly understand the role of a project in their organizations and to master project management tools/techniques and interpersonal skills necessary to orchestrate projects to completion.

Audience

This book was written for a professional audience. We see three types of people who would benefit from reading and understanding the content of the book: professionals who are finding that projects are becoming a major part of their work, practicing project managers, and those who are studying for the Project Management Institute (PMI) certification examination. We believe we have presented the most important aspects needed to be a successful project manager.

1. Professionals who have realized that projects are becoming a major part of their work will find the book helpful for learning real-world answers to project problems and for getting a start in developing the skills and tools needed to succeed in this new millennium. Managers with limited project experience will find the book useful to understand why organizations have developed formal project management processes to gain a competitive advantage. Readers will find the concepts and techniques discussed in enough detail to be immediately useful in new project situations.

2. Practicing project managers will find the text a useful guide, handbook, and reference for typical problems that pop up. Practicing project managers often find blank spots in their project management knowledge as they accept larger and riskier projects. Managers will also find the book useful to understand the role of the project in the mission of their organization. This book should serve these managers well.

3. Project management professionals will find the book is well structured to meet the needs of those wishing to prepare for PMP (Project Management Professional) certification. The book has excellent in-depth coverage of the

most critical topics found in PMI's *Project Management Body of Knowledge* (PIMBOK).

Today, it is difficult to imagine anyone at any level in the organization who would not benefit from some degree of expertise in the process of managing projects.

Content

This text is written to provide the reader with a comprehensive, integrative understanding of the project management process. The text focuses both on the science of project management and the art of managing projects. Chapter 1 defines project management and describes the forces that are making project management critical to future business success. Chapter 2 focuses on how organizations go about evaluating and selecting projects. Special attention is devoted to the importance of linking project selection to the mission and strategy of the firm. The organizational environment in which projects are implemented is the focus of Chapter 3. The traditional discussion of matrix management and other organizational forms is augmented by a discussion of the role the culture of the organization plays in the implementation of projects.

The next six chapters focus on developing a plan for the project; after all, project success begins with a good plan. Chapter 4 deals with defining the scope of the project and developing a work breakdown structure (WBS). The challenge of formulating cost and time estimates is the subject of Chapter 5. Chapter 6 focuses on utilizing the information from the WBS to create a project plan in the form of a timed and sequenced network of activities. Risks are a potential threat to project management, and Chapter 7 examines how organizations and managers identify and manage risks associated with project work. Resource allocation is added to the project plan in Chapter 8 with special attention devoted to how resource limitations impact the schedule and budget of the project. Finally, Chapter 9 examines strategies for reducing ("crashing") project duration either prior to the initiation of the project or in response to problems or new demands placed on the project.

Chapters 10 through 12 focus on project implementation and the sociocultural side of project management. Chapter 10 begins by focusing on the role of the project manager as a leader and stresses the importance of managing project stakeholders within the organization. Chapter 11 focuses on the core project team. It combines the latest information on team dynamics with leadership skills/techniques for developing a high-performing project team. Chapter 12 continues the theme of managing project stakeholders by extending it to the management of extra-organizational project relationships (i.e., contractors, customers, suppliers). This chapter also focuses on the art of negotiating, which is a core competency for project management.

Chapter 13 focuses on the kinds of information managers use to monitor project progress, with special attention devoted to the key concept of earned value. Issues surrounding termination or completion of the project are dealt with in Chapter 14. The final chapter looks toward the future of project management, expands on the discussion of project management maturity models, and includes a special segment on pursuing a career in project management.

Throughout this book you will be exposed to the major aspects of the project management system. However, a true understanding of project management comes not from what a scope statement is, or the critical path, or partnering with contractors, but from trying to understand how the different elements of the project management system interact to determine the fate of a project.

The key to success, then, becomes managing conflicting demands and the interaction between different elements of a project (scope, plans, schedule, risk, customer, team, and other stakeholders) not the elements themselves. For example, project managers must manage the interaction among scope, cost, schedule, and customer expectations. They must manage the interaction between the project management information system and the people who provide the data and use it. They must manage the interaction between the core project team and outsiders they are dependent upon.

If by the end of this book, you come to appreciate these key points of balancing your skills in the technical and sociocultural dimensions and managing the interaction among them, you should be better equipped to lead projects.

Acknowledgments

We are grateful to all of the people who helped us complete this project. The book includes contributions from numerous students, colleagues, friends, and managers gleaned from professional conversations. We want them to know we sincerely appreciate their counsel and suggestions.

We want to extend our thanks to all the people at McGraw-Hill for their efforts and support. We'd like to thank Anne G. Seitz and Laura S. Horowitz of Hearthside Publishing Services for managing the final development/production phase of the project.

In addition, we would like to thank our colleagues in the College of Business, Oregon State University, for their support and help. Special thanks go to Karen Bruder, Sharon Carlson, Neil Young, Ann Leen, and Alice Johnson who helped prepare the manuscript.

Finally, we thank all the project managers and professionals who have shared their trials and tribulations over the years—especially those who repeatedly reminded us that it is the people not the tools that complete projects. We have tried to keep this in mind, and we hope that our balanced approach will contribute to future project success.

Clifford F. Gray
Erik W. Larson

1

PROJECT MANAGEMENT TODAY

DaimlerChrysler Introduced New Model
Breakthrough in Hydrogen Fuel Cell Technology Announced
Microsoft Launches New Operating System
State of the Art Football Stadium On Track for Season Opener
FARM AID Concert Raises Millions for Family Farmers
Potential Cure for Leukemia Found

What do the above headlines have in common? They all resulted from project management.

Characteristics of Projects

A **project** is a

- Complex
- Nonroutine
- One-time effort

And the one-time effort is limited by

- Time
- Budget
- Resources
- Performance specifications

All of the work done in most organizations is geared toward satisfying a customer's need. But the characteristics of a project help differentiate it from other corporate endeavors. The major characteristics of projects are:

1. Projects have defined objectives.
2. Projects have a defined life span with a beginning and an end.
3. Projects usually involve several departments and professionals.
4. Projects typically haven't been done before.
5. Projects have specific time, cost, and performance requirements.

Defined Objective

First, projects have a defined objective—for example, constructing a 12-story apartment complex by January 1 or releasing version 4.0 of a specific software package as quickly as possible. This singular purpose is often lacking in daily organizational life in which workers perform repetitive operations each day.

A Beginning and an End

Since there is a specified objective, projects have a defined end point. This is contrary to the ongoing duties and responsibilities of traditional jobs. In many cases, people involved in project management move from one project to the next as opposed to staying in one job. For example, after adding special effects to a sci-fi action film in Miami, a computer graphics engineer may be assigned next to a virtual reality ride in Los Angeles.

Involve Several Professionals

Unlike much organizational work that is segmented according to functional specialty, projects typically require the combined efforts of a variety of specialists. Instead of working in separate offices under separate managers, project participants, whether they are engineers, financial analysts, marketing professionals, or quality control specialists, work closely together under the guidance of a project manager to complete a project.

Haven't Been Done Before

Another distinguishing characteristic of a project is that it is nonroutine and has some unique elements. This is not an either/or issue but a matter of degree. Accomplishing something that has never been done before, such as putting an astronaut on the moon, requires solving previously unsolved problems and using breakthrough technology. On the other hand, even basic construction projects that involve established sets of routines and procedures require some degree of customization that makes them unique.

Specific Time, Cost, and Performance Requirements

Finally, specific time, cost, and performance requirements bind projects. Projects are evaluated according to what they accomplished, at what cost, and how much time they took. These triple constraints impose a higher degree of accountability than you typically find in most jobs. These three also highlight one of the primary functions of project management: balancing the trade-offs between time, cost, and performance while ultimately satisfying the customer.

The Project Approach

The project approach has long been the style of doing business in the construction industry, Department of Defense contracts, and Hollywood as well as at big consulting firms. Now project management is spreading to all avenues of work.

Today project teams carry out everything from port expansions to hospital restructuring to upgrading information systems. The Big Three automakers credit their ability to recapture a significant share of the auto market to the use of project management teams that quickly develop new cars incorporating the latest automotive technology.

The impact of project management is most profound in the area of information technology where the new folk heroes are young professionals whose Herculean efforts lead to the constant flow of new hardware and software products. For a description of some recent management projects, see *Project Management in Action: A Project Management Sampler.*

Project management is not limited to the private sector. Project management is also used for doing good deeds and solving social problems. Organizing a march against cancer, putting on a local soccer tournament, or implementing a campaign against teenage smoking are projects that benefit from the application of modern project management skills and techniques.

The Project Life Cycle

The project life cycle recognizes that projects have a limited life span and that there are predictable changes in level of effort and focus over the life of a project. There are a number of different life-cycle models in project management. Many are unique to a specific industry or kind of project. For example, a new software development

-----

Project Management in Action

A Project Management Sampler

Examples

Projects cut across all business functions and industries. A few recent projects are described below.

  1. Company: Paccar* (number two truck maker in the United States [Peterbilt and Kenworth lines])

  Marketing project: Make the truck industry technically savvy by shifting parts purchasing online, building Web-powered engine-monitoring equipment in each truck, and investing in net start-ups

  Payoff: Cut parts costs by $500,000 a year and expect venture investment payoffs of $20 million

  The system monitors performance of big rigs as they are driven. If a problem is diagnosed, the system fires off an alert to the driver and the next dealership so the parts can be on hand. The system also includes online ordering to eliminate paper pushing with customers, suppliers, and parts sellers.

  2. Company: Cisco*

  Streamlining project: Sales and inventory tracking system linking Cisco with suppliers, manufacturers, and customers

  Payoff: Savings of more than $800 million annually, or 20 percent of its yearly profit

  Orders are input directly by the customer, zapped to the Web ordering system, and fulfilled by outside suppliers. Because suppliers can see the order, they can maintain their inventory in real time with their parts suppliers who operate just-in-time systems.

  3. Company: Science Ministry of North Rhine-Westphalia

  Project: Prototype delivery drone (called Cargo Cap) and test track for 45 miles of tunnel

  Payoff: Traffic problem through the 40-mile corridor between Duisburg and Dortmund (Germany) that sometimes has 200-mile backups

  Ruhr University professors are developing prototypes of conveyance vehicles, infrastructure for the proposed tunnel, and sidetracks. The initial route is to be built under existing highways, will cost about $450 million, and will be paid for by user tolls

  4. Company: FPL, a subsidiary of Florida Power and Light

  Project: Window of opportunity—83 windmill electric generators

  Payoff: 300 megawatts of electric power to meet U.S. energy crunch—one megawatt of power on average is capable of powering 1,000 houses

A Project Management Sampler (continued)

Building and installing 83 wind generators near the Columbia River gorge, located near what is sometimes called the windsailing capital of the world. The cost of electricity should be near 5 cents per megawatt hour and capable of servicing a small city. The generators will be conveniently located near aluminum factories that have been forced to reduce electric power consumption from nearby hydropower dams.

5. Company: United Parcel Service*

Moving the goods project: Expand from delivering packages to helping Net companies with everything from managing inventory to tracking shipments

Payoff: About 500,000 companies worldwide use the full package of UPS online logistic services, generating $1.4 billion in revenue

UPS developed an online system for e-tailers for everything from product delivery and tracking, managing inventories, and dealing with suppliers, to handling billings and payments. Costs are slashed for all stakeholders in the supply chain to the final customer. The UPS system leaves competitors in a catch-up mode.

6. Company: Southwest Airlines*

Customer service project: To make buying tickets online irresistible by emphasizing simplicity and speed over whizzy features

Payoff: Web sales are almost 30 percent of revenues, saving $80 million on agent commissions and other overhead

The Southwest Airlines Web site followed its no-frills, simplicity philosophy of business. The system was so simple, some customers thought they were being scammed. Today its online booking is about 30 percent of its revenue, compared to about 6 percent to 7 percent for other big carriers.

7. Company: Nortel Networks*

Management project: Speed up product development—key tactic: have development teams share ideas and documents on private Web sites

Payoff: Product development time has been cut 90 percent

Nortel uses small work groups to that use customized Web portals to share ideas and documents; for example, collaboration between software developers in India and Canada. The system has reduced the average new product development time to 24 weeks, from the 240 weeks it used to take. In addition, Nortel launched *e2open* that informs suppliers the moment the company receives an order; this system has cut lead time in half.

*See *BusinessWeek,* "Web Smart 50," September 18, 2000, pp. EB43-104 for more detailed descriptions of projects. The report included 50 innovative projects in six major areas: products, streamlining, customer service, marketing, moving goods, and management.

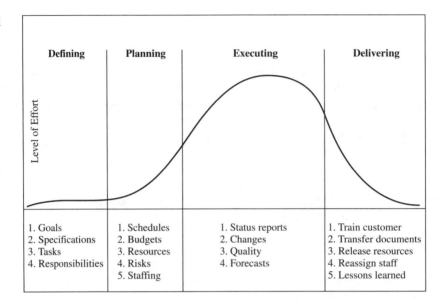

project may consist of five phases: definition, design, code, integration/test, and maintenance. Figure 1–1 shows a typical life cycle for a project.

The project life cycle passes sequentially through four stages:

1. Defining
2. Planning
3. Executing
4. Delivering

The starting point begins the moment the project is given the go ahead. Project effort starts slowly, builds to a peak, and then declines to delivery of the project to the customer.

The Defining Stage

In the *defining* stage, specifications of the project are defined, project objectives are established, teams are formed, and major responsibilities are assigned.

The Planning Stage

In the *planning* stage the level of effort increases and plans are developed that answer such questions as What? When? Who? Quality? Budgets?

The Executing Stage

During the *executing* stage a major portion of the project work takes place—both physical and mental. In this stage the physical product is produced—a bridge, a report, a software program. Time, cost, and specification measures are used for control. Is the project on schedule, on budget, and meeting specifications? What are the forecasts of each of these measures? What revisions/changes are necessary?

The Delivering Stage

The *delivering* stage usually includes two activities: (1) delivering the completed project to the customer, and (2) redeploying the project resources. Delivery of the project might include customer training and transferring documents. Redeployment usually involves releasing project equipment/materials to other projects and finding new assignments for team members.

In practice, the project life cycle is used to outline the timing of major tasks over the life of the project. For example, the design team might plan a major commitment of resources in the defining stage, while the quality team would expect their major effort to increase in the latter stages of the project life cycle. Since most organizations have a number projects going on simultaneously, each at a different stage of its life cycle, careful planning and management are needed for each project and in the total organization.

The Project Manager

Various types of managers exist because they fill special needs. For example, the marketing manager specializes in distributing a product or service, the production manager specializes in conversion of resource inputs to outputs, and the financial manager ensures adequate funds are available to keep the organization viable. In this book, we will call these managers "functional managers."

Project managers have many of the same responsibilities as functional managers: they plan, schedule, motivate, and control. But project managers are unique because they manage temporary, *nonrepetitive* activities and frequently act independently of the formal organization.

Unique functions of project managers

- Project managers are expected to marshal resources to complete a defined project on time, on budget, and within specifications.
- Project managers are the direct link to the customer and must fulfill the customer's expectations while staying within the project specifications.

- Project managers direct, coordinate, and integrate the project team, which is often made up of part-time participants loyal to their functional departments.
- Project managers are responsible for performance (frequently with too little authority). They must ensure that appropriate trade-offs are made between the time, cost, and performance requirements of the project.
- At the same time, unlike their functional counterparts, project managers generally possess only a small proportion of the technical knowledge to make decisions. Instead they must orchestrate the completion of the project by inducing the right people, at the right time, to address the right issues, and to make the right decisions.

Clearly project management is a unique and challenging profession. In this book we will cover the necessary knowledge, perspective, and tools you need for project management.

The Age of Project Management

Project management is no longer a special-need management. It is rapidly becoming a standard way of doing business. Many firms are devoting an increasing percentage of their efforts to defined projects. The future promises an increase in the importance and the role of projects in contributing to the strategic direction of organizations. An influential project management scholar, David Cleland, has declared that this is the dawning of the "Age of Project Management."[1] Below are some of the major driving forces that are providing the momentum and impetus for this new age:

- Compression of product life cycle
- Speed is competitive advantage
- Global competition
- Knowledge explosion
- Corporate downsizing
- Industry consolidation and restructuring

Compressed Life Cycles and Speed

Compression of the product life cycle is perhaps the most significant driving force behind the demand for project managers and management of projects. Speed is becoming an important mode for gaining competitive advantage. Speed also increases the number of new products developed each year, and thus, more projects.

Project Management in Action

The Best Wireless Phone on the Market[2]

In the spring of 1996, a tense team of Nokia Corp. researchers gathered outside of Helsinki, Finland. Their charter: to create a new "icon" among cell phones—something jazzy, like Apple Computer Inc.'s first Macintosh. The marketing division presented a wish list of grueling specs: featherweight, long battery life, and whizzy new features to attract techies. Then came the clincher: It was to be unveiled in Beijing in November 1997—just 20 months away. "We knew that time was our enemy," says project manager Arto Kiema.

What they came up with is Nokia's 6100 series—powerful 4.5-ounce phones about the size and shape of a slim pack of cigarettes.

The saga of the 6100 set a new standard for conquering high-tech markets. Developers began with a simple precept: First, to save money and time, they recycled everything from the complex decoding software to ring menus from earlier, 2100 series phones. For panache, they added new features. But, they confined the innovations to things that wouldn't tax the battery, such as simple computer games, an alarm clock, and an infrared modem for downloading e-mail from data networks.

Most important, Nokia listened to key customers. The Finns went straight to big service providers, such as AT&T, which buys thousands of cell phones and resells them in subscription packages. Such providers want their customers to be able to communicate across frequency bands used by different formats, such as analog and digital cellular and PCs. They also want phones switched on for as many hours as possible to maximize the number of calls received.

Nokia concentrated on ratcheting down power consumption in the handset. For help, it enlisted Texas Instruments Inc. The Dallas-based chip giant came up with proprietary power-saving circuits that brought Nokia handsets from six volts down to three. Nokia then scrambled to redesign other components to run on less power.

The most arduous task Nokia faced was customizing the phone for every major market. Developers built in rudimentary voice recognition for Asia, where keyboards are problematic, and raised the ring volume so the phone could be heard on crowded Asian streets. A bigger challenge was building in extra receivers so the regional models could accommodate all the different formats: GSM digital in Europe and much of Asia and one analog and two digital modes for the splintered U.S. market. "To work through all of the protocols was painful," says Kiema. "Sometimes they're in conflict."

The phones debuted on schedule in China and since then consumers from Sidney to Seville have snapped up an estimated 3 million plus units. Daniel Hesse, CEO of AT&T Wireless proclaimed that the Nokia 6100 was ". . . the best wireless phone on the market, bar none."

The Knowledge Explosion and Global Competition

The knowledge explosion has increased the number of new products each year. The divergent technologies and complexities included in these products have also increased. Coordinating the specialists needed to develop these products is ideally suited to project management.

Increased global competition naturally leads to more attention on customer needs. Meeting the needs of customers frequently means customizing the product. Customizing results in more demand for project management.

Corporate Downsizing and Restructuring

Corporate downsizing and "rightsizing" has left middle management a mere skeleton of its past, with corporations sticking to their core competencies. Project management is replacing middle management.

Industry consolidation is resulting in more cross-culture projects that require close coordination. Project management is ideally suited to manage such international projects.

These driving forces are contributing to the increased demand for project management across all industries and sectors. Membership in the Project Management Institute (PMI), a professional organization for project managers, quadrupled between 1993 and 1997 to 24,000 members. Today PMI membership is more than 83,000 and growing rapidly. Project management appears to be ideally suited for a business environment requiring accountability, flexibility, innovation, speed, and continuous improvement. For example, see *Project Management in Action: The Best Wireless Phone on the Market.*

Today, more and more organizations have come to realize that managing projects can be a vital part of everyone's job. Many companies are beginning to recognize that their entire staff can benefit from being trained in project management. For example, Brian Vannoni, formerly of General Electric Plastics, states:

> We have very few dedicated project managers. Our project managers might be process engineers, they might be scientists, they might be process control technicians, maintenance mechanics, degreed and nondegreed people. A short answer for GE Plastics is that anyone, any level, any function could be a project manager.[3]

Project Management Today—An Integrative Approach

As the world becomes more competitive, it is increasingly important to "get it right the first time" when managing a project. Piecemeal project management systems fail in a number of areas. They often fail to tie to the overall strategies of the firm. Piecemeal priority systems fail to prioritize project selection and allot resources to the projects that contribute most to the strategic plan. Piecemeal tools and techniques fail to be integrated throughout the project life cycle. Piecemeal approaches fail to balance project management with an organization's culture.

Studies consistently point out that about 30 to 45 percent of software development projects fail before completion. These kinds of projects often incur budget and schedule overruns in excess of 200 percent. Surveys show failure to integrate project management processes, absence of management support, and a nonsupportive organization culture to be top reasons for projects failing to reach their objectives.[4]

Fortunately, many organizations are attempting to address these issues by creating an integrated approach to project management. At the organizational level, they emphasize developing an integrated project management process that focuses all efforts toward the strategic plan of the organization. At the individual level, they require project managers to master both project management tools/techniques and the interpersonal skills necessary to orchestrate successful project completion.

For some organizations, integrating projects with strategy requires reengineering the entire business management process. For others, integration means carefully establishing links among the piecemeal systems already in place to focus on one total system. At the individual level, for some professionals to become effective project managers they must augment their leadership and team-building skills with modern project planning and control methods. Others need to complement their administrative skills with the capacity to inspire and lead a divergent cast of professionals to project completion.

Integration in project management directs attention to three key areas. The first area is integration of projects with the strategic plan of the organization. The second area is mastering the process of managing actual projects. The third is evolution of project-driven organization.

Integrating Projects with the Strategic Plan

In some companies, assignments treated as projects often fail to support the strategic plan of the organization. Strategic plans are written by one group of managers, projects are selected by another group, and the projects are implemented by a third. These independent decisions by different groups of managers create a set of conditions that leads to conflict, confusion, and frequently an unsatisfied customer. Under these conditions, the resources of the organization are wasted in non-value-added activities/projects.

An integrated project management system is one in which all of the parts are interrelated. Any change in one of the parts will influence the whole. Every organization has a customer they are seeking to satisfy. The customer sets the *raison d'être* for the organization. Mission, objectives, and strategies are set to meet the needs of customer(s). Developing the mission, objectives, and organization strategies is dependent on external and internal environmental factors. External environmental factors are political, social, economic, and technological: They signal opportunities or threats in setting the direction for the organization. Internal environmental factors are strengths and weaknesses, such as management, facilities, core competencies, and financial condition. Analyzing these environmental factors yields a strategy designed to best meet the needs of customers. But this is only the first step. See Figure 1–2.

Implementing strategies is the most difficult step, and strategies are typically implemented through projects. Creative minds always propose more projects than there are resources. The key is selecting from the many proposals those projects that make the largest and most balanced contribution to the objectives and strategies (and thus, the customer) of the organization. This means prioritizing projects so scarce resources are allocated to the right projects. Once a project has been

FIGURE 1–2

Integrated management of projects

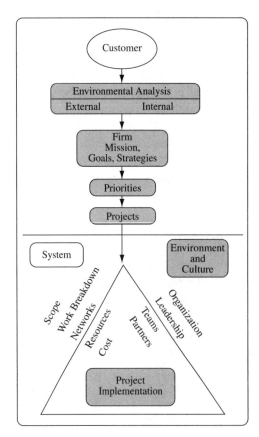

selected for implementation, the focus should switch to the project management process that sets the stage for how the project will be implemented or delivered.

The Process of Managing Projects

There are two dimensions within the project management process: technical and sociocultural.

The Technical Dimension. The first dimension is the technical side of the management process, which consists of the formal, disciplined, pure logic parts of the process. The technical side relies on the formal information system available. This dimension includes planning, scheduling, and controlling projects.

Clear project scope statements should be written to link the project and customer, and to facilitate planning and control. Creating the deliverables and work breakdown structures facilitates planning and monitoring the progress of the project. The work breakdown structure serves as a database that links all levels in the organization, major deliverables, and all work—down to the tasks in a work package.

The impacts of project changes should be documented and traceable. So any change in one part of the project is traceable to the source by the integrated linkages of the system. This integrated information approach can provide all project managers and the customer with decision information appropriate to their level and needs. A successful project manager will be well trained in the technical side of managing projects. See Figure 1–3.

FIGURE 1–3

The technical and socio-cultural dimensions of the project management process

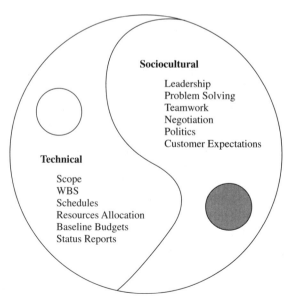

Sociocultural

Leadership
Problem Solving
Teamwork
Negotiation
Politics
Customer Expectations

Technical

Scope
WBS
Schedules
Resources Allocation
Baseline Budgets
Status Reports

The Sociocultural Dimension. The second dimension is the sociocultural side of the project management process. In contrast with the orderly world of project planning, this dimension involves the much messier, often contradictory, and paradoxical world of implementation. It centers on creating a temporary social system within a larger organizational environment tocombine the talents of a divergent set of professionals working to complete the project.

Project managers must shape a project culture that stimulates teamwork and high levels of personal motivation as well as a capacity to quickly identify and resolve problems that threaten project work. This dimension also involves managing the interface between the project and the external environment. Project managers have to assess and shape expectations of customers, sustain the political support of top management, negotiate with their functional counterparts, monitor subcontractors, and so on. Overall the manager must build a cooperative social network among a divergent set of allies with different standards, commitments, and perspectives.

Some suggest that the technical dimension represents the "science" of project management while the sociocultural dimension represents the "art" of managing a project. To be successful, managers must be a master of both. Unfortunately, some project managers become preoccupied with the planning and technical dimension of project management. Often their first real exposure to project management is through project management software, and they become infatuated with network charts, Gantt diagrams, and performance variances and attempt to manage a project from a distance. Conversely, there are other managers who manage projects by the "seat of their pants", relying heavily on the team dynamics and organizational politics to complete a project. Successful project managers balance their attention to both the technical and sociocultural dimensions of project management.

Evolution of Project Driven Organizations

Many firms have found it useful to apply project management maturity models as the foundation for directing and measuring progress toward integration, developing the skills of project managers, and creating a supportive organization culture. Project management maturity models have been around for some time—for example the capability maturity model (CMM) was developed in the late 1980s to guide organizations in implementing concrete best practices of managing software development projects.[5]

Figure 1–4 presents a typical schematic of a maturity model.[6] Each level represents an advance in the use of benchmarked project management best practices.

Following is a short description of each level:

- **Level one:** absence of, or unpredictability in, a process for developing a project plan that includes cost, time, and performance

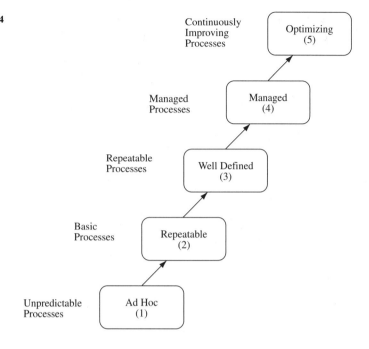

FIGURE 1–4

Capability maturity model (CMM)

- **Level two:** repeatable processes used primarily on large mission-critical projects
- **Level three:** well-defined processes that are integrated with organization processes
- **Level four:** highest level with seamless, integrated, holistic project systems and processes that include strategic decisions that take into account project selection, plans, performance, and lessons learned
- **Level five:** continuous improvement by archiving and using lessons learned to improve project management execution

Our best guess estimate is that most companies are in the throes of moving from level two to level three and that less than 10 percent of those firms that actively practice project management are at level four or five. This book is designed to provide the necessary tools and perspectives to professionals and managers so that they can lead their organization up the ladder of project management excellence.

Summary

There are powerful environmental forces contributing to the rapid expansion of project management approaches to business problems and opportunities. A project is defined as a nonroutine, one-time effort limited by time, resources, and performance specifications designed to meet customer needs. One of the distinguishing characteristics of project management is that it has both a beginning and an end. It typically consists of four phases: defining, planning, executing, and delivering. Effective project management begins with selecting and prioritizing projects that support the firm's mission and strategy. Successful implementation requires mastering both the technical and the sociocultural dimensions of the process.

2

ALIGNING PROJECTS WITH ORGANIZATION STRATEGIES

If you don't know where you are going, any road will take you there.
Confucius

Projects and the Strategic Plan

A strong linkage between the strategic plan and projects is important. Making that linkage happen requires continuous attention from top and middle management. There are many medium and large organizations in which the managers cannot identify a project's priority and link it with the strategic plan. The larger and more diverse an organization, the more difficult it is to create and maintain this strong link. A commonly heard complaint of project managers is that projects seem to appear out of nowhere.

Every project should contribute value to the organization's strategic plan, which is designed to meet the future needs of its customers. There is ample evidence that many organizations have not developed a process that clearly aligns project selection to the strategic plan. The result is that the organization's resources—people, money, equipment, and core competencies are poorly used. Conversely, there is ample evidence that organizations with a coherent link between projects and strategy have more cooperation across the organization, perform better on projects, and have fewer projects.

How can an organization ensure this link and alignment? The answer requires integrating projects with the strategic plan. To do so, an organization must have a strategic plan and a process for prioritizing projects according to their contribution to the plan. It is crucial to create a process that is open and published for all participants to review.

This chapter presents an overview of the importance of strategic planning and the process for developing a strategic plan. Typical problems encountered when strategy and projects are not linked are outlined. We will give a generic methodology that ensures integration by creating very strong linkages of project selection and priority to the strategic plan. The intended outcomes are:

- Clear organization focus
- Best use of scarce organization resources (people, equipment, capital)
- Improved communication across projects and departments

Why Project Managers Need to Understand the Strategic Management Process

In today's world of organization *downsizing,* the process of strategic planning has come to include participants from nearly every level of the organization—as opposed to only senior management. There is a distinct trend toward a top-down *and* bottom-up approach to strategic management that encourages commitment from stakeholders at every level. Project managers are finding themselves a part of this process and are becoming more involved in strategic planning and the project selection process. This participation is good for several reasons:

- Involvement gives the project manager an overall perspective of the organization focus, which typically leads to professional growth and more reasoned decisions.
- Experienced project managers can provide valuable insights concerning organizational capabilities and resource constraints.
- Each project manager can see his or her project in relation to other projects.
- Awareness of the selection criteria and process facilitates reassignment of resources and priorities among projects in a less hostile manner.
- Every project manager must be prepared to identify and justify how his or her project contributes to the organization focus and direction.

Project managers should find it valuable to have a keen understanding of strategic management and the project selection process.

The Strategic Management Process: An Overview

Strategic management is the process of assessing "what we are" and deciding and implementing "what we intend to be and how we are going to get there." Strategy describes how an organization intends to compete with the resources available in the existing and perceived future environment.

Two major dimensions of strategic management are:

1. Responding to changes in the external environment
2. Allocating scarce resources of the firm to improve its competitive position

The first dimension means that organizations must constantly scan the external environment for changes to survive in a hostile competitive environment. The second dimension is the internal responses to new action programs aimed at enhancing the competitive position of the firm. The nature of the responses depends on the type of business, environment volatility, competition, and the organizational culture.

Strategic management provides the theme and focus of the future direction of the organization:

- It supports consistency of action at every level of the organization.
- It encourages integration because effort and resources are committed to common goals and strategies.
- It is a continuous, iterative process aimed at developing an integrated and coordinated long-term plan of action.

Strategic management positions the organization to meet the needs and requirements of its customers for the long term. With the long-term position identified, objectives are set, and strategies are developed to achieve objectives and then translated into actions by implementing projects. Strategy can decide the survival of an organization. Most organizations are successful in *formulating* strategies for what courses they should pursue. However, the problem in many organizations is *implementing* strategies—that is, making them happen. Integration of strategy formulation and implementation often does not exist.

The components of strategic management are closely linked, and all are directed toward the future success of the organization. Strategic management requires strong links among mission, goals, objectives, strategy, and implementation.

- The *mission* gives the general purpose of the organization.
- *Goals* give global targets within the mission.
- *Objectives* give specific targets to goals.
- Objectives give rise to formulation of *strategies* to reach those objectives.
- Finally, strategies require actions and tasks to be *implemented.*

In most cases the actions to be taken represent projects. Figure 2–1 shows a schematic of the strategic management process and major activities required. *Project Management in Action: Sample Strategies to Recapture Market Growth* shows examples of strategies formulated to reach specified objectives.

FIGURE 2–1

*Strategic
Management
Process*

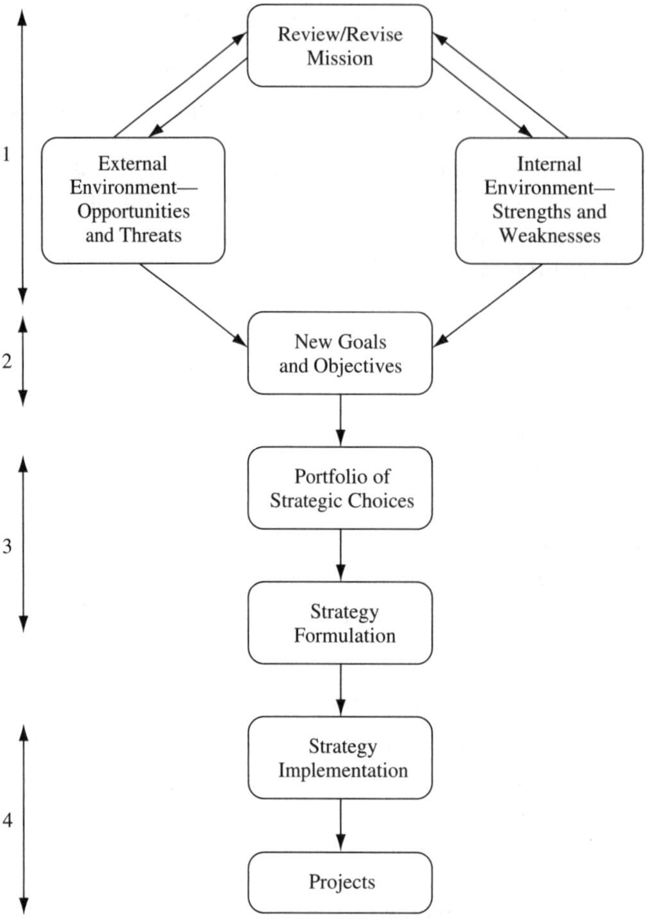

The Strategic Management Process: Four Activities

The typical strategic management process includes four activities:

1. Review and define the organizational mission.
2. Set long-range goals and objectives.
3. Analyze and formulate strategies to reach the objectives.
4. Implement strategies through projects.

These four activities are described below.

Activity 1: Review and Define the Organizational Mission.   The mission identifies "what we want to become" or the *raison d'être*. Mission statements identify the scope of the organization in terms of its product or service. Everyone in the

Project Management in Action

Sample Strategies to Recapture Market Growth

There are many strategies designed to gain a competitive advantage. For example, price leadership, cost leadership, franchising, quality, innovation, design, and niche markets are only a few of the hundreds you might find in practice. Two design strategies to recapture market growth are described here.

Apple Steps Back to Recapture the Student Education Market

Apple's approach was to appeal to the niche student market by emphasizing design and a plethora of features that appeal to students. Apple, known for high-risk strategies, developed the iBook for this niche market. The new 2001 iBook includes features such as DVDs, read and write CDs, wireless Ethernet, a full complement of ports, an attractive white box small enough to fit into a backpack, and lighter (4.9 pounds) than most textbooks to meet the needs of students and educators. Apple's development of PowerSchool® used by more than 3,000 schools encourages sales of iBook.

Apple's design strategy has also resulted in the gold award for best product design of the year—2001 for their Titanium Powerbook G4 for mobile computing.

Thermos Changes Its Approach to Product Development When Market Growth Fades

With market growth going flat, Thermos CEO Monte Peterson wanted a completely new concept in grilling. His solution to the problem was to break down the highly functional, bureaucratic organization culture by creating a cross-functional team charged with the collective responsibility to think out of the box and develop a new type of electric grill. Up front the team knew it would be responsible for the complete design, manufacture, and marketing of the new product. The team came up with a new type of electric grill that is hot enough to sear foods and produce a cookout taste. The dedicated team and collective responsibility facilitated solutions to many problems usually encountered in the traditional functional approach where each department worked independently in the design, building, and marketing phases of the new product. The new grill won four design awards and company grill sales increased 13 percent the first year.

organization should be keenly aware of the organization's mission. For example, one consulting firm requires partners who fail to recite the mission statement on demand to buy lunch. A written mission statement provides focus for decision making when shared by organizational managers and employees. The mission statement communicates and identifies the purpose of the organization to all stakeholders. Mission statements can be used for evaluating organization performance.

Traditional components of mission statements are:

- Major products and services
- Target customers and markets
- Geographical domain

In addition, statements frequently include organizational philosophy, key technologies, public image, and contribution to society. Researchers Pearce and David found that mention of such factors in mission statements related to business success.[1] Mission statements change infrequently. However, when the nature of the business changes or shifts, it may require a revised mission statement. For example, the break up of American Telephone and Telegraph (AT&T) required a shift in mission from telecommunications to information handling.

More specific mission statements tend to give better results because of a tighter focus. Mission statements decrease the chance of false directions by stakeholders. For example, compare the phrasing of the following mission statements:

- Provide bridge design services.
- Provide waste plant design services.
- Provide engineering services.
- Increase shareholder value.
- Providing high value products to our customer.

Clearly, the first two statements leave less chance for misinterpretation than the others. A rule-of-thumb test for a mission statement is, *if the statement can be anybody's mission statement, it will not provide the guidance and focus intended.* It is important that the mission statement be clear and concise, because the mission sets the parameters for developing objectives.

Activity 2: Set Long-Range Goals and Objectives.   Objectives translate the organization mission into specific, concrete, measurable terms:

- Organizational objectives set targets for all levels of the organization.
- Objectives pinpoint the direction managers believe the organization should move toward.
- Objectives answer in detail *where* the firm is headed and *when* it is going to get there.

Typically, objectives for the organization cover markets, products, innovation, productivity, quality, finance, profitability, and people. In every case, objectives should be as operational as possible. That is, objectives should include a time frame, be measurable, be an identifiable state, and be realistic. Doran created a memory device—SMART—that is useful when writing objectives:[2]

S	**Specific**	Be specific in targeting an objective
M	**Measurable**	Establish a measurable indicator(s) of progress
A	**Assignable**	Make the objective assignable to one person for completion
R	**Realistic**	State what realistically can be done with available resources
T	**Time related**	State when the objective can be achieved, that is, its duration

Each level below the organizational objectives should support the higher level objectives in more detail. For example, if a firm making leather luggage sets an objective of achieving a 40 percent increase in sales through a research and development strategy, this charge is passed to the marketing, production, and R&D (research and development) departments. The R&D department accepts the firm's strategy as its objective, and its strategy becomes the design and development of a new "pull-type luggage with hidden retractable wheels." At this point the objective becomes a project to be implemented—to develop the retractable wheel luggage for market within 6 months and within a budget of $200,000. See Figure 2–2 for a schematic of the linkages.

A similar schematic is also shown for an engineering firm in Figure 2–2. The engineering firm sets an objective to diversify by entering the waste treatment plant market. This objective becomes the strategy for its design department. In turn, this strategy becomes an objective for the engineering department that decides on a strategy of specializing in the design and construction management of solid waste plants. Implementation becomes a project of designing three technologically advanced solid waste plants to meet the needs of local governmental groups, within 8 months at a budget of $500,000.

Activity 3: Analyze and Formulate Strategies to Reach Objectives. Formulating a strategy answers the question of *what* needs to be done to reach objectives. Strategy formulation includes determining and evaluating alternatives that support the organization's objectives and selecting the best alternative.

The first step is a realistic evaluation of the past and current position of the enterprise. This step typically includes an analysis of who the customers are and what their needs are as they (the *customers)* see them.

SWOT Analysis. The next step is an assessment of the internal and external environments. The goal of this analysis is to attempt to forecast fundamental

FIGURE 2–2

*Strategy,
Objectives,
and Project
Linkages*

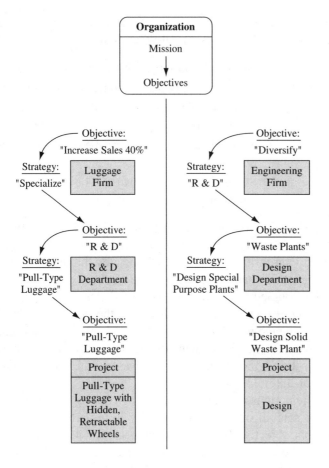

industry changes and stay in a proactive mode rather than a reactive one. This assessment is known as the SWOT analysis:

S	**Strengths**
W	**Weaknesses**
O	**Opportunities**
T	**Threats**

Strengths and Weaknesses.   What are the internal strengths and weaknesses of the enterprise? Examples of internal strengths or weaknesses could be core competencies such as technology, product quality, management talent, low debt, and dealer networks. Managers can alter the strengths and weaknesses.

Opportunities and Threats.   The external environment is viewed as opportunities and threats. They are the flip sides of the same coin. That is, a threat can be perceived as an opportunity, or vice versa. Examples of perceived external threats could be a slowing of the economy, a maturing life cycle, exchange rates, or government regulation. Typical opportunities are increasing demand, emerging markets, and demographics. Managers or individual firms have limited opportunities to influence such external environmental factors; however, in recent years, notable exceptions have been new technologies (laser scanning, computers) and alliances (Kodak's and Fuji's joint development of film standards for the industry).[3]

SWOT Conclusions.   From this analysis, critical issues and an assortment of strategic alternatives are identified. These alternatives are compared with the current portfolio and available resources; strategies are then selected that should support the basic mission and objectives of the organization. Critical analysis of the strategies includes asking questions:

- Does the strategy take advantage of our core competencies?
- Does the strategy exploit our competitive advantage?
- Does the strategy maximize meeting customers' needs?
- Does the strategy fit within our acceptable risk range?

Strategy formulation ends with cascading objectives or tasks assigned to lower divisions, departments, or individuals. Strategy formulation is a relatively straightforward process when compared with planning how strategies will be implemented. A rule of thumb for management effort in formulating strategy might range around 20 percent, while determining *how* strategy will be implemented might consume 80 percent of management's effort.

Activity 4: Implement Strategies through Projects.   Implementation answers the question of *how* strategies will be realized, given available resources. The conceptual framework for strategy implementation lacks the structure and discipline found in strategy formulation. Implementation requires action and completing tasks; the latter frequently means mission-critical projects. Therefore, implementation must include attention to several key areas.

Allocating Resources.   First, completing tasks requires allocation of resources. Resources typically represent funds, people, management talents, technological skills, and equipment. Multiple objectives place conflicting demands on organizational resources, so it is important to allocate resources carefully.

Organizational Support.   Second, implementation requires both the formal and informal structures within an organization to complement and support strategy and projects. Authority, responsibility, and performance all depend on organization structure and culture.

Planning and Control.   Third, planning and control systems must be in place. These systems are necessary to be certain that project activities are effectively performed.

Motivating Project Teams.   Fourth, motivating project contributors (managers and teams) is a major factor for achieving project success.

Prioritizing Projects.   Finally, an area receiving more attention in recent years is prioritizing projects. Although the strategy implementation process is not as clear as strategy formulation, all managers realize that without implementation success is impossible.

Absence of a Priority System Linked to Strategy Creates Problems

We have identified three main problems that result from the absence of a priority system that is linked to the organizational strategy:

1. The implementation gap
2. The organizational politics of project selection
3. Multiple projects, resource contentions, and multitasking

Problem 1: The Implementation Gap

In organizations with short product life cycles, it is interesting to note that participation in strategic planning and implementation frequently includes participants from all levels within the organization. However, in perhaps 80 percent of the remaining product and service organizations, top management pretty much formulates strategy and then leaves the strategy implementation to functional managers. The functional managers then develop more detailed strategies and objectives. The fact that these objectives and strategies are made *independently* at different levels by functional groups within the organizational hierarchy causes manifold problems.

Some symptoms of organizations struggling with strategy disconnect and unclear priorities are:

- Frequent conflicts among functional managers and lack of trust
- Frequent meetings to establish or renegotiate priorities

- Frequent shifting of people among projects, depending on current priority
- People assigned to multiple projects
- People feeling inefficient because of multiple assignments
- Inadequate resources

Since clear linkages do not exist, the organizational environment becomes dysfunctional and confused the organization strategy is ineffectively implemented, and the projects lose focus. Well documented by researchers, these phenomena are categorized as the **"implementation gap."** The implementation gap refers to the lack of understanding and consensus of organization strategy among top and middle-level managers.[4]

Example of an Implementation Gap. We have seen the following scenario many times: Top management identifies 20 projects for the next planning period, without prioritizing them. Each functional department—marketing, finance, operations, engineering, information technology, and human resources—selects projects from the list to implement. But, the departments don't choose the same projects in the same order. So a project that rates first in the IT department could rate tenth in the finance department. Implementing the projects then causes conflicts of interest, and animosities develop over organization resources.

The Implementation Gap Is a Serious Problem. Unfortunately, this type of information gap and lack of uniform priorities across departments is not uncommon. The problem is serious and widespread. One study found that about only 25 percent of *Fortune* 500 executives believe there is a strong linkage, consistency, and/or agreement between the strategies they formulate and implementation.[5] Another large study found that middle managers considered organizational strategy to be under the purview of others or not in their realm of influence.[6]

The research of Fusco suggests the implementation gap and prioritizing projects are still overlooked by many organizations. He surveyed 280 project managers and found that 24 percent of their organizations did not even publish or circulate their objectives; in addition, 40 percent of the respondents reported that priorities among competing projects were not clear, while only 17 percent reported clear priorities.[7] The link between strategy and projects cannot be overlooked if the firm intends to compete in today's turbulent, competitive world.

It is the responsibility of senior management to set policies that show a distinct link between organizational strategy and objectives and projects that implement those strategies. *Project Management in Action: The SAS Turnaround* describes the results that a well-implemented strategy can bring.

Project Management in Action

The SAS Turnaround

During the early 1980s Jan Carlzon was appointed chief operating officer for Scandinavian Airlines (SAS). At this time the entire airline industry was in the middle of a slump, and SAS was about to record a second straight year of losses. Carlzon halted the practice of instituting across-the-board cuts and instead focused on developing a strategic mission that would make SAS profitable during a time of zero market growth. The strategy was to make SAS known as the best airline in the world for the frequent business traveler. SAS realized that business travelers were the most stable part of the market and tended to purchase full-fare tickets as opposed to discounted tickets. Furthermore, business travelers tended to have unique needs that would allow SAS to develop services to attract their full-fare business.

Under Carlzon's leadership, SAS scrutinized every project and expense as to whether it contributed to improving the service to the frequent business traveler. If the answer was no, no matter what it was or how dear it was to those within SAS, it was cut. Projects such as developing vacation packages to the Mediterranean were eliminated, and overall SAS was able to cut $40 million in nonessential expenses. At the same time, Carlzon persuaded the SAS board to invest $45 million and increase operating expenses $12 million a year for 147 different projects designed to attract and serve the frequent business traveler. They launched a comprehensive punctuality campaign, improved the traffic hub in Copenhagen, and offered customer service courses for more than 12,000 staff members.

SAS dropped first class seating and created "Euro-Class" at full-fare coach prices. They installed movable partitions in their aircraft to separate the Euro-Class section from the others. They were among the first airlines to create comfortable lounges at the terminals with telephone and telex services for Euro-Class passengers. They gave Euro-Class travelers separate, express check-in counters, more comfortable seats, and better food.

The results were startling. Within 3 years SAS increased the number of full-fare business passengers by 23 percent at a time when the overall market was stagnant. *Fortune* magazine conducted a survey that named SAS the best airline for business travelers in the world. The SAS story illustrates how a clear mission allows an organization to concentrate its limited resources on those projects that increase the profitability and success of the firm.

Problem 2: Organizational Politics and Project Selection

Politics and projects are inextricably linked in most organizations. Politics can play a role not only in project selection but also in the aspirations behind projects. Individuals can enhance their power within an organization by managing extraordinary and critical projects.[8] Power and status naturally accrue to successful innovators and risk takers rather than to steady producers. Similarly, managers can become heroes within their organization by leading projects that contribute significantly to the organization's mission or solve a pressing crisis. Many ambitious managers pursue high-profile projects as a means for moving quickly up the corporate ladder. For example, Lee Iacocca's career was built on successfully leading the design and development of the highly successful Ford Mustang.

Studies on innovation highlight the role that *project sponsors* play in the selection and successful execution of projects.[9] Project sponsors are typically high-ranking managers who endorse and lend political support for the completion of a specific project. They are instrumental in winning approval of the project and in protecting the project during the critical development stage. Savvy project managers recognize the importance of having "friends in higher courts" who can advocate for their case and protect their interests.

Within companies, the term "sacred cow" is often used to denote a project that a powerful, high-ranking official is advocating. For example, a marketing consultant confided that he was once hired by the marketing director of a large firm to conduct an independent, external market analysis for a new product the firm was interested in developing. His extensive research indicated that there was insufficient demand to warrant the financing of this new product. The marketing director chose to bury the report and made the consultant promise never to share this information with anyone. The director explained that this new product was the "pet idea" of the new CEO, who saw it as his legacy to the firm. He went on to describe the CEO's irrational obsession with the project and how he constantly referred to it as his "new baby." Like a parent fiercely protecting his child, the CEO might fire the marketing director if such critical information ever became known.

An Example of Destructive Organizational Politics. The significance of corporate politics can be seen in the ill-fated ALTO computer project at Xerox during the mid-1970s. The project was a tremendous technological success; it developed the first workable mouse, the first laser printer, the first user-friendly software, and the first local area network. All of these developments were 5 years ahead of their nearest competitor. During the next 5 years this opportunity to dominate the nascent personal computer market was squandered because of infighting at Xerox and the absence of a strong project sponsor.[10]

All Projects Have Political Ramifications. Some would argue that politics and project management should not mix. A more proactive response is that projects and politics invariably mix and that effective project managers recognize that any significant project has political ramifications. Likewise, top management needs to develop a system for identifying and selecting projects that reduces the impact of internal politics and fosters the selection of the best projects for achieving the mission and strategy of the firm.

Problem 3: Multiple Projects, Resource Contentions, and Multitasking

Most organizations work on many projects at once. This environment creates the problems of project interdependency and the need to share resources. For example, if a construction company wins a new contract it is bidding on, what impact will it have on the labor resource pool? Will existing labor be adequate to deal with the new project given the completion date? Will current projects be delayed? Will subcontracting help? Which projects will have priority?

Competition among project managers can be contentious. All projects managers seek to have the best people for their projects. The problems of sharing resources and scheduling resources across projects grow exponentially as the number of projects rises. In multiproject environments, the stakes are higher and the benefits or penalties for good or bad resource scheduling become even more significant than in most single projects.

Resource sharing also leads to multitasking. Multitasking involves starting and stopping work on one task to go and work on another project, and then returning to the work on the original task. People working on several tasks concurrently are far less efficient, especially where conceptual or physical shutdown and start-up are significant. Multitasking adds to delays and costs. Changing priorities exacerbate the multitasking problem even more. Likewise, multitasking is more evident in organizations that have too many projects for the resources they command.

The number of small and large projects in a portfolio almost always exceeds the available resources (typically by a factor of three to four times the available resources). This capacity overload inevitably leads to confusion and inefficient use of scarce organizational resources. The presence of an implementation gap, of power politics, and of multitasking adds to the problem of which projects are allocated resources first. Employee morale and confidence suffer because it is difficult to make sense of an ambiguous system. A multiproject organization environment faces major problems without a priority system that is clearly linked to the strategic plan.

Moving to an Effective Project Selection System

To this point we have suggested that many organizations do not effectively address the problems we have described. The issues that need to be resolved are:

- How can the implementation gap be narrowed so that understanding and consensus of organizational strategies run through all levels of management?

- How can power politics be minimized?
- Can a process be developed in which projects are consistently prioritized to support organizational strategies?
- Can the prioritized projects be used to allocate scarce organizational resources—for example, people and equipment?
- Can the process encourage bottom-up initiation of projects that support clear organizational targets?

The first and most important change that will go a long way in addressing these and other problems is the development and use of a meaningful project priority process for project selection. To do so, you need a set of integrative criteria and a process for evaluating and selecting projects that support higher level strategies and objectives. A single project priority system that ranks projects by their contribution to the strategic plan would make life easier. This is easily said, but is sometimes difficult to accomplish in practice. Gaining support for a project priority system is a major step forward.

Creating Support for a Central Portfolio Management System

Survey the Stakeholders. The suggestion that a rigorous project priority system be used to select which projects will be budgeted and staffed is frequently met with skepticism and resistance.[11] Typical responses include the following:

1. We already have a priority system. All of our projects are very important.
2. Come on. We all know which projects have first priority.
3. Our business world changes each day. We don't need a system that locks us out of opportunities. Priorities change.
4. Let's not rock the boat. We're getting along. The cream projects always rise to the top.

Resistance responses such as these almost always suggest a deep need for a project priority system. Developing a project priority system will not happen without top management support and a demonstrated need for all stakeholders. Individuals and small groups at *all* levels in the organization need to be asked to address the general problem of why projects do not achieve their desired impact. This can be accomplished through a questionnaire or by having consultants interview staff. The outcomes can be consolidated into a table or a fishbone diagram that is then communicated to major stakeholders.

The following answers are typical when a survey asks "Why don't projects achieve their desired impact?"

1. No consistent project approval system exists.
2. Many individuals can approve projects.

3. There is little evidence that project priority is communicated downward.
4. Priorities are set outside the chain of command—several priority systems exist.
5. Functional areas protect turf.
6. Human resources for projects are not budgeted.
7. Priorities are set without regard to strategic plan.
8. No consistency in applying criteria to projects exists.
9. It is not acceptable to refuse project assignments because of lack of resources.
10. No feedback system exists to gauge the effect of new projects on current projects.
11. Pet projects of powerful individuals receive higher priority.
12. No central clearing system of projects exists.
13. Production is always first.

Sometimes the same information can be more clearly summarized in a fishbone diagram to demonstrate the need for a priority system, as shown in Figure 2–3. The fishbone diagram is also an excellent tool for analyzing and isolating symptoms and causes of problems.

It is interesting to see the commonality of answers, regardless of industry or organization size; all groups tend to identify similar problems and even major classifications of problems. The survey results reinforce the issue of project problems and identify some of the causes of the problem, which is the lack of a uniform priority system. Using a survey questionnaire helps major stakeholders agree that there is a problem and helps them reach a consensus that change is needed.

Survey of Projects in Process.   Another factor that can support buy-in of stakeholders to a project priority system is an additional survey of projects in process and proposed projects accepted. Consultants or an internal task force collect a list of all of the projects in process and planned for an organization. The outcome is usually enlightening and startling! The projects easily fall into three categories. Here are the figures for one such survey:

1. Repetitive operations that are not projects—e.g., quarterly financial statements	180
2. Projects less than $50,000 or projects less than 500 labor hours	109
3. "Real" projects	72
Total	361

FIGURE 2–3

Cause-and-Effect Worksheet Example

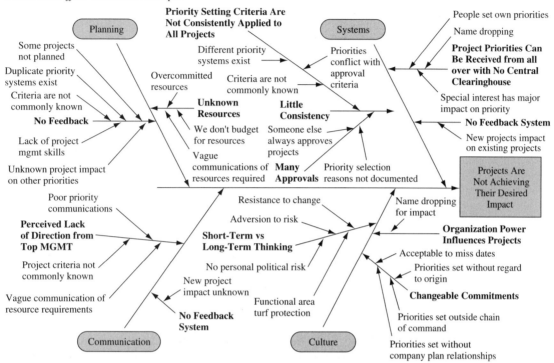

These results are typical in product and service organizations.[12] First, many projects are repetitive and represent the basic daily operations of the organization. These recurring activities should be handled and scheduled by the departments responsible and not be treated as projects.

Second, projects that require few labor hours or represent a relatively small dollar value do not individually sabotage implementation of high-impact projects. However, such projects in total can have a profound effect on important projects by gobbling up critical resources. Analyzing these small projects regularly may point out that they contribute little or nothing to the strategic plan or to meeting the needs of the customer. Many can then be eliminated.

Finally, the remaining "real" projects are those that clearly contribute significantly to the organization's mission, goals, and strategies. The linkage can be identified. Figure 2–4 assigns several projects to two categories with similar results.

FIGURE 2–4

*Project
Portfolio
Matrix*

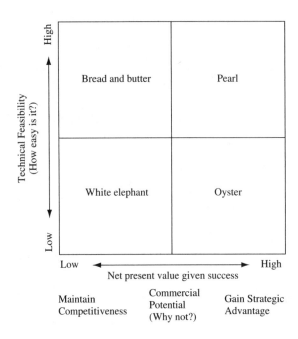

Getting Buy-In from Stakeholders.   The results and implications of our survey are serious! Planned and proposed *real* projects typically overcommit resources by a factor of four over a 5-year planning horizon. Some projects need to be eliminated. The total set of real projects lacks focus. This situation suggests the strategic plan had not been communicated effectively to middle management. The hierarchical arrangement of objectives and strategies had not taken place, and the middle managers were not active contributors to the process. No formal system existed for prioritizing projects to optimize their contribution to the strategic plan. The results of using the processes just described are usually earth shaking enough to gain buy-in that some kind of priority system is needed to select and monitor projects.

A Generic Project Portfolio Management System

Now that all stakeholders have agreed that a project portfolio management system is needed, it is time to design one. Design of a project portfolio system should include the following:

- Classification of projects
- Selection criteria depending upon classification

- Sources and solicitation of project proposals
- Responsibility for prioritizing
- Managing the portfolio system
- Balancing risk within the portfolio

Classification of Project

Most organizations find they have three different kinds of projects in their portfolio:

- Compliance and emergency (must do) projects
- Operational projects
- Strategic projects

Figure 2–5 shows a portfolio of projects by type. Anyone generating a project proposal should classify their proposal by type, so the appropriate criteria can be used to evaluate their proposal.

Compliance Projects.   Compliance projects are typically those needed to meet regulatory conditions required to operate in a region, so they are called "must do" projects. Emergency projects, such as rebuilding a soybean factory destroyed by fire, meet the must do criterion. Compliance and emergency projects usually have penalties if they are not implemented.

Operational Projects.   Operational projects are those that are needed to support current operations. These projects are designed to improve efficiency of delivery systems, reduce product costs, or improve performance. TQM projects are examples of operational projects.

FIGURE 2–5

Portfolio of Projects by Type

Strategic Projects.   Finally, strategic projects are those that directly support the organization's long-run mission. They frequently are directed toward increasing revenue or market share. Examples of strategic projects are new products, research, and development.

Selection Criteria Depending on Classification

It is not necessary to have exactly the same criteria across the different types of projects discussed above (strategic and operations). However, experience shows most organizations use similar criteria across all types of projects, with perhaps one or two criteria specific to the type of project. Regardless of criteria differences among different types of projects, the most important criterion for selection is the project's fit to the organization strategy. Therefore, this criterion should be consistent across all types of projects and carry a high priority, relative to other criteria. This uniformity across all priority models used can keep departments from suboptimizing the use of organization resources.

The variety of models available to practitioners is unlimited. Picking a selection model depends on the nature of the organization. For example, factors such as industry, organization size, risk-aversion level, technology, competition, markets, and management style may strongly influence the form of the model used to select projects. Some organizations use three models as suggested earlier: must do, operations, and strategic. Regardless, the processes for selection and implementation are very similar.

In the past, financial criteria were used almost to the exclusion of other criteria. However, in the last two decades we have witnessed a dramatic shift to include multiple criteria in project selection that are strongly aligned to organization strategy. For example, having a product line to serve the complete needs of the customer could mean adding a product (project) that has no direct return on investment, but will ultimately increase total sales.

Succinctly, profitability alone simply is not an adequate measure of contribution; however, it is still an important criterion, especially for projects that enhance revenue and market share such as breakthrough R&D projects. A detailed discussion of financial models is beyond the scope of this text; however, two financial models are briefly mentioned here to give the reader a sense of the nature and potential problems of financial models.

Financial Model: Payback.   The *payback model* measures the time it will take to recover the project investment. Shorter paybacks are more desirable. Payback is the simplest and most widely used model. Payback emphasizes cash flows, a key factor in business. Some managers use the payback model to eliminate unusually risky projects (those with lengthy payback periods). The major limitations of payback are that it ignores the time value of money, assumes constant cash flows for the investment period (and not beyond), and does not consider profitability.

Financial Model: NPV. The *net present value (NPV) model* uses management's minimum desired discount rate of return (for example, 20 percent) to compute the present value of all cash inflows and outflows. If the result is positive, and the project meets the minimum desired rate of return, it is eligible for further consideration. Higher positive NPVs are desirable. Figure 2–6 presents simple examples of the payback and NPV models.

FIGURE 2–6

Financial Project Selection Criteria

Given Data for Two Potential Projects:		
	Project A	*Project B*
Cost of project	$720,000	$600,000
Estimated annual cash inflow	125,000	180,000
Estimated useful life of project	5 years	5 years
Required rate of return	20%	20%
$\text{Payback Period} = \dfrac{\textbf{Investment}}{\textbf{Annual Net Savings}} = $ **5.8 years**		**3.3 years**
Rate of return*	17.4%	30.0%

NPV (Net Present Value)

Present value of annual net cash inflows

Project A $125,000 × 2.991[†]	$383,870	
Project B $180,000 × 2.991		$538,380
Investment	(−720,000)	(−600,000)
NPV	($−346,130)	($−61,620)

Outcomes:

Payback:

Project A is 5.8 years. Reject, longer than life of project (5 years)

Project B is 3.3 years. Accept, less than 5 years and exceeds 20% desired rate of return

Net Present Value:

Reject both projects because they have negative net present values.

* The reciprocal of payback yields the average rate of return (e.g., 125/720 × 100 = 17.4%).

[†] Present value of an annuity of $1 for 5 years at percent. These values can be found in annuity tables of standard accounting and finance texts.

Project Management in Action

Y2K Projects

Anecdotal remarks of Y2K pundits and informal surveys suggested that about 80 percent of Y2K project managers believed they had too little time to complete proper testing of their projects by December 31, 1999. Advocates of multiple screening criteria for selection of projects were quick to point out that many Y2K projects were started too late. Their explanation was that Y2K projects did not add to the bottom line. Therefore, those organizations depending on the return on investment (ROI) criterion for project selection never allowed Y2K projects to rise to the top of the priority list. Finally, when national attention focused on the seriousness of the problem and the year 2000 neared, organizations bypassed the ROI criterion and used criteria such as urgency, improved customer service, minimization of loss, and must do projects to justify Y2K projects.

Most of the Y2K latecomers found their projects costing much more because of the necessity to crash activity times and the unavailability of qualified human resources. In fact, some IT managers found it necessary to visit retirement homes to recruit old-timers who had COBOL programming skills that could be used to reprogram older business programs. Because the cost of Y2K projects ran into billions of dollars, earlier recognition of the seriousness of the problem and earlier implementation of Y2K projects would have resulted in significant savings and avoided the very real business risks of not meeting the year 2000 deadlines.

From Figure 2–6 the payback method suggests accepting project B because it has a payback of 3.3 years. However, the NPV model rejects both projects, which have negative present values of −$346,130 and −$61,620, because it considers the time value of money. The NPV model is more realistic because it considers the time value of money, cash flows, and profitability. This example demonstrates the major shortcoming of the payback model and why model selection is important. *Project Management in Action: Y2K Projects* shows the value of viewing projects from a number of perspectives before accepting or rejecting them.

Today, senior management is interested in identifying the potential mix of projects that will yield the best use of human and capital resources to maximize return on investment in the long run. Factors such as researching new technology, public image, ethical position, protection of the environment, core competencies, and strategic fit might be important criteria for selecting projects. Multiple screening criteria seem the best alternative to meet this need.[13] After selection criteria have been determined, project proposals can be solicited.

Sources and Solicitation of Project Proposals

As you would guess, projects should come from anyone who believes his or her project will add value to the organization. However, many organizations restrict proposals from specific levels or groups within the organization. This could be an opportunity lost. Good ideas are not limited to certain types or classes of organization stakeholders. Encourage and keep solicitations open to all sources, both internal and external.

It is a rare organization that does not have more project proposals than are feasible. This is especially true in project-driven organizations. Culling through so many proposals to identify those that add the most value requires a structured process. Figure 2–7 shows a flow chart of a screening process beginning with the creation of an idea for a project.

FIGURE 2–7

Project Screening Process

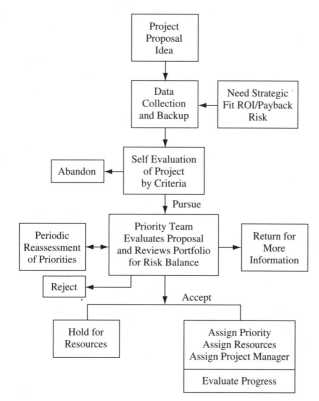

Data and information are collected to assess the value of the proposed project to the organization and for future backup. If the sponsor decides to pursue the project on the basis of the collected data, it is forwarded to the project priority team (or the project office). Note that the sponsor knows which criteria will be used to accept or reject the project. Given the selection criteria and current portfolio of projects, the priority team rejects or accepts the project. If accepted, the priority team sets implementation of the project in motion.

Selection Process.   The strategic value of a proposed project must be determined before it can be placed in the project portfolio. Under rare circumstances, there are projects that must be selected. These compliance or emergency projects are those that must be implemented or the firm will fail or suffer dire penalties or consequences. For example, a manufacturing plant must install an electrostatic filter on top of a smokestack in 6 months or close down. French courts are trying to force Microsoft to open their software architecture to allow competing software firms to be compatible and interact with Microsoft. This decision may become a compliance project for Microsoft. Any project placed in the "must" category ignores other selection criteria. A rule of thumb for placing proposed project in this category is that 99 percent of the organization stakeholders would agree that the project must be implemented; there is no choice but to implement the project.

All other projects are selected using criteria linked to organization strategy. Examples of multiple selection criteria are described next.

Applying Selection Criteria.   Selection criteria need to mirror the critical success factors of an organization. For example, 3M set a target that 25 percent of the company's sales would come from products fewer than 4 years old versus the old target of 20 percent. Their priority system for project selection strongly reflects this new target. On the other hand, failure to pick the right factors will render the screening process useless in short order.

Figure 2–8 represents a hypothetical project screening matrix. The screening criteria selected are shown across the top of the matrix (stay within core competencies, ROI [return on investment] of 8 percent plus). Management weights each criterion (a value of 0 to a high of, say, 3) by its relative importance to the organization's objectives and strategic plan. Project proposals are then submitted to a project priority team or project office.

Each project proposal is then evaluated by its relative contribution/value added to the selected criteria. Values of 0 to a high of 10 are assigned to each criterion for each project. This value represents the project's fit to the specific criterion. For example, project 1 appears to fit well with the strategy of the organization because it is given a value of 8. Conversely, project 1 does nothing to support

FIGURE 2–8

*Project
Screening
Matrix*

Criteria Weight	Stay within core competencies	Strategic fit	Urgency	25% of sales from new products	Reduce defects to less than 1%	Improve customer loyalty	ROI of 18% plus	Weighted Total
	2.0	3.0	2.0	2.5	1.0	1.0	3.0	
Project 1	1	8	2	6	0	6	5	66
Project 2	3	3	2	0	0	5	1	27
Project 3	9	5	2	0	2	2	5	56
Project 4	3	0	10	0	0	6	0	32
Project 5	1	10	5	10	0	8	9	102
Project 6	6	5	0	2	0	2	7	55
Project *n*	5	5	7	0	10	10	8	83

reducing defects (its value is 0). Finally, this model applies the management weights to each criterion by importance using a value of 1 to 3. For example, ROI and strategic fit have a weight of 3, while urgency and core competencies have weights of 2. Applying the weight to each criterion, the priority team derives the weighted total points for each project. For example, project 5 has the highest value of 102 $[(2 \times 1) + (3 \times 10) + (2 \times 5) + (2.5 \times 10) + (1 \times 0) + (1 \times 8) + (3 \times 9) = 102]$ and project 2 a low value of 27. If the resources available create a cutoff threshold of 50 points, the priority team would eliminate project 2 and project 4. Project 5 would receive first priority, project *n* second, and so on. In rare cases where resources are severely limited and project proposals are similar in weighted rank, it is prudent to pick the project placing less demand on resources. Weighted multiple criteria models similar to this one are rapidly becoming the dominant choice for prioritizing projects.[14,15]

Responsibility for Prioritizing

Prioritizing can be an uncomfortable exercise for managers. Prioritizing means discipline, accountability, responsibility, constraints, reduced flexibility, and loss of power. Top management commitment means more than giving a blessing to the priority system; it means management will have to rank and weigh, in concrete terms, the objectives and strategies they believe to be most critical to the organization. This public declaration of commitment can be risky if the ranked objectives later prove to be poor choices, but setting the course for the organization is top management's job. The good news is, if management truly is trying to direct the organization to a strong future position, a good project priority system supports their efforts and develops a culture in which everyone feels a part of contributing to the goals of the organization.

Managing the Portfolio System

Managing the portfolio requires constant effort. The priority system can be managed by a small group of key employees in a small organization. Or, in larger organizations, the priority system can be managed by the project office or the enterprise management group.

Senior Management Input.   Management of a portfolio system requires two major inputs from senior management. First, senior management must provide guidance in establishing selection criteria that strongly align with the current organization strategies. Second, senior management must decide annually how they wish to balance the available organizational resources (people and capital) among the different types of projects. A preliminary decision of balance must be made by top management (e.g., 20 percent compliance, 50 percent strategic, and 30 percent operational) before project selection takes place, although the balance may be changed when the projects submitted are reviewed. Given these inputs the priority team or project office can carry out their many responsibilities, which include supporting project sponsors and representing the interests of the total organization.

Priority Team Responsibilities.   The *priority team,* or *project office,* is responsible for publishing the priority of every project and ensuring the process is open and free of power politics. For example, most organizations using a priority team or project office use an electronic bulletin board to disperse the current portfolio of projects, the current status of each project, and current issues. This open communication discourages power plays. Over time the priority team evaluates the progress of the projects in the portfolio. The priority team is also responsible for reassessing organization goals and priorities and changing priorities if conditions dictate. How well this whole process is managed can have a profound impact on the success of an organization.

Constant scanning of the external environment to determine if organizational focus and/or selection criteria need to be changed is imperative! Periodic priority review and changes need to keep current with the changing environment and keep a unified vision of organization focus. Regardless of the criteria used for selection, each project should be evaluated by the same criteria. If projects are classified as must do, operation, and strategic, each project in its class should be evaluated by the same criteria. Enforcing the project priority system is crucial. Keeping the whole system open and aboveboard is important to maintaining the integrity of the system and keeping executives from going around the system. For example, communicating which projects are approved, project ranks, current status of in-process projects, and any changes in priority criteria will discourage people from bypassing the system.

Balancing Risk within the Portfolio

A major responsibility of the priority team is to balance projects by type and by risk. This requires a total organization perspective. Hence, a proposed project that satisfies most criteria may not be selected because the organization portfolio already includes too many projects with the same characteristics—e.g., project risk level, use of key resources, competency based projects, capability based projects, high cost, non-revenue-producing, long durations. Balancing the portfolio of projects is as important as project selection. David and Jim Matheson studied R&D organizations and found the typical portfolio of projects includes too many projects with low probability of success and/or low expected strategic value or commercial success. They developed a project portfolio matrix that could be used for assessing a project portfolio. They labeled the matrix quadrants "white elephants," "bread and butter," "pearl," and "oyster" projects. Revisit their matrix in Figure 2–4. The Mathesons believe the portfolio mix should include more projects in the "pearl" and "oyster" quadrants.[16] Although their research centers on R&D organizations, their observations appear to hold over all types of project organizations.

Some projects may have to be put on hold. If a project meets all the selection criteria and is deemed worthwhile, the reasons for placing the project on hold or even rejecting the project should be carefully explained to the project sponsor. Also, some form of appreciation and recognition should be given for creativity and innovation.

In summary, centralized project priority systems support a holistic approach to aligning projects with organizational strategy. The system is proactive rather than reactive. The project portfolio represents a process for controlling the use of scarce resources and balancing risk across the organization. Today, project-driven organizations are using project offices to integrate organizational goals and strategy with projects using a portfolio of projects selected by a proactive project priority system. The important point is that some project priority system must to be in place, managed by some group within the organization.

Only one priority system can exist for each type of project—for example, operational or strategic. It is important to ensure all projects of a class are evaluated by the same consistent criteria. It is critical to communicate priority criteria to all organizational stakeholders. Every project selected should be ranked and the results published. Senior management must take an active role in setting priorities and supporting the priority system. Going around the priority system will destroy its effectiveness. The project priority team needs to consist of seasoned managers who are capable of asking tough questions and distinguishing facts from fiction. Resources (people, equipment, and capital) for major projects must be clearly allocated and not conflict with daily operations or become an overload task. The priority system must respond quickly to changes. An appeal process should be included in the system; all appeals and responses should be open and documented.

Assessing the Effectiveness of the Priority System over the Long Haul—The Balanced Scorecard Model

Project priority models select which actions (projects) best support organizational strategy. The balanced scorecard model complements the project priority selection process. It is more "macro" in perspective than project priority selection models. This model measures the *results* of major activities taken to support the overall vision, mission, and goals of the organization. It helps answer the question, "Did we succeed in what we intended to do?" American Express, the U.S. Department of Transportation, Mobil, Kaiser Permanente, National Semiconductor, and others are known to be using their own customized models of the balanced scorecard.

The scorecard model limits measures of performance to goals in four main areas:[17,18]

1. Customer measures
2. Internal measures
3. Innovation and learning measures
4. Financial measures

For example, a performance measure for a customer might be industry ranking for sales, quality, or on-time projects. Internal measures that influence employees' actions could be time-to-market or reduction of design time to final product. Innovation and learning measures frequently deal with process and product innovation and improvement. For example, the percentage of sales or profit from new products is often used as a performance goal and measure. Project improvement savings from partnering agreements are another example of an innovation and learning measure. Finally, financial measures such as ROI, cash flow, and projects on budget reflect improvement and actions that contribute value to the bottom line.

These four perspectives and performance measures keep vision and strategy at the forefront of employees' actions. The basic assumption underlying the balanced scorecard model is that people will take the necessary actions to improve the performance of the organization on the given measures and goals. The balanced scorecard model and project priority selection models should never be in conflict with each other. If a conflict exists, both models should be reviewed and conflicts eliminated. When both models are used in project-driven organizations, focus on vision, strategy, and implementation are reinforced. Both models encourage employees to determine the actions needed to improve performance.

Summary

Project portfolio management systems have emerged out of pressure from multiple competing projects, limited skilled resources, dispersed virtual teams, time-to-market pressures, and limited capital. This systems approach serves as the infrastructure for handling multiple projects and linking upper management and the project manager. The most important pieces to this systems approach are creation of criteria that are used to select and prioritize projects among competing needs.

The priority system focuses attention on the mission and major goals of the organization. The system forces management to develop a mission and goals that are highly operative, not motherhood and apple pie statements such as "maximize shareholder's wealth." A single project priority system that links strategy formulation and implementation fills a void found in many product and service organizations. Most importantly, a relative ranking system must be developed that ties the long range plan to projects. The major value of a project priority system is not in the numbers but rather in identifying areas of disagreement and gaining consensus on direction. The resultant priority system provides focus at all levels in the organization and furnishes the basis for effective allocation of scarce human and non-human resources. The system results in bottom-up proposals from front line managers who have the expertise, who are closest to the customer, and who have a clear vision of where the organization is headed. The process encourages the entrepreneurial spirit and allows individual project initiators to flourish.

When strategy and projects are closely aligned and projects are readily recognized as the primary vehicle to implement strategy, the next challenge is to establish a consistent, formal, disciplined process for managing the implementation of projects. In theory this may appear to be a contradiction since all projects are different and teams need autonomy to act freely. However, the absence of strategy linkage and a consistent process for managing projects creates serious problems. It is possible to meet both conditions and not strangle organization innovation and the motivation of self-directed teams. The balanced score card method is useful as a reality check on your priority system over the long run.

3

ORGANIZATION: STRUCTURE AND CULTURE

Successful project management can flourish within any structure, no matter how terrible the structure looks on paper, but the culture within the organization must support the four basic values of project management: cooperation, teamwork, trust, and effective communication.
Harold Kerzner[1]

Once an organization decides to initiate a project, the question then becomes: how should we implement the project? This chapter examines three different project management structures commonly used by firms to implement projects:

- Functional organization
- Dedicated project teams
- Matrix structure

In addition, the emergence of what is being called the *virtual organization* will be discussed. Although not exhaustive, these structures represent the major approaches for organizing projects. The advantages and disadvantages of each of these structures are briefly discussed as well as some of the critical factors that might lead a firm to choose one form over the others.

Whether a firm chooses to complete projects with independent project teams, within the traditional functional organization, or through some form of matrix arrangement is only part of the story. Anyone who has worked for more than one organization realizes that there are often considerable differences in how projects are managed within certain firms with similar structures. Working in a matrix system at IBM is significantly different from working in a matrix environment at

Motorola. Many researchers would attribute these differences to the *organizational culture* at IBM and Motorola. A simple explanation of organizational culture is that it reflects the "personality" of an organization. Just as each individual has a unique personality, so each organization has a unique culture. Toward the end of this chapter, we will examine in more detail what organizational culture is and the impact that the culture of the parent organization has on organizing and managing projects.

Both the project management structure and the culture of the organization constitute major elements of the environment in which projects are implemented. It is important for project managers and participants to know the "lay of the land" so that they can avoid obstacles and take advantage of pathways to complete their projects.

Organizing Projects within the Functional Organization

One approach to organizing projects is simply to manage them within the existing functional hierarchy of the organization. Once management decides to implement a project, the different segments of the project are delegated to the respective functional units with each unit responsible for completing its segment of the project. (see Figure 3–1). Coordination is maintained through normal management

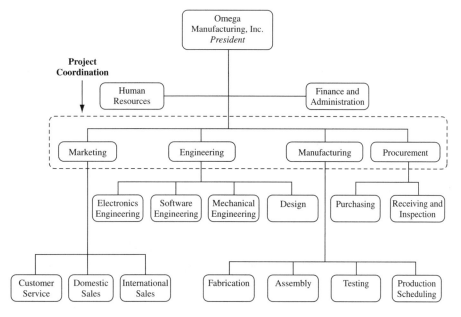

FIGURE 3–1

Functional Organization

channels. For example, a tool manufacturing firm decides to differentiate its product line by offering a series of tools specially designed for left-handed individuals. Top management decides to implement the project, and different segments of the project are distributed to appropriate areas. The industrial design department is responsible for modifying specifications to conform to the needs of left-handed users. The production department is responsible for devising the means for producing new tools according to these new design specifications. The marketing department is responsible for gauging demand and price as well as identifying distribution outlets. The overall project will be managed within the normal hierarchy, with the project being part of the working agenda of top management.

The functional organization is also commonly used when, given the nature of the project, one functional area plays a dominant role in completing the project or has a dominant interest in the success of the project. Under these circumstances, a high-ranking manager in that area is given the responsibility of coordinating the project. For example, a top-ranking manager in the firm's facilities department would manage the transfer of equipment and personnel to a new office. Likewise, the information systems department would manage a project involving the upgrading of the management information system. In both cases, most of the project work would be done within the specified department and coordination with other departments would occur through normal channels.

Advantages

There are several advantages to organizing projects within the existing functional organization.[2] First, unlike what we will see with matrix management, there is no radical alteration in the design and operation of the parent organization. Second, there is flexibility in the use of staff. Appropriate specialists in different functional units can be assigned temporarily to work on the project and then return to their normal work. Finally, normal career paths within a functional division are maintained. While specialists can make significant contributions to projects, their functional field is their professional home and the focus of their professional growth and advancement.

Disadvantages

Just as there are advantages for organizing projects within the existing functional organization, there are also disadvantages. These disadvantages are particularly pronounced when the scope of the project is broad and one functional department does not take the dominant technological and managerial lead on the project. For example, projects implemented within the functional organization often suffer from a lack of project focus. Each functional unit has its own core routine work to do; sometimes project responsibilities get pushed aside to meet primary obligations. Another serious weakness is poor integration across functional units. There is a tendency to suboptimize the project with respective functional specialists being concerned with their segment of the project only and not the total project. Another disadvantage is that it generally takes longer to complete projects through this functional arrangement. This is in part attributable to slow response time—project information and decisions have to be circulated through normal management channels. Furthermore, the lack of direct communication among functional groups contributes to rework as specialists realize the implications of others' actions after the fact.

Organizing Projects As Dedicated Teams

At the other end of the spectrum is the creation of independent project teams. These teams operate as separate units from the rest of the parent organization. Usually a full-time project manager is designated to pull together a core group of specialists who work full-time on the project. The subsequent team is physically separated from the parent organization and given the primary directive of accomplishing the objectives of the project (see Figure 3–2).

FIGURE 3–2

Dedicated Project Team

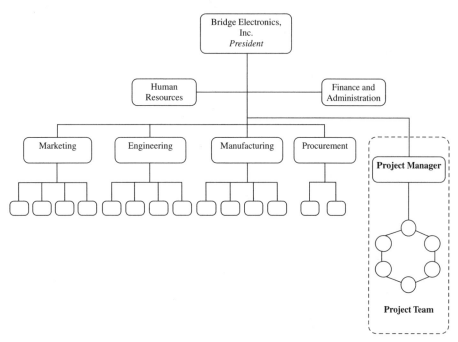

The interface between the parent organization and the project team will vary. In some cases the parent organization prescribes administrative and financial control procedures over the project. In other cases, firms allow the project manager maximum freedom to get the project done given the resources originally assigned to the project. At Apple, the project team that developed the Macintosh computer was isolated in a separate building, away from corporate noise and interference, and given the prime directive to develop a breakthrough computer as quickly as possible.

In the case of firms where projects are the dominant form of business, such as a construction firm or a consulting firm, the entire organization is designed to support project teams. Instead of one or two special projects, the organization consists of sets of quasi-independent teams working on specific projects. The main responsibility of traditional functional departments is to assist and support these project teams. For example, the marketing department is directed at generating new business that will lead to more projects, while the human resources department is responsible for managing a variety of personnel issues as well as recruiting and training new employees. This type of organization is referred to in the literature as a *projectized* form of organization and is graphically portrayed in Figure 3–3.

FIGURE 3–3

Projectized Organization Structure

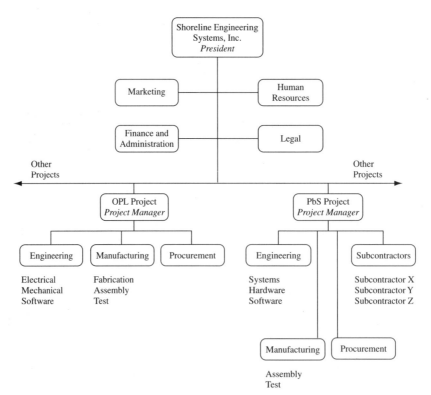

Advantages

As in the case of functional organization, the dedicated project team approach has advantages and disadvantages. One advantage is that it is a relatively simple means for completing a project that does not directly disrupt ongoing operations. Other than taking away resources in the form of specialists assigned to the project, the functional organization remains intact with the project team operating independently. A second advantage is speed. Projects tend to get done more quickly when dedicated teams are created. Participants devote their full attention to the project and are not distracted by other obligations and duties. Furthermore, response time tends to be quicker because most decisions are made within the team and are not deferred up the hierarchy. Another factor that contributes to speed of completion is the high level of motivation and cohesiveness that often emerges within the project team. Participants share a common goal that contributes to improved cross-functional integration.

Disadvantages

In many cases, the project team approach is the optimum approach for completing a project when you view it solely from the standpoint of what is best for completing the project. Its disadvantages become more evident when the needs of the parent organization are taken into account. For example, creating self-contained project teams to complete projects is expensive. Not only have you created a new management position (project manager), but resources are also assigned on a full-time basis. This can result in duplication of efforts across projects and a loss of economies of scale.

Another disadvantage is that sometimes dedicated project teams become an entity of their own and a disease known as *projectitis* develops (see *Project Management in Action: Projectitis: The Dark Side of Project Teams*). A strong we–they divisiveness emerges between the project team and the parent organization. This divisiveness can undermine not only the integration of the eventual outcomes of the project into mainstream operations but also the assimilation of project team members back into their functional units once the project is completed. Assigning full-time personnel to a project also creates the dilemma of what to do with personnel after the project is completed. If other project work is not available, then the transition back to their original functional departments may be difficult due to their prolonged absence and the need to catch up with recent developments in their functional area.

Organizing Projects within a Matrix Arrangement

Matrix management is a hybrid organizational form in which a horizontal project management structure is "overlaid" on the normal functional hierarchy. In a matrix system, there are usually two chains of command, one along functional lines

Project Management in Action

Projectitis: The Dark Side of Project Teams

One of the advantages of creating dedicated project teams is that participants from different functional areas develop into a highly cohesive work team that is strongly committed to completing the project. While such teams often produce Herculean efforts in pursuit of project completion, there is a negative dimension to this commitment that is often referred to in the literature as *projectitis*. A we–they attitude can emerge between project team members and the rest of the organization. The project team succumbs to *hubris* and develops a holier-than-thou attitude that antagonizes the parent organization. People not assigned to the project become jealous of the attention and prestige being showered on the project team, especially when they believe that their hard work is financing the endeavor. The gap between the project team and the parent organization tends to widen when the teams are given special perks and exotic titles such as "Silver Bullets" and "Tiger Teams."

Such appears to have been the case with Apple's highly successful Macintosh development team. Steve Jobs, who at the time was both the chairman of Apple and the project manager for the Mac team, pampered his team with perks including at-the-desk massages, coolers stocked with freshly squeezed orange juice, a Bosendorfer grand piano, and first-class plane tickets. No other employees at Apple got to travel first class. Jobs considered his team to be the elite of Apple and had a tendency to refer to everyone else as "Bozos" who "didn't get it." Engineers from the Apple II division, which was the bread and butter of Apple's sales, became incensed with the special treatment their colleagues were getting.

One evening at Ely McFly's, a local watering hole, the tensions between Apple II engineers seated at one table and those of a Mac team at another boiled over. Aaron Goldberg, a long-time industry consultant, watched from his barstool as the squabbling escalated. "The Mac guys were screaming, 'We're the future!' The Apple II guys were screaming, 'We're the money!' Then there was a geek brawl. Pocket protectors and pens were flying. I was waiting for a notebook to drop, so they would stop and pick up the papers."[3]

Although comical from a distance, the discord between the Apple II and Mac groups severely hampered Apple's performance during the 1980s. John Sculley, who replaced Steve Jobs as chairman of Apple, observed that Apple had evolved into two "warring companies" and referred to the street between the Apple II and Macintosh buildings as "the DMZ" (demilitarized zone).[4]

and the other along project lines. Instead of delegating segments of a project to different units or creating an autonomous team, project participants report simultaneously to both functional and project managers.

Companies apply this matrix arrangement in a variety of ways. Some organizations set up temporary matrix systems to deal with specific projects, while the matrix may be a permanent fixture in other organizations. Let us first look at its general application and then proceed to a more detailed discussion of the finer points. Consider Figure 3–4. There are three projects currently underway: A, B, and C. All three project managers (PM A–C) report to a director of project management, who supervises all projects. Each project has an administrative assistant although the one for project C is only part-time.

Project A involves the design and expansion of an existing production line to accommodate new metal alloys. To accomplish this objective, Project A has assigned to it 3½ people from manufacturing and 6 people from engineering. These individuals are assigned to the project on a part-time or full-time basis, depending on the project's needs during various phases of the project.

Project B involves the development of a new product that requires the heavy representation of engineering, manufacturing, and marketing. Project C involves forecasting changing needs of an existing customer base. While these three projects, as well as others, are being completed, the functional divisions continue performing their basic core activities.

The matrix structure is designed to utilize resources optimally by having individuals work on multiple projects while being capable of performing normal functional duties. At the same time it attempts to achieve greater integration by creating and legitimizing the authority of a project manager.

FIGURE 3–4

Matrix Organization Structure

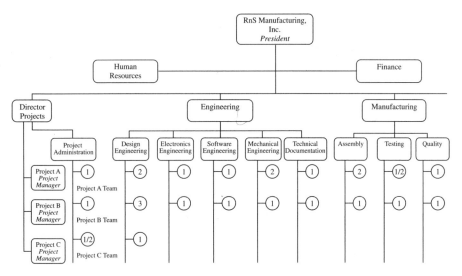

Different Matrix Forms

In practice there are really different kinds of matrix systems, depending on the relative authority of the project and functional managers.[5] *Lightweight matrix* or *functional matrix* are titles given to matrices in which the balance of authority strongly favors the functional managers. *Balanced matrix* or *middleweight matrix* is used to describe the traditional matrix arrangement. *Heavyweight matrix* or *project matrix* is used to describe a matrix in which the balance of authority is strongly on the side of the project manager.

The relative difference in power between functional managers and project managers is reflected along a number of related dimensions. One such dimension is level of reporting relationship. A project manager who reports directly to the chief executive officer (CEO) has more clout than a marketing manager who reports to the vice president (VP) of marketing. Location of project activities is another subtle but important factor that determines relative influence. A project manager wields considerably more influence over project participants if they work in his or her office than if they perform their project-related activities in their functional offices. Likewise, the percentage of full-time staff assigned to the project contributes to relative influence. Full-time status implies transfer of obligations from functional activities to the project.

Ultimately, whether the matrix is weak or strong, a functional or project matrix is determined by the extent to which the project manager has direct authority over participants. Authority may be determined informally by the persuasive powers of managers involved and the perceived importance of the project or formally by the prescribed powers of the project manager. Below is a thumbnail sketch of the three kinds of matrices:

- **Functional matrix:** This form is very similar to a functional approach with the exception that there is a formally designated project manager responsible for coordinating project activities. Functional managers are responsible for managing their segment of the project. The project manager basically acts as a staff assistant who draws the schedules and checklists, collects information on status of work, and facilitates project completion. The project manager has indirect authority to expedite and monitor the project. Functional managers call most of the shots and decide who does what and when the work is completed.
- **Balanced matrix:** This is the classic matrix in which the project manager is responsible for defining what needs to be accomplished while the functional managers are concerned with how it will be accomplished. More specifically, the project manager establishes the overall plan for completing the project, integrates the contribution of the different disciplines, sets schedules, and monitors progress. The functional

managers are responsible for assigning personnel and executing their segment of the project according to the standards and schedules set by the project manager. The merger of "what and how" requires both parties to work closely together and jointly approve technical and operational decisions.

- **Project matrix:** This form attempts to create the "feel" of a project team within a matrix environment. The project manager controls most aspects of the project, including scope trade-offs and assignment of functional personnel. The project manager controls when and what specialists do and has final say on major project decisions. The functional manager has title over her people and is consulted on a need basis. In some situations a functional manager's department may serve as a "subcontractor" for the project, in which case they have more control over specialized work. For example, the development of a new series of laptop computers may require a team of experts from different disciplines working on the basic design and performance requirements within a project matrix arrangement. Once the specifications have been determined, final design and production of certain components (i.e., power source) may be assigned to respective functional groups to complete.

One of the primary advantages matrix has over the project team approach is that resources can be shared across multiple projects as well as within functional divisions. Individuals can divide their energy across multiple projects on an as-needed basis. This reduces duplication required in a pure project team structure. Because the project organization is overlaid on the functional divisions, the project has reasonable access to the entire reservoir of technology and expertise of functional divisions. Furthermore, unlike dedicated project teams, specialists maintain ties with their functional group, so they have a homeport to return to once the project is completed.

Advantages and Disadvantages

The strengths of matrix structure are considerable. Unfortunately, so are the potential weaknesses. This is due in large part to the fact that matrix is more complicated and the creation of multiple bosses represents a radical departure from the traditional hierarchical authority system. For example, matrix is predicated on tension between functional managers and project managers who bring critical expertise and perspectives to the project. Such tension is viewed as a necessary mechanism for achieving an appropriate balance between complex technical issues and unique project requirements. While the intent is noble, the effect is sometimes analogous to opening Pandora's box. Legitimate conflict resulting from conflicting agendas and accountabilities can spill over to a more personal level. Worthy discussions can degenerate into heated arguments that engender animosity among the managers involved. Decision making can get bogged down, as agreements have to be forged across multiple groups.

When the three variant forms of matrix are considered, we can see that advantages and disadvantages are not necessarily true for all three forms of matrix. The project matrix is likely to enhance project integration, increase reaction time, diminish internal power struggles, and ultimately improve control of project activities and costs. On the down side, technical quality may suffer since functional areas have less control over their contributions. Likewise, projectitis may emerge as the members develop a strong team identity.

The functional matrix is likely to improve technical quality as well as provide a better system for managing conflict across projects because the functional manager assigns personnel to different projects. The problem is that functional control is often maintained at the expense of poor project integration. The balanced matrix can achieve better balance between technical and project requirements, but it is a very delicate system to create and manage and is more likely to succumb to many of the problems associated with matrix structures.[6]

Organizing Projects within Virtual Organizations

The turn of the century has seen a radical shift in the organizational architecture of business firms. Corporate downsizing and cost control have produced what we call "virtual organizations." In theory, a virtual organization is an alliance of several organizations for the purpose of creating products or services for customers. This collaborative structure typically consists of several satellite organizations "bee hived" around a hub or core firm. The core firm coordinates the network process and provides one or two core competencies, such as marketing or product development. For example, Cisco Systems mainly designs new products and utilizes a constellation of suppliers, contract manufacturers, assemblers, and other partners to deliver products to their customers. Likewise, Nike, another prime example of a virtual organization, provides marketing expertise for its sports footwear and apparel. The key organizing principle is that, instead of doing everything in-house, a firm outsources key activities to other businesses with the requisite competencies.

The shift toward virtual organizations is readily apparent in the film industry. During the golden age of Hollywood, huge, vertically integrated corporations made movies. Studios such as MGM, Warner Brothers, and Twentieth Century Fox owned large movie lots and employed thousands of full-time specialists—set designers, camera people, film editors, directors, and even actors. Today, most movies are made by a collection of individuals and small companies who come together to make films project-by-project. This structure allows each project to be staffed with the talent most suited to its demands rather than choosing only from those people the studio employs.

Virtual projects have been the bread and butter of the construction industry. Whether it is building a dream house or a desalination plant, clients typically hire general contracting firms who subcontract tradespeople and professional organizations to perform specific segments of construction. This approach is now being applied to a wide range of projects.

Figure 3–5 depicts a situation in which a new electronic toy is being developed. The genesis for the toy comes from an electronics engineer who developed the idea in her garage. The inventor negotiates a contract with a toy company to develop and manufacture the toy. The toy company in turn creates a project team of manufacturers, suppliers, and marketing firms to create the new toy. Each participant adds the requisite expertise to the project. The toy company brings its brand name and distribution network to the project. Plastics and chip manufacturers provide customized parts. Marketing firms refine the design, develop packaging, and

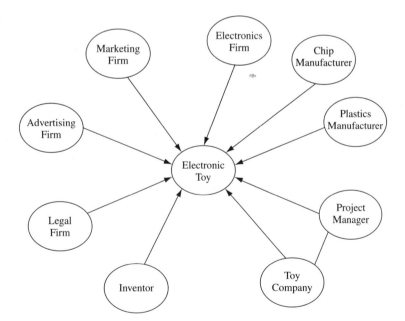

FIGURE 3–5

Electronic Toy Virtual Project

test-market potential names. A project manager is assigned by the toy company to work with the inventor and the other parties to complete the project.

Advantages

The advantages of virtual projects are many. The most noteworthy is cost reduction. Companies can secure competitive prices for contracted services, especially if the work can be outsourced offshore. Furthermore, overheads costs are cut dramatically since the company no longer has to maintain internally the contracted services. A second advantage is the level of expertise and technology that can be brought to bear on the project. A company no longer has to keep up with technological advances. Instead, it can focus on developing its core competencies and hire firms with the know-how to work on relevant segments of the project. A final major advantage is increased flexibility. Organizations are no longer constrained by their own resources but can pursue a wide range of projects by combining their resources with talents of other companies.

Disadvantages

The disadvantages of virtual projects are less well documented. Coordination of professionals from different organizations can be challenging, especially if the project work requires close collaboration and mutual adjustment. This form of project management structure tends to work best when each party is responsible for a well-defined, independent deliverable, as in the case of most construction projects. A second disadvantage is loss of control over the project. The core team depends on other organizations over which they do not have direct authority. While long-term survival of participating organizations depends upon performance, a project may falter when one partner fails to deliver. Finally, networked projects are more prone to interpersonal conflict since the different participants do not share the same values, priorities, and culture. Trust, which is essential to project success, can be difficult to forge when interactions are limited and people come from different organizations.

Many virtual projects operate in an electronic environment in which people are linked by computers, faxes, computer-aided design systems, and video teleconferencing and rarely, if ever, see one another face-to-face. On other projects participants from different organizations work closely together, for example at a construction site or in shared office space. In either case, people come and go as services are needed, much like a matrix structure, but they are not formal members of one organization, merely technical experts who form a temporary alliance with an organization, fulfill their contractual obligations, and then move on to the next project.

Since projects involving collaboration of partners from different organizations is quickly becoming the norm, Chapter 12 is devoted to this subject.

Choosing the Right Project Management Structure

So what project structure should an organization use? This is a complicated question with no precise answers. A number of issues need to be considered at both the organization and project level.

At the organization level, the first question that needs to be asked is: How important is project management to the success of the firm? What percentage of core work involves projects? If more than 75 percent of work involves projects, then an organization should consider a fully projectized organization. If an organization has both standard products and projects, then a matrix arrangement would appear to be appropriate. If an organization has very few projects, then a less formal arrangement is probably all that is required. Temporary task forces could be created on an as-needed basis and the organization could outsource project work.

A second key question is resource availability. Remember, matrix evolved out of the necessity to share resources across multiple projects and functional domains while at the same time creating legitimate project leadership. For organizations that cannot afford to tie up critical personnel on individual projects, a matrix system would appear to be appropriate. An alternative would be to create a dedicated team but outsource project work when resources are not available internally

Within the context of the first two questions, an organization needs to assess current practices and changes that are needed to manage projects more effectively. A strong, project matrix is not installed overnight. The shift toward a greater emphasis on projects has a host of political implications that need to be worked through, requiring time and strong leadership. For example, we have observed many companies who make the transition from a functional organization to a matrix organization begin with a weak functional matrix. This beginning is due in part to resistance on the part of functional and department managers to transferring authority to project mangers. With time, these matrix structures eventually evolve into a project matrix. Many organizations have created project management offices to support project management efforts (see *Project Management in Action: The Project Management Office*).

At the project level, the question is how much autonomy does the project need in order to be successfully completed. Hobbs and Ménard[7] identify seven factors that should influence the choice of project management structure:

1. Size of project
2. Strategic importance
3. Novelty and need for innovation
4. Need for integration (number of departments involved)
5. Environmental complexity (number of external interfaces)
6. Budget and time constraints
7. Stability of resource requirements

The Project Management Office

As more and more companies embrace project management as a critical vehicle for realizing corporate objectives, they are creating centralized project management offices (PMOs) to oversee and improve the management of projects. PMO functions vary widely by organization and need. In some cases, they serve as a simple clearinghouse for project management information. In other cases, they recruit, train, and assign managers to specific projects. As PMOs mature and evolve over time, they become full-service providers of project management expertise within a firm. The different services that PMOs may provide include the following:

- Creating and maintaining the internal project management information system
- Recruiting and selecting project managers both within and outside of the organization
- Establishing standardized project planning and reporting methodologies
- Training in project management techniques and tools
- Auditing ongoing and recently completed projects
- Developing comprehensive risk management programs
- In-house project management consulting and mentoring services
- Maintaining an internal project management library containing critical documents including project plans, funding papers, test plans, and audit reports
- Establishing and benchmarking *best practices* in project management
- Maintaining and tracking the portfolio of projects within an organization

A good example of how project management offices evolve is the Global Project Office (GPO) at Citibank's Global Corporate Bank. GPO originated at the grass-roots level within the small world of Operations and Technology for Global Cash Management. Committed to bringing order to the chaos of managing projects, GPO instituted training programs and professional project management practices on a very small scale. Soon the success of GPO-supported projects caught the eye of upper management. Within 3 years the department was expanded to offer a full range of PMO services across Citibank's entire banking operation. GPO's mission is to establish project management as a core competency throughout the entire Citibank organization.[8]

The higher the levels of these seven factors, the more autonomy and authority the project manager and project team need to be successful. This translates into using either a dedicated project team or a project matrix structure. For example, these structures should be used for large projects that are strategically critical and are new to the company, thus requiring much innovation. These structures would also be appropriate for complex, multidisciplinary projects that require input from many departments, as well as for projects that require constant contact with customers to assess their expectations. Dedicated project teams should also be used for urgent projects in which the nature of the work requires people working steadily from beginning to end.

Many firms that are heavily involved in project management have created a flexible management system that organizes projects according to project requirements. For example, Chaparral Steel, a mini-mill that produces steel bars and beams from scrap metal, classifies projects into three categories: advanced development, platform, and incremental. Advanced development projects are high-risk endeavors involving the creation of a breakthrough product or process. Platform projects are medium risk-projects involving system upgrades that yield new products and processes. Incremental projects are low-risk, short-term projects that involve minor adjustments in existing products and processes. At any point in time, Chaparral might have 40 to 50 projects underway, of which only one or two are advanced, three to five are platform projects, and the remainder are small, incremental projects. The incremental projects are almost all done within a functional matrix with the project manager coordinating the work of functional subgroups. A project matrix is used to complete the platform projects, while dedicated project teams are typically created to complete the advanced development projects.[9] More and more companies are using this "mix and match" approach to managing projects.

Organizational Culture

The decision for combining a discussion of project management structures and organizational cultures in this chapter can be traced to a conversation the authors had with two project managers who work for a medium-sized information technology firm. The managers were currently developing a new operating platform that would be critical to the future success of their company. When they tried to describe how this project was organized, one manager began to sketch out on a napkin a complicated structure involving 52 different teams, each with a project leader and a technical leader! After we probed to understand how this system worked, the manager stopped short and proclaimed, "The key to making this structure work is the culture in our company. This approach would never work at Company Y, where I worked before. But because of our culture here we are able to pull it off."

This comment, our observations of other firms and research suggest there is a strong connection between project management structure, organizational culture, and project success.[10] We have observed organizations successfully manage complex projects within the traditional functional organization because the culture encouraged cross-functional cooperation. Conversely we have seen matrix structures break down because the culture of the organization did not support the division of authority between project managers and functional managers.

What Is Organizational Culture?

Organizational culture refers to a system of shared norms, beliefs, values, and assumptions, which bind people together thereby creating shared meanings.[11] This system is manifested by customs, norms, and habits that exemplify the values and beliefs of the organization. You might think of it as the organization's DNA—invisible to the naked eye, yet a powerful template that shapes what happens in the workplace.

Much has been written about organizational culture. Different schemes and means for classifying or characterizing culture have been developed. Below is our attempt at identifying some of the key cultural dimensions that affect project management.[12]

1. **Member identity:** the degree to which employees identify with the organization as a whole rather than with their type of job or profession
2. **Team emphasis:** the degree to which activities are organized around groups rather than individuals
3. **Interunit relations:** the degree to which units collaborate with each other rather than compete against each other
4. **Control:** the degree to which rules, policies, and direct supervision are used to oversee and control employee behavior
5. **Social distance:** the degree to which superior-subordinate relationships are distant and hierarchical rather than close and egalitarian
6. **Reward criteria:** the degree to which rewards such as promotion and salary increases are allocated according to performance rather than seniority, favoritism, or other nonperformance factors
7. **Conflict tolerance:** the degree to which employees are encouraged to air conflicts and criticisms openly
8. **Level of effort:** the degree to which employees put forth 110 percent effort rather than bare minimum effort
9. **Sharing information:** the degree to which employees openly share information in pursuit of the truth rather than withholding information and protecting their self-interest.
10. **External orientation:** the degree to which outsiders are embraced as potential partners rather than competitors.

FIGURE 3–6

Organizational Culture

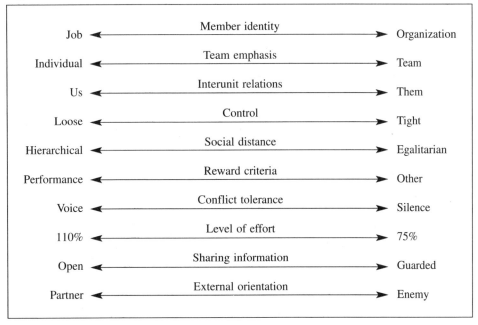

Assessing an organization according to these 10 dimensions (see Figure 3–6) provides a composite picture of the organization's culture. This picture becomes the basis for feelings of shared understanding that the members have about the organization, how things are done, and the way members behave.

Although our discussion of organization culture may appear to suggest one culture dominates the entire organization, in reality this is rarely the case. "Strong" or "thick" are adjectives used to denote a culture in which the organization's core values and customs are widely held and widely shared within the entire organization. Conversely a "weak" or "thin" culture is one that is not widely shared or practiced within a firm.

Even within a strong organizational culture, there are likely to be subcultures often aligned within specific departments or specialty areas. As noted earlier in our discussion of project management structures, it is not uncommon for norms, values, and customs to develop within a specific field or profession such as marketing, finance, or operations. Likewise, countercultures can emerge within organizations that reflect a different set of values, beliefs, and customs—often in direct contradiction with the culture espoused by top management. How pervasive these subcultures and countercultures are affects the strength of the culture of the organization and the extent to which culture influences members' actions and responses.

Identifying Cultural Characteristics

Organizational culture operates beneath the surface of organizational behavior, as shown in Figure 3–7. Deciphering an organization's culture is a highly interpretative, subjective process that requires assessment of both current activities and past history. The student of culture simply cannot rely on what people report about their culture. The physical environment in which people work, as well as how people act and respond to different events that occur, must be examined. Although by no means exhaustive, the checklist of 5 yields clues about the norms, customs, and values of an organization.

   1. Study the physical characteristics of an organization. What does the external architecture look like? What image does it convey? Is it unique? For example, a visit to corporate headquarters for Oakley, Inc., the maker of high-end, ultra-hip eyewear and footwear, would suggest that Oakley is engaged in some form of intergalactic battle with its competition. The lobby of the $40 million building located in Foothill Ranch, California, looks like a bomb shelter—sleek pipes, watertight doors, and towering metallic walls studded with oversize bolts suggest a fortress mentality. Ejection seats from a B-52 bomber in the waiting

FIGURE 3–7

Organizational Culture

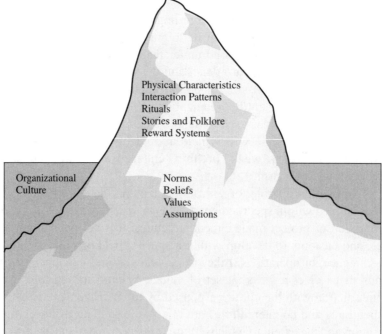

room and a full-size torpedo in a rack behind the receptionist's armored desk reinforce a warrior mentality.[13]

Physical layout also yields insights into the social structure of a firm. Are the buildings and offices the same quality for all employees? Or are modern buildings and fancier offices reserved for senior executives or managers from a specific department? What are the customs concerning dress? What symbols does the organization use to signal authority and status within the organization? These physical characteristics can shed light on who has real power within the organization, the extent to which the organization is internally differentiated, and how formal the organization is in its business dealings.

2. Observe how people interact within the organization. What is their pace—is it slow and methodical or urgent and spontaneous? What language is used? For instance, when Monsanto Company CEO Robert Shapiro met with American Home Products CEO John Stafford about a possible merger, Monsanto employees referred to "Bob," whereas American Home products executives addressed "Mr. Stafford." The contrast between Monsanto's egalitarian culture and American Home's hierarchical culture was soon evident to everyone at the conference.[14]

Meetings often can yield insightful information. Who are the people at the meetings? Who does the talking? To whom do they talk? How candid is the conversation? Do people speak for the organization or for the individual department? What is the focus of the meetings? How much time is spent on various issues? Issues that are discussed repeatedly and at length are clues about the values of the organization's culture.

3. Analyze organizational rituals. Organizational rituals are defined as formal and customarily repeated acts that convey basic norms and values throughout the organization. Although organizations do not have the equivalent of baptism, Holy Communion, or bar mitzvah, they do engage in a variety of ritualistic behavior including the annual company picnic or holiday party, employee morale surveys, TGIF gatherings, weekly staff meetings, and going-away parties. Companies that are committed to building a strong culture that supports their basic values and principles invest considerable attention to organizational rituals. The Sequent Corporation, an information technology firm located in Portland, Oregon, is a good example. As it turns out, 85 percent of their business typically is shipped out during the last week of the quarter. It has become the custom for everyone at Sequent, from the president down to the janitor, to volunteer to work one shift in the loading area during this time. According to the president, this custom reinforces a variety of important corporate values including "We're in the business of building products," and "None of us is too big to get our hands dirty."

4. Interpret stories and folklore surrounding the organization. Either through talking directly to people from other organizations or in daily conversations with coworkers, an observer can begin to gain a deeper sense of an organization's culture. Pay particular attention to the stories and anecdotes that are passed on within the organization for they often yield useful evidence about the important qualities of the culture. Look for similarities among stories told by different people. The subjects highlighted in recurring stories often reflect what is important to an organization's culture. For example, many of the stories that are repeated at Versatec, a Xerox subsidiary that makes graphic plotters for computers, involve their flamboyant cofounder Renn Zaphiropoulos. According to company folklore, one of the very first things Renn did when the company was formed was to assemble the top management team at his home. They then devoted the weekend to making a beautiful teak conference table by hand around which all future decisions would be made. This table came to symbolize the importance of teamwork and maintaining high standards of performance, two essential qualities of the culture at Versatec.

Try to identify who the heroes and villains are in the company folklore. What do they suggest about the culture's ideals? Returning to the Versatec story, when the company was eventually purchased by Xerox, many employees expressed concern that Versatec's informal, play hard/work hard culture would be overwhelmed by the bureaucracy at Xerox. Renn rallied the employees to superior levels of performance by arguing that if they exceeded Xerox's expectations they would be left alone. Autonomy has remained a fixture of Versatec's culture long after Renn's retirement.

5. Assess the organization's informal and formal reward system. Finally, it is also important to pay close attention to the basis for promotions and rewards. Are promotions based on accomplishments and performance or tenure and loyalty to the organization? What do people see as the keys to getting ahead within the organization? What contributes to downfalls? These last two questions can yield important insights into the qualities and behaviors that the organization honors as well as the cultural taboos and behavioral land mines that can derail a career. For example, one project manager confided that a former colleague was sent to project management purgatory soon after publicly questioning the validity of a marketing report. From that point on, the project manager was careful to consult privately with the marketing department whenever she had questions about their data.

With practice an observer can assess how strong the dominant culture of an organization is and the significance of subcultures and countercultures. Furthermore, learners can discern and identify where the culture of an organization stands on the cultural dimensions presented earlier, and in essence, begin to build a cultural profile for a firm. Based on this profile, conclusions can be drawn about specific customs and norms that need to be adhered to as well as those behaviors and actions that violate the cultural norms of a firm.

Implications of Organizational Culture for Organizing Projects

Project managers have to be able to operate in several potentially diverse organizational cultures. First, they have to interact with the culture of their parent organization as well as the subcultures of various departments (marketing, accounting). Second, they have to interact with the project's client or customer organizations. Finally, they have to interact in varying degrees with a host of other organizations connected to the project. These organizations include suppliers and vendors, subcontractors, consulting firms, government and regulatory agencies, and, in many cases, community groups. Many of these organizations are likely to have very different cultures. Project managers have to be sensitive to cultural differences in order to work effectively with each of these organizations. Project managers have to be able to read and speak the culture they are working in to develop strategies, plans, and responses that are likely to be understood and accepted.[15]

Earlier we stated that we believe there are strong relationships among project management structure, organizational culture, and successful project management. The metaphor we choose to describe this relationship is that of a boat trip on a river. Culture is the river and the project is the boat. Organizing and completing projects within an organization in which the culture is conducive to project management is like paddling downstream: much less effort is required, and the natural force of the river generates progress toward the destination. In many cases, the current can be so strong that steering is all that is required. Such is the case for projects that operate in a project-friendly environment where teamwork and cross-functional cooperation are the norms, where there is a deep commitment to excellence, and healthy conflict is voiced and dealt with quickly and effectively.

One organization that appears to approach this ideal profile is 3M. 3M has received acclaim for creating an entrepreneurial culture within a large corporate framework. The essence of its culture is captured in phrases that have been chanted often by 3Mers throughout its history: "Encourage experimental doodling." "Hire good people and leave them alone." "If you put fences around people, you get sheep. Give people the room they need." Freedom and autonomy to experiment are reflected in the "15 percent rule," which encourages technical people to spend up to 15 percent of their time on projects of their own choosing and initiative. This fertile culture has contributed to 3M's branching out into more than 60,000 products and 40 separate product divisions.[16]

Conversely, trying to complete a project in an organization in which several important features of the dominant culture inhibit effective project management is like paddling upstream: much more time, effort, and attention are needed to reach the destination. This would be the situation in cultures that discourage teamwork and cooperation, that have a low tolerance for conflict, where risks are to be avoided, and where getting ahead is based less on performance and more on cultivating favorable relationships with superiors. In such cases, the project manager and his or her people not only have to overcome the natural obstacles of the project but also have to overcome the prevailing negative forces inherent in the culture of the organization. (See *Project Management in Action: Matrix Problems at DEC*.)

The implications of this analogy are obvious but important. Greater project authority and resources are necessary to complete projects that encounter a strong, negative cultural current. Conversely, less formal authority and fewer dedicated resources are needed to complete projects in which the cultural currents generate behavior and cooperation essential to project success. The key issue is the degree of interdependence between the parent organization and the project team and the

---

Project Management in Action

Matrix Problems at DEC

After a decade of declining sales and profits, Digital Equipment Corporation (DEC) was acquired in 1998 by Compaq Computer. Many analysts attributed the decline at DEC to the management of the company's structure prior to the ousting of its founder and CEO, Kenneth H. Olsen, in 1992.

Olsen created a matrix structure to manage DEC's new-product development. In the early days of the computer industry, companies had the time and opportunity to perfect a product's technical capabilities because the product cycles were slow. In the matrix, rival product teams worked side by side on different designs. When one superior design emerged, it was chosen for further development. The winning teams became organizational heroes and rose quickly in the corporation, earning the right to lead future product teams and claim a larger share of the company resources. The other teams were disbanded so that their members could work on other products.

At first this system worked well and led to early successes. But soon DEC began to lose ground as a result of increased competition in the computer industry that placed a premium on speed to market. As DEC faltered, resources tightened, and the product teams began to compete with each other for scarce company resources such as marketing and engineering support. Intense rivalries broke out between product teams. Many key members left because they felt that their careers were in jeopardy because DEC rewarded only winners.

As a result of the increased competition among teams, the product teams did not pool knowledge and expertise, and integration between functions declined. Instead of providing flexibility and efficient use of resources, the matrix structure at DEC resulted in inertia, infighting, and slow development time.[17]

corresponding need to create a unique project culture conducive to successful project completion.

In cases where the prevalent organizational culture supports the behaviors essential to project completion, a project management structure that is aligned within the structure of the parent organization would be appropriate. Such would be the case for both the functional and balanced matrices. One of the major reasons why Chaparral Steel is able to use a functional matrix successfully to complete incremental projects is that its culture contains strong norms for cooperation. Conversely, one of the reasons behind the failure of Kodak's "Factory of the Future" project in the mid-1980s was that the culture at that time did not support project management.[18]

When the parent organization possesses a dominant culture that inhibits collaboration and innovation among disciplines and groups of people, it is advisable to insulate the project team from the dominant culture by creating a self-sufficient dedicated project team. If a dedicated project team is impossible because of resource constraints, then at least a project matrix should be used where the project manager has centralized control over the project. Another option is to create a networked project by hiring people from other organizations. In all of these cases, the managerial strategy is to create a distinct subculture within the project team in which a new set of norms, customs, and values evolve that will be conducive to project completion.

Under extreme circumstance this project culture could even represent a counterculture in that many of the norms and values are the antithesis of the dominant, parent culture. Such was the case of the original "Skunk Works" established by Kelly Johnson at Lockheed. Kelly and a small, isolated band of Lockheed mavericks developed the revolutionary U-2 spy plane during the early 1950s. The malodorous reference symbolized the departure from normal operations. Likewise when IBM decided to develop their personal computer quickly in 1980, they knew the overabundance of computer knowledge and bureaucracy in the company could bog down the project. They also realized that they would have to work closely with suppliers and make use of many non-IBM parts if they were to get to the market quickly. This was not the IBM way at the time, so IBM established the PC project team in a warehouse in Boca Raton, Florida, far from corporate headquarters and other corporate development facilities that existed within the organization.[19]

Summary

This chapter examined two major characteristics of the parent organization that impact the implementation and completion of projects. The first is the formal structure of the organization and how it chooses to organize and manage projects.

Although the individual project manager may have very little say about how the firm chooses to manage projects, she or he must be able to recognize the options available as well as the inherent strengths and weaknesses of different approaches.

The second major characteristic of the parent organization that was discussed in this chapter is the concept of organizational culture. Organizational culture is the pattern of beliefs and expectations shared by an organization's members. Culture includes the behavioral norms, customs, shared values, and the "rules of the game" for getting along and getting ahead within the organization. It is important for project managers to be "culturally sensitive" so that they can develop strategies and responses that are likely to be understood and accepted as well as avoid violating key customs and norms that would jeopardize their effectiveness within the organization.

The interaction between project management structure and organizational culture is a complicated one. We have argued that in certain organizations, culture encourages the implementation of projects. In this environment the project management structure used plays a less decisive role in the success of the project. Conversely, for other organizations in which the culture stresses internal competition and differentiation, just the opposite may be true. The prevailing norms, customs, and attitudes inhibit effective project management, and the project management structure plays a more decisive role in the successful implementation of projects. At a minimum, under adverse cultural conditions, the project manager needs to have significant authority and autonomy over the project team; under more extreme conditions firms should use dedicated project teams to complete critical projects. In both cases, the managerial strategy should be used to insulate project work from the dominant culture so that a more positive "subculture" can emerge among project participants.

The project management structure of the organization and the culture of the organization are major elements of the environment in which a project is initiated. Subsequent chapters will examine how project managers and professionals work within this environment to successfully complete projects.

4

DEFINING
THE PROJECT

Select a dream
Use your dream to set a goal
Create a plan
Consider resources
Enhance skills and abilities
Spend time wisely
Start! Get organized and go

. . . it is one of those acro-what evers,
said Pooh.[1]

One of the best ways to meet the needs of the customer and major project stake-holders is to use an integrated project planning and control system that requires selective information. Project managers who manage a single, small project can plan and schedule the project tasks without a formal planning and information system. However, when project managers must manage several small projects or a large, complex project, they quickly reach a threshold where they can no longer cope with the level of detail.

This chapter describes a disciplined, structured method for selectively collecting information to use through all phases of the project life cycle, to meet the needs of all stakeholders (e.g., customer, project manager), and to measure performance against the strategic plan of the organization. The method suggested is a selective outline of the project called the *work breakdown structure (WBS)*. The early stages of developing the outline serve to ensure that all tasks are identified and that participants in the project have an understanding of what is to be done.

Once the outline and its details are defined, an integrated information system can be developed to schedule work and allocate budgets. This baseline information is later used for control.

The five generic steps provide a structured approach for collecting the project information that is necessary for planning, scheduling, and controlling the project. These steps and the development of project networks found in the next chapters all take place concurrently, and several iterations are typically required to develop dates and budgets that can be used for control of the project. The old saying, "We can control only what we have planned," is true; therefore, defining the project is the first step.

Step 1: Defining the Project Scope

Defining the project scope sets the stage for developing a project plan. *Project scope* is a definition of the end result or mission of your project—a product or service for your client or customer. The primary purpose is to define as clearly as possible the deliverable(s) for the end user and to focus project plans. As fundamental and essential as scope definition appears, it is frequently overlooked by project leaders of well-managed, large corporations.

Research clearly shows that a poorly defined scope or mission is the most frequently mentioned barrier to project success. Smith and Tucker's study of a large petroleum refinery plant project found that poor scope definition for major segments of the project had the greatest negative impact on cost and schedule.[2] Pinto and Slevin found that a clear mission statement is a predictor of more than 50 percent of project success in the concept, planning, and execution stages of the project.[3] Ashley et al., found outstanding, successful projects exhibit clear scope and work definitions.[4] A survey by Posner found lack of clear goals as a major problem mentioned by more than 60 percent of project manager respondents.[5] In a large study of more than 1,400 project managers in the United States and Canada, Gobeli and Larson found that approximately 50 percent of the planning problems relate to unclear definition of scope and goals.[6] These studies suggest a strong correlation between project success and clear scope definition. The scope document directs focus on the project purpose throughout the life of the project for the customer and project participants.

The scope should be developed under the direction of the project manager and customer. The project manager is responsible for seeing that there is agreement with the owner on project objectives, deliverables at each stage of the project, technical requirements, and so forth. For example, a deliverable in the early stage might be specifications; for the second stage, three prototypes for production; for the third, a sufficient quantity to introduce to market; and finally, marketing promotion and training.

Your project scope definition is a document that will be published and used by the project owner and project participants for planning and measuring project success. *Scope* describes what you expect to deliver to your customer when the project is complete. Your project scope should define the results to be achieved in specific, tangible, and measurable terms.

Employing a Project Scope Checklist

Clearly, project scope is the keystone interlocking all elements of a project plan. To ensure that scope definition is complete, you may wish to use the following checklist:

Project Scope Checklist
1. Project objectives
2. Deliverables
3. Milestones
4. Technical requirements
5. Limits and exclusions
6. Reviews with customer

1. Project objectives. The first step of project scope definition is to define the major objectives to meet your customer's need(s). For example, as a result of extensive market research a computer software company decides to develop a program that automatically translates verbal sentences in English to Russian. The project should be completed within 3 years at a cost not to exceed $1.5 million. Another example is a project to design and produce a completely portable, hazardous waste, thermal treatment system in 13 months at a cost not to exceed $13 million. Project objectives clarify the questions of what, when, and how much.

2. Deliverables. The next step is to define major deliverables—the expected outputs over the life of the project. For example, deliverables in the early design phase of a project might be a list of specifications. In the second phase deliverables could be software coding and a technical manual. The next phase could be prototype testing. The final phase could be final tests and approved software. Deliverables typically include time, quantity, and cost estimates.

3. Milestones. A milestone is a significant event in a project that occurs at a point in time. The milestone schedule shows only major segments of work; it represents first, rough-cut estimates of time, cost, and resources for the project. The milestone schedule is built using the deliverables as a platform to identify major segments of work and an end date—for example, testing complete and finished by July 1 of the same year. Milestones should be natural, important control points in the project. Milestones should be easy for all project participants to recognize. The milestone schedule should identify which major organizational divisions will assume responsibility for the major segments of work and provide the necessary resources and technical expertise. The organizational units may be internal or external—for example, companies may rely on consultants to randomly test a new drug.

4. Technical requirements. More frequently than not, a product or service will have technical requirements to ensure proper performance. For example, a technical requirement for a personal computer might be the ability to accept 120-volt alternating current or 240-volt direct current without any adapters or user switches. Another well-known example is the ability of 911 emergency systems to identify the caller's phone number and location. Examples from information system projects include the speed and capacity of database systems and connectivity with alternative systems. For an unusual set of technical requirements, see *Project Management in Action: Operation Keiko Lift.*

5. Limits and exclusions. The limits of scope should be defined. Failure to define limits can lead to false expectations and to expending resources and time on the wrong problem. Examples of limits include local air transportation to and from base camps will be outsourced; system maintenance and repair only up to 1 month after final inspection; client will be billed for additional training beyond that prescribed in the contract. In addition exclusions should also be noted. Exclusions further define the boundaries of a project by stating what is not included in the project. Examples include: data will be collected by client, not the contractor; a house will be built, but no landscaping or security devices; software will be installed, but no training given.

6. Reviews with customer. Completion of the scope checklist ends with a review with your customer—internal or external. The main concern here is the understanding and agreement of expectations. Is the customer getting what he or she desires in deliverables? Does the project definition identify key accomplishments, budgets, timing, and performance requirements? Are questions of limits and exclusions covered? Clear communication in all these issues is imperative to avoid claims or misunderstanding.

The six points above constitute a generic scope checklist. Different industries and companies will develop unique checklists and templates to fit their needs and specific kinds of projects. Many companies engaged in contracted work refer to scope statements as *statements of work* (SOW). Other organizations use the term *project charter.* However, *project charter* has different meanings in the world of project management. One meaning is an expanded version of the scope statement described above that might include such items as risk limits, customer needs, spending limits and even team composition.[7] A second meaning, which dates back to the original use of the word "charter," is a document that is used to legitimize the authority of the project manager to initiate and lead the project. This may take the form of a simple announcement that the project has been approved by top management has approved the project and Jane Doe is in charge. In other cases it may include a scope statement with a statement of the business case (why the

Project Management in Action

Operation Keiko Lift

Imagine being assigned the project of transporting a 21-foot, 10,000-pound Orca whale 8,630 miles from Newport, Oregon, to the Westman Islands in Iceland. Such was the challenge of the Free Willy Keiko Foundation whose mission ultimately is to return Keiko, the star of the popular children's film *Free Willy,* to his natural habitat.

The project posed several major technical challenges. Keiko's trainers had to coax him into a small medical pool adjacent to his 2-million gallon tank at the aquarium. They gradually lowered the water level, and Keiko was gingerly placed in a nylon sling. He was then hoisted into a special 28-foot container filled with ice to maintain constant 50-52 degree water temperature. A UPS truck then took him 3 miles to the local municipal airport.

At the airport, Keiko was loaded onto a huge U.S. Air Force C-17. The C-17 Globemaster is the only aircraft in the world capable of both flying a large payload like Keiko and landing on short, rough airstrips. The C-17 was equipped to carry the 10,000-pound whale in his 35,000-pound transport container and land on the 3,900-foot airstrip adjacent to his bay pen in Iceland. Since the objective was to get Keiko to his new pen as soon as possible, the C-17 was refueled twice in mid-air.

Because Keiko could not be sedated, there was grave concern that the whale would go into shock during his trip. A small army of trainers and veterinarians traveled with Keiko throughout the flight to comfort him and slather moisturizing balm on his back and his famous droopy dorsal fin.

Nine hours after taking off, Keiko arrived in Iceland and was transported to his new home. There he began an elaborate rehabilitation program to prepare him for life in the open seas. In total, the price for what the U.S. Air Force called Operation Keiko Lift was $2 million.

project is important) and a priority ranking. In either case, authority is transferred to the project manager not only formally by the charter, but also informally by the stature of the sponsors of the project.

In summary, close liaison with your customer is necessary to develop a project definition that meets all the requirements of the customer. Clear scope definition ensures you will know when a change in scope occurs. A clear project scope definition is the primary prerequisite for development of your work breakdown structure. Scope definition provides an administrative plan that is used to develop your operational plan. Scope definition should be as brief as possible but complete; one or two pages are typical for small projects. Partial scope statements for three different projects are profiled in *Project Management in Action: Examples of Project Scope Statements.*

Project Management in Action

Examples of Project Scope Statements

Silver Fiddle Construction Project Scope Statement

Project Objective.   To construct a high-quality, custom home within 5 months at a cost not to exceed $320,000.

Deliverables
- A 2,500 square foot, 2½ bath, 3-bedroom, finished home
- A finished garage, insulated and sheet-rocked
- Kitchen appliances to include range, oven, microwave, and dishwasher
- High-efficiency gas furnace with programmable thermostat

Milestones
1. Permits approved July 5
2. Foundation poured July 12
3. "Dry in"—framing, sheathing, plumbing, electrical, and mechanical inspections—passed September 25
4. Final inspection November 7

Technical Requirements
1. Home must meet local building codes
2. All windows and doors must pass NFRC class 40 energy ratings
3. Exterior wall insulation must meet an "R" factor of 21
4. Ceiling insulation must meet an "R" factor of 38
5. Floor insulation must meet an "R" factor of 25
6. Garage will accommodate two cars and one 28-foot-long Winnebago
7. Structure must pass seismic stability codes

Limits and Exclusions
1. The home will be built to the specifications and design of the original blueprints provided by the customer
2. Owner responsible for landscaping
3. Refrigerator not included among kitchen appliances
4. Air conditioning not included, but house is prewired for it
5. SFC reserves the right to contract out services

Customer Review.   Bolo and Izabella Czopek

Javacom LAN Project Scope Statement*

Project Objective.   To design and install a local area network (LAN) within 1 month with a budget not to exceed $82,000 for the Meridian Social Service Agency.

Deliverables

- Twenty workstations
- Server with dual Pentium processors
- Two Hewlett-Packard Laser Jet Si/Si MX Printers
- Windows NT server and workstation operating system
- Four hours of introduction training for client's personnel
- Sixteen hours training for client network administrator
- Fully operational LAN system

Milestones

1. Hardware January 22
2. Setting users priority and authorization January 26
3. In-house whole network test completed February 1
4. Client site test completed February 2
5. Training completed February 16

Technical Requirements

1. Workstations with 17-inch monitors, Pentium II processor, 128 MB RAM, 4 MB SVGA, 32X CD-Rom, Zip drive, Ethernet card, 4.0 GB hard drive
2. PCI 64 Ethernet LAN interface cards and Ethernet connections (must transmit at least 100 mbps)
3. System must support Windows NT platform

Limits and Exclusions

1. System maintenance and repair only up to 1 month after final inspection
2. Warranties transferred to client
3. Only responsible for installing software designated by the client 2 weeks before the start of the project
4. Client will be billed for additional training beyond that prescribed in the contract

Customer Review.   Director of the Meridian Social Service Agency

---

*This case was prepared with the assistance of Budiyoso Kuriawai.

Great Alaskan Fly-Fishing Expedition Project Scope Statement[†]

Project Objective.   To organize and lead a 5-day fly-fishing expedition down the Tikchik River System in Alaska from June 21 to 25 at a cost not to exceed $18,000.

Deliverables

- Provide air transportation: from Dillingham, Alaska, to Camp I and from Camp II back to Dillingham
- Provide river transportation: 2 eight-person drift boats with outboard motors
- Provide food: 3 meals a day for the 5 days spent on the river
- Provide training: 4 hours in fly-fishing instruction
- Provide lodging: overnight accommodations at the Dillingham Lodge, 3 four-person tents with cots, bedding, and lanterns
- Provide guides: 4 experienced river guides and fly fishermen
- Provide fishing licenses: for all guests

Milestones

1. Contract signed January 22
2. Guests arrive in Dillingham June 20
3. Depart by plane to Base Camp I June 21
4. Depart by plane from Base Camp II to Dillingham June 25

Technical Requirements

1. Fly-in air transportation to and from base camps
2. Boat transportation within the Tikchik River system
3. Digital satellite communication devices
4. Camps and fishing conform to State of Alaska requirements

Limits and Exclusions

1. Guests responsible for travel arrangements to and from Dillingham, Alaska
2. Guests responsible for their own fly-fishing equipment and clothing
3. Local air transportation to and from base camps will be outsourced
4. Tour guides not responsible for the number of king salmon caught by guests

Customer Review.   The president of BlueNote Inc.

[†] This case was prepared with the assistance of Stuart Morigeau.

Step 2: Establishing Project Priorities

Quality and the ultimate success of a project are traditionally defined as meeting and/or exceeding the expectations of the customer and/or upper management in terms of cost (budget), time (schedule), and performance (scope) of the project (see Figure 4–1). The interrelationship among these criteria varies. For example, sometimes it is necessary to compromise the performance and scope of the project to get the project done quickly or less expensively. Often, the longer a project takes, the more expensive it becomes. However, a positive correlation between cost and schedule may not always be true. Sometimes project costs can be reduced by using cheaper, less efficient labor or equipment that extends the duration of the project. Likewise, as will be seen in Chapter 9, project managers are often forced to expedite or "crash" certain key activities by adding additional labor, thereby raising the original cost of the project.

One of the primary jobs of a project manager is to manage the trade-offs among time, cost, and performance. To do so, project managers must define and understand the nature of the priorities of the project. They need to have a candid discussion with the project customer and upper management to establish the relative importance of each criterion. One technique that is useful for this purpose is completing a priority matrix for the project that identifies which criterion is constrained, which should be enhanced, and which can be accepted:

Constrain: The original parameter is fixed. The project must meet the completion date, specifications and scope of the project, or budget.

Enhance: Given the scope of the project, which criterion should be optimized? In the case of time and cost, this usually means taking advantage of opportunities either to reduce costs or shorten the schedule. Conversely, with regard to performance, enhancing means adding value to the project.

FIGURE 4–1

Project Management Trade-offs

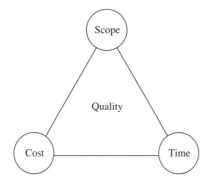

FIGURE 4–2

*Project
Priority
Matrix*

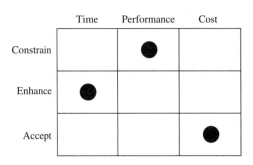

Accept: For which criterion is it tolerable not to meet the original parameters? When trade-offs have to be made, is it permissible for the schedule to slip, to reduce the scope and performance of the project, or to go over budget?

Figure 4–2 displays the priority matrix for the development of a new high-speed modem. Since *time* to market is important to sales, the project manager is instructed to take advantage of every opportunity to reduce completion time. In doing so, going over *cost* is acceptable, though not desirable. At the same time, the original *performance* specifications for the modem as well as reliability standards cannot be compromised.

Priorities vary from project to project. For example, for many software projects time to market is critical and companies like Microsoft may defer original scope requirements to later versions in order to get to the market first. Alternatively, for special event projects (conferences, parades, tournaments) time is constrained once the date has been announced, and if the budget is tight, the project manager will compromise the scope of the project in order to complete the project on time.

Some would argue that all three criteria are always constrained and that good project managers should seek to optimize each criterion. If everything goes well on a project and no major problems or setbacks are encountered, their argument may be valid. However, this situation is rare, and project managers are often forced to make tough decisions that benefit one criterion while compromising the other two. The purpose of this exercise is to define and agree on what the priorities and constraints of the project are so that when "push comes to shove," the right decisions are made.

There are likely to be natural limits to the extent managers can constrain, optimize, or accept any one criterion. It may be acceptable for the project to slip 1 month behind schedule but no further or to exceed the planned budget by as much as $20,000. Likewise, it may be desirable to finish a project 1 month early, but after that cost conservation should be the primary goal. Some project managers document these limits as part of creating the priority matrix.

In summary, developing a decision priority matrix for a project is a useful exercise. (*Note:* This matrix is also useful midway in the project for approaching any problem or decision that must be made.) It provides a forum for clearly establishing priorities with customers and top management so as to create shared expectations and to avoid misunderstandings. The priority information is essential to the planning process, where adjustments can be made in the scope, schedule, and budget allocation. Finally, the matrix provides a basis for monitoring and evaluating progress so that appropriate corrective action can be taken. Still, one caveat must be mentioned: during the course of a project, priorities may change. The customer may suddenly need the project completed 1 month sooner, or new directives from top management may emphasize cost saving initiatives. The project manager needs to be vigilant in order to anticipate and confirm changes in priorities and make appropriate adjustments. See *Project Management in Action: Year 2000 Olympic Games—Sydney, Australia.*

Project Management in Action

Year 2000 Olympic Games—Sydney, Australia[8]

In the realm of event project management, the Olympic Games rank as one of the premier achievements.

Project Objective

To stage the Year 2000 Olympic Games at specified locations in Sydney beginning September 1 at a cost of $1.4 billion

Client

No clearly defined client. Activities were underwritten by the New South Wales (NSW) Government. Many stakeholders and customers, e.g., citizens of New South Wales, the NSW Government, the Australian people, the International Olympic Committee, the international community as a whole, the athletes, and Australian and international business communities.

Scope

Organizing all games and ceremonies. Putting in place all technology and resources required to stage the Games. Handling public relations and fund raising.

Criteria for Success

Trouble-free performance of games. Level of public enthusiasm and enjoyment. Economic activity generated within NSW and Australia. Continued interest in future Olympic Games.

Project Team

The **Sydney Organizing Committee for Olympic Games** (SOCOG) was appointed as the project managers by legislation. Other organizations directly contributing to the success of the Games, such as the International Olympic Committee, Australian Olympic Committee, Sydney City Council, and Olympic Coordination Authority (NSW Government) were made party to the Host City Contract. Olympic Coordination Authority is responsible for all the infrastructure projects, most of which were either under way or were being reprogrammed to accommodate the Games. Completion of these projects on time was vital to the success of the Olympic Games.

Work Breakdown Structure

The WBS for the project included the following major areas: events; venues and facilities including accommodation; transport; media facilities and coordination; telecommunications; security arrangements; medical care; human resources including volunteers; cultural olympiad; pregames training; information technology projects; opening and closing ceremonies; public relations; financing; test games and trial events; and sponsorship management and control of ambush marketing. Each of these items could be treated as a project in its own right. Precision coordination was necessary to ensure that these, and therefore the entire Games project, are delivered on time.

Priorities

Time, obviously, was the most critical dimension of the Sydney 2000 Olympic Games project. Any shortcomings in the time dimension would have to be offset by sacrificing either cost or quality. However, performance on all three dimensions is vital to success of the Games. Worldwide opinion is shaped by the perceived quality of the facilities, the efficacy of event management, and the treatment of foreign athletes and spectators. The Games budget in nominal terms is $1.4 billion, and any major cost overruns will alienate the public and overshadow the spectacle. Still, if a compromise has to be made, the cost aspect will be the first dimension sacrificed.

Step 3: Creating the Work Breakdown Structure

Once the scope and deliverables have been identified, the work of the project can be successively subdivided into smaller and smaller work elements. The outcome of this hierarchical process is called the *work breakdown structure (WBS)*. The WBS is a map of the project. Use of a WBS helps to assure project managers that all products and work elements are identified, to integrate the project with the current organization, and to establish a basis for control. Basically, the WBS is an outline of the project with different levels of detail. Figure 4–3 shows the major groupings commonly used in the field to develop a hierarchical WBS.

The WBS begins with the project as the *final deliverable*. Major project work deliverables/systems are identified first; then the *subdeliverables* necessary to accomplish the larger deliverables are defined. The process is repeated until the subdeliverable detail is small enough to be manageable and one person can be responsible. This subdeliverable is further divided into *work packages*. Because the lowest subdeliverable usually includes several work packages, the work packages are grouped by type of work—for example, hardware, programming, and testing.

FIGURE 4–3

Hierarchical Breakdown for WBS

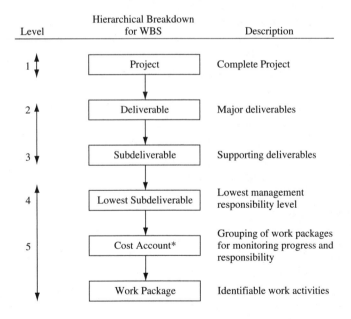

Level	Hierarchical Breakdown for WBS	Description
1	Project	Complete Project
2	Deliverable	Major deliverables
3	Subdeliverable	Supporting deliverables
4	Lowest Subdeliverable	Lowest management responsibility level
5	Cost Account*	Grouping of work packages for monitoring progress and responsibility
	Work Package	Identifiable work activities

*This breakdown groups work packages by type of work within a deliverable and allows assignment of responsibility to an organization unit. This extra step facilitates a system for monitoring project progress (discussed in Chapter 13).

These groupings within a subdeliverable are called *cost accounts*. This grouping facilitates a system for monitoring project progress by work and responsibility.

The hierarchical structure later provides management with a database for planning, executing, monitoring, and controlling the work of the project. In addition, the hierarchical structure provides management with information appropriate to each level. For example, top management deals primarily with major deliverables, while first-line supervisors deal with smaller subdeliverables and work packages.

How a WBS Helps the Project Manager

• The WBS defines all the elements of the project in a hierarchical framework and establishes their relationships to the project end item(s). Think of the project as a large work package that is successively broken down into smaller work packages; the total project is the summation of all the smaller work packages. This hierarchical structure facilitates evaluation of cost, time, and technical performance at all levels in the organization over the life of the project.

• While WBS is developed, organizational units and individuals are assigned responsibility for accomplishment of work packages. This integrates the work and the organization. In practice, this process is sometimes called OBS, the organization breakdown structure, which will be discussed later in the chapter.

• WBS makes it possible to plan, schedule, and budget. It gives a framework for tracking cost and work performance. Use of the structure provides the opportunity to "rollup" (sum) the budget and actual costs of the smaller work packages into larger work elements so that performance can be measured by organizational units and work accomplishment.

• The WBS defines communication channels and assists in understanding and coordinating many parts of the project. The structure shows the work and organizational units responsible and suggests where written communication should be directed. Problems can be quickly addressed and coordinated because the structure integrates work and responsibility.

WBS Development

Figure 4–4 shows a simplified WBS for development of a new Voice Data Recognition project to be used by field personnel to collect and analyze data. At the top of the chart (level 1) is the project end item—a deliverable product or service. Note how the levels of the structure can represent information for different levels of management. For example, level 1 information represents the total project objective and is useful to top management; levels 2, 3, and 4 are suitable for middle management; and level 5 is for first-line managers.

Level 2 shows a partial list of deliverables necessary to develop the new product—*Design Specifications, Software Development, Integration, Hardware*

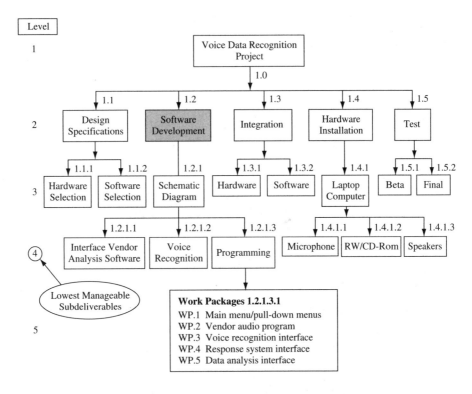

FIGURE 4–4

Work Breakdown Structure

Level

1 — Voice Data Recognition Project — 1.0

2 — 1.1 Design Specifications | 1.2 Software Development | 1.3 Integration | 1.4 Hardware Installation | 1.5 Test

3 — 1.1.1 Hardware Selection | 1.1.2 Software Selection | 1.2.1 Schematic Diagram | 1.3.1 Hardware | 1.3.2 Software | 1.4.1 Laptop Computer | 1.5.1 Beta | 1.5.2 Final

4 — 1.2.1.1 Interface Vendor Analysis Software | 1.2.1.2 Voice Recognition | 1.2.1.3 Programming | 1.4.1.1 Microphone | 1.4.1.2 RW/CD-Rom | 1.4.1.3 Speakers

Lowest Manageable Subdeliverables

5 —

Work Packages 1.2.1.3.1
WP.1 Main menu/pull-down menus
WP.2 Vendor audio program
WP.3 Voice recognition interface
WP.4 Response system interface
WP.5 Data analysis interface

Installation, and *Test.* The *Software Development* deliverable (shaded), has been extended down to level 5 work packages. Level 4 subdeliverables represent the lowest manageable elements of the project. Each subdeliverable requires work packages that will be completed by an assigned organizational unit. Each deliverable will be successively divided in this manner. It is not necessary to divide all elements of the WBS to the same level.

The lowest level of the WBS is called a *work package.* Work packages are short-duration tasks that have a definite start and stop point, consume resources, and represent cost. Each work package is a control point. A work package manager is responsible for seeing that the package is completed on time, within budget, and according to technical specifications. Practice suggests a work package should not exceed 10 work days or 1 reporting period. If a work package has a duration exceeding 10 days, check or monitoring points should be established within the duration, say every 3 to 5 days, so progress and problems can be identified before too much time has passed. Each work package of the WBS should be as independent of other packages of the project as possible. No work package is described in more than one subdeliverable of the WBS.

There is an important difference between the last work breakdown subdeliverable and a work package. Typically, a work breakdown subdeliverable includes the outcomes of more than one work package from perhaps two or three departments. Therefore, the subdeliverable does not have a duration of its own and does not consume resources or cost money directly. (In a sense, of course, a duration for a particular work breakdown element can be derived from identifying which work package must start first [earliest] and which package will be the latest to finish; the difference becomes the duration for the subdeliverable.) The resources and costs for the subdeliverable are simply the summation of the resources and costs for all the work packages in the work subdeliverable. This is the basis for the term *project rollup*; starting with the work package, costs and resources can be "rolled up" into the higher elements. The higher elements are used to identify deliverables at different phases in the project and to develop status reports during the execution stage of the project life cycle. Thus, the work package is the basic unit used for planning, scheduling, and controlling the project.

To review, each work package in the WBS

1. Defines work (what).
2. Identifies time to complete a work package (how long).
3. Identifies a time-phased budget to complete a work package (cost).
4. Identifies resources needed to complete a work package (how much).
5. Identifies a single person responsible for units of work (who).
6. Identifies monitoring points for measuring progress.

Creating a WBS from scratch can be a daunting task. Project managers should take advantage of relevant examples to facilitate the process. WBS's are products of group efforts. If the project is small, the entire project team may be involved breaking down the project into its components. For large, complex projects the people responsible for the major deliverables are likely to meet to establish the first two levels of deliverables. In turn, further detail would be delegated to the people responsible for the specific work. Collectively this information would be gathered and integrated into a formal WBS by a project support person. The final version would be reviewed by the inner echelon of the project team. Relevant stakeholders (most notably customers) would be consulted to confirm agreement and revise when appropriate.

Project managers developing their first WBS frequently forget that the structure should be end-item, output oriented. First attempts often result in a WBS that follows the organization structure—design, marketing, production, finance. If a WBS follows the organization structure, the focus will be on the organization function and processes rather than the project output or deliverables. In addition, a WBS with a process focus will become an accounting tool that records costs by function rather than a tool for "output" management. Every effort should be made to develop a WBS that is output oriented in order to concentrate on concrete deliverables. Organizational unit responsibility can be tied to the WBS by grouping the work packages of a deliverable into a cost account while still maintaining the focus on completing the deliverable. This process is discussed next.

Step 4: Integrating the WBS with the Organization

An integral part of creating the WBS is to define the organizational units responsible for performing the work. In practice, the outcome of this process is the organization breakdown structure (OBS). The OBS depicts how the firm has organized to discharge work responsibility. The purposes of the OBS are to provide a framework to summarize organization unit work performance, to identify organization units responsible for work packages, and to tie the organizational unit to cost control accounts. Recall, cost accounts group similar work packages (usually under the purview of a department). The OBS defines the organization

FIGURE 4–5

Integration of WBS and OBS

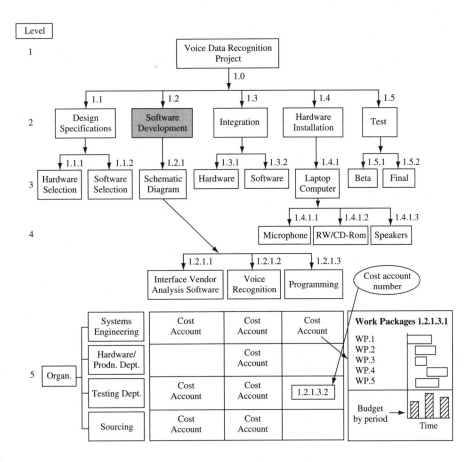

subdeliverables in a hierarchical pattern in successively smaller and smaller units. Frequently, the traditional organization structure can be used. Even if the project is performed entirely by a team, it is necessary to break down the team structure for assigning responsibility for budgets, time, and technical performance.

As in the WBS, the OBS assigns the lowest organizational unit the responsibility for work packages within a cost account. Herein lies one major strength of using WBS and OBS; they can be *integrated* as shown in Figure 4–5. The intersection of work packages and the organizational unit creates a project control point (cost account) that integrates work and responsibility. The intersection of the WBS and OBS represents the set of work packages necessary to complete the subdeliverable located immediately above and the organizational unit on the left responsible for accomplishing the packages at the intersection. Later we will use the intersection as a cost account for management control of projects. For example, the department is responsible for the work packages in two cost accounts—under deliverables *Interface Vendor Analysis Software* and *Voice Recognition*. Control can be checked from two directions—outcomes and responsibility. In the execution phase of the project, progress can be tracked vertically on deliverables (client's interest) and tracked horizontally by organization responsibility (management's interest). Although it is possible to graphically show an integrated WBS/OBS (e.g., Figure 4–5) for demonstration purposes, software programs do not draw diagrams as we have shown. The graphic output requirements for large projects make such graphic descriptions impractical by sheer size alone. Typical software packages allow project managers to sort by WBS and/or OBS, which simply presents the information in another form—columns or lists. See Tables 4–1A and 4–1B.

TABLE 4–1A   Work Packages Sorted by WBS

	Sorted by WBS	Direct Labor Budget		
1.2.1	Schematic diagram	$185		
1.2.1.1	Interface vendor			
	Data analysis software		40	
	Systems engineering			15
	Test			5
	Sourcing			20
1.2.1.2	Voice recognition		50	
	Systems engineering			15
	Hardware/prodn. dept.			10
	Test			15
	Sourcing			10
1.2.1.3	Programing		95	
	Systems engineering			60
	Test			35

TABLE 4–1B   **Work Packages Sorted by OBS**

Sorted by OBS		Direct Labor Budget	
Systems Engineering		90	
1.2.1.1	Interface vendor		
	Data analysis software		15
1.2.1.2	Voice recognition		15
1.2.1.3	Programing		60
Hardware/Prodn. Dept.		10	
1.2.1.2	Voice recognition		10
Test		55	
1.2.1.1	Interface vendor		
	Data analysis software		5
1.2.1.2	Voice recognition		15
1.2.1.3	Programing		35
Sourcing		30	
1.2.1.1	Interface vendor		
	Data analysis software		20
1.2.1.2	Voice recognition		10
Total		185	

Step 5: Coding the WBS for the Information System

Gaining the maximum usefulness of a breakdown structure depends on a coding system. The codes are used to define levels and elements in the WBS, organization elements, work packages, and budget and cost information. The codes allow reports to be consolidated at any level in the structure. The most commonly used scheme in practice is numeric indention. An example for our Voice Data Recognition project and the Software Development deliverable in Figure 4–5 is presented below:

1.0 Voice Data Recognition Project

    1.2 Software Development

        1.2.1 Schematic Diagram

            1.2.1.1 Interface Vendor Data Analysis Software

            1.2.1.2 Voice Recognition

            1.2.1.3 Programming

                1.2.1.3.1 Work package—Main menu/pull-down menus

                1.2.1.3.2 Work package—Vendor audio program

                1.2.1.3.3 Work package—Voice recognition interface

                1.2.1.3.4 Work package—Response system interface

                1.2.1.3.5 Work package—Data analysis interface

Note the project identification is 1.0. Each successive indention represents a lower element or work package. Ultimately the numeric scheme reaches down to the work package level, and all tasks and elements in the structure have an identification code. The "cost account" is the focal point because all budgets, work assignments, time, cost, and technical performance come together at this point.

This coding system can be extended to cover large projects. Additional schemes can be added for special reports. For example, adding a "−3" after the code could indicate a site location, an elevation, or a special account such as labor. Some letters can be used as special identifiers, such as "M" for materials or "E" for engineers. You are not limited to only 10 subdivisions (0–9); you can extend each subdivision to large numbers—for example, .1–.99 or .1–.9999. If the project is small, you can use whole numbers. The following example is from a large, complex project:

3R–237A–P2–3.6

"3R" identifies the facility, 237A represents elevation and the area, P2 represents pipe two inches wide, and 33.6 represents the work package number. In practice most organizations are creative in combining letters and numbers to minimize the length of WBS codes.

Project Rollup

Figure 4–6 shows hypothetical labor costs and work packages for the schematic diagram deliverable of the *Voice Data Recognition* project. The intersection of the systems engineering and programming shows five work packages in the cost account with budgets of $18, $12, $10, $13, and $7, which total $60. Rollup to the programming element (summation of all cost accounts below the element) is $95. The schematic diagram element that includes all first level elements has a budget of $185. The rollup for the organizational units operates in a similar fashion. For example, the systems engineering department has responsibility for the work packages found in interface vendor analysis software, voice recognition, and programming cost accounts. These accounts each have a labor budget of $15, $15, and $60 respectively, or a total of $90. The test department has a total budget of $55. Of course the total for the organization units delivering the schematic diagram element is the same as the total budget of all elements rolled up to the schematic diagram element. This ability to consolidate and integrate using the rollup process demonstrates the potential value of the WBS for managing the project. Remember, the units do not have to be money; the units can be resources, labor hours, materials, time, or any units that contribute to the completion of deliverables. However, at the cost account level the units have to be the same throughout the structure.

FIGURE 4–6

Direct Labor Budget Rollup

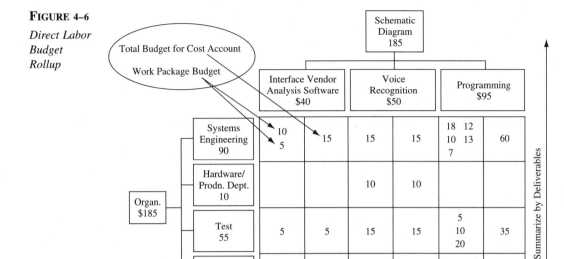

Summarize by Deliverables

Summarize by Organization Units

Process Breakdown Structure

The WBS is best suited for design and build projects that have tangible outcomes, such as an offshore mining facility or a new car prototype. The project can be decomposed or broken down into major deliverables, subdeliverables, further subdeliverables, and ultimately to work packages. It is more difficult to apply WBS to less tangible, *process-oriented* projects in which the final outcome is a product of a series of steps or phases. Here the big difference is that the project evolves over time with each phase affecting the next phase. IT projects typically fall in this category—for example, creating an extranet Web site or an internal software database system. These projects are driven by performance requirements, not by plans or blueprints. Some practitioners choose to utilize what we refer to as a Process Breakdown Structure (PBS) instead of the classic WBS.

Figure 4–7 provides an example of a PBS for a software development project. Instead of being organized around deliverables, the project is organized around phases. Each of the five major phases can be broken down into more specific activities until a sufficient level of detail is achieved to communicate what needs to be done to complete that phase. People can be assigned to specific activities and

FIGURE 4–7

*PBS for
Software
Development
Project*

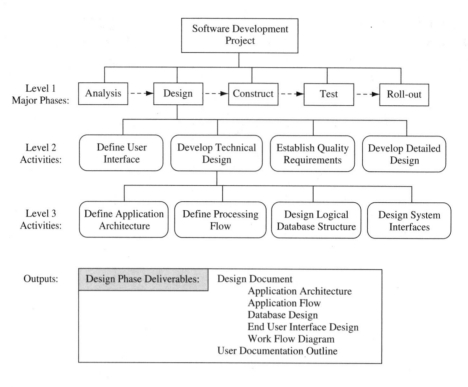

a complementary OBS can be created just as is done for the WBS. Deliverables are not ignored but are defined as outputs required to move to the next phase.

Checklists that contain the phase exit requirements are developed to manage project progress. These checklists provide the means to support phase walk-throughs and reviews. Each phase checklist defines the exit requirement for a phase. Checklists vary depending upon the project and activities involved but typically include the following details:

- Deliverables needed to exit a phase and begin a new one
- Quality checkpoints to ensure that deliverables are complete and accurate
- Sign-offs by all responsible stakeholders to indicate that the phase has been successfully completed and that the project should move on to the next phase

As long as exit requirements are firmly established and deliverables for each phase are well defined, the PBS provides a suitable alternative to the WBS for projects that involve extensive development work.

Responsibility Matrices

In many cases, the size and scope of the project do not warrant an elaborate WBS or OBS. One tool that is widely used by project managers and task force leaders of small projects is the *responsibility matrix* (RM). The RM (sometimes called a linear responsibility chart) summarizes the tasks to be accomplished and who is responsible for what on a project. In its simplest form an RM consists of a chart listing all the project activities and the participants responsible for each activity. For example, Figure 4–8 illustrates an RM for a market research study. In this matrix the R is used to identify the committee member who is responsible for co-ordinating the efforts of other team members assigned to the task and making sure that the task is completed. The S is used to identify members of the five-person team who will support and/or assist the individual responsible. Simple RMs like

FIGURE 4–8

Responsibility Matrix for a Market Research Project

	R = RESPONSIBLE S = SUPPORTS/ASSISTS				
	Project Team				
Task	*Richard*	*Dan*	*Dave*	*Linda*	*Elizabeth*
Identify Target Customers	R	S		S	
Develop Draft Questionnaire	R	S	S		
Pilot-test Questionnaire		R		S	
Finalize Questionnaire	R	S	S	S	
Print Questionnaire					R
Prepare Mailing Labels					R
Mail Questionnaires					R
Receive and Monitor Returned Questionnaires				R	S
Input Response Data			R		
Analyze Results		R	S	S	
Prepare Draft of Report	S	R	S	S	
Prepare Final Report	R		S		

this one are useful not only for organizing and assigning responsibilities for small projects but also for subprojects of large, more complex projects.

More complex RMs not only identify individual responsibilities but also clarify critical interfaces between units and individuals that require coordination. For example, Figure 4–9 is an RM for a larger, more complex project to develop a new piece of test equipment. Notice that within each cell a numeric coding scheme is used to define the nature of involvement on that specific task. Such an RM extends the WBS/OBS and provides a clear and concise method for depicting responsibility, authority, and communication channels.

FIGURE 4–9

Responsibility Matrix for the Computer-Controlled Conveyor Belt Project

Legend

1 Responsible
2 Support
3 Consult
4 Notification
5 Approval

ORGANIZATION

DELIVERABLES	Design	Development	Documentation	Assembly	Testing	Purchasing	Quality Assur.	Manufacturing
Architectural Design	1	2			2		3	3
Hardware Specifications	2	1				2	3	
Kernel Specifications	1	3						3
Utilities Specification	2	1			3			
Hardware Design	1			3		3		3
Disk Drivers	3	1	2					
Memory Management	1	3			3			
Operating System Documentation	2	2	1					3
Prototypes	5		4	1	3	3	3	4
Integrated Acceptance Test	5	2	2		1		5	5

Responsibility matrices provide a means for all participants in a project to view their responsibilities and agree on their assignments. They also help clarify the extent or type of authority exercised by each participant in performing an activity in which two or more parties have overlapping involvement. By using an RM and by defining authority, responsibility, and communications within its framework, the relationship between different organizational units and the work content of the project are made clear.

Summary

The project scope definition and breakdown structure are the keys to nearly every aspect of managing the project. The scope definition provides focus and emphasis on the end item(s) of the project. The structure helps ensure all tasks of the project are identified and provides two views of the project—one on deliverables and one on organization responsibility. The WBS avoids having the project driven by organization function or a finance system. The structure forces attention to realistic requirements of personnel, hardware, and budgets. Use of the structure provides a powerful framework for project control that identifies deviations from plan, identifies responsibility, and spots areas for improved performance. No well-developed project plan or control system is possible without a disciplined, structured approach. The WBS, OBS, and cost account codes provide this discipline. This same discipline can be achieved by creating a PBS for development projects and a responsibility matrix for smaller projects.

The next step in the project management process is to develop the project network to time-phase work, resources, and budgets. *In practice the WBS, network, schedule, and baseline are all developed in one step.* Since many projects have an imposed duration and budget, making times and budgets match these requirements can cause several preplanning passes. The integration of the WBS and project network development is a complex step that requires the full attention of the project manager.

5

THE CHALLENGE OF ESTIMATING PROJECT TIMES AND COSTS

Project estimation is indeed a yardstick for project cost control. And if the yardstick is faulty, you start on the "wrong foot." It is in this context that we exhort you not to underestimate the estimate.
O. P. Kharbanda and Jeffrey K. Pinto

Estimating is the process of forecasting the time and cost of completing project deliverables. The processes used are unique to each organization; you can't buy them off the shelf. However, in practice, estimating processes are frequently classified as top down (macro) or bottom up (micro). Top-down estimates are usually derived from analogy or mathematical relationships. Bottom-up estimates are typically based on estimates of elements found in the work breakdown structure (WBS). In a few situations both methods are used and reasons for any differences are reconciled.

Everyone prefers accurate cost and time estimates, but most understand the inherent uncertainty in all projects. Inaccurate estimates lead to false expectations and consumer dissatisfaction. Accuracy is improved with greater effort, but is it worth the time and cost? Estimating effort costs money! Many factors impact estimating accuracy and effort.

Costs, times, and budgets are the lifelines for control; they serve as the standards for comparison between the plan and the actual throughout the life of the project. Project rollup and project status reports depend on reliable estimates as the major input for measuring variances and taking corrective action. Thus, getting accurate time estimates is important for project schedule *and* cost. Ideally, the project manager, and in most cases the customer, would prefer to have a database of detailed schedule and cost estimates for every work package in the project. Regrettably, such detailed data gathering is not always possible or practical, and other methods are used to develop project estimates. Project estimating becomes a task of balancing the expectations of major stakeholders and the need for control while the project is implemented.

Factors Influencing the Quality of Estimates

Many factors influence the quality of estimates. The most important are:

- Past experience
- The planning horizon
- Use of new technology
- The people factor

Past Experience

A typical statement in the field is the desire to ". . . have a 95 percent probability of meeting time and cost estimates." Past experience is a good starting point for developing time and cost estimates. But past experience estimates almost always must be refined by other considerations to reach the 95 percent probability level. Factors related to the uniqueness of the project will have a strong influence on the accuracy of estimates. Project, people, and external factors all need to be considered to improve quality of estimates for project times and costs.

The Planning Horizon

The quality of the estimate depends on the planning horizon; estimates of current events are close to 100 percent but are reduced for more distant events. The accuracy of time and cost estimates should improve as you move from the conceptual phase to the point where individual work packages are defined.

New Technology

Time to implement new technology has a habit of expanding in an increasing, nonlinear fashion. Sometimes poorly written scope specifications for new technology result in errors in estimating times and costs. Environmental conditions for a project also can produce errors. Long-duration projects increase the uncertainty in estimates. A predetermined imposed time-to-market duration can profoundly influence time and cost estimates for the project.

The People Factor

The people factor can also introduce errors in estimating times and cost. For example, accuracy of estimates depends on the skills of the people making the estimates. A close match of people skills to the task will influence productivity and learning time. Similarly, whether members of the project team have worked together before on similar projects will influence the time it takes to coalesce into an effective team. Sometimes factors such as staff turnover can influence estimates. It should be noted that increasing the number of new people on a project increases time spent communicating.

Project Structure

Which project structure is chosen to manage the project will influence time and cost estimates. One of the major advantages of a dedicated project team discussed earlier is the speed gained from concentrated focus and localized project decision making. This speed comes at an additional cost of tying up personnel full-time. Conversely, projects operating in a matrix environment may reduce costs by more efficiently sharing personnel across projects but may take longer to complete since attention is divided and coordination demands are higher.

Padding Estimates

In work situations that ask for time and cost estimates, most of us are inclined to add a little padding to increase the probability and reduce the risk of being late or over budget. If everyone at all levels of the project adds a little padding to reduce risk, the project duration and cost are seriously overstated. This phenomenon causes some managers or owners to call for a 10 to 15 percent cut in time and/or cost for the project. Of course the next time the game is played, the person estimating cost and/or time will pad the estimate to 20 percent or more. Clearly such games defeat chances for realistic estimates, which is what is needed to be competitive.

Organization Culture

Organization culture can significantly influence project estimates. In some organizations padding estimates is tolerated and even privately encouraged. Other organizations place a premium on accuracy and strongly discourage estimating gamesmanship. The political environment in some organizations allows senior executives to go around the project priority process by underestimating project cost to gain approval and commitment during the conceptual stage.

Organizations vary in the importance they attach to estimates. The prevailing belief in some organizations is that detailed estimating takes too much time and is not worth the effort or that it's impossible to predict the future. Other organizations subscribe to the belief that accurate estimates are the bedrock of effective project management. Organization culture shapes every dimension of project management; estimating is not immune to this influence.

Nonproject Factors

Finally, nonproject factors can refine time and cost estimates. For example, equipment downtime can alter time estimates. National holidays, vacations, and legal limits can influence project estimates. Project priority can influence resource assignment and impact time and cost.

Project estimating is a complex process. The quality of time and cost estimates can be improved when these variables are considered in making the estimates. Estimates of time and cost together allow the manager to develop a time-phased budget baseline.

Macro versus Micro Estimating

Since estimating effort costs money, the time and detail devoted to estimating is an important decision. Statements similar to those below strongly influence the decision to use macro estimates (top-down) or micro estimates (bottom-up).

"Rough order of magnitude is good enough. Spending time on detailed estimating wastes money."

"Time is everything; our survival depends on getting there first! Time and cost accuracy is not an issue."

"The project is internal. We don't need to worry about cost."

"The uncertainty is so great, spending time and money on estimates is a waste."

"The project is so small; we don't need to bother with estimates. Just do it."

"They used an initial estimate 'for strategic decisions' and then we had to live with it."

"This is our key client. We come in on time and on budget or we are finished."

"We were burned once. I want a detailed estimate of every task by the people responsible."

These statements indicate there are sound reasons for using macro or micro estimates. Table 5–1 depicts conditions that suggest one approach is preferred over another.

TABLE 5–1   Conditions for Preferring Top-Down or Bottom-Up Time and Cost Estimates

Condition	Macroestimates	Microestimates
Strategic decision making	X	
Cost and time important		X
High uncertainty	X	
Internal, small project	X	
Fixed-price contract		X
Customer wants details		X
Unstable scope	X	

Top-down estimates usually are derived from someone who uses experience and/or information to determine the project duration and total cost. These estimates are sometimes made by top managers who have very little knowledge of the processes used to complete the project. For example, a mayor of a major city making a speech noted that a new law building would be constructed at a cost of $23 million and be ready for occupancy in 2½ years. Although the mayor probably asked for an estimate from someone, the estimate could have come from a luncheon meeting with a local contractor who wrote an estimate (guesstimate) on a napkin. This is an extreme example, but in a relative sense this scenario is frequently played out in practice. The question is, *do these estimates represent low-cost, efficient methods?* Do the top-down estimates of project time and cost become a self-fulfilling prophecy in terms of setting time and cost parameters?

It is important to recognize that these first macro estimates are only a rough cut and typically occur in the "conceptual" stage of the project. The top-down estimates are helpful in initial development of a complete plan. However, such estimates are sometimes significantly off the mark because little detailed information is gathered. At this level individual work items are not identified. Or, in a few cases, the top-down estimates are not realistic because top management "wants the project." Nevertheless, the initial top-down estimates are helpful in determining whether the project warrants more formal planning, which would include more detailed estimates.

The next step, if possible and practical, is to push the estimating process down to the work package level for bottom-up estimates that establish low-cost, efficient methods. This process can take place after the project has been defined in detail. Good sense suggests project estimates should come from the people most knowledgable about the estimate needed. The bottom-up approach at the work package level can serve as a check on cost elements in the WBS by rolling up the work packages and associated cost accounts. Similarly, resource requirements can be checked. Later, the time, resource, and cost estimates from the work packages can be consolidated into time-phased networks, resource schedules, and budgets that are used for control.

The ideal approach is for the project manager to allow enough time for both the top-down and bottom-up estimates to be worked out so a complete plan based on reliable estimates can be offered to the customer. In this way false expectations are minimized for all stakeholders and negotiation is reduced. The bottom-up approach also provides the customer with an opportunity to compare the low-cost, efficient method approach with any imposed restrictions. For example, if the project completion duration is imposed at 2 years and your bottom-up analysis tells you the project will take 2½ years, the client can now consider the trade-off of the low-cost method versus compressing the project to 2 years—or in rare cases canceling the project. Similar trade-offs can be compared for different levels of resources or increases in technical performance. The assumption is that any movement away from the low-cost, efficient method will increase costs—e.g., overtime.

The best approach is to make rough top-down estimates, develop the WBS/OBS, make bottom-up estimates, develop schedules and budgets, and reconcile differences between top-down and bottom-up estimates. Hopefully, these steps are done *before* final negotiation with either an internal or external customer. With both top-down and bottom-up approaches, managers must be sensitive to factors that can influence project estimates.

Estimating Project Times and Costs

Macro Approaches

At the strategic level macro estimating methods are used to evaluate the project proposal. Sometimes much of the information needed to derive accurate time and cost estimates is not available in the initial phase of the project—for example, design is not finalized. In these situations, macro estimates are used until the tasks in the WBS are clearly defined.

Ratio Methods. Macro methods (sometimes called parametric methods) are usually top down and use surrogates or ratios to estimate project times or costs. Macro approaches are often used in the concept or "need" phase of a project to get an initial duration and cost estimate for the project. For example, contractors frequently use the number of square feet to estimate the cost and time to build a house; that is, a house of 2700 square feet might cost might cost $110 per square foot (2,700 feet × $110 per foot equals $297,000) and take approximately 100 days to complete. Two other common examples of macro cost estimates are the cost for a new plant estimated by capacity size or a software product estimated by features and complexity.

Apportion Method.   This method is an extension of the ratio method. Apportionment is used when projects closely follow past projects in features and costs. Given good historical data, estimates can be made quickly with little effort and reasonable accuracy. This method is very common in projects that are relatively standard but have some small variation or customization.

Anyone who has borrowed money from a bank to build a house has been exposed to this process. Given an estimated total cost for the house, banks and the FHA pay out money to the contractor by completion of specific segments of the house. For example, the foundation might represent 3 percent of the total loan, framing 25 percent, electric plumbing and heating 15 percent, etc. Payments are made as these items are completed. An analogous process is used by some companies that apportion costs to deliverables in the WBS—given average cost percentages from past projects. Figure 5–1 presents an example similar to one found in practice. Assuming the total project cost is estimated using a macro estimate to be $500,000, the costs are apportioned as shown.

For example, the costs apportioned to the "Document" deliverable are 5 percent or $25,000. The subdeliverables "Doc-1" and "Doc-2" are allocated $10,000 and $15,000 respectively.

FIGURE 5–1

Apportion Method of Allocating Project Costs Using the Work Breakdown Structure

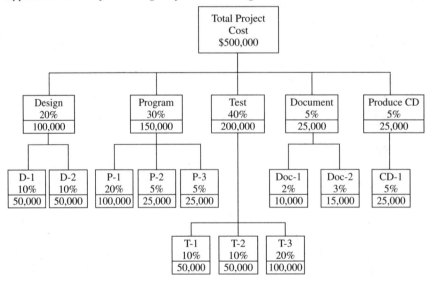

Function Point Methods for Software and System Projects. In the software industry, software development projects are frequently estimated using weighted macro variables called "function points" or major parameters such as number of inputs, number of outputs, number of inquires, number of data files, and number of interfaces. These weighted variables are adjusted for a complexity factor and added. The total adjusted count provides the basis for estimating the labor effort and cost for a project (usually using a regression formula derived from data of past projects). This latter method assumes adequate historical data for the industry and by type of software project—for example, MIS systems. In the U.S. software industry 1 person-month represents on average 5 function points. Such historical data provide a basis for estimating the project duration.[1] Variations of this top-down approach are used by companies such as IBM, Bank of America, Sears Roebuck, HP, AT & T, Ford Motors, GE, Du Pont, and many others. See Table 5–2 and Table 5–3 for a simplified example of function point count methodology.

Given the function point count (e.g., 660) and regression weights from past projects, the cost and duration (in person-months and number of people) of a project is easily computed. For example, given 660 function points and good historical data, the average person-months might be 130 (13 people, a duration of 10 months), and a total cost of $1.2 million. Although functional point metrics are useful, their accuracy depends on adequate historical data, currency of data, and relevancy of the project to past averages.[1,3]

Learning Curves. Some projects require the same task, group of tasks, or product be repeated several times. Managers know intuitively that the time to perform a task improves with repetition. This phenomenon is especially true of tasks that are labor intensive. In these circumstances the pattern of improvement phenomenon can be used to predict the reduction in time to perform the task. From empirical

---

TABLE 5–2 Simplified Basic Function Point Count Process for a Prospective Project

Element	Low	Average	High	Total
	Complexity Weighting			
Number of *inputs*	___ × 2 +	___ × 3 +	___ × 4	= ___
Number of *outputs*	___ × 3 +	___ × 6 +	___ × 9	= ___
Number of *inquiries*	___ × 2 +	___ × 4 +	___ × 6	= ___
Number of *files*	___ × 5 +	___ × 8 +	___ × 12	= ___
Number of *interfaces*	___ × 5 +	___ × 10 +	___ × 15	= ___

TABLE 5–3   **Example: Function Point Count Method**

Software Project 13: Patient Admitting and Billing

15	Inputs	Rated complexity as low	(2)
5	Outputs	Rated complexity as average	(6)
10	Inquiries	Rated complexity as average	(4)
30	Files	Rated complexity as high	(12)
20	Interfaces	Rated complexity as average	(10)

Application of Complexity Factor

Element	Count	Low	Average	High	Total
Inputs	15	× 2			= 30
Outputs	5		× 6		= 30
Inquiries	10		× 4		= 40
Files	30			× 12	= 360
Interfaces	20		× 10		= 200
				Total	660

evidence across *all* industries, the pattern of this improvement has been quantified in the **learning curve** (also known as *improvement curve, experience curve,* and *industrial progress curve*), which is described by the following relationship:

> Each time the output quantity doubles, the unit labor hours are reduced at constant rate.

In practice the improvement ratio may vary from 60 percent, representing very large improvement, to 100 percent representing no improvement that all. Generally, as the difficulty of the work decreases, the expected improvement also decreases and the improvement ratio that is used becomes greater. One significant factor to consider is the proportion of labor in the task in relation to machine paced work. Obviously, a lower percentage of improvement can occur only in operations with high labor content.

The main disadvantage of macro approaches to estimating is simply that the time and cost for a specific task are not considered. Grouping many tasks into a common basket encourages errors of omission and the use of imposed times and costs.

Micro Approaches

Template Method.   If the project is similar to past projects, the costs from past projects can be used as a starting point for the new project. Differences in the new project can be noted and past times and costs adjusted to reflect these differences.

For example, a ship repair dry dock firm has a set of estimates for standard repair projects (i.e., templates for overhaul, electrical, mechanical) that they use as a *starting point* for estimating the cost and duration of any new project. The differences between the standard project and the new project are noted, and changes are made to the estimate as necessary. This approach enables the firm to develop a potential schedule, estimate costs, and develop a budget in a very short time. Developing such templates in a database can quickly reduce estimate errors.

Parametric Procedures Applied to Specific Tasks.   Just as parametric techniques such as cost per square foot can be the source of macro estimates, the same technique can be applied to specific tasks. For example, as part of an MS Office XP conversion project, 36 different computer workstations needed to be converted. Based on past conversion projects, the project manager determined that on average one person could convert 3 workstations per day. Therefore the task of converting the 36 workstations would take 3 technicians 4 days [(36/3)/3]. Similarly, to estimate the wallpapering allowance on a house remodel, the contractor figured a cost of $5 per square yard of wallpaper and $2 per yard to install it, for a total cost of $7. By measuring the length and height of all the walls, she was able to calculate the total area in square yards and multiply it by $7.

Detailed Estimates for the WBS Work Packages.   Probably the most reliable method for estimating time and cost is to use the WBS and to ask the people responsible for the work package to make the estimates. They know from experience or know where to find the information to estimate work package durations—especially those that depend on labor hours and costs. When work packages have significant uncertainty associated with the time to completion, it is a prudent policy to require three time estimates—low, average, and high. Figure 5–2 presents a hypothetical example using three time estimates for a work package. This time

FIGURE 5–2

*Read/Write
Head Design*

Work Package Cost Estimate			
	Cost		
DIRECT COSTS	*Low*	*Average*	*High*
Design engineers	80	100	150
Proto engineers	130	150	280
Materials	25	25	25
Equipment Rental	25	25	30
TOTAL DIRECT COSTS	260	300	485

estimating approach gives the project manager and client an opportunity to assess the risks associated with project times (and thus, costs). The approach helps to reduce surprises as the project progresses. The three-time estimate approach also provides a basis for assessing risk and determining the contingency fund. (See Chapter 7 for a discussion of contingency funds.)

A Hybrid: Phase Estimating.   This approach begins with a macro estimate for the project and then refines estimates for phases of the project as they are implemented. Some projects by their nature cannot be rigorously defined because of the uncertainty of design or the final product. Although rare, such projects do exist such as aerospace projects, IT projects, new technology projects, and construction projects where the design is incomplete. In these projects, phase or life-cycle estimating is frequently used. *Project Management in Action: Estimate Accuracy During Project Life Cycle* illustrates the difficulty of accurately estimating projects.

Project Management in Action

Estimate Accuracy During Project Life Cycle

The authors have found this phenomenon in the field and developed the table below to approximate our observations

Time and Cost Estimate Accuracy during Project Life Cycle and by Type of Project

	Bricks and Mortar	*Information Technology*
Conceptual stage	+60 percent to −30%	+200 percent to −30 percent
Deliverables defined	+30 percent to −15 percent	+100 percent to −15 percent
Work packages defined	+15 percent to −5 percent	+50 percent to −5 percent

For example, information technology projects that determine their time and cost estimates in the conceptual stage can expect their "actuals" to err up to 200 percent over cost and duration, and perhaps as much as 30 percent under estimates. Conversely, estimates for buildings, roads, etc., made after the work packages are clearly defined have a smaller error in actual costs and times of 15 percent over estimate and 5 percent less than estimate. Although these estimates vary by project, they can serve as ballpark numbers for project stakeholders selecting how project time and cost estimates will be derived.

Phase estimating is used when an unusual amount of uncertainty surrounds a project and it is impractical to estimate times and costs for the entire project. Phase estimating uses a two-estimate system over the life of the project. A detailed estimate is developed for the immediate phase and a macro estimate is made for the remaining phases of the project. Figure 5–3 depicts the phases of a project and the progression of estimates over its life.

For example, when the project need is determined, a macro estimate of the project cost and duration is made so analysis and decisions can be made. Simultaneously a detailed estimate is made for deriving project specifications and for a macro estimate for the remainder of the project. As the project progresses and specifications are solidified, a detailed estimate for design is made, and a macro estimate is made for the remainder of the project. Clearly, as the project progresses through its life cycle and more information is available, the reliability of the estimates should improve.

Phase estimating is preferred by people working on projects where the final product is not known and the uncertainty is very large—for example, the integration of wireless phones and computers. The commitment to cost and schedule is necessary only for the next phase of the project, and commitment to unrealistic future schedules and costs based on poor information is avoided. This progressive macro/micro method provides a stronger basis for using schedule and cost estimates to manage progress during the next phase.

Unfortunately, your customer—internal or external—will want an accurate estimate of schedule and cost the moment the decision is made to implement the project. Additionally, the customer who is paying for the project often perceives

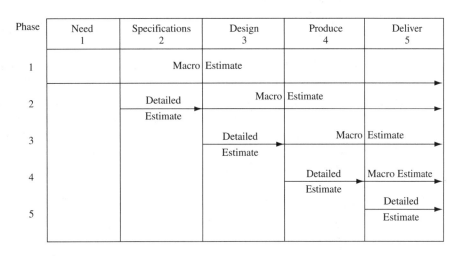

FIGURE 5–3

Phase Estimating over Project Life Cycle

phase estimating as a blank check because costs and schedules are not firm over most of the project life cycle. Even though the reasons for phase estimating are sound and legitimate, most customers have to be sold on its legitimacy. A major advantage for the customer is the opportunity to change features, reevaluate, or even cancel the project in each new phase. In conclusion, phase estimating is very useful for projects that have an uncertain final product.

Level of Detail

Level of Detail for Top and Middle Management

Level of detail is different for different levels of management. At any level the detail should be no more than is necessary and sufficient. Top management interests usually center on the total project and major milestone events that mark major accomplishments—e.g., "build oil platform in the North Sea" or "complete prototype." Middle management might center on one segment of the project or one milestone. First-line managers' interests may be limited to one task or work package. One of the beauties of WBS is the ability to aggregate network information so each level of management can have the kind of information it needs to make decisions.

Level of Detail for Project Managers

Practicing project managers advocate keeping the level of detail to a minimum. But there are limits to this suggestion. One of the most frequent errors of new project managers is to forget that the task time estimate will be used to control schedule and cost performance. A rule of thumb frequently used by practicing project managers says that a task duration should not exceed 5 workdays or at the most 10 workdays, if workdays are the time units used for the project. Such a rule probably will result in a more detailed network, but the additional detail pays off in controlling schedule and cost as the project progresses.

For example, suppose the task is "build prototype computer-controlled conveyor belt," the time estimate is 40 workdays, and the budget $300,000. It may be better to divide the task into seven or eight smaller tasks for control purposes. If one of the smaller tasks gets behind because of problems or a poor time estimate, it will be possible to take corrective action quickly and avoid delaying successive tasks and the project. If the single task of 40 workdays is used, it is possible that no corrective action would be taken until day 40, since many people have a tendency to "wait and see" or avoid admitting they are behind or passing on bad news; the result may mean far more than 5 days behind schedule. The 5–10 day rule of thumb applies to cost and performance goals. A similar check is needed on cost and performance goals at short time intervals to avoid losing control.

If using the rule of thumb suggested above results in too many network tasks, an alternative is available, but it has conditions. The activity time can be extended beyond the 5 to 10 day rule only *if* control monitoring check points for segments of the task can be established so clear measures of progress can be identified by a specific percentage complete. This information is invaluable to the control process of measuring schedule and cost performance—for example, payments for contract work are paid on "percentage complete." Defining a task with clear start, intermediate, and end points enhances the chances of early detection of problems, corrective action, and on-time project completion.

Getting the level of detail in the WBS to match management needs for effective implementation is crucial, but the delicate balance is difficult to find. The level of detail in the WBS varies with the complexity of the project; the need for control; the project size, cost, and duration; and other factors. If the structure reflects excessive detail, there is a tendency to break the work effort into department assignments. This tendency can become a barrier to success since the emphasis will be on departmental outcomes rather than on deliverable outcomes. Excessive detail also means more unproductive paperwork. Note that if the level of the WBS is increased by one, the number of cost accounts may increase geometrically. On the other hand, if the level of detail is not adequate, an organization unit may find the structure falls short of meeting its needs. Fortunately, the WBS has built-in flexibility. Participating organization units may expand their portion of the structure to meet their special needs. For example, the engineering department may wish to break down their work on a deliverable into smaller packages by electrical, civil, and mechanical. Alternatively, the marketing department may wish to break their new product promotion into TV, radio, periodicals, and newspapers.

Developing Budgets

Time-Phased Budgets

Cost estimates are not a budget. A cost estimate becomes a budget when it is time-phased. *If the estimate is not time-phased, it is impossible to control project costs!* For example, the budget for a project may be $500,000. The money is dispensed as the project is implemented. A procedure is needed to determine *when* the money must be available. Each work package estimate requires a time-phased budget. In Figure 5–4 the work package has a duration of 3 weeks; at this point there is *no way of knowing when* the work package time-phased expenses will be incurred.

FIGURE 5–4

*Work Package
Estimates*

WP Descript. _Final Version_						Page _1_ of _1_
WP ID _1.1.3.2_						Project _PC Proto_
Deliverable _Circuit Board_						Date _9/29/02_
Orgn. Unit _Software_						Estimator _RMG_
WP Duration _3_ Work Weeks						Total Budget _$ 465_

Time-Phased Budget($)

		WORK PERIODS					
DIRECT COSTS	RATE	1	2	3	4	5	TOTAL
Code	$XX/hr	50	30	20			$100
Document	$XX/hr		10	15			25
Publish	$XX/hr			5			5
TOTAL LABOR		50	40	40			$130
Materials			20				20
Equipment	$XX/hr	50	15	50			115
Other _____							
TOTAL DIRECT		100	75	90			$265

This work package duration and others are used to develop the project network that schedules when work packages will start and finish. The time-phased budgets for work packages are then assigned to scheduled time periods to determine the financial requirements for each period over the life of the project. These time-phased budgets should mirror how the actual cash needs will occur.

Perceptions of costs and budgets vary depending on their users. The project manager must be aware of these differences when setting up the project budget and when communicating these differences to others. Figure 5–5 depicts these different perceptions.[2] The project manager can commit costs months before the resource is used. This information is useful to the financial officer of the organization in forecasting future cash outflows. The project manager is interested in when the budgeted cost is expected to occur, when the budgeted cost actually is charged (earned), and when the actual cost emerges; the respective timings of these three cost figures are used to measure project schedule and cost variances.

FIGURE 5–5

Three Views of Cost

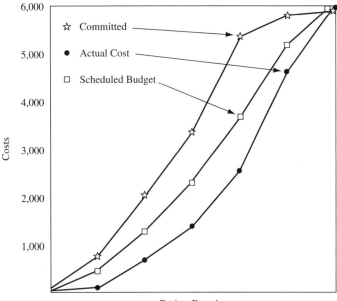

Project Duration

Types of Costs

The accuracy of the cost estimate improves as you move from the conceptual phase of the project to the point where you define individual items (work packages). Assuming work packages are defined, detailed cost estimates can be made. Here are typical kinds of costs found in a project:

1. Direct costs
    a. Labor
    b. Materials
    c. Equipment
    d. Other
2. Project overhead costs
3. General and administrative (G&A) overhead costs

The total project cost estimate is broken out in this fashion to sharpen the control process and improve decision making.

Direct Costs.   These costs are clearly chargeable to a specific work package. Direct costs can be influenced by the project manager, project team, and individuals implementing the work package. These costs represent real cash outflows and must be paid as the project progresses; therefore direct costs are usually separated from overhead costs. Lower level project rollups frequently include only direct costs.

Direct Overhead Costs.   Direct overhead rates more closely pinpoint which resources of the organization are being used in the project. Direct overhead costs can be tied to project deliverables or work packages. Examples include the salary of the project manager and temporary rental space for the project team. Although overhead is not an immediate out-of-pocket expense, it is *real* and must be covered in the long run if the firm is to remain viable. These rates are usually a ratio of the dollar value of the resources used—e.g., direct labor, materials, equipment. For example, a direct labor burden rate of 20 percent would add a direct overhead charge of 20 percent to the direct labor cost estimate. A direct charge rate of 50 percent for materials would carry a charge of 50 percent to the direct material cost estimate. Selective direct overhead charges provide a more accurate project (job or work package) cost, rather than using a blanket overhead rate for the whole project.

General and Administrative (G&A) Overhead Costs.   These represent organization costs that are not directly linked to a specific project. These costs are carried for the duration of the project. Examples include organization costs across all products and projects such as advertising, accounting, and senior management above the project level. Allocation of G&A costs varies from organization to organization. However, G & A costs usually are allocated as a percentage of the total direct cost, or a percentage of a specific direct cost such as labor, materials, or equipment.[2]

Given the totals of direct and overhead costs for individual work packages, it is possible to cumulate the costs for any deliverable or for the entire project. A percentage can be added for profit if you are a contractor. A breakdown of costs for a proposed contract bid is presented in Figure 5–6.

FIGURE 5–6

Contract Bid Summary Costs

Direct Costs	$ 80,000
Direct Overhead	$ 20,000
G&A Overhead (20%)	$ 20,000
Profit (20%)	$ 24,000
Total Bid	**$144,000**

Estimating Guidelines for Times, Costs, and Resources

Managers recognize time, cost, and resource estimates must be accurate if project planning, scheduling, and controlling are to be effective. However, there is substantial evidence suggesting poor estimates are a major contributor to projects that have failed.[1] Therefore, every effort should be made to see that initial estimates are as accurate as possible since the choice of no estimates leaves a great deal to luck and is not palatable to serious project managers. Even though a project has never been done before, a manager can follow five guidelines to develop useful work package estimates.

1. Responsibility. *At the work package level, estimates should be made by the persons most familiar with the task.* Draw on their expertise! Except for supertechnical tasks, those responsible for getting the job done on schedule and within budget are usually first-line supervisors or technicians who are experienced and familiar with the type of work involved. These people will not have some preconceived, imposed duration for a deliverable in mind. They will give an estimate based on experience and best judgment. A secondary benefit of using those responsible is the hope they will "buy in" to seeing that the estimate materializes when they implement the work package. If those involved are not consulted, it will be difficult to hold them responsible for failure to achieve the estimated time. Reliable time estimates deserve the careful attention of those responsible. Finally, drawing on the expertise of team members who will be responsible helps to build communication channels early.

Since projects represent one-time efforts, depending on other sources for task time, resource, and cost estimates has some inherent dangers. Historical data are good for highly repetitive, stable activities, but repetitive operations are uncommon in projects. A custom contractor who builds homes may consider every home to be the same—foundation, floor, walls, roof, plumbing, electricity, and finishing. But the repetition should end there. The methods for accomplishing the task (e.g., walls) and duration should differ. If the activities are indeed highly repetitive, there are other scheduling techniques that are more appropriate. Historical estimates, although low cost and easy to obtain, assume the past represents the future and may miss uncertainties that go with a new task.

2. Normal conditions. When task time, cost, and resource estimates are determined, they are based on certain assumptions. *Estimates should be based on normal conditions, efficient methods, and a normal level of resources.* Normal conditions are sometimes difficult to discern, but it is necessary to have a consensus in the organization as to what normal conditions mean in this project. If the normal workday is 8 hours, the time estimate should be based on an 8-hour day. Similarly, if the normal workday is two shifts, the time estimate should be based on a two-shift workday. Any time estimate should reflect efficient methods for the resources normally available. The time estimate should represent the normal level of resources—people or equipment. For example, if three programmers are available for coding or two road graders are available for road construction, time and cost estimates should be based on the normal level of resources unless it is anticipated the project will change what is currently viewed as normal. In addition, possible conflicts in demand for resources on parallel or concurrent activities should not be considered at this stage. The need for adding resources will be examined when the resource scheduling is discussed in Chapter 8.

3. Time units. Time units to use should be selected early in the development phase of the project network. *All task time estimates need consistent time units.* Estimates of time must consider if normal time is calendar days, workdays, workweeks, person days, single shift, hours, minutes, etc. In practice, the use of workday is the dominant choice for expressing task duration. However, in projects such as a heart transplant operation, minutes probably would be more appropriate as a time unit. One such project that used minutes as the time unit was the movement of patients from an old hospital to an elegant new one across town. Since there were several life-endangering moves, minutes were used to ensure patient safety so proper emergency life-support systems would be available if needed. The point is, network analysis requires a standard unit of time. When computer programs allow more than one option, some notation should be made of the variance from the standard unit of time. If the standard unit of time is a 5-day workweek and the estimated activity duration is in calendar days, it must be converted to the normal workweek. For example, if the shipment of a large pump to an Alaskan oilfield takes 14 calendar days from a Seattle port, the activity duration would be 10 workdays (5/7 × 14 = 10).

4. Independence. Estimators should treat the task as independent of other tasks that might be integrated by the WBS. Use of first-line managers usually results in considering tasks independently; this is good. Top managers are prone to aggregate many tasks into one time estimate and then deductively make the individual task time estimates add to the total. If tasks are in a chain and performed by the same group or department, it is best not to ask for all the time estimates in the sequence at once to avoid the tendency for a planner or a supervisor to look at the whole path and try to adjust individual task times in the sequence to meet an arbitrary imposed schedule or some rough "guesstimate" of the total time for the whole path or segment of the project. This tendency does not reflect the uncertainties of individual activities and generally results in optimistic task time estimates. In summary, each task time estimate should be considered *independently* of other activities.

5. Contingencies. *Work package estimates should not include allowances for contingencies.* The estimate should assume normal or average conditions even though every work package will not materialize as planned. For this reason top management has an extra fund for contingencies that can be used to cover unforeseen events.

Refining Estimates and Contingency Funds

As described in Chapter 4, detailed work package estimates are aggregated and "rolled up" by deliverable to estimate the total direct cost of the project. Similarly, estimated durations are entered into the project network to establish the project schedule and determine the overall duration of the project. Experience tells us that for many projects the total estimates do not materialize and the actual costs and schedule of some projects significantly exceed original work package-based estimates. (See *Project Management in Action: How Do You Estimate the Cost of a Nuclear Power Plant?*) This has lead some project managers to adjust total costs by some multiplier (i.e., total estimated costs $\times$ 1.20).

Project Management in Action

How Do You Estimate the Cost of a Nuclear Power Plant?

O. P. Kharbanda in his book (co-authored with Jeffrey K. Pinto), *What Made Gertie Gallop: Learning from Project Failures** makes the important point that estimating is as much an art as a skill. For example, early on in his career (in the 1960s), he was involved with the fabrication of a nuclear reactor in India at a time when the local facilities were not geared for such sophisticated jobs. Having had no experience in building complex equipment with (almost) unheard-of tolerances and precision, it was virtually impossible to create a reasonable advance estimate of the cost. The estimators did the best they could, then added a little more than normal margin before quoting a price to the client.

Soon after, Kharbanda happened to attend a week-long international nuclear power conference that included stalwarts in this field from all over the world. About midweek, he was fortunate to meet the chief engineer of the company that had supplied the first reactor to India, identical in design to the one his company had recently bid. This was the chance of a lifetime to finally get the inside information on accurate cost estimating. In fact, the expert confessed that his company "lost their shirt" on the Indian reactor. Then in reply to the innocent question, "How do you estimate a nuclear reactor?" the expert answered with cool confidence, "Do your normal cautious estimating, add more than normal margin and then after a short pause, double it!" Kharbanda confessed that in their ignorance they had skipped the last vital step, but this short, casual conversation proved most valuable. "We were forewarned, we took it seriously, and got forearmed. It saved us several millions of dollars."

**What Made Gertie Gallop: Learning from Project Failures,* New York: Van Nostrand Reinhold, 1996, by O. P. Kharbanda and Jeffrey K. Pinto, p. 73.

Why Are Estimates Sometimes Wrong?

The practice of adjusting original estimates by 20 or even 100 percent begs the question, "why, after investing so much time and energy on detailed estimates, could the numbers be so far off?" There are a number of reasons for this, most of which can be traced to the estimating process and the inherent uncertainty of predicting the future. Some of these reasons are discussed below:

Interaction Costs Are Hidden in Estimates.   According to the guidelines, each task estimate is supposed to be done independently. However, tasks rarely are completed in a vacuum. Work on one task is dependent upon prior tasks, and the hand-off between tasks requires time and attention. For example, people working on prototype development need to interact with design engineers after the design is completed, whether simply to ask clarifying questions, or to make adjustments in the original design. Similarly, the time necessary to coordinate activities typically is not reflected in independent estimates. Coordination is reflected in meetings and briefings as well as time necessary to resolve disconnects between tasks. Time, and therefore cost, devoted to managing interactions rises exponentially as the number of people and different disciplines involved increases on a project.

Normal Conditions Do Not Apply.   Estimates are supposed to be based on normal conditions. While this is a good starting point it rarely holds true in real life. This is especially true when it comes to the availability of resources. Resource shortages, whether in the form of people, equipment, or materials, can extend original estimates. For example, under normal conditions four bulldozers are typically used to clear a certain site size in 5 days, but the availability of only three bulldozers would extend the task duration to 8 days. Similarly, the decision to outsource certain tasks can increase costs as well as extend task durations since time is added to acclimating outsiders to the particulars of the project and the culture of the organization.

Things Go Wrong on Projects.   Design flaws are revealed after the fact, extreme weather conditions occur, accidents happen, and so forth. Although you shouldn't plan for these risks to happen when estimating a particular task, the likelihood and impact of such events need to be considered.

Project Scope and Plans Change.   As a manager gets further and further into the project he or she obtains a better understanding of what needs to be done to accomplish the project. This may lead to major changes in project plans and costs. Likewise, if it is a commercial project, changes often have to be made midstream to respond to new demands by the customer and/or competition. Unstable project scopes are a major source of cost overruns; while every effort should be made up front to nail down the project scope, it is becoming increasingly difficult to do so in our rapidly changing world.

The reality is that, for many projects, not all of the information needed to make accurate estimates is available and it is impossible to predict the future. The dilemma is that without solid estimates, the credibility of the project plan is eroded. Deadlines become meaningless. Budgets become rubbery. Accountability becomes problematic.

What Can Be Done About Incorrect Estimates?

So how do organizations deal with these challenges? First, they do the best job they can revising estimates based on relevant information prior to establishing the baseline schedule and budget. Second, they create contingency funds and time buffers to deal with uncertainty. Finally, they have a change management system in placed so that the baseline budget and schedule can be revised when events warrant it. Each of these actions will be briefly discussed below.

Adjusting Estimates.   Effective organizations adjust estimates of specific tasks once risks, resources, and particulars of the situation have been more clearly defined. They recognize that the rolled up estimates generated from a detailed estimate based on the WBS is just the starting point. As they delve further into the project planning process they make appropriate revisions both in the time and cost of specific activities. They factor the final assignment of resources into the project budget and schedule. For example, when they realize that only three instead of four bulldozers are available to clear a site they adjust both the time and cost of that activity. They adjust estimates to account for specific actions to mitigate potential risks on the project. For example, to reduce the chances of design code errors, they would add the cost of independent testers to the schedule and budget. Finally, they adjust estimates to take into account abnormal conditions. For example, if soil samples reveal excessive ground water, then they adjust foundation costs and times.

Contingency Funds and Time Buffers.   Contingency funds and time buffers are created to offset uncertainty. Adding contingency reduces the likelihood that actual costs will overrun estimates and the project will take longer than planned. In general, the less well-defined the project, the greater the contingency.

Contingency can be added to specific activities or work packages or to the project as a whole. Activity contingency is an amount added by the estimator to the initial estimate of an activity or work package to account for known uncertainties. Contingencies include such things as design changes, unreliable estimates, and risks associated with specific activities. For example, the backup plan against the risk that the project is behind schedule is to use the more expensive overnight delivery service. Note that once the risk has passed, then the specific contingency fund should be cut from the project budget and not used elsewhere. This practice discourages the tendency to expend whatever is available in the budget when costs rise.

In addition to assigning contingencies for specific tasks or activities, project managers create an overall project contingency. The amount both in terms of time and cost is proportional to the uncertainty inherent in the project, so projects with greater uncertainty are allotted a higher contingency amount. When possible the percentage contingency is derived from historical records of similar projects. For example, if previous software development projects on the average take 25 percent longer than planned, then this percentage would be added as a contingency. This contingency is used to account for hidden interaction costs as well as risks and uncertainties that cannot be pinpointed to specific tasks such as fluctuation in exchange rates, resource shortages, untested assumptions, and changes in the market.

Changing Baseline Schedule and Budget.   Sometimes events dictate reformulating the budget and schedule. Examples of such events include changes in the product concept, insurmountable technical barriers, labor strikes, legal entanglements, political upheaval, and skyrocketing wage and material costs. In these cases the original estimates no longer apply and a new baseline budget and schedule need to be created. This should only be done after careful consultation with all of the major stakeholders and should be implemented through a formal change management system. Change management and contingency funds will be further discussed in Chapter 7.

Obtaining accurate estimates is a challenge. Committed organizations accept the challenge of coming up with meaningful estimates and invest heavily in developing their capacity to do so. They understand that without an honest attempt to come up with the best estimates possible, then all else is a crapshoot. Accurate estimates reduce uncertainty and provide a discipline for effectively managing projects.

Creating a Database for Estimating

The best way to improve estimates is to collect and archive data on past project estimates and actuals. Saving historical data—estimates and actuals—provides a knowledge base for improving project time and cost estimating. Creating an estimating database is a "best practice" among leading project management organizations.

FIGURE 5–7

Estimating Database Templates

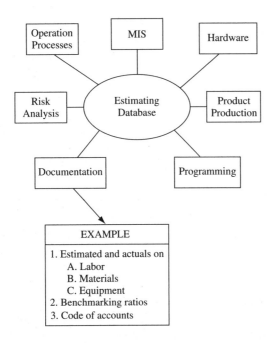

Some organizations have large estimating departments of professional estimators—e.g., Boeing, Kodak, IBM—that have developed large time and cost databases. Others collect these data through the project office. This database approach allows the project estimator to select a specific work package item from the database for inclusion. The estimator then makes any necessary adjustments concerning the materials, labor, and equipment. Of course any items not found in the database can be added to the project—and ultimately to the database if desired. Again, clearly, the quality of the database estimates depends on the experience of the estimators, but over time the data quality should improve. Such structured databases serve as estimating feedback and as benchmarks for cost and time for each project. In addition, comparison of estimate and actual for different projects can suggest the degree of risk inherent in estimates. See Figure 5–7 for the structure of a database similar to those found in practice.

Summary

Quality time and cost estimates are the bedrock of project control. Past experience is the best starting point for these estimates. The quality of estimates is influenced by other factors such as people, technology, and downtimes. The key for getting estimates that represent realistic average times and costs is to have an organization culture that allows errors in estimates without incriminations. If times represent average time, we should expect that 50 percent will be less than the estimate and 50 percent will exceed the estimate. It should also be recognized that once work gets behind, it tends to stay behind. The use of teams that are highly motivated can help in keeping task times and costs near the average. For this reason it is crucial to get team buy-in on time and cost estimates.

Using top-down (macro) estimates is good for initial and strategic decision making or in situations where the costs associated with developing better estimates have little benefit. However, in most cases the bottom-up approach (micro) to estimating is preferred and more reliable because it assesses each work package, rather than the whole project, section, or deliverable of a project. Estimating time and costs for each work package facilitates development of the project network and a time-phased budget, which are needed to control schedule and cost as the project is implemented. Using the estimating guidelines will help eliminate many common mistakes made by those unacquainted with estimating times and costs for project control. Establishing a time and cost estimating database fits well with the learning organization philosophy.

The level of time and cost detail should follow the old saying of "no more than is necessary and sufficient." Managers must remember to differentiate between committed outlays, actual costs, and scheduled costs. Finally, it is well known that up-front efforts in clearly defining project objectives, scope, and specifications vastly improve time and cost estimate accuracy.

How estimates are gathered and how they are used can affect their usefulness for planning and control. The team climate, organization culture, and organization structure can strongly influence the importance attached to time and cost estimates and how they are used in managing projects.

6

DEVELOPING A NETWORK PLAN

I had six honest serving men who taught me all I know: their names were what and how and why, and when and where and who.
Rudyard Kipling

The Project Network

The project network is the tool used for planning, scheduling, and monitoring project progress. The network is developed from the information collected for the WBS and is a graphic flowchart of the project job plan. The network depicts:

- The project activities that must be completed
- The logical sequences for the activities
- The interdependencies of the activities to be completed
- In most cases, the times for the activities to start and finish along with the longest path(s) through the network—the critical path.

The network is the framework for the project information system that will be used by the project managers to make decisions concerning project time, cost, and performance.

Importance of the Network

Developing a project network takes time for someone or some group to develop; therefore it costs money! Are networks really worth the struggle? The answer is definitely yes, except in cases where the project is considered trivial or very short in duration. The network is easily understood by others because the network presents a graphic display of the flow and sequence of work through the project. Once the network is developed, it is very easy to modify or change when unexpected events occur as the project progresses. For example, if materials for an activity are delayed, the impact can be assessed quickly and the whole project can be revised in only a few minutes with the computer. These revisions can be communicated to all project participants quickly (for example, via e-mail or the project Web site).

Information and Insights

The project network provides other invaluable information and insights. Networks provide:

- The basis for scheduling labor and equipment
- A communication device that melds all managers and groups together in meeting the time, cost, and performance objectives of the project
- An estimate of project duration rather than picking a project completion date from a hat or someone's preferred date
- The times when activities can start and finish and when they can be delayed
- The basis for budgeting the cash flow of the project
- A way for identifying which activities are "critical" and, therefore, should not be delayed if the project is to be completed as planned

There are other reasons project networks are worth their weight in gold. Basically, project networks minimize surprises by getting the plan out early and allowing corrective feedback. A commonly heard statement from practitioners is that the project network represents three-quarters of the planning process. Perhaps this is an exaggeration, but it signals the perceived importance of the network to project managers in the field.

From Work Package to Network

Networks are built using nodes (boxes) and arrows. In Figure 6–1 the node (box) depicts an activity, and the arrow shows dependency and project flow. The activity represents one or more tasks that consume time.

The network process is similar to the WBS process. That is, the work packages are used to develop a detailed network for the first-line managers (see "Level 3 Plans" in Figure 6–1). The detailed network of two projects can be shown in a more aggregate network, which includes additional projects, for the department

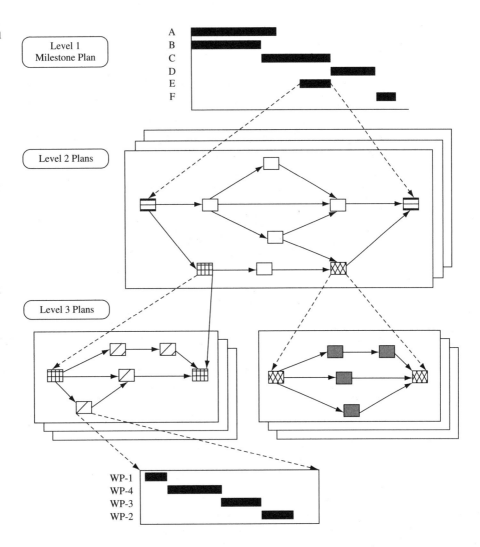

FIGURE 6–1

Rollup of Network Plans

manager (level 2) and, in turn, is summarized to a level needed for the project manager, top management, and the client. This top level is usually depicted as a bar chart of *several projects for top management*. Validity of the information at each summary level relies on the accuracy of the work packages and activities.

Integrating the work packages and the network represents a point where the management process often fails in practice. The primary explanations for this failure are that (1) different groups (people) are used to define work packages and activities, and (2) the WBS is poorly constructed and not deliverable/output oriented. Integrating the WBS and project network is crucial to effective project management. The project manager must be careful to guarantee continuity by having some of the same people who defined the WBS and work packages develop the network activities.

Networks provide the project schedule by identifying dependencies, sequencing, and timing of activities, which the WBS is not designed to do. The primary inputs for developing a project network plan are work packages. Remember, a work package is defined independently of other work packages, has definite start and finish points, requires specific resources, includes technical specifications, and has cost estimates for the package. However, a work package does not include dependency, sequencing, and timing of each of these factors. A network activity can include one or more work packages.

Figure 6–2 shows a segment of the WBS example from Chapter 4 and how the information is used to develop a project network. The lowest level deliverable

FIGURE 6–2

WBS/Work Packages to Network

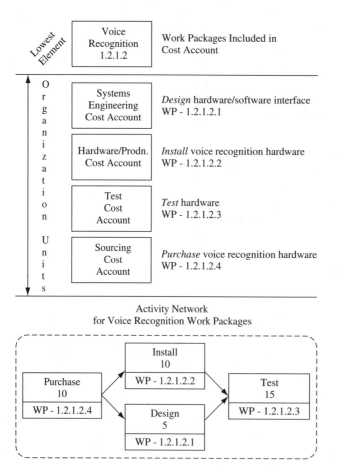

in Figure 6–2 is "Voice Recognition." The cost accounts by department (systems engineering, hardware/prodn., test, and sourcing) denote project work, organization unit responsible, and time-phased budgets for the work packages. Each cost account represents one or more work packages. For example, the test cost account has work package (WP–1.2.1.2.3)—test hardware. Developing a network requires sequencing tasks from all work packages that have measurable work.

Figure 6–2 traces how work packages are used to develop a project network. You can trace the use of work packages by the coding scheme. For example, purchase uses work package WP–1.2.1.2.4 (purchase voice recognition hardware), while design uses work package WP–1.2.1.2.1. This methodology of selecting work packages to describe activities also is used to develop the total project network, which sequences and times project activities. Care must be taken to include all work packages. *The manager derives activity time estimates from the task times in the work package.* For example, the install activity requires 10 workdays to complete; test requires 15 workdays to complete. Given the sequence and time for all the activities, the activity early and late times can be computed, which allows the manager to schedule resources and develop time-phase budgets (with dates).

Constructing a Project Network

Terminology

Every field has its jargon that allows colleagues to communicate comfortably with each other about the techniques they use. Project managers are no exception. Here are some terms used in building project networks.

Activity. For project managers, an *activity* is an element of the project that requires time. It may or may not require resources. Typically an activity consumes time—either while people work or while people wait. Examples of waiting are time waiting for contracts to be signed, materials to arrive, drug approval from the government, budget clearance, etc. Activities usually represent one or more tasks from a work package. Descriptions of activities should use a verb/noun format: for example, "develop product specifications."

Merge activity. This is an activity that has more than one activity immediately preceding it (more than one dependency arrow flowing to it).

Parallel activities. These are activities that can take place at the same time, if the manager wishes. However, the manager may choose *not* to have parallel activities occur simultaneously.

Path. A sequence of connected, dependent activities.

Critical path. When this term is used, it means the longest path(s) through the network; if an activity on the critical path is delayed, the entire project is delayed the same amount of time.

Event. This term is used to represent a point in time when an activity is started or completed. It does not consume time.

Burst activity. This activity has more than one activity immediately following it (more than one dependency arrow flowing from it).

Two Approaches

The two approaches used to develop project networks are known as *activity-on-node (AON)* and *activity-on-arrow (AOA)*. Both methods use two building blocks—the arrow and the node. Their names derive from the fact that the AON method uses a node to depict an activity, while AOA uses an arrow to depict an activity. From the first use of these two approaches in the late 1950s, practitioners have offered many enhancements; however, in practice the activity-on-node (AON) method has come to dominate most projects—it is used in perhaps 99 percent of projects. Hence, this chapter will discuss AON.

Basic Rules to Follow in Developing Project Networks

The following eight rules apply in general when developing a project network:

1. Networks flow typically from left to right (except for some computer printouts that need to fit a network to a page size).
2. An activity cannot begin until all preceding connected activities have been completed.
3. Arrows on networks indicate precedence and flow. Arrows can cross over each other.
4. Each activity should have a unique identification number.
5. An activity identification number must be larger than that of any activities that precede it.
6. Looping is not allowed. In other words, recycling through a set of activities cannot take place.
7. Conditional statements are not allowed. That is, this type of statement should not appear: "If successful, do something; if not, do nothing."
8. Experience suggests that when there are multiple starts, a common start node can be used to indicate a clear project beginning on the network. Similarly, a single project end node can be used to indicate a clear ending.

Activity-On-Node (AON) Fundamentals

The wide availability of personal computers and graphics programs has served as an impetus for use of the activity-on-node (AON) method (sometimes called the *precedence diagram method*). Figure 6–3 shows a few typical uses of building blocks

FIGURE 6–3

Activity-On-Node Network Fundamentals

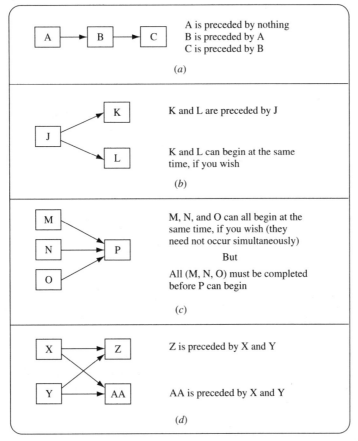

A is preceded by nothing
B is preceded by A
C is preceded by B

(a)

K and L are preceded by J

K and L can begin at the same time, if you wish

(b)

M, N, and O can all begin at the same time, if you wish (they need not occur simultaneously)

But

All (M, N, O) must be completed before P can begin

(c)

Z is preceded by X and Y

AA is preceded by X and Y

(d)

for the AON network construction. An *activity* is represented by a *node* (box). The node can take many forms, but in recent years the node represented as a rectangle (box) has dominated. The dependencies among activities are depicted by *arrows* between the rectangles (boxes) on the AON network. The arrows indicate how the activities are related and the sequence in which things must be accomplished. The length and slope of the arrow are arbitrary. The letters in the boxes serve here to identify the activities while you learn the fundamentals of network construction and analysis. In practice, activities have identification numbers and descriptions.

There are three basic relationships that must be established for activities included in a project network. The relationships can be found by answering the following three questions for each activity:

1. Which activities must be completed immediately *before* this activity? These activities are called *predecessor* activities.

2. Which activities must immediately *follow* this activity? These activities are called *successor* activities.

3. Which activities can occur *while* this activity is taking place? These activities are called *concurrent* or *parallel* activities.

Sometimes a manager can use only questions one and three to establish relationships. This information allows the network analyst to construct a graphic flowchart of the sequence and logical interdependencies of project activities.

Figure 6–3*a* is analogous to a list of things to do where you complete the task at the top of the list first and then move to the second task, etc. This figure tells the project manager that activity A must be completed before activity B can begin, and activity B must be completed before activity C can begin.

Figure 6–3*b* tells us that activities K and L cannot begin until activity J is completed. This figure also indicates that activities K and L can occur concurrently or simultaneously if the project manager wishes; however, it is not a necessary condition. For example, pouring concrete driveway (activity K) can take place while landscape planting (activity L) is being accomplished, but land clearing (activity J) must be completed before activities K and L can start. Activities K and L are considered *parallel* activities. Parallel paths allow concurrent effort, which may shorten time to do a series of activities. Activity J is sometimes referred to as a *burst* activity since more than one arrow bursts from the node. The number of arrows indicates how many activities immediately follow activity J.

Figure 6–3*c* shows us activities M, N, and O can occur simultaneously if desired, and activity P cannot begin until activities M, N, and O are all completed. Activities M, N, and O are parallel activities. Activity P is called a *merge* activity since more than one activity must be completed before P can begin. Activity P could also be called a milestone. A *milestone* activity is one that, when completed, represents the accomplishment of a significant, identifiable segment of the project.

In Figure 6–3*d*, activities X and Y are parallel activities that can take place at the same time; activities Z and AA are also parallel activities. But activities Z and AA cannot begin until X and Y are both completed.

An Example of AON Fundamentals

Given these fundamentals of AON, we can practice developing a simple network. See also *Project Management in Action: The Yellow Sticky Approach.* Remember, the arrows can cross over each other (e.g., Figure 6–3*d*), be bent, or be any length or slope. Neatness is not required for a valid, useful network, but you must include all project activities, their dependencies, and time estimates. Information for a simplified project network is given in Table 6–1. This project represents a

---

Project Management in Action

The Yellow Sticky Approach

In practice small project networks (25–100 activities) are frequently developed using yellow Post-it® Note stickers.

You need the following:

1. Project team members and a facilitator.
2. One yellow sticker (3 × 4 inches or larger) for each activity with the description of the activity printed on the sticker.
3. Erasable whiteboard with marker pen (a long 4-feet wide piece of butcher paper can be used in place of a whiteboard).

All of the yellow stickers are placed in easy view of all team members. The team begins by identifying those activity stickers that have no predecessors. Each of these activity stickers is then attached to the whiteboard. A start node is drawn, and a dependency arrow is connected to each activity.

After the start activities are identified, each is examined for immediate successor activities. These activities are attached to the whiteboard and dependency arrows are drawn. This process is continued until all of the yellow stickers are attached to the whiteboard with dependency arrows. (Note: The process can be reversed, beginning with those activities that have no successor activities and connecting them to a project end node. The predecessor activities are selected for each activity and attached to the whiteboard with dependency arrows marked.)

When the process is complete, the dependencies are recorded in the project software, which develops a computer-designed network along with the critical path(s) and early, late, and slack times. This methodology sensitizes team members early to the interdependencies among project activities.

custom order for a computer-managed air control system—heating, exhaust, and air conditioning for a twelve-story hotel.

Figure 6–4 shows the first steps in constructing the AON project network from the information in Table 6–1. We see that activity 1 (Order Review) has nothing preceding it; therefore, it is the first node to be drawn. Next, we note that activities 2, 3, 4, and 5 (Order Vendor Parts, Produce Other Standard Parts, Design Custom Parts, and Software Development) are all preceded by activity 1. We draw four arrows from activity 1 and connect them to activities 2, 3, 4, and 5. This segment shows the project manager that activity 1 must be completed before

TABLE 6–1 **Network Information**

Air Control Project

Activity	Description	Preceding Activity
1.	Order review	None
2.	Order vendor parts	1
3.	Produce other standard parts	1
4.	Design custom parts	1
5.	Software development	1
6.	Manufacture custom parts	4
7.	Assemble	2, 3, & 6
8.	Test	5 & 7

FIGURE 6–4

Air Control Project

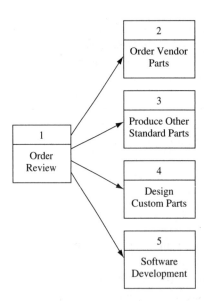

FIGURE 6–5

Air Control Project

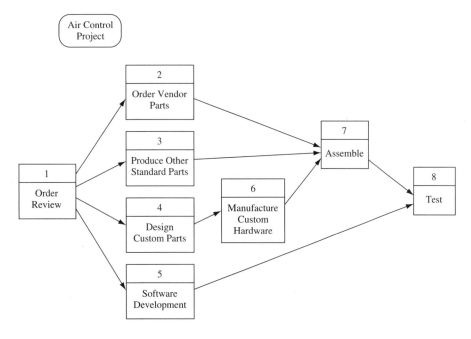

activities 2, 3, 4, and 5 can begin. After activity 1 is complete, activities 2, 3, 4, and 5 can go on concurrently, if desired. Figure 6–5 shows the completed network with all of the activities and precedences depicted.

Start and Finish Network Computations

At this point our project network is a graphic map of the project activities with sequences and dependencies. This information is tremendously valuable to those managing the project. However, estimating the duration for each activity will further increase the value of the network. A realistic project plan and schedule require reliable time estimates for project activities. The addition of time to the network allows you to estimate how long the project will take and allows you to determine:

- When activities can or must start
- When resources must be available
- Which activities can be delayed
- When the project is estimated to be complete

To derive an activity time estimate, you need to make an early assessment of resource needs: material, equipment, and people. In essence the project network with activity time estimates links project planning, scheduling, and controlling.

The Network Computation Process

Drawing the project network places the activities in the right *sequence* for computing start and finish times of activities. Activity time estimates are taken from the task times in the work package and added to the network (review Figure 6–2). Performing a few simple computations allows the project manager to complete a process known as the *forward and backward pass*. Completing the forward and backward pass will answer the following questions (the terms in parentheses represent the acronyms used in most texts and computer programs and by project managers):

Forward Pass—Earliest Times
1. How soon can the activity start? (early start—*ES*)
2. How soon can the activity finish? (early finish—*EF*)
3. How soon can the project be finished? (time expected—*TE*)

Backward Pass—Latest Times
1. How late can the activity start? (late start—*LS*)
2. How late can the activity finish? (late finish—*LF*)
3. Which activities represent the critical path *(CP)*? This is the longest path in the network which, when delayed, will delay the project.
4. How long can the activity be delayed? (slack or float—*SL*)

Forward Pass—Earliest Times

The forward pass starts with the first project activity and traces each path (chain of sequential activities) through the network to the last project activity. As you trace along the path, you *add* the activity times. The longest path denotes the project completion time for the plan and is called the critical path (CP). Table 6–2

TABLE 6–2   Network Information

Air Control Project

Activity	Description	Preceding Activity	Activity Time
1.	Order review	None	2
2.	Order vendor parts	1	15
3.	Produce other standard parts	1	18
4.	Design custom parts	1	13
5.	Software development	1	18
6.	Manufacture custom parts	4	15
7.	Assemble	2, 3, & 6	10
8.	Test	5 & 7	5

lists the activity times in workdays for the Air Control Project example we used for drawing a network.

Figure 6–6 shows the network with the activity time estimate found in the node. (See "Dur." for duration in the legend.) For example, activity 1 has an activity duration of 2 workdays, and activity 7 has a duration of 10 workdays.

The forward pass begins with the project start time, which is usually time zero. (Note: calendar times can be computed for the project later in the planning phase.) In our Air Control Project example, the early start time for the first activity (activity 1) is zero (not at the midpoint of zero to one, but at zero). This time is found in the upper left corner of the activity 1 node in Figure 6–7.

The early finish for activity 1 is 2 (ES + DUR = EF or 0 + 2 = 2). Next, we see that activity 1 is the predecessor for activities 2, 3, 4, and 5. (Remember, the forward pass assumes every activity will start the instant in time when the last of its predecessors is finished.) Therefore, the earliest these activities can begin is when activity 1 is completed; this time is 2 workdays. You can now see in Figure 6–7 activities 2, 3, 4, and 5 can all start the moment activity 1 is complete and, therefore, have an early start (ES) of 2. Again, the ES + DUR = EF for each of these activities. The results are early finish (EF) times of 17, 20, 15, and 20 for activities 2, 3, 4, and 5 respectively. What is the ES for activity 7, which is a merge activity? Is it 17, 20, or 30? The answer is 30 because activities 4 and 6 will take the longest to complete; they control the ES of activity 7.

FIGURE 6–6

*Activity-
On-Node
Network*

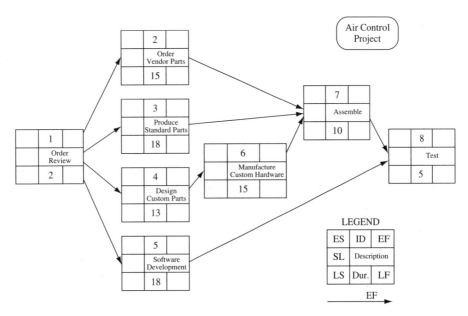

FIGURE 6–7

Activity-On-Node Network, Forward Pass

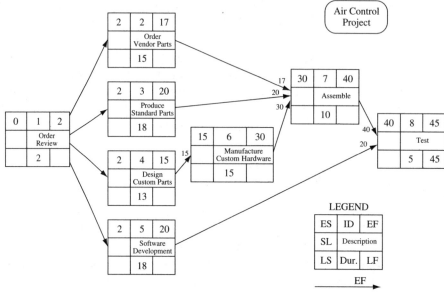

The forward pass requires that you remember just three things when computing early activity times:

1. You *add* activity times along each path in the network (ES + DUR = EF).
2. You carry the early finish (EF) to the next activity where it becomes its early start (ES), *unless*
3. The next succeeding activity is a *merge* activity. In this case you select the *largest* early finish number (EF) of *all* its immediate predecessor activities.

We see activity 8 is a merge activity and therefore find the largest EF of its immediate predecessors (activities 5 and 7). In this case the choice is between the EF times of 20 and 40; the choice for the ES of activity 8 is 40 workdays. The EF for activity 8 (45 workdays) becomes the earliest the project can be expected to be completed (TE) under normal conditions. The three questions derived from the forward pass have been answered; that is, early start (ES), early finish (EF), and the project duration (TE) times have been computed. The backward pass is the next process to learn.

Backward Pass—Latest Times

The backward pass starts with the last project activity on the network. You trace backward on each path *subtracting* activity times to find the late start (LS) and finish times (LF) for each activity. Before the backward pass can be computed, the late finish for the last project activity must be selected. In early planning stages, this time is usually set equal to the early finish (EF) of the last project activity (or in the case of multiple finish activities, the activity with the largest EF). In some cases an imposed project duration deadline exists, and this date will be used. Let us assume for planning purposes we can accept the EF project duration (TE) equal to 45 workdays. The LF for activity 8 becomes 45 workdays (EF = LF). See Figure 6–8.

The backward pass is similar to the forward pass; you need to remember three things:

1. You *subtract* activity times along each path starting with the project end activity (LF − DUR = LS).
2. You carry the LS to the next preceding activity to establish its LF, *unless*
3. The next preceding activity is a *burst* activity; in this case you select the *smallest* LS of all its immediate successor activities to establish its LF.

Let's apply these rules to our Air Control Project example. Beginning with activity 8 (test) and an LF of 45 workdays, the LS for activity 8 is 40 workdays (LF − DUR = LS or 45 − 5 = 40). The LS for activity 8 becomes the LF for activities 5 and 7. The LS for activities 5 and 7 becomes 22 (40 − 18 = 22) and

FIGURE 6–8

*Activity-
On-Node
Network,
Backward
Pass*

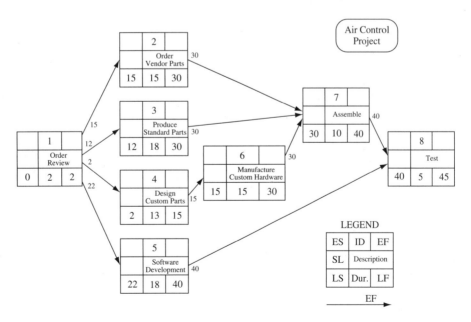

30 workdays (40 − 10 = 30) respectively. Next, the LS for activity 7 (30) becomes the LF for activities 2, 3, and 6; their LS become 15, 12, and 15. The LF
for activity 4 is controlled by activity 6, which has a LS of 15 that becomes the
LF for activity 4. Activity 1 is a *burst* activity that ties to activities 2, 3, 4, and 5.
The late finish for activity 1 is controlled by the LS of these activities. Since the
LS for activities 2, 3, 4, and 5 are 15, 12, 2, and 22, the LF for activity 1 is
the *smallest* LS, which is 2. Note: the LS times for activity 1 have been placed
to the right of the node so you can select the *smallest* time—2 weeks. The backward pass is complete, and the latest activity times are known.

Determining Slack (or Float)

When the forward and backward passes have been computed, it is possible to
determine which activities can be delayed by computing "slack" or "float."
Total slack or float for an activity is simply the difference between the LS and
ES (LS − ES = SL) or between LF and EF (LF − EF = SL). For example, the
slack for activity 2 is 13 days, for activity 5 is 20 days, and for activity 6 is zero.
See Figure 6–9. *Total slack* tells us the amount of time an activity can be delayed
and yet not delay the project. If slack of one activity in a path is used, the ES for
all activities that follow in the chain will be delayed and their slack reduced by
the same amount. Use of total slack must be coordinated with all participants in
the activities that follow in the chain.

FIGURE 6–9

*Activity-On-
Node Network
with Slack*

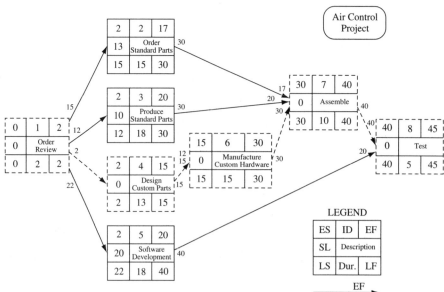

After slack for each activity is computed, the critical path(s) is (are) easily identified. When the LF = EF for the end project activity, the critical path can be identified as those activities that also have LF = EF or a slack of zero (LF − EF = 0) (or LS − ES = 0). *The critical path is the network path(s) that has (have) the least slack in common.* This awkward arrangement of words is necessary because a problem arises when the project finish activity has an LF that differs from the EF found in the forward pass—for example, an imposed duration date. If this is the case, the slack on the critical path will *not* be zero; it will be the difference between the project EF and the imposed LF of the last project activity. For example, if the EF for the project is 45 days, but the imposed LF or target date is set at 40 days, all activities on the critical path would have a slack of *minus* 5 days. Of course, this would result in a late start of negative 5 days for the first project activity—a good trick if the project is to start now. Negative slack occurs in practice when the critical path is delayed. See *Project Management in Action: The Critical Path* for some insight into just how important the critical path is.

In Figure 6–9 the critical path is marked with dashed arrows and nodes—activities 1, 4, 6, 7, and 8. Delay of any of these activities will delay the total project by the same number of days. Critical activities typically represent about 10 percent of the activities of the project. Therefore, project managers pay close attention to the critical path activities to be sure they are not delayed.

Free Slack (Float)

An activity with free slack is unique because the activity can be delayed without delaying the ES of activities following it. Free slack is defined as the difference between the EF of an activity and the ES of the activity that follows it. Free slack can never be negative. Only activities that occur at the *end* of a chain of activities (usually where you have a merge activity) can have free slack. For example, if a single chain (path) of activities has 14 days slack, the last activity will have free slack, and the others will have none. Sometimes the chain is not very long; it can be only one activity. For example, in the Air Control network (Figure 6–9), activity 5 is a chain of one and has free slack of 20 days ($22 − 2 = 20$ or $40 − 20 = 20$). Activities 2 and 3 also have free slack of 10 and 13 days respectively. The beauty of free slack is that changes in start and finish times for the free slack activity require less coordination with other participants in the project and give the project manager more flexibility than total slack. For example, assume a chain of 10 activities. Because the tenth activity is the last in the chain, delaying this activity up to the slack amount will not influence any following activities. However, delaying any of the other nine activities in the chain requires notifying the managers of the remaining activities in the chain that you will be late, so they can adjust their schedules and not have the slack available to them.

Project Management in Action

The Critical Path

The critical path method (CPM) has long been considered the "Holy Grail" of project management. Here are comments made by veteran project managers when asked about the significance of the critical path in managing projects:

- I try to make it a point whenever possible to put my best people on critical activities or on those activities that stand the greatest chance of becoming critical.
- I pay extra attention when doing risk assessment to identifying those risks that can impact the critical path, either directly or indirectly, by making a noncritical activity so late that it becomes critical. When I've got money to spend to reduce risks, it usually gets spent on critical tasks.
- I don't have time to monitor all the activities on a big project, but I make it a point to keep in touch with the people who are working on critical activities. When I have the time, they are the ones I visit to find out firsthand how things are going. It's amazing how much more I can find out from talking to the rank and file who are doing the work and by reading the facial expressions of people—much more than I can gain from a number-driven status report.
- When I get calls from other managers asking to "borrow" people or equipment, I'm much more generous when it involves resources working on noncritical activities. For example, if another project manager needs an electrical engineer who is assigned to a task with five days of slack, I'm willing to share that engineer with another project manager for two to three days.
- The most obvious reason the critical path is important is because these are the activities that impact completion time. If I suddenly get a call from above saying they need my project done two weeks earlier than planned, the critical path is where I schedule the overtime and add extra resources to get the project done more quickly. In the same way, if the project schedule begins to slip, it's the critical activities I focus on to get back on schedule.

How the Information of the Forward and Backward Pass Is Used

What does a slack of 20 workdays for activity 5 mean for the project manager? In this specific case it means activity 5 can be delayed 20 workdays. In a larger sense the project manager soon learns that slack is important because it allows flexibility in scheduling scarce project resources—personnel and equipment—that are used on more than one parallel activity.

Knowing the four activity times of ES, LS, EF, and LF is invaluable for planning, scheduling, and controlling the project. The ES and LF tell the project manager the time interval in which the activity should be completed. For example, activity 2 (order vendor parts) must be completed within the time interval 2 and 30 workdays; the activity can start as early as day 2 or as late as day 15. Conversely, activity 7, (assemble), has an ES and LS of 30; hence the activity must start on day 30 or the project will be delayed.

When the critical path is known, it is possible to manage the resources of the activities on the critical path tightly so no mistakes are made that will result in delays. In addition, if for some reason the project must be expedited to meet an earlier date, it is possible to select those activities, or combination of activities, that will cost the least to shorten the project. Similarly, if the critical path is delayed and the time must be made up by shortening some activity or activities on the critical path to make up any negative slack, it is possible to identify the activities on the critical path that cost the least to shorten. If there are other paths with very little slack, it may be necessary to shorten activities on those paths also.

Loose Ends

Network Logic Errors

Project network techniques have certain logic rules that must be followed. One rule is that conditional statements such as "if test successful, build proto; if failure, redesign" are not permitted. The network is not a decision tree; it is a project plan that you assume will materialize. If conditional statements were allowed, the forward and backward pass would make little sense. Although in reality a plan seldom materializes as you expect in every detail, it is a reasonable initial assumption. You will see that once a network plan is developed, it is easy to make revisions to accommodate changes.

Another rule that defeats the project network and computation process is *looping*. Looping is an attempt by the planner to return to an earlier activity. Recall that the activity identification numbers should always be higher for the activities following an activity in question; this rule helps to avoid the illogical precedence relationships among the activities. An activity should occur only once; if it is to occur again, the activity should have a new name and identification number and should be placed in the right sequence on the network. Figure 6–10 shows an

FIGURE 6–10

Illogical Loop

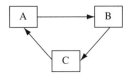

illogical loop. If this loop were allowed to exist, this path would repeat itself per-
petually. Many computer programs catch this type of logic error.

Activity Numbering

Each activity needs a unique identification code—usually a number. In practice,
very elegant schemes exist. Most schemes number activities in ascending order,
that is, each succeeding activity has a larger number so that the flow of the project activities is toward project completion. It is customary to leave gaps between
numbers (1, 5, 10, 15 . . .). Gaps are desirable so you can add missing or new activities later. Because it is nearly impossible to draw a project network perfectly,
numbering networks frequently is not done until after the network is complete.

In practice you will find computer programs that accept numeric, alphabetic,
or a combination of activity designations. Combination designations often are used
to identify cost, work skill, departments, and locations. As a general rule, activity numbering systems should be ascending and as simple as possible. The intent
is to make it as easy as you can for project participants to follow work through
the network and locate specific activities.

Using Computers to Develop Networks

All of the tools and techniques discussed in this chapter can be used with computer software currently available. Two examples are shown in Figures 6–11 and
6–12. Figure 6–11 presents an AON computer output for the Air Control Project
with calendar dates. The nonshaded activities are critical and represent the
critical path − activities 1, 4, 6, 7, and 8. Noncritical activities are shaded. The
activity description is identified on the top line of the node box. The activity identification is found below the description and below that is the duration. Immediately below the activity description are the activity times—ES and EF. For example, activity 5 has a duration of 18 days, an early start of January 3, 2002, and
an early finish of January 20, 2002. "RES" is left blank; it represents activity resources such as people, teams, and equipment.

Figure 6–12 presents a Gantt bar chart generated by Microsoft Project 2000®.
Bar charts are popular because they present an easy-to-understand, clear picture
on a time-scaled horizon. They are used during planning, resource scheduling, and
status reporting. The format is a two-dimensional representation of the project
schedule, with activities down the columns and time across the horizontal axis of
the bar chart (the bars are shown in the top right corner). For example, for software development (activity 5) the thick bar represents a duration of 18 days and
the thin line following the bar represents 20 days of slack. In this particular project the ES, LS, EF, LF, and slack times are shown left of the bar chart for each
activity. For example, this chart indicates activity 5 can start at time 1/3/02 and

FIGURE 6-11

Air Control Project

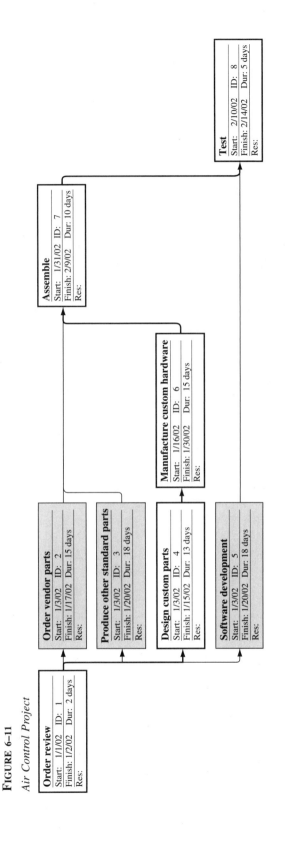

FIGURE 6–12

Air Control Project

ID	Task Name	Start	Finish	Late Start	Late Finish	Fee Slack	Total Slack
1	Order review	Tue 1/1/02	Wed 1/2/02	Tue 1/1/02	Wed 1/2/02	0 days	0 days
2	Order vendor parts	Thu 1/3/02	Thu 1/17/02	Wed 1/16/02	Wed 1/30/02	13 days	13 days
3	Produce other standard parts	Thu 1/3/02	Sun 1/20/02	Sun 1/13/02	Wed 1/30/02	10 days	10 days
4	Design custom parts	Thu 1/3/02	Tue 1/15/02	Thu 1/3/02	Tue 1/15/02	0 days	0 days
5	Software development	Thu 1/3/02	Sun 1/20/02	Wed 1/23/02	Sat 2/9/02	20 days	20 days
6	Manufacture custom hardware	Wed 1/16/02	Wed 1/30/02	Wed 1/16/02	Wed 1/30/02	0 days	0 days
7	Assemble	Thu 1/31/02	Sat 2/9/02	Thu 1/31/02	Sat 2/9/02	0 days	0 days
8	Test	Sun 2/10/02	Thu 2/14/02	Sun 2/10/02	Thu 2/14/02	0 days	0 days

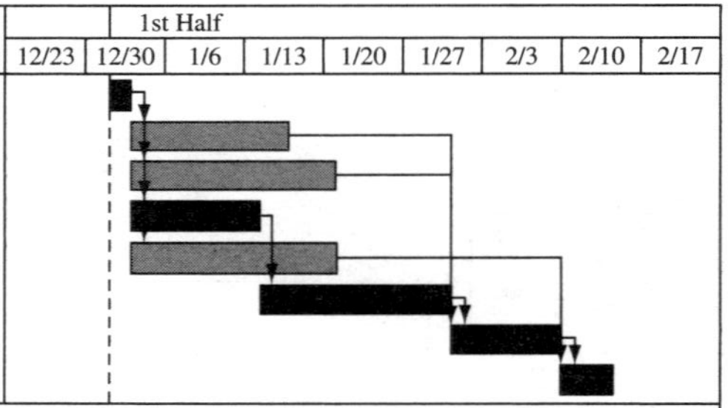
1st Half
12/23
12/30
1/6
1/13
1/20
1/27
2/3
2/10
2/17

Air Control Project
Start Date: January 1, 2002

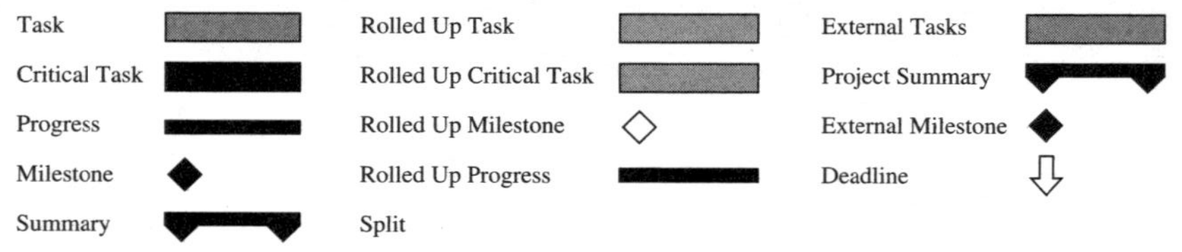
Task
Critical Task
Progress
Milestone
Summary
Rolled Up Task
Rolled Up Critical Task
Rolled Up Milestone
Rolled Up Progress
Split
External Tasks
Project Summary
External Milestone
Deadline

can finish by 1/20/02, or have a LS of 1/23/02 and a LF of 2/9/02. Gantt charts provide a clear overview of the project schedule and often can be found posted on the walls of project offices. The major weakness of the bar chart format is the difficulty of tracing dependency relationships among project activities on a cluttered chart. The dependency lines can soon become overwhelming and defeat the simplicity of the bar chart. Note that the bar chart is derived from the project network—not vice versa.

Project management software can be a tremendous help in the hands of those who understand and are familiar with the tools and techniques discussed in this text. However, there is nothing more dangerous than someone using the software with little or no knowledge of how the software derives its output. Mistakes in input are very common and require someone skilled in the concepts, tools, and information system to recognize where errors exist so that false actions are avoided.

Calendar Dates

Ultimately you will want to assign calendar dates to your project activities. If a computer program is not used, dates are assigned manually. Lay out a calendar of workdays or workweeks (exclude nonworkdays), and number them. Then relate the calendar workdays to the workdays on your project network. Most computer programs will assign calendar dates automatically after you identify start dates, time units, and nonworkdays. See Figures 6–11 and 6–12. Most computer software also allows you to set holidays, vacations for individuals, workday hours, efficiency rates, and other information tailored to the individual project.

Multiple Starts and Multiple Projects

Some computer programs require a common start and finish event in the form of a node—usually a circle or rectangle—for a project network. Even if this is not a requirement, it is a good idea because it avoids "dangler" paths. Dangler paths give the impression that the project does not have a clear beginning or ending. If a project has more than one activity that can begin when the project is to start, each path is a dangler path. The same is true if a project network ends with more than one activity; these unconnected paths are also called danglers. Danglers can be avoided by tying dangler activities to a common project start or finish node.

When several projects are tied together in an organization, using a common start and end node helps to identify the total planning period of all projects. Using pseudo or dummy wait activities from the common start node allows different start dates for each project.

Extended Network Techniques from Practice

The method for showing relationships among activities in the previous section is called the finish-to-start relationship because it assumes all immediate preceding connected activities must be completed before the next activity can begin. In an effort to come closer to the realities of projects, some useful extensions have been added. The use of *laddering* was the first obvious extension practitioners found very useful.

Laddering

The assumption that all immediate preceding activities must be 100 percent complete is too restrictive for some situations found in practice. This restriction occurs most frequently when one activity overlaps the start of another and has a long duration. Under the standard finish-to-start relationship, when an activity has a long duration and will delay the start of an activity immediately following it, the activity can be broken into segments and the network drawn using a *laddering* approach so the following activity can begin sooner and not delay the work. This segmenting of the larger activity gives the appearance of steps or a ladder on the network, thus the name. The classic example used in many texts and articles is laying pipe, because it is easy to visualize. The trench must be dug, pipe laid, and the trench refilled. If the pipeline is one mile long, it is not necessary to dig one mile of trench before the laying of pipe can begin or to lay one mile of pipe before refill can begin. Figure 6–13 shows how these overlapping activities might appear in an AON network using the standard finish-to-start approach.

FIGURE 6–13

Example of Laddering Using Finish-to-Start Relationship

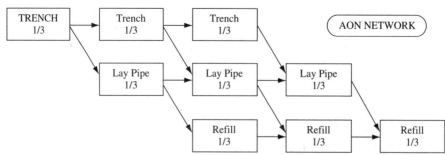

Lags

The use of *lags* has been developed to offer greater flexibility in network construction. *A lag is the minimum amount of time a dependent activity must be delayed to begin or end.* The use of lags in project networks occurs for two primary reasons:

1. When activities of long duration delay the start or finish of successor activities, the network designer normally breaks the activity into smaller activities to avoid the long delay of the successor activity. Use of lags can avoid such delays and reduce network detail.
2. Lags can be used to constrain the start and finish of an activity. The most commonly used relationship extensions are start-to-start, finish-to-finish, and combinations of these two.

Finish-to-Start Relationship. The finish-to-start relationship represents the typical, generic network style used in the early part of the chapter. However, there are situations in which the next activity in a sequence must be delayed even when the preceding activity is complete. For example, removing concrete forms cannot begin until the poured cement has cured for 2 time units. Figure 6–14 shows this lag relationship for AON networks. Finish-to-start lags frequently are used when ordering materials. For example, it may take 1 day to place orders but take 19 days to receive the goods. The use of finish-to-start allows the activity duration to be only 1 day and the lag 19 days. This approach ensures the activity cost is tied to placing the order only rather than charging the activity for 20 days of work. This same finish-to-start lag relationship is useful to depict transportation, legal, and mail lags.

The use of finish-to-start lags should be carefully checked to ensure their validity. Conservative project managers have been known to use lags as a means of building in a "slush" factor to reduce the risk of being late. A simple rule to follow is that the use of finish-to-start lags must be justified and approved by someone responsible for a large section of the project. The legitimacy of lags usually

FIGURE 6–14

Finish-to-Start Relationship

is not difficult to discern. The legitimate use of the additional relationship shown can greatly enhance the network by more closely representing the realities of the project.

Start-to-Start Relationship.   An alternative to segmenting the activities as we did earlier is to use a start-to-start relationship. Typical start-to-start relationships are shown in Figure 6–15. Part A of the figure shows the start-to-start relationship with zero lag, while Part B shows the same relationship with a *lag* of five time units. It is important to note that the relationship may be used with or without a lag. If time is assigned, it is usually shown on the dependency arrow of an AON network.

In Part B of Figure 6–15 activity Q cannot begin until 5 time units after activity P begins. This type of relationship typically depicts a situation in which you can perform a portion of one activity and begin a following activity before completing the first. This relationship can be used on the pipe laying project. Figure 6–16 shows the project using an AON network. The start-to-start relationship reduces network detail and project delays by using lag relationships.

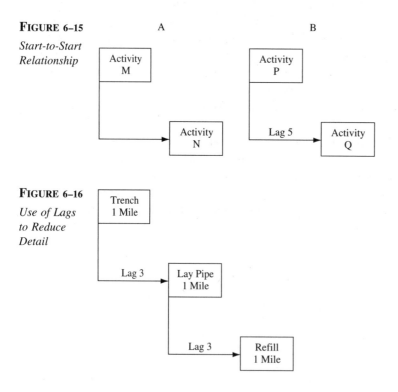

FIGURE 6–15

Start-to-Start Relationship

FIGURE 6–16

Use of Lags to Reduce Detail

It is possible to find compression opportunities by changing finish-to-start relationships to start-to-start relationships. A review of finish-to-start critical activities may reveal opportunities that can be revised to be parallel by using start-to-start relationships. For example, in place of a finish-to start activity "design house, then build foundation," a start-to-start relationship could be used in which the foundation can be started, say, 5 days (lag) after design has started—assuming the design of the foundation is the first part of the total design activity. This start-to-start relationship with a small lag allows a sequential activity to be worked on in parallel and to compress the duration of the critical path. This same concept is found frequently in construction projects in which concurrent engineering is used to speed completion of a project. Concurrent engineering, which is highlighted in *Project Management in Action: Concurrent Engineering*, basically breaks activities into smaller segments so that work can be done in parallel and the project expedited.[1] Start-to-start relationships can depict the concurrent engineering conditions and reduce network detail. Of course the same result can be accomplished by breaking an activity into small packages that can be implemented in parallel, but this latter approach increases the network and tracking detail significantly.

Project Management in Action

Concurrent Engineering

In the old days, when a new product development project was initiated by a firm, it would start its sequential journey in the R&D department. Concepts and ideas would be worked out and the results passed to the engineering department that sometimes reworked the whole product. This result would be passed to manufacturing, where it might be reworked once more in order to ensure the product could be manufactured using existing machinery and operations. Quality improvements were initiated after the fact once defects and improvement opportunities were discovered during production. This sequential approach to product development required a great deal of time, and it was not uncommon for the final product to be totally unrecognizable when compared to original specifications.

Given the emphasis on speed to the market, companies have abandoned the sequential approach to product development and have adopted a more holistic approach titled *concurrent engineering*. In a nutshell, concurrent engineering actively involves all the relevant specialty areas throughout the design and development process. The traditional chain-like sequence of finish-to-start relationships is replaced by a series of start-to-start lag relationships as soon as meaningful work can be initiated for the next phase. Figure 6–17 summarizes the dramatic gains in time to market achieved by this approach.

Concurrent Engineering (continued)

FIGURE 6–17

New Product Development Process

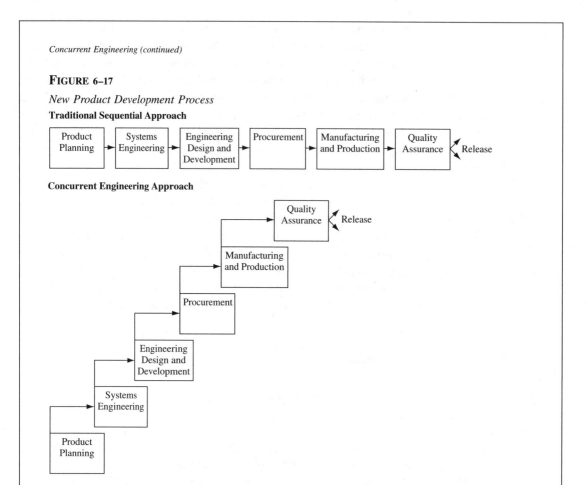

For example, this approach was used by Chrysler Corporation to design its new line of SC cars including the popular *Neon* sedan. From the very beginning specialists from marketing, engineering, design, manufacturing, quality assurance, and other relevant departments were involved in every stage of the project. Not only did the project meet all of its objectives, it was completed six months ahead of schedule.[1]

Finish-to-Finish Relationship. This relationship is shown in Figure 6–18. The finish of one activity depends on the finish of another activity. For example, testing cannot be completed any earlier than 4 days after the prototype is complete. It is not a finish-to-start relationship because the testing of subcomponents can begin before the prototype is completed, but will require 4 days of "system" testing after the prototype is finished

Start-to-Finish Relationship. This relationship represents situations in which the finish of an activity depends on the start of another activity. For example, system documentation cannot end until 3 days after testing has started. Here all the relevant information to complete the documentation is obtained after the first 3 days of testing. See Figure 6–19.

Combinations of Lag Relationships. More than one lag relationship can be attached to an activity. These relationships are usually start-to-start and finish-to-finish combinations tied to two activities. For example, debugging cannot begin until 2 days after coding has started. Coding must be finished 4 days before debugging can be finished (see Figure 6–20).

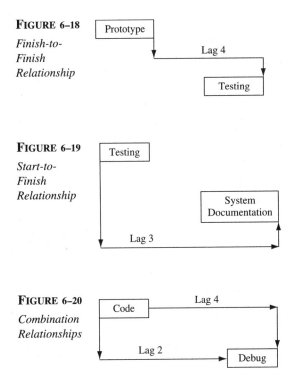

FIGURE 6–18

Finish-to-Finish Relationship

FIGURE 6–19

Start-to-Finish Relationship

FIGURE 6–20

Combination Relationships

An Example Using Lag Relationships

The Forward and Backward Pass

The forward and backward pass procedures are the same as those explained earlier in the chapter for finish-to-start relationships (without lags). The modifying technique lies in the need to check each new relationship to see if it alters the start or finish time of another activity.

An example of the outcome of the forward and backward pass is shown in Figure 6–21. Order hardware depends on the design of the system (start-to-start). Three days into the design of the system (activity A), it is possible to order the required hardware (activity B). It takes 4 days after the order is placed (activity B) for the hardware to arrive so it can begin to be installed (activity C). After two days of installing the software system (activity D), the testing of the system can begin (activity E). System testing (activity E) can be completed two days after the software is installed (activity D). Preparing system documentation (activity F) can begin once the design is completed (activity A), but it cannot be completed until 2 days after testing the system (activity E). This final relationship is an example of a finish-to-finish lag.

FIGURE 6–21

Network Using Lags

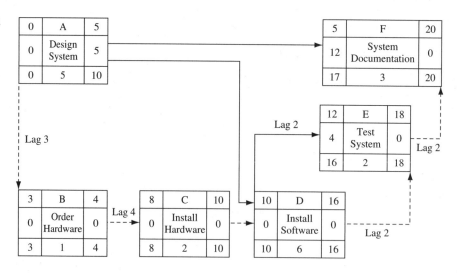

Note how an activity can have a critical finish and/or start. Activities E and F have critical finishes (zero slack), but their activity starts have 4 and 12 units of slack. It is only the finish of activities E and F that are critical. Conversely, activity A has zero slack to start but has 5 time units of slack to finish. The critical path follows activity start and finish constraints that occur due to the use of the additional relationships available and the imposed lags. You can identify the critical path in Figure 6–21 by following the dotted line on the network.

If a lag relationship exists, each activity must be checked to see if the start or finish is constrained. For example, in the forward pass the EF of activity E (test system) (18) is controlled by the finish of activity D (install software) and the lag of 2 time units (16 + 2 lag = 18). Finally, in the backward pass, the LS of activity A (design system) is controlled by activity B (order hardware) and the lag relationship to activity A (3 − 3 = 0).

Hammock Activities

Another of the extended techniques uses a *hammock activity*. The major use of a hammock activity is to identify the use of fixed resources or costs over a segment of the project. Typical examples of hammock activities are inspection services, consultants, or construction management services. A hammock activity derives its duration from the time span between other activities. For example, a special color copy machine is needed for a segment of a trade show publication project. A hammock activity can be used to indicate the need for this resource and to apply costs over this segment of the project. This hammock is linked from the start of the first activity in the segment that uses the color copy machine to the end of the last activity that uses it. The hammock duration is simply the difference between the EF for the last activity and the ES of the first activity. The duration is computed after the forward pass and hence has no influence on other activity times. The hammock duration will change if any ES or EF in the chain sequence changes. Hammock activities are very useful in assigning and controlling indirect project costs.

Another major use of hammock activities is to aggregate sections of a project. This is similar to developing a subnetwork, but the precedence is still preserved. This approach is sometimes used to present a macro network for upper management levels. Using a hammock activity to group activities can facilitate getting the right level of detail for specific sections of a project.

Summary

Many project managers feel the project network is their most valuable exercise and planning document. Project networks sequence and time phase the project work, resources, and budgets. Work package tasks are used to develop activities for networks. Every project manager should feel comfortable working in an AON environment. The AON method uses nodes (boxes) for activities and arrows for dependencies. The forward and backward passes establish early and late times for activities. Although most project managers use computers to generate networks and activity times, they find a keen understanding of network development and the ability to compute activity times manually is invaluable in the field. Computers break down; input errors give false information; some decisions must be made without computer "what if" analysis. Project managers who are well acquainted with network development and AON methods and who are able to compute activity times will encounter fewer problems than project managers less well acquainted. Project networks help to ensure there are no surprises.

Several extensions and modifications have been appended to the original AON method. Lags allow the project planner to replicate more closely the actual conditions found in practice. Using lags can result in the start or finish of an activity becoming critical. Some computer software simply calls the whole activity critical rather than identifying the start or finish as being critical. Be careful not to use lags as buffers for possible errors in estimating time. Finally, hammock activities are useful in tracking costs of resources used for a particular segment of a project. Hammock activities can also be used to reduce the size of a project network by grouping activities. All of the refinements to the original AON methodology contribute to better planning and control of projects.

7   MANAGING RISK

When fate hands you a lemon, make lemonade.
Dale Carnegie

Every project manager understands that risks are inherent in projects. It is not possible to eliminate all risks, and no amount of planning can overcome all risks. Project risk events typically have a negative impact on the project objectives of schedule, cost, and specification. (Note: It is possible to have positive risk events, but project managers' major concerns center on *what can go wrong?*) Project risks are those events, which, if they materialize, can delay or kill a project. Some of these possible undesirable events can be identified *before* the project starts, while a few may be unforeseen and beyond imagination. The goals of risk management are to:

- Identify as many risk events as possible (What can go wrong?)
- Minimize their impact (What can be done about the event before the project begins?)
- Manage responses to those events that do materialize (create contingency plans)
- Provide contingency funds to cover risk events that actually materialize

Risk Management Process

Figure 7–1 presents a graphic model of the risk management dilemma.[1] The chances of a risk event occurring (e.g., an error in time estimates, cost estimates,

FIGURE 7–1

*Risk Event
Graph*

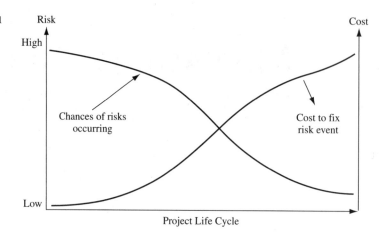

or design technology) are greatest in the concept, planning, and start-up phases of the project. The cost impact of a risk event in the project is less if the event occurs earlier rather than later. The early stages of the project represent the period when the opportunity for minimizing the impact or working around a potential risk exists. Conversely, as the project passes the halfway mark, the cost of a risk event occurring increases rapidly. For example, the risk event of a design flaw occurring after a prototype has been made has a greater cost or time impact than if the event occurred in the start-up phase of the project.

The cost of mismanaged risk control early on in the project is illustrated by the ill-fated 1999 NASA Mars Climate Orbiter. Investigations revealed that Lockheed Martin botched the design of critical navigation software. While flight computers on the ground did calculations based on pounds of thrust per second, the spacecraft's computer software used the metric system unit of measure called newtons. A check to see if the values were compatible was never done.

"Our check and balances processes did not catch an error like this that should have been caught," said Ed Weiler, NASA's associate administrator for space science. "That is the bottom line. Processes that were in place were not followed." After the 9-month journey to the Red Planet, the $125 million probe approached Mars at too low an altitude and burned up in the planet's atmosphere.[2]

Planning for project risk is a proactive approach rather than a reactive one. It is designed to ensure that surprises are reduced and that negative consequences are minimized. It also prepares the project manager to take risks when time, cost, and/or technical advantages are possible. Successful risk management gives the project manager better control over the future and can significantly improve your chances of reaching your project objectives of on time and within budget.[3]

The sources of project risks are unlimited. There are external sources such as inflation, market acceptance, exchange rates, and government regulations.

External risks are sometimes called threats because they are beyond the control of the project manager. Since such external risks are usually considered before the decision to go ahead with the project, we will not cover them here.

Other risk sources depend on the specific type of project—e.g., construction, design, software, system, process. Space prevents us from covering them here. We will discuss generic risk situations that apply to most projects.

The major components of the risk management process are depicted in Figure 7–2. Each component will be examined in more detail in the remainder of the chapter.

FIGURE 7–2

The Risk Management Process

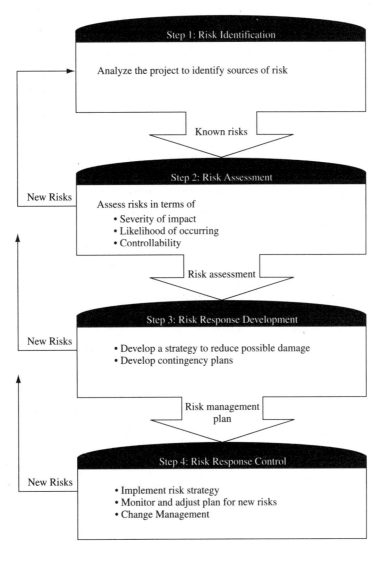

Step 1: Identifying Sources of Risk

Generate a List of Risks

The first step of the risk management process is to generate a list of all the possible risks that could affect the project. During the planning phase, the project manager pulls together a risk management team consisting of core team members and other relevant stakeholders. The team uses brainstorming and other problem-identifying techniques to list possible risks. Participants are encouraged to keep an open mind and generate as many risks as possible. Later, during the assessment phase, the team will analyze and filter out unreasonable risks.

One common mistake made early on in the risk identification process is to focus on consequences and not on the events that could produce consequences. For example, team members may identify "failing to meet schedule" as a major risk. What they need to focus on are the events that could cause this to happen (e.g., poor estimates, adverse weather, shipping delays, etc.).

The focus in the beginning should be on risks that can affect the whole project as opposed to a specific section of the project or network. After the macro risks have been identified, specific areas can be checked. An effective tool for identifying specific risks is the work breakdown structure (WBS). Using the WBS reduces the chance a risk event will be missed. On large projects, multiple risk teams are organized around specific deliverables, and they submit their risk management reports to the project manager. In some projects, practitioners use a technical breakdown structure (TBS) to ensure that all technical risks are examined. A TBS uses the WBS as the framework and identifies technical risk events for tasks and deliverables.

The Risk Profile

A risk profile is another tool that can help management teams identify and eventually analyze risks. A risk profile is a list of questions that addresses traditional areas of uncertainty on a project. These questions have been developed and refined from previous, similar projects. Figure 7–3 provides a partial example of a risk profile.

Good risk profiles are tailored to the type of project in question. For example, building an information system is different from building a new car. Risk profiles are organization specific. They recognize the unique strengths and weaknesses of the firm. Risk profiles address both technical and management risks. For example, the profile shown in Figure 7–3 asks questions about design (*Does the design depend on unrealistic assumptions?*) and work environment (*Do people cooperate across functional boundaries?*).

FIGURE 7–3

Partial Risk Profile for Product Development Project

Technical Requirements	**Quality**
Are the requirements stable?	Are quality considerations built into the design?
Design	**Management**
Does any of the design depend on unrealistic or optimistic assumptions?	Do people know who has authority for what?
Testing	**Work Environment**
Will testing equipment be available when needed?	Do people work cooperatively across functional boundaries?
Development	**Staffing**
Is the development process supported by a compatible set of procedures, methods, and tools?	Is staff inexperienced? Is the project understaffed?
Schedule	**Customer**
Is the schedule dependent upon the completion of other projects?	Does the customer understand what it will take to complete the project?
Budget	**Contractors**
How reliable are the cost estimates?	Are there any ambiguities in contractor task definitions?

Risk profiles are usually generated and maintained by personnel from the project office. They are updated and refined during the postproject audit (see Chapter 14). These profiles, when kept up to date, can be a powerful resource in the risk management process. The collective experience of the firm's past projects resides in their questions.

It is even possible to acquire good risk profiles. Many consulting firms sell them as part of their project management services. The Software Engineering Institute offers in its *Continuous Risk Management Guidebook* a detailed list of questions for evaluating risks on software projects.[4]

Historical records can complement risk profiles or be used when formal risk profiles are not available. Project teams can investigate what happened on similar projects in the past to identify potential risks. For example, a project manager can check the on-time performance of selected vendors to gauge the threat of shipping delays. IT project managers can access "best practices" papers detailing other company's experiences converting software systems. Inquiries should not be limited to recorded data. Savvy project managers tap the wisdom of others by seeking the advice of veteran project managers.

Leave No Stones Unturned

The risk identification process should not be limited to the core team. Smart project managers get input from customers, sponsors, subcontractors, vendors, and other stakeholders. They can be interviewed formally or included on the risk management team. Not only do these players have a valuable perspective, but also by involving them in the risk management process they become more committed to the success of the project.

One of the keys to success in risk identification is attitude. While optimism and a "can do" attitude are essential during implementation, project managers have to encourage critical thinking when it comes to risk identification. The goal is to find problems before they happen, and participants need to believe in Murphy's Law—"anything that can go wrong, will go wrong." The WBS and risk profiles are useful tools for making sure no stones are left unturned. At the same time, when done well the number of risks identified can be overwhelming and a bit discouraging. Initial optimism can be replaced with griping and cries of "what have we gotten ourselves into?" It is important that project managers set the right tone and complete the risk management process so members regain confidence in themselves and the project.

Step 2: Risk Analysis and Assessment

Step 1 produces a list of potential risks. Not all of these risks deserve attention. Some are trivial and can be ignored while others pose serious threats to the welfare of the project. Managers have to develop methods for sifting through the list of risks, eliminating inconsequential or redundant ones, and stratifying worthy ones in terms of importance and need for attention. So Step 2 of the risk management process is analyzing and assessing the risks that have been identified.

Scenario Analysis

Scenario analysis is the easiest and most commonly used technique for analyzing risks. Team members assess each risk in terms of:

1. The undesirable event
2. All the outcomes of the event's occurrence
3. The magnitude or severity of the event's impact
4. Chances/probability of the event happening
5. When the event might occur in the project

For example, assume the chances of a resource shortage of a particular skill are about 80 percent. The outcomes could be a delayed project, tighter scheduling and less flexibility, increased cost, etc. The impact could be a 10 percent increase in cost and 5 percent delay in project duration. The shortage will show up in the design stage of the project. A delay in this project may delay other projects or require a change in priorities. Having this information available facilitates the assessment of each risk event worthy of attention.

The scenario analysis can be seen in various risk assessment forms used by companies. Figure 7–4 is an example of a partial risk assessment form used on an IS project involving the upgrade from Windows Office 97 to Windows Office XP. The project team identified risks, including interface problems with current software systems, the system freezing after installation, end-users resisting and complaining about the changes, and hardware equipment malfunctioning. In addition to assessing the chances, severity, and when the event is likely to occur, the project team also assessed whether they would be able to detect that the event was going to occur in time to take mitigating action. Notice that the team rated the "detection difficulty" high (5) for the system freezing since systems crash without warning, while "user backlash" was rated medium (3) because a ground swell of resistance could be detected before such a backlash reached disastrous proportions.

Risk Assessment Matrix

Often organizations find it useful to categorize the severity of different risks into some form of risk assessment matrix. The matrix is typically structured around the impact and likelihood of the risk event. For example, the risk matrix presented in Figure 7–5 consists of a 5×5 array of elements with each element representing a different set of impact and likelihood values.

The matrix is divided into red, yellow, and green zones representing major, moderate, and minor risks, respectively. The red zone is centered on the top right corner of the matrix (high impact/high likelihood), while the green zone is

FIGURE 7–4

Risk Assessment Form

Risk Event	Likelihood	Impact	Detection Difficulty	When
Interface Problems	4	4	4	Conversion
System Freezing	2	5	5	Start-up
User Backlash	4	3	3	Postinstallation
Hardware Malfunctioning	1	5	5	Installation
Low 1 → 5 High				

FIGURE 7–5

Risk Severity Matrix

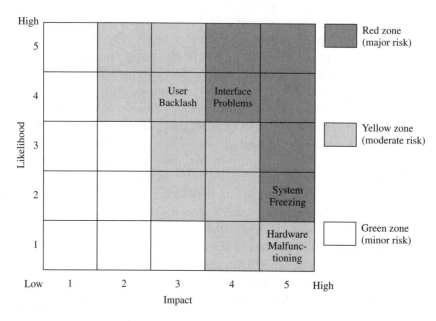

centered on the bottom left corner (low impact/low likelihood). The moderate risk, yellow zone extends down the middle of the matrix. Since impact generally is considered more important than likelihood (a 10 percent chance of losing $1,000,000 is usually considered a more severe risk than a 90 percent chance of losing $1,000), the red zone (major risk) extends farther down the high-impact column.[5]

Using the Windows Office XP project again as an example, interface problems and system freezing would be placed in the red zone (major risk), while user backlash and hardware malfunctioning would be placed in the yellow zone (moderate risk).

The risk severity matrix provides a basis for prioritizing which risks to address. Red zone risks receive first priority followed by yellow zone risks. Green zone risks are typically considered inconsequential and are ignored unless their status changes.

Scenario analysis is one of many approaches to risk assessment. Basically, assessments are either subjective or quantitative. "Expert opinion" or "gut feeling" estimates are used most, but they can carry serious errors depending on the skill of the person(s) making the judgment call. Quantitative methods usually require more detailed analysis of facts and tend to be more reliable. Typical quantitative methods are ratio analysis, probability analysis, and sensitivity analysis. Unfortunately, quantitative methods require serious data collection, are frequently limited in scope, and have low acceptance levels by practicing managers. Hybrid expert systems, which utilize quantitative data and rules of thumb derived from experience, are being used more today. Whether a subjective or quantitative approach is used depends on the source of risk, possible outcomes, effects of a risk event, and management's attitude toward risk assessment.

A few of the most recognized techniques will be examined to give the flavor of approaches used by some project managers. Techniques that require sophisticated and elegant mathematical analysis have been excluded—not because they are invalid, but because they require specialized training and data that are often very difficult and expensive to collect, and are used less frequently. In addition, the accuracy of data for a project never done before leaves the numerical answer of questionable value to some practitioners.

Ratio/Range Analysis

This technique is widely used by some project managers. The technique uses data from prior projects that are similar to the proposed project. It assumes a ratio between the old and new project to make a point estimate of time, cost, or technology and a low and high range for the estimate. The ratio typically serves as a constant. For example, if past projects have taken 10 minutes per line of computer code, a constant of 1.10 (which represents a 10 percent increase) would be used for the proposed project time estimates because the new project will be more difficult than prior projects. Given the computed estimate for the new project, the percentage ranges for past projects can also be reviewed and the downside risk of the range assessed.

Hybrid Analysis Approaches

Managers are often reluctant to accept quantitative methods because of their restrictive assumptions and scope. To these managers such models fail to utilize the full breadth and knowledge they have gained from experience. Acceptance of heuristic models that utilize the manager's knowledge and rules of thumb is increasing. Managers are comfortable using rules of thumb combined with subjective judgments and will continue to use them. A few researchers have included these rules of thumb in knowledge-based expert systems to pick up the benefits of the manager's experience/knowledge and historical quantitative databases. The expert system uses a hierarchical inference network for the manager to select general risk factors and ultimately work through to courses of action.[6]

Failure Mode and Effects Analysis (FMEA)

This quality tool is a variation of the risk severity matrix discussed earlier. Each risk is assessed in terms of the following score:

$$\text{Impact} \times \text{Probability} \times \text{Detection} = \text{Risk Value}$$

Each of the three dimensions is rated according to a 5-point scale. For example, detection is defined as the ability of the project team to discern that the risk event is imminent. A score of 1 would be given if even a chimpanzee could spot the risk coming. The highest detection score of 5 would be given to events that could be discovered only after it is too late (i.e., system freezing). Similar anchored scales would be applied for severity of impact and the probability of the event occurring. The weighting of the risks is then based on their overall score. For example, a risk with an impact in the "1" zone with a very low probability and an easy detection score might score a 1 ($1 \times 1 \times 1 = 1$). Conversely, a high impact risk with a high probability and impossible to detect would score 125 ($5 \times 5 \times 5 = 125$).[7] This broad range of numerical scores allows for easy stratification of risk according to overall significance.

Probability Analysis

There are many statistical techniques available to the project manager that can assist in assessing project risk. Decision trees have been used to assess alternative courses of action using expected values. Statistical variations of net present value (NPV) have been used to assess cash flow risks in projects. Correlation between past projects' cash flow and S-curves (cumulative project cost curve—baseline—over the life of the project) have been used to assess cash-flow risks. Finally, PERT (program evaluation review technique) and PERT simulation can be used to review activity and project risk. The use of PERT simulation is increasing because it uses the same data required for PERT and software to perform the simulation is readily available. Basically PERT simulation assumes a statistical distribution (range between optimistic and pessimistic) for each activity duration; it then simulates the network (perhaps over 1,000 simulations) using a random number generator. The outcome is the relative probability, called a criticality index, of an activity becoming critical under the many different, possible activity durations for each activity. PERT simulation also provides a list of potential critical paths and their respective probabilities of occurring. Having this information available can greatly facilitate identifying and assessing schedule risk.[8]

Semiquantitative Scenario Analysis

The authors have found that project managers are reluctant to use or provide probabilities for risk analysis. Such information would allow risk analysis to be more rigorous, robust, and valuable. The challenge is to get the project team to articulate risk in words. This information can be very practical and, at the same time provide some of the benefits of probability and utility theory.

One approach used by practicing project managers, which the authors have chosen to call semiquantitative scenario analysis, is described *Project Management in Action: Semiquantitative Risk Approaches*. This approach uses time as a

Semiquantitative Risk Approach

The scenario analysis begins with the *baseline* schedule that typically represents average time and implies there is a 50/50 chance of completing the project schedule early or late. Risk team members are checked to be sure they are 90 (or 95) percent confident this schedule duration is about average.

Second, the risk team assesses the baseline schedule assuming "everything goes right." A new *best case* schedule is developed. The team is asked to confirm they are 90 percent confident there is at least a 10 percent chance that the best case schedule can be reached if everything goes right. Note that this schedule actually represents an opportunity for project compression by taking steps to avoid or reduce risks.

Third, the risk team assumes the worst case, which implies the identified risk events will occur. Murphy's Law will dominate the project. A *worst case* schedule is developed. The team is asked to confirm they are 90 percent confident there is a 90 percent chance they can meet the worst case schedule if the risk events occur.

Finally, as a reality check on the three schedules—best, baseline, and worst—team members are asked to suggest how much of their own money they would be willing to wager on each schedule. This open process usually results in some small revisions of schedules, but it also brings the team close to agreement that the schedules are reasonable. Figure 7–6 depicts three hypothetical schedules for a project, known as 10, 50, and 90 percent schedules. That is, the team is 90 percent confident there is a 10 percent chance of reaching the best-case schedule of 470 days, a 50 percent chance of meeting the baseline schedule of 500 days and a 90 percent chance of meeting the worst-case schedule of 590 days. Graphing these three schedules and documenting time estimates, costs, and assumptions is a powerful mechanism that is very useful in explaining to the customer and senior management the uncertainties and effects of risk on a project.

risk factor because most risk events are time dependent and impact project delays. Time is easily understood by risk team members. (Note that a similar approach can be used for budget.)

This quasiquantitative scenario approach takes basic scenario analysis one step further. By using numbers to verify impacts, it serves as a reality check on identified risks and analysis. A major outcome of the process is a "bracketing" of the project risk and possible durations. By running the three schedules before the project begins, it is possible to examine what decisions may have to be made; "what if . . ." questions can be addressed. For example, if a risk event occurs, what impact will it have on other projects? This approach is also very useful in explaining to project members the risks inherent in a project.

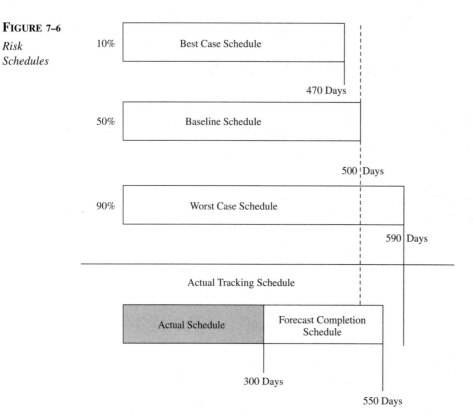

FIGURE 7–6

Risk Schedules

Sensitivity Analysis

This approach can incorporate techniques from the very simple to the highly complex. Fundamentally, project variables are given different values to identify different outcomes and the severity of each. It is similar to scenario analysis, but it typically uses a modeling approach that is very detailed and numerically oriented.

Step 3: Responding to Risks

When a risk event is identified and assessed, a decision must be made concerning which response is appropriate for the specific event. So Step 3 of the risk management process is responding to the identified risks. Responses to risk can be classified as mitigating, transferring, sharing or retaining.

Mitigating Risk

Reducing risk is usually the first alternative considered. There are basically two strategies for mitigating risk: (1) reduce the likelihood that the event will occur and (2) reduce the impact that the adverse event would have on the project. An example of the former can be found in the following description of an information systems project.

The project team was responsible for installing a new operating system in their parent company. Before implementing the project, the team tested the new system on a smaller isolated network. By doing so they discovered a variety of problems and were able to come up with solutions in advance of implementation. The team still encountered problems with the installation but the number and severity were greatly reduced. Other examples of reducing the probability of risks occurring is scheduling outdoor work during the summer months, investing in up-front safety training, and choosing high-quality materials and equipment.

An alternative strategy is to reduce the severity of the risk if it occurs. For example, a new bridge project for a coastal port was to use an innovative, continuous cement pouring process developed by an Australian firm to save large sums of money and time. The major risk was that the continuous pouring process for each major section of the bridge could not be interrupted. Any interruption would require the whole cement section (hundreds of cubic yards) be torn down and started over. An assessment of possible risks centered on delivery of the cement from the cement factory. Trucks could be delayed or the factory could break down. Such risks would result in tremendous rework costs and delays. Having two additional portable cement plants built nearby on different highways within 20 miles of the bridge project in case the main factory supply was interrupted reduced risk. These two portable plants carried raw materials for a whole bridge section and extra trucks were on immediate standby each time continuous pouring was required.

Similar risk reduction scenarios are apparent in system and software development projects where parallel innovation processes are used in case one fails. Finally, the *Project Management in Action: From Dome to Dust* details the steps Controlled Demolition took to minimize damage when they imploded the Seattle Kingdome.

Transferring Risk

Passing risk to another party is common; this transfer does not change risk. Passing risk to another party almost always results in paying a premium for this exemption. Fixed-price contracts are the classic example of transferring risk from an owner to a contractor. The contractor understands his or her firm will pay for any risk event that materializes; therefore, a monetary risk factor is added to the contract bid price. Before deciding to transfer risk, the owner should decide which party could best control activities that would lead to the risk occurring. The owner should ask, "Is the contractor capable of absorbing the risk?" Clearly identifying and documenting responsibility for absorbing risk is imperative.

Project Management in Action

From Dome to Dust

On March 26, 2000 the largest concrete domed structure in the world was reduced to a pile of rubble in a dramatic implosion lasting less than 20 seconds. According to Mark Loizeaux, whose Maryland-based Controlled Demolition Inc. was hired to bring the 24-year-old Seattle Kingdome down, "We don't blow things up. We use explosives as an engine, but gravity is the catalyst that will bring it down."

Destroying the Kingdome was the most complicated of the 7,000 demolitions Loizeaux's company has undertaken. Nearly 3 months of preparations were needed to implode the dome at a total cost of $9 million. The Kingdome was considered to be one of the strongest structures in the world, containing over 25,000 tons of concrete with each of its 40 vaulted ribs incorporating seven lengths of $2\frac{1}{4}$-inch reinforcing steel bar.

Strands of orange detonating cord—basically dynamite in a string that explodes at the lightning pace of 24,000 feet per second—connected six pie-like divisions of the Kingdome to a nearby control center. Throughout each section, Controlled Demolition workers drilled nearly 1,000 holes and packed them with high-velocity gelatin explosives the size of hot dogs. Large charges were placed about $\frac{1}{3}$ of the way up each dome rib, smaller charges were put farther up the ribs. When the detonation button was pushed, blasting caps set off a chain reaction of explosions in each section, reducing the stadium to rubble.

While the actual implosion was a technical tour-de-force, risk management was a critical part of the project's success. To minimize damage to surrounding buildings, the explosive charges were wrapped in a layer of chain-link fencing covered with thick sheets of geotextile polypropylene fabric to contain flying concrete. Nearby buildings were protected in various manners depending on the structure and proximity to the Dome. Measures included sealing air-handling units, taping seams on doors and windows, covering floors and windows with plywood and draping reinforced polyethylene sheeting around the outside.

To help absorb the impact, air conditioning units removed from the interior were stacked with other material to create a barrier around the perimeter of the work area.

Hundreds of policemen and security personnel were used to cordon off an area extending roughly 1,000 feet from the Dome from overzealous spectators. Traffic was closed for a larger area. Accommodations were provided for people and pets who lived within the restricted zone.

Eight water trucks, eight sweeper units and more than 100 workers were deployed immediately after the blast to control dust and begin the cleanup.

As a side note, one-third of the concrete will be crushed and used in the foundation of a new $430 million outdoor football stadium that is being built in its place. The rest of the concrete will be carted away and used in roadbeds and foundations throughout the Seattle area.[9]

Another more obvious way to transfer risk is insurance. However, in most cases this is impractical because defining the project risk event and conditions to an insurance broker who is unfamiliar with the project is difficult and usually expensive. Of course, low-probability and high-consequence risk events such as acts of God are more easily defined and insured. Finally, performance bonds, warranties, and guarantees are other financial instruments used to transfer risk.

Sharing Risk

Risk sharing allocates proportions of risk to different parties. An example of risk sharing was the Airbus A300B. Research and development risks were allocated among European countries including Britain and France. Alternatively, the entertainment industry formed a consortium to define a common operating format for digital video disc (DVD). Other forms of risk sharing are emerging.

Sharing risk has drawn more attention in recent years as a motivation for reducing risk and, in some cases, cutting project costs. Partnering (see Chapter 12) between an owner and contractors has prompted the development of continuous improvement procedures to encourage contractors to suggest innovative ways for project implementation. The new method will probably include additional start-up costs and the risk that the new process may not work. Usually the costs and benefits of the improved process are shared on a 50/50 basis between the owner and contracting firms.

Retaining Risk

In some cases a conscious decision is made to retain the risk of an event occurring. Some risks are so large it is not feasible to consider transferring or reducing the event (e.g., an earthquake or flood). The project owner assumes the risk because the chance of such an event occurring is slim. In other cases risks identified in the budget reserve can simply be absorbed if they materialize. The risk is retained by developing a contingency plan to implement if the risk materializes. In a few cases a risk event can be ignored and a cost overrun accepted should the risk event occur.

The more effort given to risk response before the project begins, the better the chances are for minimizing project surprises. Knowing that the response to a risk event will be retained, transferred, or shared greatly reduces stress and uncertainty when the risk event occurs. Again, control is possible with this structured approach.

Contingency Planning

A contingency plan is an alternative plan that will be used if a possible foreseen risk event becomes a reality. The contingency plan represents preventive actions that will reduce or mitigate the negative impact of the risk event. Like all plans, the contingency plan answers the questions of what, where, when, and how much action will take place. The absence of a contingency plan, when a risk event occurs, can cause a manger to delay or postpone the decision to implement a remedy. This postponement can lead to panic, crisis mismanagement, and acceptance of the first remedy suggested. Such after-the-event decision making under pressure potentially can be dangerous and costly. Contingency planning evaluates alternative remedies for possible foreseen events before the risk event occurs and selects the best plan among alternatives. This early contingency planning facilitates a smooth transition to the remedy or work-around plan. The availability of a contingency plan can significantly increase the chances for project success.

Conditions for activating the contingency plan should be decided and clearly documented. The plan should include a cost estimate and identify the source of funding. All parties affected should agree to the contingency plan and have authority to make commitments. Because implementation of a contingency plan embodies disruption in the sequence of work, all contingency plans should be communicated to team members so surprise and resistance are minimized.

Here is an example: a high-tech niche computer company intends to introduce a new "platform" product at a very specific target date. The project's 47 teams all agree delays will not be acceptable. Their contingency plans for two large component suppliers demonstrate how seriously risk management is viewed. One supplier's plant sits on the San Andreas Fault. The contingency plan has an alternative supplier, who is constantly updated, producing a replica of the component in another plant. Another supplier in Toronto, Canada, presents a delivery risk on their due date because of potential bad weather. This contingency plan calls for a chartered plane (already contracted to be on standby) if overland transportation presents a delay problem. To outsiders these plans must seem a bit extreme, but in high-tech industries where time to market is king, risks of identified events are taken seriously.

Risk response matrices such as the one shown in Figure 7–7 are useful for summarizing how the project team plans to manage risks that have been identified. Again, the Windows Office XP project (see Figure 7–4) is used to illustrate this kind of matrix. The first step is to identify whether to reduce, share, transfer, or accept the risk. The team decided to reduce the chances of experiencing interface problems and the system freezing by experimenting with a prototype of the system. Prototype experimentation not only would allow them to identify and fix conversion "bugs" before the actual installation, but it would also yield information that would be useful in enhancing acceptance by end users. The project team would be able to identify and document changes between the old and new system that would be incorporated in the training the users receive. The risk of equipment malfunctioning is transferred by choosing a reliable supplier with a strong warranty program.

FIGURE 7–7

*Risk
Response
Matrix*

Risk Event	Response	Contingency Plan	Trigger	Who Is Responsible
Interface Problems	Reduce	Work around until help comes	Not solved within 24 hours	Nils
System Freezing	Reduce	Reinstall OS	Still frozen after 1 hour	Emmylou
User backlash	Reduce	Increase staff support	Call from top management	Eddie
Equipment malfunctions	Transfer	Order different brand	Replacement doesn't work	Jim

The next step is to identify contingency plans in case the risk still occurs. For example, if interface problems prove insurmountable then the team would attempt a work around until vendor experts arrived to help solve the problem. If the system freezes after installation, the team will first try to reinstall the software. If user dissatisfaction is high, then the IS department will provide more staff support. If the team is unable to get reliable equipment from the original supplier, then it will order a different brand from a second dealer.

The team needs to discuss and agree what would trigger implementation of the contingency plan. In the case of the system freezing, it would be not being able to unfreeze the system within an hour or in the case of user backlash it would be anticipating an angry call from top management. Finally, the individual responsible for monitoring the potential risk and initiating the contingency plan needs to be assigned. Smart project managers establish protocols for contingency response before they are needed.

Unplanned Risk Events—Go/No-Go Situations

Sometimes unforeseen risk events occur midway in a project. Since no contingency plan is available, one must quickly be developed. For example, a new computer chip plant halfway through construction faced an injunction to stop construction because of an environmental lawsuit claiming damage to wetlands. Development of a contingency plan required a go/no-go decision and an additional set of new players in the project—biologists, hydrologists, lawyers, etc. The new contingency plan involved heavy damage control and a go ahead on construction with significant changes in design and cost. As in this example, risk events which arise from sources external to the project tend to cause more disruption than internal risk events. Contingency plans that respond to external events frequently involve new team players. Such players (although necessary) may be unfamiliar with the project organization and have goals in conflict with project goals, presenting still another problem.

Contingency plans are designed to ensure that project goals are reached. Plans typically cover schedule, cost, and technical risks. Some considerations for teams developing contingency plans are discussed next. Some are caveats that represent misdirections managers often take. Clearly, all projects are different; therefore, project managers will need to pick and choose which considerations are relevant to their project. (See *Project Management in Action: Risk Management at the Top of the World.*)

Schedule Risks

Use of Slack.   When some managers see network slack, they cease to worry about completing their activity on time. *Why worry if there is 10 days' slack!* Unfortunately, that slack may be needed by another activity on the path, which now must start later and leave little or no slack available because the path slack has already been used up. Managing slack can be an excellent method for reducing schedule risk.[10] Remember, use of slack moves more activities nearer their late start, and thus the risk of project delay is increased.

Managing scheduling risk usually requires trade-off decisions. It is ironic that practicing managers actually increase risk by some of their decisions. Two of those situations are examined below.

Imposed Duration Dates.   Our experience suggests about 80 percent of all projects have imposed duration dates. Usually this means someone (with authority) has determined the project or milestones can or must be completed by a specific date. Examples might be completing a road by January 1 or developing a video-game for the Christmas market. The specified project duration is frequently a top-down decision that does not include bottom-up planning and often understates the normal time required to complete the project. If this is the case, meeting the required, specified project duration would result in activities being performed more rapidly than the normal, low-cost method. This hurried approach increases cost and the chance of activities being late. There are times when completing a project by an imposed duration is necessary (e.g., time to market to beat competition), but in almost all cases of imposed project duration, both risks of being late and greater costs are increased. The question is, "Is this simply poor planning or is there a real necessity to manage projects by imposed durations?"

Compression of Project Schedules.   Sometimes before or midway through the project, the need to shorten the project duration arises. Shortening project duration is accomplished by shortening (compressing) one or more activities on the

Risk Management at the Top of the World

Into Thin Air, Jon Krakauer's gripping account of an ill-fated attempt to climb Mount Everest in which six climbers died, provides testimony to the risks of extreme mountain climbing. Thirteen days after the tragedy, David Breashears successfully led a film crew to the summit. Their footage can be seen in the spectacular IMAX film, *Everest.*

Accounts of Everest expeditions provide unique insights into planning for project risk management. First, most climbers spend more than three weeks acclimating their bodies to high-altitude conditions. Native Sherpas are used extensively to carry supplies and set up each of the four base camps that will be used during the final stages of the climb. To reduce the impact of hypoxia, light-headiness, and disorientation caused by shortage of oxygen, most climbers use oxygen masks and bottles during the final ascent. If one is lucky enough not to be one of the first expeditions of the season, the path to the summit should be staked out and roped by previous climbers. Climbing guides receive last-minute weather reports by radio to confirm whether the weather conditions warrant the risk. Finally, for added insurance most climbers join their Sherpas in an elaborate *puja* ritual intended to summon the divine support of the gods before beginning their ascent.

All of these efforts pale next to the sheer physical and mental rigors of making the final climb from base camp IV to the summit. This is what climbers refer to as the "death zone" because beyond 26,000 feet one's mind and body begin to deteriorate quickly despite supplemental oxygen. Under fair conditions it takes around 18 hours to make the round trip to the top and back to the base camp. Climbers leave as early as 1:00 am in order to make it back before night falls and total exhaustion sets in.

The greatest danger in climbing Mount Everest is not reaching the summit, but making it back to the base camp. One out of every five climbers who makes it to the summit dies during the descent. The key is establishing a contingency plan in case the climbers encounter hard going or the weather changes. Guides establish a predetermined turn-around time (i.e., 2:00 pm) to ensure a safe return no matter how close the climbers are to the summit. Accepting the time takes tremendous discipline. One who was caught up by time was solo climber Goran Krupp—a 29-year old Swede who had bicycled 8,000 miles from Stockholm to Katmandu. He turned back 1,000 feet from the top! Many lives have been lost by failing to adhere to the turn back-time and pushing forward to the summit. As one climber put it, "With enough determination, any bloody idiot can get up the hill. The trick is to get back down alive."[11]

critical path. Shortening an activity/work package duration increases direct cost. In addition, compressing the critical path decreases total slack on other paths and more paths become critical or near critical. The more critical activities or near-critical activities there are, the higher the risk of delaying project completion. Some contingency plans can avoid costly procedures. For example, schedules can be altered by working activities in parallel or using start-to-start lag relationships. Also, using the best people for high-risk tasks can relieve or lessen the chance of some risk events occurring. Techniques for managing this situation are discussed in Chapter 9.

Cost Risks

Given some of the reported cost overruns, cost risks are significant and carry heavy consequences. Most cost risks are created in schedule and technical estimate errors and omissions. In addition, some management decisions actually increase cost risks. A few selected cost risks found in practice are discussed here.

Time/Cost Dependency Link.   There is a dependency link between time and cost and technical problems and cost. For example, if the activity "develop process prototype" requires 50 percent more time than the original estimate, it can be expected that costs will also increase. Thus, time and cost do not occur independently. Neglecting to consider this interactive dependency can result in significant cost risk errors.

Cash Flow Decisions.   Some cash flow decisions can heighten schedule risks. For example, financial analysts will make comparisons of an early start schedule versus a late start schedule. Theoretically, they conclude that by delaying activities, the future value of the money is greater than its value today (the money can earn interest). Alternatively, the money can be used elsewhere. The increased risk of reducing slack is sometimes ignored or significantly underestimated. Using the schedule to solve cash flow problems should be avoided if possible. If the schedule is used, it should be done with clear recognition of an increase in schedule risk and the fact that late schedules usually result in higher costs.

Price Protection Risks.   Long-duration projects need some contingency for price changes—which are usually upward. The important point to remember when reviewing price is to avoid the trap of using one lump sum to cover price risks. For example, if inflation has been running about 3 percent, some managers add 3 percent for all materials used in the project. This lump sum approach does not address exactly where price protection is needed and fails to provide for tracking and control. Price risks should be evaluated item by item. Some purchases and contracts will not change over the life of the project. Those that may change should be identified and estimates made of the magnitude of change. This approach ensures control of the contingency funds as the project is implemented.

Technical Risks

Technical risks are problematic; such risks often can cause the project to be shut down. What if the system or process does not work? Contingency or backup plans are made for those possibilities that are foreseen. For example, Carrier Transicold was involved in developing a new Phoenix refrigeration unit for truck-trailer applications. This new unit was to use rounded panels made of bonded metals, which at the time was new technology for Transicold. Furthermore, one of its competitors had tried unsuccessfully to incorporate similar bonded metals in their products. The project team was eager to make the new technology work, but it wasn't until the very end of the project that they were able to get the new adhesives to bond adequately to complete the project.[11] Throughout the duration of the project the team maintained a welded-panel fabrication approach just in case they were unsuccessful. This contingency approach would have increased production costs, but the project still would have been completed on time.

In addition to backup strategies, project managers need to develop methods to assess quickly whether technical uncertainties can be resolved. The use of sophisticated CAD programs has greatly helped resolve design problems. At the same time, Smith and Reinertsen, in their book, *Developing Products in Half the Time*,[12] argue that there is no substitute for making something and seeing how it works, feels, or looks. They suggest that one should first identify the high-risk technical areas, then build models or design experiments to resolve the risk as quickly as possible. By isolating and testing the key technical questions early on in a project, one can quickly determine project feasibility and make necessary adjustments such as reworking the process or in some cases closing down the project.[13] Usually the owner and project manager make decisions concerning technical risks.

Funding Risks

What if the funding for the project is cut by 25 percent or completion projections indicate that costs will greatly exceed available funds? What are the chances of the project being canceled before completion? Seasoned projects managers recognize that a complete risk assessment must include an evaluation of funding supply. This is especially true for publicly funded projects. A case in point was the Superconducting Super Collider (SSC) that was initiated in Dallas, Texas, by the U.S. government in the early 1980s. This $11 billion project was designed to conduct experiments within a 54-mile underground circular chamber, accelerating subatomic particicles to 99.9999 percent of the speed of light and smashing them together at combined energies of 40 trillion electron volts. In October 1993 Congress—after spending more than $2 billion on the SSC—unceremoniously pulled the pug, ending 11 years of effort and putting 2000 people out of work. As Congressman Joe Barton, R-Texas, described what killed the SSC: "If you boil it down to one word, Clinton."[14] Clinton assumed the presidency in 1992 after 12 years of Republican rule and had a different agenda than former presidents Bush and Reagan. Moreover, Texas's 32 electoral votes had gone to native son George Bush in the 1992 presidential election.

Just as government projects are subject to changes in political structure and national agenda so do business firms frequently undergo changes in priorities and top management. The "pet projects" of the new CEO replace the "pet projects" of the former CEO. Resources become tight and one way to fund new projects is to cancel other projects.

Severe budget cuts or lack of adequate funding can have a devastating effect on a project. Typically when such a fate occurs there is a need to scale back the scope of the project to what is possible. Here the "chunkability" of the project can be an advantage. For example, freeway projects can fall short of the original intentions but still add value for each mile completed. This was not the case for the SSC project. The 54-mile donut was not a flexible thing; one couldn't stop, say at mile 50, and have a useful result.

On a much smaller scale, similar funding risks may exist for more mundane projects. For example, a building contractor may find that due to a sudden downturn in the stock market the owners can no longer afford to build their dream house. Or, an IS consulting firm may be left empty handed when a client files for bankruptcy. In the former case the contractor may have as a contingency selling the house on the open market, while unfortunately the consulting firm will have to join the long line of creditors.

Establishing Contingency Reserves

Contingency funds are established to cover errors in estimates, omissions, and uncertainties that may materialize as the project is implemented. When, where, and how much money will be spent is not known until the risk event occurs. Project "owners" are often reluctant to set up project contingency funds that seem to imply the project plan might be a poor one. Some perceive the contingency fund as an add-on slush fund. Some say they will face the risk when it materializes. Usually such reluctance to establish contingency reserves can be overcome with documented risk identification, assessment, contingency plans, and plans for when and how funds will be disbursed.

The size and amount of contingency reserves depends on "newness" of the project, inaccurate time and cost estimates, technical problems, minor changes in scope, and problems not anticipated. In practice, contingencies run from 1 to 10 percent in projects similar to past projects. However, in unique and high-technology projects it is not uncommon to find contingencies running in the 20 to 60 percent range. Use and rate of consumption of reserves must be closely monitored and controlled. Simply picking a percentage of the baseline, say 5 percent, and calling it the contingency reserve is not a sound approach. Also, adding up all the identified contingency allotments and throwing them in one pot is not conducive to sound control of the reserve fund. In practice, the contingency reserve fund typically is divided into budget and management reserve funds for control purposes. Budget reserves are those allocated to specific segments of the project. Management reserves are those allocated to risks associated with the total project.

Budget Reserves

These reserves are identified for specific work packages or segments of a project found in the baseline budget or work breakdown structure. Budget reserves are for *identified* risks that have a low chance of occurring. Examples of variations covered by budget reserves are small design changes and time and cost estimate errors. For example, a reserve amount might be added to "computer coding" to cover the risk of "testing" showing a coding problem. The reserve amount is determined by costing out the accepted contingency or recovery plan. The budget reserve should be communicated to the project team. This openness suggests trust and encourages good cost performance. However, distributing budget reserves should be the responsibility of both the project manager and the team members responsible for implementing the specific segment of the project. If the risk does not materialize, the funds are returned to the management reserve. Thus, budget reserves decrease as the project progresses.[15]

Management Reserves

These reserve funds are needed to cover major unforeseen and potential risks, and hence are applied to the total project. For example, a major scope change may appear necessary midway in the project. Because this change was not anticipated or identified, it is covered from the management reserve. Management reserves are established *after* budget reserves are identified and funds established. These reserves are independent of budget reserves and are controlled by the project manager and the "owner" of the project. The "owner" can be internal (top management) or external to the project organization. Most management reserves are set using historical data and judgments concerning the uniqueness of the project.

TABLE 7–1   **Contingency Fund Estimate (Thousands of dollars)**

Activity	Budget Baseline	Budget Reserve	Project Budget
Design	$ 500	$15	$ 515
Code	$ 900	$80	$ 980
Test	$ 20	$ 2	$ 22
Subtotal	$1,420	$97	$1,517
Mgmt. Reserve	——	——	$ 50
Total	$1,420	$97	$1,567

Placing technical contingencies in the management reserve is a special case. Identifying possible technical (functional) risks is often associated with a new, untried, innovative process or product. Since there is a chance the innovation may not work out, a fallback plan is necessary. This type of risk is beyond the control of the project manager. Hence, technical reserves are held in the management reserve and controlled by the owner or top management. The owner and project manager decide when the contingency plan will be implemented and the reserve funds used. It is assumed there is a high probability these funds will never be used.

Table 7–1 shows the development of a contingency fund estimate for a hypothetical project. Note how budget and management reserves are kept separate; control is easily tracked using this format.

Step 4: Risk Control

Step 4 in the risk management process is risk control—executing the risk response strategy, monitoring risks, initiating contingency plans, and watching for new risks. Establishing a change management system to deal with events that require formal changes in the scope, budget, and/or schedule of the project is also an essential element of risk control.

Project managers need to monitor risks just like they track project progress. Risk assessment and updating needs to be part of every status meeting and progress report system. The project team needs to be on constant alert for new, unforeseen risks. Management needs to be sensitive that others may not be forthright in acknowledging new risks and problems. Admitting that there might be a bug in the design code or that different components are not compatible reflects poorly on individual performance. If the prevailing organizational culture is one where mistakes are punished severely then it is only human nature to protect oneself. Similarly, if bad news is greeted harshly, and there is a propensity to "kill the messenger" then participants will be reluctant to speak freely. The tendency to suppress bad news is compounded when individual responsibility is vague and the project team is under extreme pressure from top management to get the project done quickly.

Project managers need to establish an environment in which participants feel comfortable raising concerns and admitting mistakes. The norm should be that mistakes are acceptable, hiding mistakes is intolerable. Problems should be embraced not denied. Participants should be encouraged to identify problems and new risks. Here a project manager's positive attitude toward risks is a key.

On large, complex projects it may be prudent to repeat the risk identification/ assessment exercise with fresh information. Risk profiles should be reviewed to test to see if the original responses held true. Relevant stakeholders should be brought into the discussion. While this may not be practical on an ongoing basis, project managers should touch base with them on a regular basis or hold special stakeholder meetings to review the status of risks on the project.

A second key for controlling the cost of risks is documenting responsibility. This can be problematic in networked projects involving multiple organizations and contractors. Responsibility for risk is frequently passed on to others with the statement, "That is not my worry." This mentality is dangerous. Each identified risk should be assigned (or shared) by mutual agreement of the owner, project manager, and the contractor or person having line responsibility for the work package or segment of the project. It is best to have the line person responsible approve the use of budget reserve funds and monitor their rate of usage. If management reserve funds are required, the line person should play an active role in estimating additional costs and funds needed to complete the project. Having line personnel participate in the process focuses attention on the management reserve, controls of its rate of usage, and serves as early warning of potential risk events. If risk management is not formalized, responsibility and responses to risk will be ignored—"it is not my area."

The bottom line is that project managers and team members need to be vigilant in monitoring potential risks and identifying new road mines that can derail a project. Risk assessment has to be part of the working agenda of status meetings and when new risks emerge they need to be analyzed and incorporated into the risk management process.

Change Control Management

A major element of the risk control process is change management. Every detail of a project plan will not materialize as expected. Coping with and controlling project changes present a formidable challenge for most project managers. Changes come from many sources such as the project customer, owner, project manager, team members, and occurrence of risk events. Most changes easily fall into three categories. First, scope changes in the form of design or additions represent big changes—e.g., customer requests for a new feature or a redesign that will improve the product. Second, implementations of contingency plans, when risk events occur, represent changes in baseline costs and schedules. Third, improvement changes suggested by project team members represent another category of change. Since change is inevitable, a well-defined change review and control process should be set up early in the project planning cycle.

Basically, change control systems involve controlling and reporting changes to the project baseline. (Note: Some organizations consider change control systems part of configuration management.) In practice most change control systems are designed to accomplish the following:

1. Identify proposed changes.
2. List expected effects of proposed change on schedule and budget.
3. Review, evaluate, and approve or disapprove changes formally.
4. Negotiate and resolve conflicts of change, conditions, and cost.
5. Communicate changes to parties affected by change.
6. Assign responsibility for implementing change.
7. Track all changes that are to be implemented.

An example of a simplified change request form is depicted in Figure 7–8.

Change requests should be reviewed and approved or disapproved within a short time limit. If the project is large, a review team may be needed to oversee project changes. Changes more often than not increase cost, cause delays, increase stress among team members, and disrupt the sequence of work; therefore, team members often resist change proposals.

Every approved change must be identified and reflected in the project WBS and baseline. If the change control system is not integrated with the WBS and baseline, project plans and control will soon self-destruct. Thus, one of the keys to successful change control process is document, document, document! The benefits derived from change control systems are the following:

1. Inconsequential changes are discouraged by the formal process.
2. Costs of changes are maintained in a log.
3. Integrity of the WBS and performance measures is maintained.
4. Allocation and use of budget and management reserve funds are tracked.
5. Responsibility for implementation is clarified.
6. Impact of changes is visible to all parties involved.
7. Implementation of change is monitored.
8. Scope changes will be quickly reflected in baseline and performance measures.

FIGURE 7–8

Change Request

CHANGE REQUEST	

Project _____ Y2K-Machine Dept. _____   Date _____ 3/29/ _____

Originator _____ CEG _____   Phone _____ Ext. 4942 _____

Impact Areas			**Baseline Impact**		
Deliverable	# _1.3M_	Scope	☐	Contingency	☐
Work Package	# _1.313M_	Budget	☒	Staff	☒
Cost Account	# _1.31M_	Schedule	☒	Equipment	☒
Organization Unit	_IS-M Dept._				

Description of change

Install Y2K compatible chip in six computer controlled milling machines

Justification (include impact if not implemented)

Reprogramming is higher cost than estimated, and risk of old chips failing is higher than estimated.

(Eliminating reprogramming cost is −$10,000. Cost of Y2K chips installed is +$15,000)

Disposition	**Priority**	**Funding Source**	
☒ Approve			
☐ Approve as amended	☐ Emergency	Mgmt. reserve	$ _____
☐ Disapprove	☒ Urgent	Budget reserve	$ _5,000._
☐ Deferred	☐ Routine	Other	$ _____

Authorized _____ S.P _____   Scheduled start _____ 4/7/ _____

Date _____ 4/3/ _____   Scheduled finish _____ 5/10/ _____

Clearly, change control is important and requires that someone or some group be responsible for approving changes and keeping the process updated. Project control depends heavily on keeping the change control process current. This historical record can be used for satisfying customer inquiries, identifying problems in post project audits, and estimating future project costs.

Summary

To put the processes discussed in this chapter in proper perspective one should recognize that the essence of project management is risk management. Every technique in this book is really a risk management technique. Each in their own way tries to prevent something bad from happening. Project selection systems try to reduce the likelihood that projects will not contribute to the mission of the firm. Project scope statements, among other things, are designed to avoid costly misunderstandings and reduce scope creep. Work breakdown structures reduce the likelihood that some vital part of the project will be omitted or that the budget estimates are unrealistic. Team building reduces the likelihood of dysfunctional conflict and breakdowns in coordination. All of the techniques try to increase stakeholder satisfaction and increase the chances of project success.

From this perspective risk management compliments other project management processes. Managers engage risk management activities to compensate for the uncertainty inherent in project management and the reality that things never go according to plan. Risk management is proactive not reactive. It reduces the number of surprises and leads to a better understanding of the most likely outcomes of negative events.

Although many managers believe that in the final analysis, risk assessment and contingency depend on subjective judgment, some standard method for identifying, assessing, and responding to risks should be included in all projects. The very process of identifying project risks forces some discipline at all levels of project management and improves project performance.

Contingency plans increase the chance the project can be completed on time and within budget. Contingency plans can be simple "work arounds" or elaborate detailed plans. Responsibility for risks should be clearly identified and documented. It is desirable and prudent to keep a reserve as a hedge against project risks. Budget reserves are linked to the WBS and should be communicated to the project team. Control of management reserves should remain with the owner, project manager, and line person responsible. Use of contingency reserves should be closely monitored, controlled, and reviewed throughout the project life cycle.

Risk management can be handled before the project begins or when the risk occurs. Experience clearly indicates that using a formal, structured process to handle possible foreseen and unforeseen project risk events minimizes surprises, costs, delays, stress, and misunderstandings. When risk events occur or changes are necessary, using an effective change control process to approve and record changes quickly will facilitate measuring performance against schedule and cost. Ultimately successful risk management requires developing an attitude in which threats are embraced, not denied, and problems are identified not hidden.

8

RESOURCE
SCHEDULING

Project network times are not a schedule until resources have been assigned.

Scheduling Problems

One frustrated project manager listed the following questions he needed to be able to answer at any point in time:

- Will existing labor and/or equipment be adequate and available to deal with my project?
- Will outside contractors have to be used?
- Where is the critical path? Do unforeseen dependencies exist?
- If slack is used up, what happens to the risk of being late?
- Which resources have priority?
- Is the original deadline realistic?
- If another project is added to our ongoing and planned projects, will it cause delays in my project?

Clearly, this project manager has a good understanding of the problems he is facing. Any project scheduling system should facilitate finding quick, easy answers to these questions. There are many types of constraints that impinge on allocating resources to a project schedule. Some are discussed below to show the complexity managers can encounter in developing a project schedule.

Types of Project Constraints

Project constraints impede or delay the start of activities. The result is a reduction in slack shown on the planned network, a decrease in scheduling flexibility, a possible decrease in the number of parallel activities, and an increase in the likelihood of delaying the project. Three project constraints need to be considered in scheduling:

1. Technical constraints
2. Resource constraints
3. Physical constraints

Technical Constraints

These constraints address the *sequence* in which project activities must occur, assuming resources are adequate. Activities are assumed to be independent and resources will be made available and/or are interchangeable.

Resource Constraints

The absence or shortage of resources can alter technical constraints drastically. Parallel activities hold potential for resource conflicts. Because it is impossible for an individual or piece of equipment to work on two activities simultaneously, a resource dependency exists. The result is that activities that were assumed to be independent now become dependent.

Physical Constraints

In rare situations there are physical constraints that cause activities that would normally occur in parallel to be constrained by contractual or environmental conditions. For example, renovating a ship compartment might allow only one person to perform an activity because of space limitations. The procedures for handling physical constraints are similar to those used for resource constraints.

The interrelationships and interactions among time and resource constraints are complex for even small project networks. Project managers who make an effort to examine these interactions before the project begins frequently uncovers surprising problems. Those who do not consider resource availability in moderately complex projects usually learn of problems when it is too late to correct them. A deficit of resources can alter project dependency relationships, completion dates, and project costs significantly. Project managers must be careful to schedule resources to ensure availability in the right quantities and at the right time. Fortunately there are computer software programs that can identify resource problems during the early project planning phase when corrections can be considered. These programs only require activity resource needs and availability information to schedule resources.

Kinds of Resource Constraints

There are many resource constraints. The most important are:

- People
- Materials
- Equipment
- Working capital

People

This is the most obvious project resource. Human resources are usually classified by the skills they bring to the project—for example, programmer, mechanical engineer, welder, inspector, marketing director, supervisor. In rare cases some skills are interchangeable, but usually with a loss of productivity. The many differing skills of human resources add to the complexity of scheduling projects.

Materials

Lack of availability of materials can constrain the project schedule. Material shortages have been blamed for the delay of many projects. When it is known that a lack of availability of materials is important and probable, materials should be included in the project network plan and schedule. For example, the delivery and placement of an oil rig tower in a Siberian oil field had a very small time window during one summer month. Any delivery delay meant a 1-year, costly delay. Scheduling delivery of the oil rig was the problem, not people or equipment.

Scheduling materials has also become important in developing products where time-to-market can result in loss of market share.

Equipment

Equipment is often overlooked as a constraint. Equipment is usually presented by type, size, and quantity. In some cases equipment can be interchanged to improve schedules, but this is not typical for specialized equipment. The most common oversight is to assume the resource pool is more than adequate for the project. For example, if a project needs one earth-moving tractor 6 months from now and the organization owns four, it is common to assume the resource will not delay the pending project. However, when the earth-moving tractor is due on site in

6 months, all four machines in the pool might be occupied on other projects. In multiproject environments, it is prudent to use a common resource pool for all projects. This approach forces a check of resource availability across all projects and reserves the equipment for specific project needs in the future. In large organizations the project office may oversee resources used over more than one project. Recognition of equipment constraints before the project begins can avoid high crashing or delay costs.

Working Capital

In a few project situations such as construction, working capital is treated as a resource because it is limited in supply. If working capital is readily available, a project manager may work on many activities concurrently. If working capital is in short supply because progress payments are made monthly, materials and labor usage may have to be restricted to conserve cash. This situation represents a cash flow problem.

All of these constraints can significantly alter project schedules. Each additional constraint usually restricts flexibility, may cause delays, and increases the complexity of scheduling.

Scheduling Resources for Utilization and Given Availability

The planned network and activity project duration times found in previous chapters fail to deal with resource *usage* and *availability*. The time estimates for the work packages and network times were made independently with the implicit assumption that resources would be available. If resources are adequate but the demand varies widely over the life of the project, it may be desirable to even out resource demand by delaying noncritical activities (using slack) to *lower peak demand* and, thus, increase resource utilization. This process is called *resource smoothing*. On the other hand, if resources are limited and are not adequate to meet peak demands, the late start of some activities must be delayed and the duration of the project may be increased. Here, the goal is to *minimize project delay*. This process is called *resource-limited scheduling* and can create unforeseen problems. One research study of more than 50 projects reports that planned project network durations were increased 38 percent when limited resources were scheduled.[1]

Because the costs of failing to consider resource usage and availability are hidden or not obvious, resource scheduling in practice often is not done or does not get the attention it deserves. The consequences of failing to schedule limited resources are costly activity and project delays that usually manifest themselves midway in the project when quick corrective action is difficult. An additional consequence of failing to schedule resources is the failure to reduce the peaks and valleys of resource usage over the duration of the project. Because project resources usually are overcommitted and because resources seldom line up by availability and need, procedures are needed to deal with these problems. This chapter addresses methods available to project managers for identifying and dealing with resource utilization and availability through resource smoothing and resource-limited scheduling. Since these methods become very complex for even small projects, computer software must be used to implement the methods. Although the methods discussed apply to a single project, the same methods can be applied to many different resources and several projects.

Identifying the Scheduling Condition

Once the resource information for each activity is entered into the computer software, a preliminary resource loading plan is derived showing the required resources by period. At this point you need to review what condition you, as a scheduler, are dealing with. The authors have encountered four major resource allocation scenarios that capture most of the conditions facing project managers. Figure 8–1 depicts those scenarios.

1. Time-limited. These projects have an imposed duration that is considered a must. A time-to-market project is the classic example of a time-limited (constrained) project. It is assumed resources will be made available to ensure the project is completed by a specific date. Although time is the critical factor, resource usage should be no more than is necessary and sufficient.

FIGURE 8–1

Scheduling Conditions and Goals

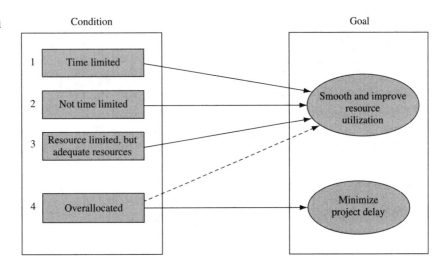

2. Time is not limited. In this condition the project plan duration is usually accepted and resources will be made available as needed.

3. Resource limited, but adequate resources. Resource availability level is limited (fixed). But the resource loading run shows that no resources are overallocated.

4. Resource limited and overallocated. The resource loading run shows resources are overallocated. Given the limited resources available, the resource conflicts make it impossible to complete the project within the planned time duration.

Resource Smoothing

Basically, all smoothing techniques delay noncritical activities by using slack to *reduce peak demand*, fill in the valleys for the resources, and increase the utilization of the resource. Reducing the peak and smoothing becomes even more important in a multiproject environment in which a portfolio of projects is managed and resources are classified into skill pools.

Condition 1: Time limited. A simple example can illustrate the smoothing procedure on a time-limited condition 1 project called Test Project. A partial network that uses only one resource, test engineers, demonstrates the basic procedure; within the class all resources are interchangeable. The starting point for smoothing resources is the early start (ES) network plan, which is found in Figure 8–2a. Figure 8–2b presents the ES bar chart plan and a loading chart that displays the resource profile for the project. The activity durations are represented by the shaded and clear bars. The shaded bars represent the critical path. The hashed bars represent slack time for the activity. The resource profile follows the typical pattern of growing to a peak and then declining. Because this project is declared time limited, the goal will be to reduce (smooth) the peak requirement for the resource and thereby increase the utilization of the resource. A quick examination of the ES resource load chart suggests only two activities have slack that can be used to reduce the resource peak—activities 2 and 4. Either one can be delayed to lower the peak resource of 3 to 2. Figure 8–2c presents the outcome of delaying activity 4 two time periods. Check the differences in the resource profiles of Figure 8–2b and Figure 8–2c. The important point is the resources needed over the life of the project have been reduced from 3 to 2 (33 percent) and the utilization of the resource has increased from 52 percent [11 total units required/(3×7)] to 86 percent [$11/(2 \times 7)$]. In addition the profile has been smoothed, which should be easier to manage.

Conditions 2 and 3 also use the same smoothing approach. That is, slack is used to minimize the peak and increase resource utilization.

Condition 2: Time is not limited. For some organizations and projects, resources and time limits may not be a major issue. Managers may wish to check

FIGURE 8-2

Time Limited Smoothing Example

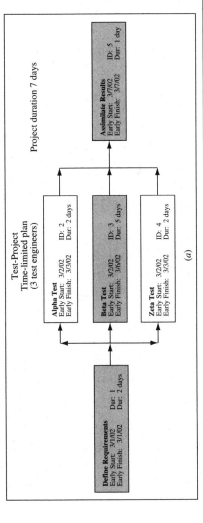

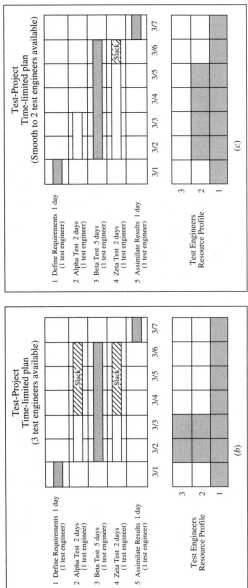

187

options available. For example, imagine that your software program has smoothed the project and indicates the coding of the system can be done with 7 coders instead of 10. Your boss doesn't have strong preferences concerning the time to complete the project—condition 2. Try reducing the number of coders to 6 or 5. Give the boss a choice. The project duration is 40 days with 7 coders or 55 days with 5 coders. The idea of using fewer coders may open up options with other projects.

Condition 3: Resource limited, but adequate resources. This condition is rare and unique. For example, when resources are limited to those available, managers of new projects assume their project plan will probably be delayed. However, the first computer run may indicate the resources needed for your project are adequate. If you encounter this fortunate situation, you may wish to smooth the resource profiles to improve resource utilization.

The downside of smoothing is a loss of flexibility that occurs from reducing slack. Also the risk of activities delaying the project increases because slack reduction can create more critical activities and/or near-critical activities. Pushing smoothing too far for a perfectly level resource profile is risky. If you were to push the resources to 100 percent utilization over the entire project duration, every activity becomes critical.

The simple, trivial example provided in condition 1 gives a sense of the time-limited problem and the smoothing approach. However, in practice the magnitude of the problem is complex for even small projects. Manual solutions are not practical. Fortunately, the software packages available today have very good routines for smoothing project resources. (Note: Some of the procedures used in the computer routines are found in the original classic studies.)[1,2,3] Typically, the programs use activities that have the most slack to level project resources. The rationale is those activities with the most slack pose the least risk. Although this is generally true, other risk factors such as reduction of flexibility to use reassigned resources on other activities or the nature of the activity (easy, complex) are not addressed using such a simple rationale. It is easy to experiment with many alternatives to find the one that best fits your project and minimizes risk of delaying the project.

Condition 4: Resource limited and overallocated. Here, the key issue is to *minimize project delay* rather than smoothing. Condition 4 projects have *resources that are limited* to those available and none are expected to be added. The project to be implemented must work within the current resources available to the organization. One simple test to determine if the project is resource limited is to ask, "If the critical path is delayed, can I add resources to get back on schedule?" If the answer is no, assume the project is resource limited. This outcome presents the most difficult and complex problems for scheduling projects. In practice more than 50 percent of non-time-to-market projects are resource limited. Because we assume the level of resources available cannot be exceeded and is inadequate, it will be necessary to delay activities and probably the project, but as little as possible. The goal is to prioritize and allocate resources to minimize project delay without exceeding the resource limit or altering the technical network relationships. If this approach is not feasible, outsourcing can be considered as an alternative. The Air Control Project is used to illustrate the resource-limited and over-allocated problem. Figure 8–3a shows the *planned* Air Control Project network without any concern for resources. That is, activities are assumed to be independent and resources will be made available and/or are interchangeable. Figure 8–3b depicts the bar chart for the project. The solid bars represent the activity durations;

FIGURE 8–3

Air Control Project, Time Plan Without Resources

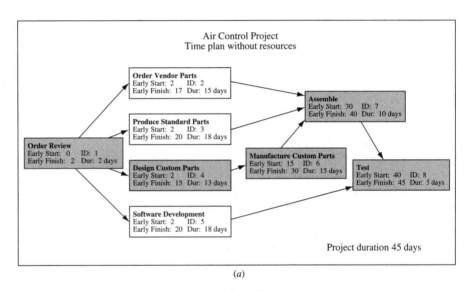

(a)

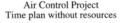

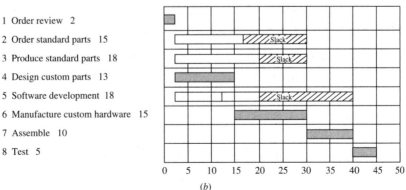

(b)

the hashed bars represent slack; the shaded bars represent the critical path. Note that the duration is 45 days and the critical path is represented by activities 1, 4, 6, 7, and 8.

Parallel activities hold potential for resource conflicts. This is the case in this project. Ryan is the resource for activities 3 and 6. If you insert Ryan in the bar chart in Figure 8–3b for activities 3 and 6, you can see activity 3 overlaps activity 6 by 5 days—an impossible situation. Because Ryan cannot work two activities simultaneously and no other person can take his place, a resource dependency exists. The result is that two activities (3 and 6) that were assumed to be independent now become dependent. Something has to give! Figure 8–4a shows the

FIGURE 8–4

Air Control Project, Schedule with Resources Limited

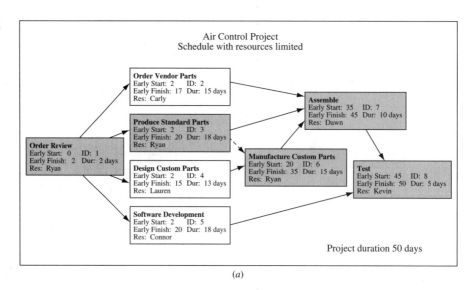

(a)

1 Order review 2

2 Order vendor parts 15

3 Produce standard parts 18

4 Design custom parts 13

5 Software development 18

6 Manufacture custom hardware 15

7 Assemble 10

8 Test 5

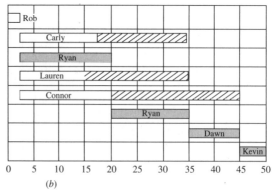

(b)

Air Control Project network with the resources included. A dashed arrow has been added to the network to indicate the resource dependency. The bar chart in Figure 8–4b reflects the revised schedule resolving the overallocation of Ryan. Given the new schedule, slack for some activities has changed. More importantly, the critical path has changed. It is now 1, 3, 6, 7, 8. The resource schedule shows the new project duration to be 50 days rather than 45 days. Project delay has been minimized.

Heuristics

Unfortunately, in practice there are many different resources working on a project and the project may share resources with other projects in the organization portfolio. The resource scheduling problem is a large combinatorial one. This means even a modest-size project network with only a few resource types might have several thousand feasible solutions. A few researchers have demonstrated *optimum* mathematical solutions to the resource allocation problem but only for small networks and very few resource types.[2] The massive data requirements for larger problems make pure mathematical solutions (e.g., linear programming) impractical. An alternative approach to the problem has been the use of heuristics (rules of thumb) to solve large combinatorial problems. These practical decision or priority rules have been in place for many years. Heuristics do not always yield an optimal schedule, but they are very capable of yielding a good schedule for very complex networks with many types of resources. The efficiency of different rules and combinations of rules has been well documented.[3] The heuristics used in computer software available today make it very easy for the project manager to create a good resource schedule for the project.

Heuristics allocate resources to activities to minimize project delay; that is, heuristics prioritize which activities are allocated resources and which activities are delayed when resources are not adequate. The following scheduling heuristics have been found to consistently minimize project delay over a large variety of projects.

1. Minimum slack
2. Smallest duration
3. Lowest activity identification number

The parallel method is the most widely used approach to apply heuristics. The parallel method is an iterative process that starts at the first time period of the project and schedules period-by-period any activities eligible to start. In any period when two or more activities require the same resource, the priority rules are applied. For example, if in period 5 three activities are eligible to start (i.e., have the same ES) and require the same resource, the first activity placed in the schedule would be the activity with the least slack (rule 1). However, if all activities have the same slack, the next rule would be invoked (rule 2), and the activity with the smallest duration would be placed in the schedule first. In very rare cases, when all eligible activities have the same slack and the same duration, the tie is broken by the lowest activity identification number (rule 3), since each activity has a unique ID number. When a resource limit has been reached, the early start (ES) for succeeding activities not yet in the schedule will be delayed (and all successor activities not having free slack) and their slack reduced. In subsequent periods the procedure is repeated until the project is scheduled. An example demonstrating the impact of resource limitations on a project schedule is the Nightingale Project, a resource-limited project.

An Example: The Nightingale Project

Nightingale was the code name given to the development of a handheld electronic medical reference guide to be used by emergency medical technicians and paramedics. Figure 8–5 contains a time-limited network for the design phase of the project. For the purpose of this example, we assume that only design engineers are required for the tasks and that the design engineers are interchangeable. The number of engineers required to perform each task is noted in the network, where 500 percent means five design engineers are needed for the activity. For example, activity 5, feature specs, requires four design engineers (400 percent). The project begins January 1, 2002 and ends February 14, 2002, a duration of 45 workdays. The time-limited bar chart for the project is shown in Figure 8–6; this chart shows the same information found on the network figure, but in a different form.

Finally, a resource usage chart is presented for a segment of the project—January 13 to January 26; see Figure 8–7. Observe that the time-limited project requires 21 design engineers on January 18 and 19 (168 hrs/8 hrs per engineer = 21 engineers). This segment represents the peak requirement for design engineers for the project.

However, due to the shortage of design engineers and commitments to other projects, only 8 engineers can be assigned to the project. To resolve this problem we use the "leveling" tool within the software and first try to solve the problem by leveling only within slack. This solution would preserve the original finish date. However, as expected, this does not solve all of the allocation problems. The next option is to allow the software to apply scheduling heuristics and level outside of slack. The new schedule is contained in the revised, resource-limited Gantt chart presented in Figure 8–8. The resource-limited project network indicates the project duration has now been extended to 2/26/02, or 57 workdays (versus 45 days time limited).

FIGURE 8–5

Nightingale Project—Time Constrained Network

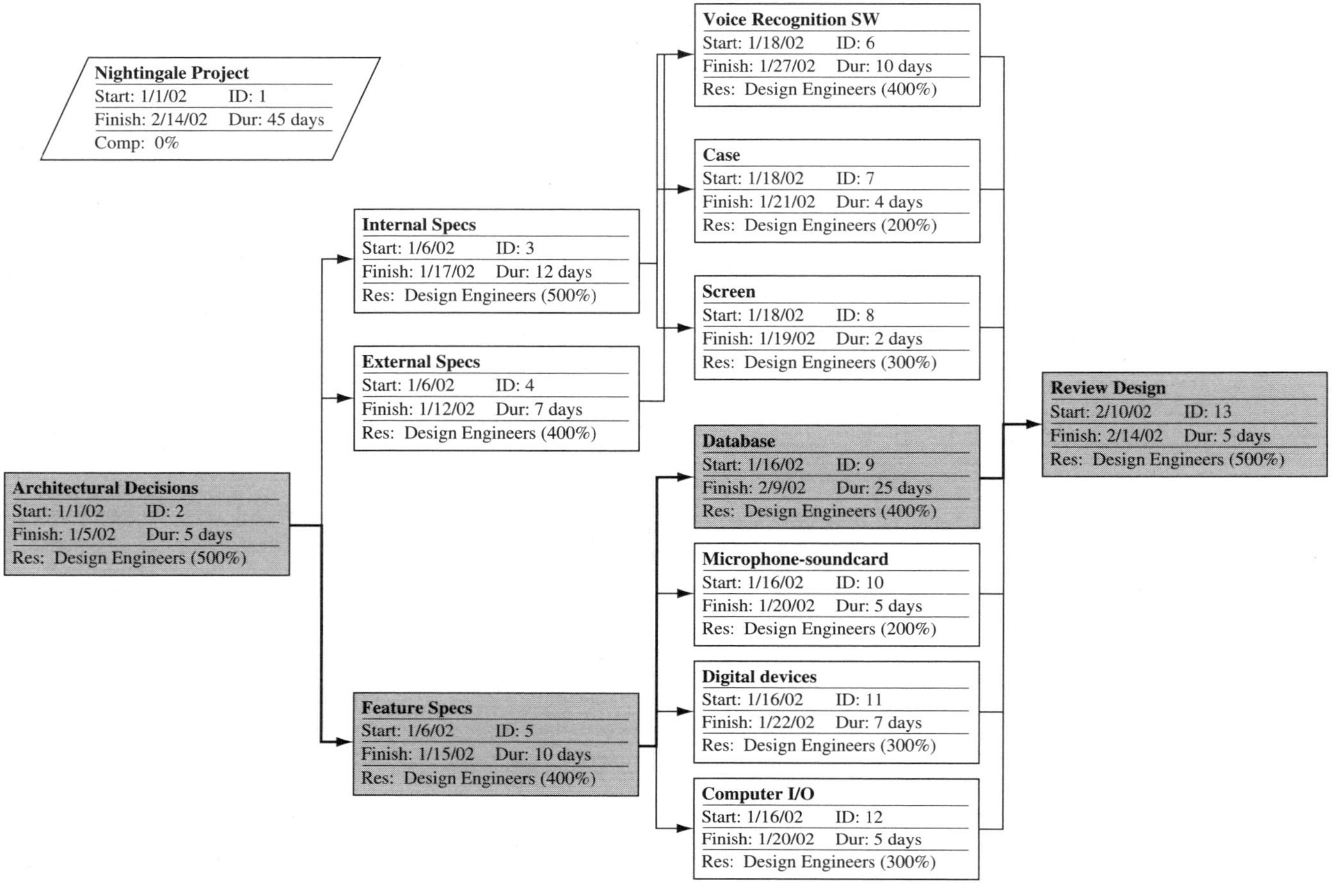

FIGURE 8–6

Nightingale Project—Time Constrained Gantt Chart

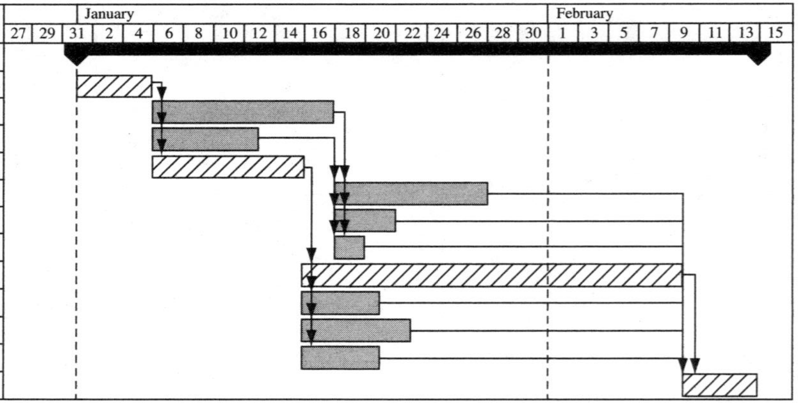

FIGURE 8–7

*Nightingale
Project—
Time
Constrained
Resource
Usage View*

ID	Resource Name	Work	Jan 13, '02							Jan 20, '02						
			S	M	T	W	T	F	S	S	M	T	W	T	F	S
1	**Design Engineers**	3,024 hrs	+72h	72h	72h	136h	136h	168h	168h	144h	104h	88h	64h	64h	64h	64h
	Architectural Decisions	200 hrs														
	Internal Specs	480 hrs	40h	40h	40h	40h	40h									
	External Specs	224 hrs														
	Feature Specs	320 hrs	32h	32h	32h											
	Voice Recognition SW	320 hrs						32h	32h	32h	32h	32h	32h	32h	32h	32h
	Case	64 hrs						16h	16h	16h	16h					
	Screen	48 hrs						24h	24h							
	Database	800 hrs				32h	32h	32h	32h	32h	32h	32h	32h	32h	32h	32h
	Microphone-soundcard	80 hrs				16h	16h	16h	16h	16h						
	Digital devices	168 hrs				24h	24h	24h	24h	24h	24h	24h				
	Computer I/O	120 hrs				24h	24h	24h	24h	24h						
	Review Design	200 hrs														

The application of the heuristics can be seen in the scheduling of the internal, external, and feature specification activities. All three activities were originally scheduled to start immediately after activity 1, architectural decisions.

This is impossible, since the three activities collectively require 14 engineers. The software chooses to schedule activity 5 first because this activity is on the original critical path and has zero slack (heuristic 1). Next, and concurrently, activity 4 is chosen over activity 3 because activity 4 has a shorter duration (heuristic 2); internal specs, activity 3, is delayed due to the limitation of 8 design engineers. Notice that the original critical path no longer applies because of the resource dependencies created by having only 8 design engineers.

Compare the bar chart in Figure 8–8 with the time-limited bar chart in Figure 8–6. For example, note the different start dates for activity 8 (screen). In the time-limited plan (Figure 8–6), the start date for activity 8 is 1/18, while the start date in the resource limited schedule (Figure 8–8) is 2/16, almost a month later! (Note: The software output shows the *leveled* delay for activity 8 is only 19 days. The 19 days is derived from the leveled internal specifications (activity 3), an immediate predecessor, finish time of 1/27 and the 2/16 start date for the screen activity.)

While resource bar graphs are commonly used to illustrate overallocation problems, we prefer to view resource usage tables like the one presented in Figure 8–7. This table tells you when you have an overallocation problem and which activities are causing the overallocation. See *Project Management in Action: Assessing Resource Allocation* for a checklist dealing with resource conflicts.

The Impacts of Resource Constrained Scheduling

Like smoothing schedules, the limited-resource schedule usually reduces slack, reduces flexibility by using slack to ensure delay is minimized, and increases the

FIGURE 8-8

Nightingale Project—Resource Constrained Gantt Chart

ID	Task Name	Duration	Start	Finish
1	**Nightingale Project**	**57 days**	**Tue 1/1/02**	**Tue 2/26/02**
2	Architectural Decisions	5 days	Tue 1/1/02	Sat 1/5/02
3	Internal Specs	12 days	Wed 1/16/02	Sun 1/27/02
4	External Specs	7 days	Sun 1/6/02	Sat 1/12/02
5	Feature Specs	10 days	Sun 1/6/02	Tue 1/15/02
6	Voice Recognition SW	10 days	Sat 2/2/02	Mon 2/11/02
7	Case	4 days	Tue 2/12/02	Fri 2/15/02
8	Screen	2 days	Sat 2/16/02	Sun 2/17/02
9	Database	25 days	Mon 1/28/02	Thu 2/21/02
10	Microphone-soundcard	5 days	Wed 1/16/02	Sun 1/20/02
11	Digital devices	7 days	Sat 1/26/02	Fri 2/1/02
12	Computer I/O	5 days	Mon 1/21/02	Fri 1/25/02
13	Review Design	5 days	Fri 2/22/02	Tue 2/26/02

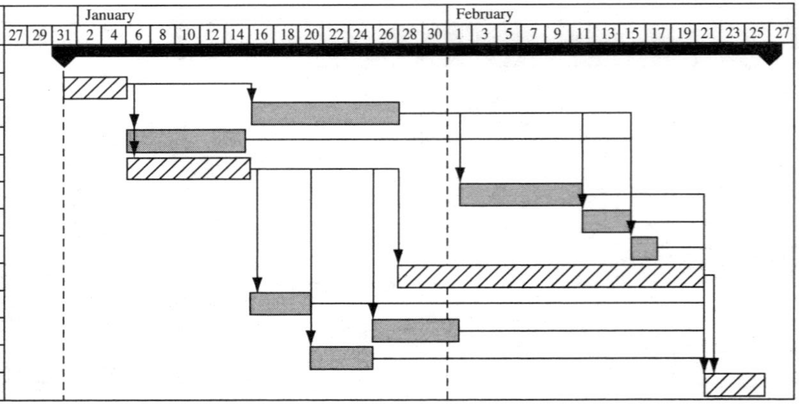

Project Management in Action

Assessing Resource Allocation

One of the strengths of today's project management software is the ability to identify and provide options for resolving resource allocation problems. A project manager who uses MS Project 2000 to plan projects shared with us the following checklist for dealing with resource conflicts after preliminary assignment of resources has been made. While this checklist makes specific references to MS Project 2000, the same steps can be used with most project management software.

1. Assess whether you have overallocation problems (see *Red* in the resource sheet view).
2. Identify where and when conflicts occur by examining the resource usage view.
3. Resolve the problem by:
   a. Replacing overallocated resources with appropriate resources that are available. Then ask if this solves the problem.
   If not:
   b. Use the leveling tool and choose the level within slack option.
      i. Does this solve the problem (are resources still overallocated)?
      ii. Check the sensitivity of the network and ask if this is acceptable.
   If not:
   c. Consider splitting tasks
      i. Make sure to re-adjust task durations to take into account additional start-up and shut-down time.
4. If 3 does not work, then either:
   a. Use the level tool default option and ask if you can live with the new completion date.
   If not:
   b. Negotiate for additional resources to complete the project.
   If not possible:
   c. Consider reducing project scope to meet deadline.

---

number of critical and near-critical activities. Scheduling complexity is increased because resource constraints are added to technical constraints; start times may now have two constraints.

The traditional critical path concept of sequential activities from the start to the end of the project is no longer meaningful. The resource constraints can break the sequence and leave the network with a set of disjointed critical activities.

Project Management in Action

U.S. Forest Service Resource Shortage

A major segment of work in managing U.S. Forest Service (USDA) forests is selling mature timber to logging companies that harvest the timber under contract conditions monitored by the Service. The proceeds are returned to the federal government. The budget allocated to each forest depends on the 2-year plan submitted to the U.S. Department of Agriculture.

Olympic Forest headquarters in Olympia, Washington, was developing a 2-year plan as a basis for funding. All of the districts in the forest submitted their timber sale projections (numbering more than 50) to headquarters, where they were compiled and aggregated into a project plan for the whole forest. The first computer run was reviewed by a small group of senior managers to determine if the plan was reasonable and "do-able." Management was pleased and relieved to note all projects appeared to be doable in the 2-year time frame until a question was raised concerning the computer printout. "Why are all the columns in these projects labeled 'RESOURCE' blank?" The response from an engineer was, "We don't use that part of the program."

The discussion that ensued recognized the importance of resources in completing the 2-year plan and ended with a request to "try the program with resources included." The new output was startling. The 2-year program turned into a $3\frac{1}{2}$-year plan because of the shortage of specific labor skills such as road engineer and environmental impact specialist. Analysis showed adding only three skilled people would allow the 2-year plan to be completed on time. In addition, further analysis showed hiring only a few more skilled people, beyond the three, would allow an extra year of projects to also be compressed into the 2-year plan. This would result in additional revenue of more than $3 million. The Department of Agriculture quickly approved the requested extra dollars for additional staff to generate the extra revenue.

Conversely, parallel activities can become sequential. Activities with slack on a time-constrained network can change from critical to noncritical, while some identified as critical activities can become noncritical with slack.

See *Project Management in Action: U.S. Forest Service Resource Shortage* for an example of the impact of resource allocation.

Splitting/Multitasking

Splitting or multitasking is a scheduling technique used to get a better project schedule and/or to increase resource utilization. A planner splits the continuous work included in an activity by interrupting the work and sending the resource to

FIGURE 8–9

Splitting/
Multitasking

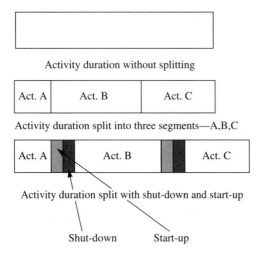

another activity for a period of time and then having the resource resume work on the original activity. Splitting can be a useful tool if the work involved does not include large start-up or shut-down costs—for example, moving equipment from one activity location to another.

The most common error is to interrupt "people work," where there are high conceptual start-up and shut-down costs. For example, having a bridge designer take time off to work on the design problem of another project may cause this individual to lose 4 days shifting conceptual gears in and out of two activities. The cost may be hidden, but it is real. Figure 8–9 depicts the nature of the splitting problem. The original activity has been split into three separate activities: A, B, and C. The start-up and shut-down times lengthen the time for the original activity. Planners should avoid splitting activities as much as possible, except in situations where splitting costs are known to be small. Computer software offers the splitting option for each activity; use it sparingly.

The Critical-Chain Approach

In practice, project managers carefully manage slack on sensitive resource-limited projects. For example, some managers use an early start schedule and prohibit use of slack on any activity or work package to be used unless authorized by the project manager. Progress by percentage complete and by remaining time are carefully monitored and reported to catch any activities that beat estimated completion times so that succeeding activities can start ahead of schedule on critical and noncritical activities. Monitoring and encouraging early completion of estimated times ensure that the time gained is used to start a succeeding activity earlier and that the time is not wasted. The intent is to save the slack as a time buffer to complete the project early or to cover delay problems that may creep up on critical activities or paths.

Eliyahu Goldratt, who championed the "theory of constraints" in his popular book *The Goal*, advocates an alternative approach to managing slack.[4] He has coined the term "critical-chain" to recognize that the project network may be constrained by both resource and technical dependencies. Each type of constraint can create task dependencies, and in the case of resource constraints, new task dependencies can be created! Remember, the critical resource shifted the critical path. Visit Figures 8–4a and 8–4b again. The critical-chain (C-C) refers to the longest string of dependencies that exist on the project. Chain is used instead of path, since the latter tends to be associated with just technical dependencies not resource dependencies. Goldratt uses the C-C concept to develop strategies for accelerating the completion of projects. These strategies are based on his observations about time estimates of individual activities.

Time Estimates

Goldratt argues that there is a natural tendency for people to add safety (just-in-case) time to their estimations. It is believed that those who estimate activity times provide an estimate that has about an 80–90 percent chance of being completed on or before the estimated time. Hence, the median time (50/50 chance) is overestimated by approximately 30–40 percent. For example, a programmer may estimate that there is a 50/50 chance that he can complete an activity in 5 days. However, to ensure success and to protect against potential problems, he adds 2 days of safety time and reports that it will take 7 days to complete the task. In this case the median (50/50) time is overestimated by approximately 40 percent. If this hidden contingency is pervasive across a project, then most activities in theory should be completed ahead of schedule. Remember, the programmer still has a 50/50 chance of completing the assignment within 5 days or less.

This situation raises an interesting paradox. Why, if there is a tendency to overestimate activity durations, do so many projects come in behind schedule? Goldratt offers several explanations:

- **Parkinson's Law:** Work fills the time available. Why hustle to complete a task today when it isn't due until tomorrow?
- **Self-protection:** Participants fail to report early finishes out of fear that management will adjust their future standards and demand more next time.

- **Three-minute egg rule:** It's not quality if it's finished before the time is up. Unnecessary time is devoted to a task in the belief that quality is being served.
- **Dropped baton:** Early finishes may not lead to the start of the next activity because people assigned to perform the next activity are not ready to start work early. The time gained is therefore lost.
- **Excessive multitasking:** This phenomenon adds time to the completion of tasks.
- **Resource bottlenecks:** Delays are caused by limited availability of critical resources.
- **Student syndrome:** There is a tendency to delay the start of tasks until you absolutely have to.

The student syndrome deserves further explanation. Goldratt asserts that just as students delay writing a term paper until the last minute, workers delay starting tasks when they perceive that they have more than enough time to complete the task. The problem with delaying the start of a task is that obstacles often are not detected until the task is underway for some time. By delaying the start of the task, the opportunity to cope with these obstacles and complete the task on time is compromised.

Critical-Chain in Action

Goldratt's solution to reducing project time overruns is to insist on people using the "true 50/50" activity time estimates (rather than estimates which have an 80 to 90 percent chance of being completed before the estimated time); the 50/50 estimates result in a project duration about one-half the low risk of 80 to 90 percent estimates. Using 50/50 estimates will discourage Parkinson's Law, the student syndrome, self-protection, and the three-minute egg rule from coming into play and in turn should increase productivity on individual tasks. Similarly, the compressed time schedule reduces the likelihood of the dropped baton effect.

Goldratt's solution to this problem is to insert time buffers into the schedule to act as "shock absorbers" to protect the project completion date against task durations taking longer than the 50/50 estimate. The rationale is that by using 50/50 estimates you are in essence taking out all of the "safety" in individual tasks. Goldratt recommends using portions of this collective safety strategically by inserting time buffers where potential problems are likely to occur.

1. First, since all activities along the critical chain have inherent *uncertainty* that is difficult to predict, project duration is uncertain. Therefore, a

project time buffer is added to the expected *project duration*—say 50 percent of the aggregate of the hidden contingencies of activity durations.

2. Second, *feeder* buffers are added to the network where noncritical paths merge with the critical-chain. These buffers serve to protect the critical path from being delayed.

3. Third, *resource* time buffers are inserted where scarce resources are needed for an activity. Resource time buffers come in at least two forms. One form is a time buffer attached to a critical resource to ensure that the resource is on call and available when needed. This preserves the relay race. The second form of time buffer is added to activities preceding the work of a scarce resource. This kind of buffer protects against resource bottlenecks by increasing the likelihood that the preceding activity will be completed when the resource is available. All buffers reduce the risk of the project duration being late and increase the chance of early project completion.

For illustrative purposes let's look at how C-C would be applied to the Air Control Project example used earlier in this chapter (see Figure 8–10). First, notice that task estimates now represent approximations of the 50/50 rule. Second, observe that not all of the activities on the critical-chain are technically linked.

FIGURE 8–10

Air Control Project Critical-Chain Network

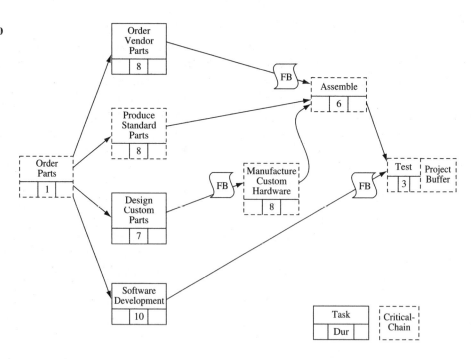

FIGURE 8–11

Air Control Project Gantt Chart Critical-Chain Approach

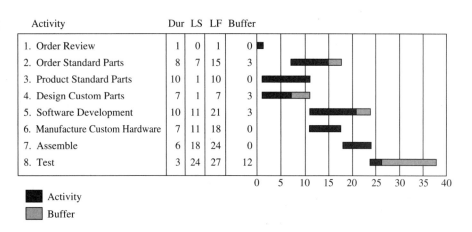

Activity	Dur	LS	LF	Buffer
1. Order Review	1	0	1	0
2. Order Standard Parts	8	7	15	3
3. Product Standard Parts	10	1	10	0
4. Design Custom Parts	7	1	7	3
5. Software Development	10	11	21	3
6. Manufacture Custom Hardware	7	11	18	0
7. Assemble	6	18	24	0
8. Test	3	24	27	12

0   5   10   15   20   25   30   35   40

■ Activity

▨ Buffer

Manufacturing custom parts is included because of previously defined resource dependency. Third, a project time buffer is added at the end of schedule. Finally, feeder buffers are inserted at each point where a noncritical activity merges with the critical-chain.

The impact the C-C approach has on the project schedule can best be seen in the Gantt chart presented in Figure 8–11. Notice first the late start times for each of the three noncritical activities. For example, under the critical path method, order vendor parts and software development would be scheduled to begin immediately after the order review. Instead they are scheduled later in the project. Three-day feeder buffers have been added to each of these activities to absorb any delays that might occur in these activities. Finally, instead of taking 50 days the project is now estimated to take only 27 days with a 10-day project buffer!

This example provides an opportunity for explaining the differences between buffers and slack. Slack is spare time inherent in the schedule of noncritical activities and can be determined by differences between the early start and late start of a specific activity. *Buffers,* on the other hand, are dedicated time blocks reserved to cover most likely contingencies and are monitored closely so if they are not needed, subsequent activities can proceed on schedule. Buffers are needed in part because the estimates are based on 50/50 approximations, and therefore roughly half of the activities will take longer than planned. To protect against these extended activity durations, buffers are inserted to minimize the impact on the schedule. Buffers are not part of the project schedule and are used only when sound management dictates it.

While not depicted in the figures, an example of a resource buffer would be to add 6 days to Ryan's schedule (remember he is the critical resource that caused the schedule to be extended). This would ensure that he could continue to work on the project beyond the eighteenth day in case either produce standard parts and/or manufacture custom hardware takes longer than planned. Progress on these two tasks would be monitored closely, and his schedule would be adjusted accordingly.

Buffers do not address the insidious effects of pervasive multitasking, especially in a multiproject environment where workers are juggling different project assignments. Goldratt has three recommendations that will help to reduce the impact of multitasking:

1. Reduce the number of projects so people are not assigned to as many projects concurrently.
2. Control start dates of projects to accommodate resource shortages. Don't start projects until sufficient resources are available to work full-time on the project.
3. Contract (lock in) for resources *before* the project begins.

The C-C Method Today

C-C has generated considerable debate within the project management community. While sound in theory, support at this time is limited but promising. For example, Harris Semiconductor was able to build a new automated wafer fabrication facility within 13 months using C-C methods when the industry standard for such a facility is 26 to 36 months. The Israeli aircraft industry has used C-C techniques to reduce average maintenance work on aircraft from 2 months to 2 weeks.[5]

C-C is not without critics. First, C-C does not address the biggest cause of project delays which is an ill-defined and unstable project scope. Second, some critics challenge Goldratt's assumptions about human behavior. They question the tendency of experts to pad estimates and the assumption that employees act deliberately against the organization for their own interest and benefit. They also object to the insinuation that trained professionals would exhibit the student syndrome habits. Right or wrong, for some there is an implied element of distrust and lack of faith in the employee's expertise in the C-C approach. The harshest critics see C-C as a highly manipulative system in which people are set up for failure with the hope that this added pressure will increase productivity.[6]

The key to implementing theory into practice is the culture of the organization. If the organization honors noble efforts that fail to meet estimates as it does efforts that do meet estimates, then greater acceptance will occur. Conversely, if management treats honest failure differently from success, then resistance will be high. Organizations adopting the C-C approach have to invest significant energy to obtaining buy-in on the part of all participants to its core principles and allaying the fears that this system may generate.

Regardless of where one stands in the debate, the C-C approach deserves credit for bringing resource dependency to the forefront, highlighting the modern ills of multitasking, and forcing us to rethink conventional methods of project scheduling.[7]

Benefits of Scheduling Resources

It is important to remember that, if resources are truly limited and activity time estimates are accurate, the resource-limited schedule *will* materialize as the project is implemented—*not* the time-constrained schedule! Therefore, failure to schedule limited resources can lead to serious problems for a project manager. The benefit of creating this schedule *before* the project begins is that time is available for considering reasonable alternatives. If the scheduled delay is unacceptable or the risk of being delayed too high, the assumption of being resource constrained can be reassessed. Time/cost trade-offs can be considered. In some cases priorities may be changed.

Resource schedules provide the information needed to prepare time-phased work package budgets with dates. Once established, they provide a quick means for a project manager to gauge the impact of unforeseen events such as turnover, equipment breakdowns, or transfer of project personnel. Resource schedules also allow project managers to assess how much flexibility they have over certain resources. This is useful when they receive requests from other managers to borrow or share resources. Honoring such requests creates goodwill and an "IOU" that can be cashed in during a time of need.

Assigning Project Work

So far the discussion of resources has been directed at analyzing how resource availability affects the project plan and schedule. Project managers must also decide who should do what on a project. Should Trevor or Lindsay do the beta testing? When making individual assignments project managers should match, as best they can, the demands and requirements of specific work with the qualifications and experience of available participants. In doing so, there is a natural tendency to assign the best people the most difficult tasks. Project managers need to be careful not to overdo this. Over time these people may grow to resent the fact that they are always given the toughest assignments. At the same time, less experienced participants may resent the fact that they are never given the opportunity to expand their skill/knowledge base. Project managers need to balance task performance with the need to develop the talents of people assigned to the project.

Project managers need to decide not only who does what but who works with whom. A number of factors need to be considered in deciding who should work together. First, to minimize unnecessary tension, managers should pick people with compatible work habits and personalities but whose skills complement each other (i.e., one person's weakness is the other person's strength). For example, Donald may be brilliant at solving complex problems but sloppy at documenting his progress. It would be wise to pair him with a person like Booker who is good at paying attention to details. Experience is another factor. Veterans should be

---
Project Management in Action

Assigning Geeks to Projects

Eric Schmidt, after a successful career at Sun Microsystems, took over struggling Novell, Inc., and helped turn it around within 2 years. One of the keys to his success is his ability to manage the technical wizards who develop the sophisticated systems, hardware, and software that are the backbone of electronically driven companies. He uses the term "geek" (and he can, since he is one, with a Ph.D. in computer science) to describe this group of technologists who rule the cyberworld.

Schmidt has some interesting ideas about assigning geeks to projects. He believes that putting geeks together in project teams with other geeks creates productive peer pressure. Geeks care a great deal about how other geeks perceive them. They are good at judging the quality of technical work and are quick to praise as well as criticize each other's work. Some geeks can be unbearably arrogant, but Schmidt claims that having them work together on projects is the best way to control them—by letting them control each other.

At the same time, Schmidt argues that too many geeks spoil the soup. By this he means that, when there are too many geeks on a development team, there is a tendency for intense technical navel gazing. Members lose sight of deadlines, and delays are inevitable. To combat this tendency, he recommends using geeks only in small groups. He urges breaking up large projects into smaller, more manageable projects so that small teams of geeks can be assigned to them. This keeps the projects on time and makes the teams responsible to each other.[8]

---

teamed up with new hires—not only so they can share their experience but also to help socialize the newcomers to the customs and norms of the organization. Finally, future needs should be considered. If managers have some people who have never worked together before but who have to later on in the project, they may be wise to take advantage of opportunities to have these people work together early on so that they can become familiar with each other. Finally, see *Project Management in Action: Assigning Geeks to Projects*, for some interesting thoughts about how Novell, Inc., put together teams.

Multiproject Resource Schedules

For clarity we have discussed key resource allocation issues within the context of a single project. In reality resource allocation generally occurs in a multiproject environment where the demands of one project have to be reconciled with the needs of other projects. Organizations must develop and manage systems for efficiently allocating and scheduling resources across several projects with different priorities, resource requirements, sets of activities, and risks. The system must be dynamic and capable of accommodating new projects as well as reallocating resources once project work is completed. While the same resource issues and principles that apply to a single project also apply to this multiproject environment, application and solutions are more complex, given the interdependency among projects.

The following lists three of the more common problems encountered in managing multiproject resource schedules. Note that these are macro manifestations of single-project problems that are now magnified in a multiproject environment:

1. Because projects often share resources, delays in one project can have a ripple effect and delay other projects. For example, work on one software development project can grind to a halt because the coders scheduled for the next critical task are late in completing their work on another development project.

2. Because projects have different schedules and requirements, there are peaks, valleys, and spikes in overall resource demands. For example, a firm may have a staff of 10 electricians to meet peak demands when, under normal conditions, only 5 electricians are required.

3. Delays and schedules are extended as a result of the shortage of critical resources that are required by multiple projects. For example, at one Lattice Semiconductor facility, project schedules were delayed because of competition over access to test equipment necessary to debug programs. Likewise, several projects at a U.S. National forest were extended because there was only one silviculturist on the staff.

One approach to multiple project resource scheduling is to use a first-come-first-served rule. A project queue system is created in which projects currently underway take precedence over new projects. New project schedules are based on the projected availability of resources. This queuing tends to lead to more reliable completion estimates and is preferred on contracted projects that have stiff penalties for being late. The disadvantages of this deceptively simple approach are that it does not optimally utilize resources nor take into account the priority of the project.

Many companies utilize more elaborate processes to schedule resources to increase the capacity of the organization to initiate projects. Most of these methods approach the problem by treating individual projects as part of one big project and adapting the scheduling heuristics previously introduced to this megaproject. Project schedulers monitor resource usage and provide updated schedules based on progress and resource availability across all projects. One major improvement in project management software in recent years is the ability to prioritize resource allocation to specific projects. Projects can be prioritized in ascending order (e.g., 1, 2, 3, 4, . . .), and these priorities will override scheduling heuristics so that resources go to the project highest on the priority list. (Note: This improvement fits nicely with organizations that use project priority models similar to those described in Chapter 2.) Centralized project scheduling also makes it easier to identify resource bottlenecks that stifle progress on projects. Once identified, the impact of the bottlenecks can be documented and used to justify acquiring additional equipment or recruiting critical personnel. Finally, many companies are using outsourcing as a means for dealing with their resource allocation problems. In some cases, a company will reduce the number of projects they have to manage internally to core projects only and outsource noncritical projects to contractors and consulting firms. In other cases, specific segments of projects are outsourced to overcome resource deficiencies and scheduling problems. Companies may hire temporary workers to expedite certain activities that are falling behind schedule or contract project work during peak periods when there are insufficient internal resources to meet the demands of all projects. The ability to more efficiently manage the ebbs and flows of project work is one of the major driving forces behind outsourcing today.

Outsourcing, however, is not a panacea for all resource problems. It means giving up control to outside specialists, who may do a smashing job or foul up the whole job. Unfortunately, when the latter occurs you often do not find out until well after the fact, which causes serious rework problems. Secondly, outsiders typically require more "management oversight" effort than having your own people doing the job. Third, finding and hiring qualified contractors takes time that can ultimately delay the project. Finally, the use of outsiders means a great deal of the learning experience of the job is lost to another firm. The key is to develop long-term relationships with contractors and service providers who are known to do quality work in the tasks you are outsourcing. This topic is explored in more detail in the chapter on partnering.

Summary

Usage and availability of resources are major problem areas for project managers. Attention to these areas in developing a project schedule can point out resource bottlenecks before the project begins. The leveling and resource techniques and computer software available allow the project manager and team to easily answer many of the problem resource questions inevitably generated by projects. The results of resource scheduling are frequently significantly different from the results of the standard CPM method. Project managers should understand the ramifications of failing to schedule resources.

With the rapid changes in technology and emphasis on time-to-market, catching resource usage and availability problems before the project starts can save the costs of crashing project activities later. Any resource deviations from plan and schedule that occur when the project is being implemented can be quickly recorded and the effect noted. Without this immediate update capability, the real negative effect of a change may not be known until it happens. Tying resource availability to a multiproject, multiresource system supports a project priority process that selects projects by their contribution to the organization's objectives and strategic plan.

Critical-chain project management has emerged as a potential alternative to critical path scheduling. While sound in theory, implementation questions remain. Time will tell if critical-chain replaces traditional scheduling techniques.

Assignment of individuals to projects may not fit well with those assigned by computer software routines. In these cases overriding the computer solution to accommodate individual differences and skill is almost always the best choice. Responsibility matrices can be effective tools for communicating and clarifying individual responsibilities on a project.

9

ACCELERATING PROJECT COMPLETION

When do you need it?
Yesterday!

The Challenge

Imagine the following scenarios:

After finalizing your project schedule you realize the estimated completion date is 2 months beyond what your boss publicly promised an important customer.

Two months into the project you realize that you are already 3 weeks behind the drop-dead date for the project.

Three months into a project top management changes its priorities and now tells you that money is not an issue. Complete the project ASAP!

What do you do?

This chapter addresses strategies for reducing project time either prior to setting the baseline for the project or in the midst of project execution. The choice of options is based on the constraints surrounding the project. Here the project priority matrix introduced in Chapter 4 comes in to play. For example, there are many more options available for reducing project time if you are not resource constrained than if you cannot spend more than your original budget. We will begin first by examining the reasons for reducing project duration followed by the classic time-cost framework. Different options for reducing project time will be discussed in terms of being resource constrained or not.

Rationale for Reducing Project Time

Reducing the time of a critical activity in a project can be done, but it almost always results in a higher direct cost; thus, the project manager faces a cost/time trade-off problem—is the reduction in time worth the additional cost? Cost/time situations focus on reducing the critical path that determines the project completion date.

There are many good reasons for attempting to reduce the duration of a project. One of the more common reasons is known in the field as an "imposed" project duration date. For example, a politician makes a public statement that a new law building will be available in 2 years. Or the president of a software company remarks in a speech that new technologically advanced software will be available in 1 year. Such statements too often become imposed project duration dates—without any consideration of the problems or cost of meeting such a date. The project duration time is set while the project is in its "concept" phase before or without any detailed scheduling of all the activities in the project. This phenomenon is very common in practice!

Another reason for reducing project time occurs when unforeseen delays—for example, adverse weather, design flaws, equipment breakdown—cause substantial delays midway in the project. Getting back on schedule usually requires compressing the time on some of the remaining critical activities. The additional costs of getting back on schedule need to be compared with the costs of being late.

In recent years emphasis on time-to-market has taken on new importance because of intense global competition and rapid technological advances. The *market* imposes a project duration date. For example, a rule of thumb for moderate-to-high-technology firms is that a 6-month delay in bringing a product to market can result in a gross profit loss or market share of about 30 percent. In these cases, the authors have found high-technology firms will typically assume that the time savings and avoidance of lost profits are worth any additional costs to reduce time without any formal analysis. It is interesting to observe how more serious analysis occurs in recession periods when cash flows are tight.

Incentive contracts and continuous improvement incentives in partnering arrangements can make reduction of project time rewarding—usually for the project contractor *and* owner. For example, a contractor finished a bridge across a lake 18 months early and received more than $6 million for the early completion. The availability of the bridge to the surrounding community 18 months early to reduce traffic gridlock made the incentive cost to the community seem small to users. In another example, in a partnering continuous improvement arrangement, the joint effort of the owner and contractor resulted in early completion of a river lock and a 50/50 split of the savings to the owner and contractor. *Project*

Management in Action: Responding to the Northridge Earthquake illustrates incentives for reducing project completion time can benefit both customers and contractors.

Sometimes very high overhead or goodwill costs are recognized before the project begins. In these cases it is prudent to examine the direct costs of shortening the critical path versus the overhead and/or goodwill cost savings. Usually there are opportunities to shorten a few critical activities at less than the daily overhead rate or perceived goodwill cost. Under specific conditions (which are not rare), huge savings are possible with little risk.

Finally there are times when it is important to reassign key equipment and/or people to new projects. Under these circumstances, the cost of compressing the project can be compared with the costs of not releasing key equipment or people.

Nothing on the horizon suggests that the need to shorten project time will change. The challenge for the project manager is to use a quick, logical method to compare the benefits of reducing project time with the cost. When sound, logical methods are absent, it is difficult to isolate those activities that will have the greatest impact on reducing project time at the least cost. This chapter describes a procedure for identifying the costs of reducing project time so that comparisons can be made with the benefits of getting the project completed sooner. The method requires gathering direct and indirect costs for specific project durations. Critical activities are searched to find the lowest direct cost activities, which will shorten the project duration. Total costs for specific project durations are computed and then compared with the benefits of reducing project time—*before the project begins or while it is in progress.*

Project Time Reduction Procedure

Cost—Time Trade-Off Logic

The general nature of project costs is illustrated in Figure 9–1. The total cost for each duration is the sum of the indirect and direct costs. Indirect costs continue for the life of the project. Hence, any reduction in project duration means a reduction in indirect costs. Direct costs on the graph grow at an increasing rate as the project duration is reduced from its original planned duration. With the information from a graph such as this for a project, managers can quickly judge any alternative such as meeting a time-to-market deadline. Further discussion of indirect and direct costs is necessary before demonstrating a procedure for developing the information for a graph similar to the one depicted in Figure 9–1.

Project Indirect Costs.   Indirect costs generally represent overhead costs such as supervision, administration, consultants, and interest. Indirect costs cannot be associated with any particular work package or activity, hence the term. Indirect

Responding to the Northridge Earthquake[1]

On January 17, 1994, a 6.8 magnitude earthquake struck the Los Angeles basin near suburban Northridge causing 60 deaths, thousands of injuries, and billions of dollars in property damage. Nowhere was the destructive power of nature more evident than in the collapsed sections of the freeway system that disrupted the daily commute of an estimated 1 million Los Angelinos. The Northridge earthquake posed one of the greatest challenges to the California Department of Transportation (CalTrans) in its nearly 100-year history. To expedite the recovery process, Governor Pete Wilson signed an emergency declaration allowing CalTrans to streamline contracting procedures and offer attractive incentives for completing work ahead of schedule. For each day that the schedule was beaten, a sizable bonus was to be awarded. Conversely, for each day over the deadline, the contractor would be penalized the same amount. The amount ($50,000–$200,000) varied depending on the importance of the work.

The incentive scheme proved to be a powerful motivator for the freeway reconstruction contractors. C.C. Myers, Inc., of Rancho Cordova, California, won the contract for the reconstruction of the Interstate 10 bridges. Myers pulled out all stops to finish the project in a blistering 66 days—a whopping 74 days ahead of schedule—and earning a $14.8 million bonus! Myers took every opportunity to save time and streamline operations. They greatly expanded the workforce. For example, 134 ironworkers were employed instead of the normal 15. Special lighting equipment was set up so that work could be performed around the clock. Likewise, the sites were prepared and special materials were used so that work could continue despite inclement weather that would normally shut down construction. The work was scheduled much like an assembly line so that critical activities were followed by the next critical activity. A generous incentive scheme was devised to reward teamwork and reach milestones early. Carpenters and ironworkers competed as teams against each other to see who could finish first.

Although C.C. Myers received a substantial bonus for finishing early, they spent a lot of money on overtime, bonuses, special equipment, and other premiums to keep the job rolling along. CalTrans supported Myers's efforts. With reconstruction work going on 24 hours a day, including jackhammering and pile-driving, CalTrans temporarily housed many families in local motels. CalTrans even erected a temporary plastic soundwall to help reduce the construction noise traveling to a nearby apartment complex. The double-layer curtain, 450 feet long and 20 feet high, was designed to reduce construction noise by 10 decibels.

Despite the difficulties and expense incurred by around-the-clock freeway building, most of Los Angeles cheered CalTrans's quake recovery efforts. The Governor's Office of Planning and Research issued a report concluding that for every day the Santa Monica Freeway was closed, it cost the local economy more than $1 million.

FIGURE 9–1

*Project
Cost–Time
Graph*

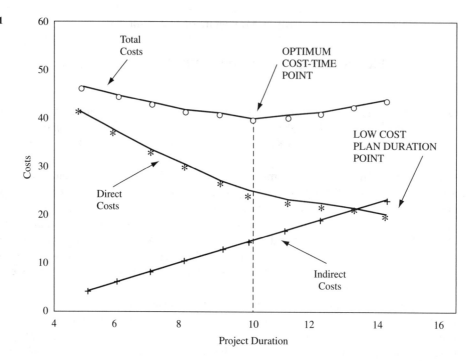

costs vary directly with time. That is, any reduction in time should result in a reduction of indirect costs. For example, if the daily costs of supervision, administration, and consultants are $2,000, any reduction in project duration would represent a savings of $2,000 per day. If indirect costs are a significant percentage of total project costs, reductions in project time can represent very real savings (assuming the indirect resources can be utilized elsewhere).

Project Direct Costs. Direct costs commonly represent labor, materials, equipment, and sometimes subcontractors. Direct costs are assigned directly to a work package and activity, hence the term. The ideal assumption is that direct costs for an activity time represent normal costs, which typically mean *low-cost, efficient methods for a normal time*. When project durations are imposed, direct costs may no longer represent low-cost, efficient methods. Costs for the imposed duration date will be higher than for a project duration developed from ideal normal times for activities. Because direct costs are assumed to be developed from normal methods and time, any reduction in activity time should add to the costs of the activity. The sum of the costs of all the work packages or activities represents the total direct costs for the project. The major plight faced in creating the information for a graph similar to Figure 9–1 is computing the direct cost of shortening individual critical activities and then finding *the total direct cost for each project duration* as project time is compressed; the process requires selecting those critical activities that cost the least to shorten.

The most difficult part of constructing a cost/time graph is finding the total direct costs for specific project durations over a relevant range. The central concern is to decide which activities to shorten and how far to carrying the shortening process. Basically, managers need to look for critical activities that can be shortened with the *smallest increase in cost per unit of time.* The rationale for selecting critical activities depends on identifying the activity's normal and crash times and corresponding costs. *Normal time* for an activity represents low-cost, realistic, efficient methods for completing the activity under normal conditions. Shortening an activity is called *crashing.* The shortest possible time in which an activity realistically can be completed is called its *crash time.* The direct cost for completing an activity in its crash time is called *crash cost.*

A Simplified Example

Figure 9–2 presents normal and maximum crash times for each activity, the estimated crash cost per day, and the project network with a duration of 25 time units. Notice the total direct cost for the 25-period duration is $450. This is an anchor point to begin the procedure of shortening the critical path(s) and finding the total direct costs for each specific duration less than 25 time units.

The network shows the critical path to be activities A, D, F, G. Because it is impossible to shorten activity G, activity A is circled because it is the least cost candidate; that is, its crash cost ($20) is less than the costs for activities D and F ($25 and $30). Reducing activity A 1 time unit cuts the project duration to 24 time units but increases the total direct costs to $470 ($450 + $20 = $470). Figure 9–2 reflects these changes. The duration of activity A has been reduced to 2 time units; the "x" indicates the activity cannot be reduced any further. Activity D is circled because it costs the least ($25) to shorten the project to 23 time units. Compare the cost of activity F. The total direct cost for a project duration of 23 time units is $495 (see Figure 9–3a).

Observe that the project network in Figure 9–3a now has two critical paths— A,C,F,G and A,D,F,G. Reducing the project to 22 time units will require that activity F be reduced; thus, it is circled. The total direct cost for 22 time units is $525. This reduction has created a third critical path—A,B,E,G; all activities are critical. The least-cost method for reducing the project duration to 21 time units is the combination of the circled activities C,D,E which cost $30, $25, $30 respectively, and increase total direct costs to $610. The results of these changes

FIGURE 9–2

*Cost/Time
Trade-Off
Example*

Activity ID	Normal Time	Maximum Crash Time	Crash Cost
A	3	1	20
B	6	2	40
C	10	1	30
D	11	4	25
E	8	2	30
F	5	1	30
G	6	0	0

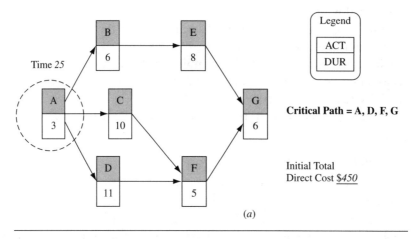

Time 25

Legend

ACT
DUR

Critical Path = A, D, F, G

Initial Total
Direct Cost $450

(a)

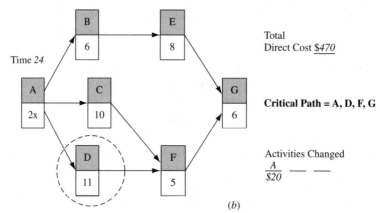

Time 24

Total
Direct Cost $470

Critical Path = A, D, F, G

Activities Changed
A
$20

(b)

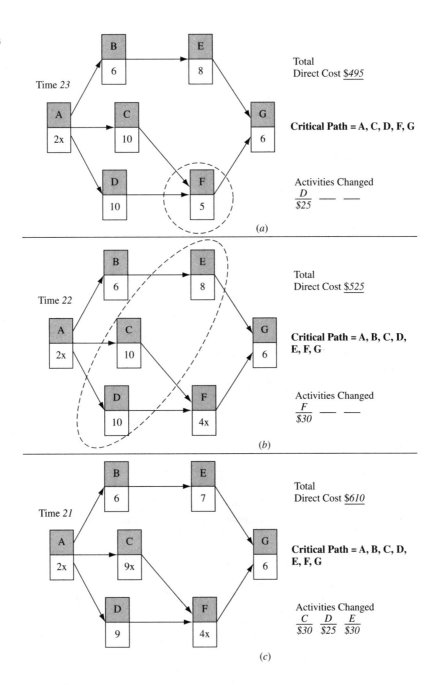

FIGURE 9–3

Cost/Time Trade-Off Example

(a)

Time *23*

B	**E**	
6	8	

A 2x   **C** 10   **G** 6

D 10   **F** 5

Total Direct Cost $495

Critical Path = A, C, D, F, G

Activities Changed

$\dfrac{D}{\$25}$ —— ——

(b)

Time *22*

B 6   **E** 8

A 2x   **C** 10   **G** 6

D 10   **F** 4x

Total Direct Cost $525

Critical Path = A, B, C, D, E, F, G

Activities Changed

$\dfrac{F}{\$30}$ —— ——

(c)

Time *21*

B 6   **E** 7

A 2x   **C** 9x   **G** 6

D 9   **F** 4x

Total Direct Cost $610

Critical Path = A, B, C, D, E, F, G

Activities Changed

$\dfrac{C}{\$30}$ $\dfrac{D}{\$25}$ $\dfrac{E}{\$30}$

FIGURE 9-4

Summary Costs by Duration

Project Duration	Direct Costs	+	Indirect Costs	=	Total Costs
25	450		400		$850
24	470		350		$820
23	495		300		$795
22	525		250		$775
21	610		200		$810

are reflected in Figure 9–4. Although some activities can still be reduced (those without the "x" next to the activity time), no activity or combination of activities will result in a reduction in the project duration.

With the total direct costs for the array of specific project durations found, the next step is to collect the indirect costs for these same durations. These costs are typically a rate per day and easily obtained from the accounting department. Figure 9–4 presents the total direct costs, total indirect costs, and total project costs. These same costs are plotted in Figure 9–5. This graph shows that the optimum cost-time duration is 22 time units and $775. Assuming the project will actually materialize as planned, any movement away from this time duration will increase project costs.

In Practice

There are good methods for developing crash times for a cost/time graph similar to the one shown in Figure 9–5. However, experience has shown the authors that project managers are reluctant to collect and analyze data. We admit to succumbing to a rough approach that requires getting the project team together and asking a few questions:

1. Could you give me a rough estimate of the overhead costs of this project?
2. Looking at all the activities on the critical path, which one would be the cheapest to shorten? (Repeat number two until a desired date is reached.)
3. Has the cost of crashing the last activity exceeded the daily overhead costs? If yes, are you willing to accept the additional project costs of shortening the project time?

This procedure works reasonably well. Nevertheless, by shortening the critical path you have increased the risk that other paths will become critical. There are projects where the procedure turns out to be a miracle. There are others where the results can be disastrous. These situations are discussed below.

FIGURE 9-5

Project Cost—Time Graph

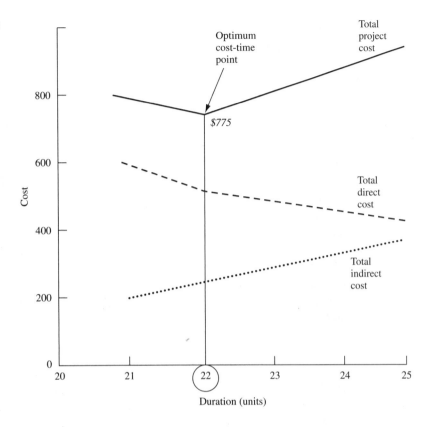

The Bottom Line

Should the project owner or project manager go for the optimum cost/time—the low point on the total cost line of Figure 9–5? The answer is, "It depends." Risk must be considered. Recall from our example that the optimum project time point represented a reduced project cost and was less than the original normal project time (review Figure 9–5). The project direct-cost line near the normal point is usually relatively flat. This phenomenon has been the case on every project the authors have witnessed. Because indirect costs for the project are usually greater in the same range, the optimum cost/time point is less than the normal time point. Logic of the cost/time procedure suggests managers should reduce the project duration to the lowest cost point and duration.

How far to reduce the project time from the normal time toward the optimum depends on the *sensitivity* of the project network. A network is sensitive if it has several critical or near-critical paths. In the simplified example, project movement toward the optimum time requires spending money to reduce critical activities, resulting in slack reduction and/or more critical paths and activities (review Figure 9–3). Slack reduction in a project with several near-critical paths increases the *risk* of being late. The practical outcome can be a higher total project cost if some near-critical activities are delayed and become critical; the money spent reducing activities on the original critical path would be wasted. Sensitive networks require careful analysis. The outcome of such analysis will probably suggest only a partial movement from the normal time toward the optimum time.

There is a positive situation where moving toward the optimum time can result in very real, large savings—when the network is *insensitive*. A project network is insensitive if it has a dominant critical path, that is, no near-critical paths. In this project circumstance movement from the normal time point toward the optimum time will *not* create new or near-critical activities. The reduction of the slack of noncritical activities increases the risk of their becoming critical only slightly when compared with the effect in a sensitive network. Insensitive networks hold the greatest potential for real, sometimes large, savings in total project costs with a minimum risk of noncritical activities becoming critical.

Insensitive networks are not a rarity in practice; they occur in perhaps 25 percent of projects. For example, a light rail project team observed from their network a dominant critical path and relatively high indirect costs. It soon became clear that by spending some dollars on a few critical activities, very large savings of indirect costs could be realized. Savings of several million dollars could be used to extend the rail line and add another station. The logic found in this example is just as applicable to small projects as large ones. Insensitive networks with high indirect costs can produce large savings.

Choice of Activities to Crash Revisited.   The cost/time crashing method relies on choosing the cheapest method for reducing the duration of the project. There are other factors besides cost that should be assessed. First, the timing of activities needs to be considered. Crashing a critical activity early in the project may result in wasted money if some other critical activity is finished early or some noncritical path becomes the new critical path. In such cases the money spent early is gone and no benefit comes from early completion by crashing the activity. Conversely, it may be wise to crash an early critical activity when later activities are likely to be delayed and absorb the time gained. Then the manager would still have the option of crashing final activities to get back on schedule.

A second consideration is the impact crashing would have on the morale and motivation of the project team. If the least-cost method repeatedly signals a subgroup to accelerate progress, fatigue and resentment may set in. Conversely, if overtime pay is involved, other team members may resent not having access to this benefit. This situation can lead to tension within the entire project team. Good project managers gauge the response that crashing activities will have on the entire project team.

Finally, the inherent risks involved in crashing particular activities need to be considered. Some activities are riskier to crash than others. For example, accelerating the completion of software design code may not be wise if it increases the likelihood of errors surfacing downstream. Conversely, it may be wise to crash a more expensive activity if there are less inherent risks involved.

Ultimately, which activities to crash is a judgment call requiring careful consideration of the options available, the risks involved, and the importance of meeting a deadline.

Options for Crashing Activity Time

Managers have found several effective methods for crashing specific project activities, which are summarized below:

Outsourcing Project Work. A common method for shortening the project time is to subcontract an activity.[2] The subcontractor may have access to superior technology or expertise that will accelerate the completion of the activity. For example, contracting for a backhoe can accomplish in 2 hours what it can take a team of laborers 2 days to do. Likewise, by hiring a consulting firm that specializes in ADSI programming, a firm may be able to cut in half the time it would take for less experienced, internal programmers to do the work. Subcontracting also frees up resources that can be assigned to a critical activity and will result in a shorter project duration. See *Project Management in Action: I'll Bet You* for other ways to accelerate tasks.

Adding Resources. The most common method for shortening project time is to assign additional staff and equipment to activities. There are limits, however, as to how much speed can be gained by adding staff. The relationship between staff size and progress is not linear; doubling the size of the workforce will not necessarily reduce completion time by half. The relationship would be correct only when tasks can be partitioned so minimal communication is needed between workers, as in harvesting a crop by hand or repaving a highway. Most projects are not set up that way; additional workers increase the communication requirements to coordinate their efforts. For example, doubling a team by adding two workers requires six times as much pair-wise intercommunication than is required in the original two-person team. Not only is more time needed to coordinate and manage a larger team, there is the additional delay of training the new people and getting them up to speed on the project. The end result is captured in Brooks' Law: *Adding manpower to a late software project makes it later.*[3]

Frederick Brooks formulated this principle based on his experience as a project manager for IBM's System/360 software project during the early 1960s. Subsequent research concluded that adding more people to a late software project

---

Project Management in Action

I'll Bet You . . .

The focus of this chapter has been on how project managers crash activities typically by assigning additional staff and equipment to cut significant time from scheduled tasks. Project managers often encounter situations in which they need to motivate individuals to accelerate the completion of a specific, critical task. Imagine the following scenario:

Pegi Young just received a priority assignment from corporate headquarters. The preliminary engineering sketches that were due tomorrow need to be e-mailed to the West Coast by 4:00 P.M. today so that the model shop can begin construction of a prototype to present to top management. She approaches Danny Whitten, the draftsman responsible for the task, whose initial response is, "That's impossible!" While she agrees that it would be very difficult she does not believe that it is as impossible as Danny suggests nor that Danny truly believes that. What should she do?

She tells Danny that she knows this is going to be a rush job, but she is confident that he can do it. When Danny balks, she responds, "I tell you what, I'll make a bet with you. If you are able to finish the design by 4:00, I'll make sure you get two of the company's tickets to tomorrow night's Celtics–Knicks basketball game." Danny accepts the challenge, works feverishly to complete the assignment, and is able to take his daughter to her first professional basketball game.

Conversations with project managers reveal that many use bets like this to motivate extraordinary performance. These bets range from tickets to sporting and entertainment events to gift certificates at high-class restaurants or to a well-deserved afternoon off. For bets to work they need to adhere to the principles of the expectancy theory of motivation.[4] Boiled down to simple terms, expectancy theory rests on three key questions:

1. Can I do it (is it possible to meet the challenge)?
2. Will I get it (can I demonstrate that I met the challenge and can I trust the project manager will deliver his/her end of the bargain)?
3. Is it worth it (is the payoff of sufficient personal value to warrant the risk and extra effort)?

does not necessarily cause the project to be later.[5] The key is whether the new staff is added early so there is sufficient time to make up for lost ground once the new members have been fully assimilated.

Scheduling Overtime.   The easiest way to add more labor to a project is not to add more people, but to schedule overtime. If a team works 50 hours a week instead of 40, it might accomplish 25 percent more. By scheduling overtime you

I'll Bet You . . . (continued)

If in the mind of the participant the answer to any of these three questions is no, then the person is unlikely to accept the challenge. However, when the answers are affirmative, then the individual is likely to accept the bet and be motivated to meet the challenge.

Bets can be effective motivational tools and add an element of excitement and fun to project work. But the following practical advice should be heeded:

1. The bet has greater significance if it also benefits family members or significant others. Being able to take a son or daughter to a professional basketball game allows that individual to "score points" at home through work. These bets also recognize and reward the support project members receive from their families and reinforces the importance of their work to loved ones.
2. Bets should be used sparingly; otherwise everything can become negotiable. They should be used only under special circumstances that require extraordinary effort.
3. Individual bets should involve clearly recognizable individual effort, otherwise others may become jealous and discord may occur within a group. As long as others see it as requiring truly remarkable, "beyond the call of duty" effort, they will consider it fair and warranted.

avoid the additional costs of coordination and communication encountered when new people are added. If people involved are salaried workers, there may be no real additional cost for the extra work. Another advantage is that there are fewer distractions when people work outside normal hours.

Overtime has disadvantages. First, hourly workers are typically paid time-and-a-half for overtime and double time for weekends and holidays. Sustained overtime work by salaried employees may incur intangible costs such as divorce, burnout, and turnover. The latter is a key organizational concern when there is a shortage of top-notch professionals. Furthermore, it is an oversimplification to assume that, over an extended period of time, a person is as productive during his eleventh hour of work as during his third hour. There are natural limits to what is humanly possible, and extended overtime may actually lead to an overall decline in productivity when fatigue sets in.

Do It Twice—Fast and Correctly. If you are in a hurry, try building a "quick and dirty" short-term solution, then go back and do it the right way. For example, the Rose Garden stadium in Portland, Oregon, was supposed to be completely finished in time for the start of the 1995–1996 National Basketball Association

(NBA) season. Delays made this impossible, so the construction crew set up temporary bleachers to accommodate the opening night crowd. The additional costs of doing it twice are more than compensated for by the benefits of satisfying the deadline.

Options for Reducing Project Duration When Resource Constrained

A project manager has fewer options for accelerating project completion when additional resources are either not available or the budget is severely constrained. This is especially true once the schedule has been established.

Fast-Tracking.   Sometimes it is possible to rearrange the logic of the project network so that critical activities are done in parallel (concurrently) rather than sequentially. This alternative is a good one if the project situation is right. When this alternative is given serious attention, it is amazing to observe how creative project team members can be in finding ways to restructure sequential activities in parallel.

As noted in Chapter 4, one of the most common methods for restructuring activities is to change a *finish-to-start* relationship to a *start-to-start* relationship. For example, instead of waiting for the final design to be approved, manufacturing engineers can begin building the production line as soon as key specifications have been established. Changing activities from sequential to parallel usually requires closer coordination among those responsible for the activities affected but can produce tremendous timesavings.

Critical-Chain.   Critical-chain (C-C) project management is designed to accelerate project completion. As discussed in Chapter 8, the jury is still out in terms of applicability. Still C-C principles appear sound and worthy of experimentation if speed is essential. At the same time, it would be difficult to apply C-C project management midstream in a project. C-C requires considerable training and a shift in habits and perspectives that takes time to adopt. Although there have been reports of immediate gains, especially in terms of completion times, a long-term management commitment is probably necessary to reap full benefits. See *Project Management in Action: The Fastest House in the World* for an extreme example of C-C application.

Virtual Tag Teams.   One novel way to reduce project durations is to take advantage of international time zones so that people work around the clock on a project. For example, team members work on a software development project during normal hours in Boston and then electronically pass their work to team

---

Project Management in Action

The Fastest House in the World[6]

On March 13, 1999, Habitat for Humanity New Zealand built a fully operational, four-bedroom house in Auckland in 3 hours, 44 minutes, and 59 seconds from floor to roof complete with curtains, running showers, lawn, and fence. In doing so they became the fastest house builders in the world.

"We made a significant decimation of the record," said Habitat New Zealand's Chief Executive Graeme Lee. "The previous record of 4 hours, 39 minutes, 8 seconds, held by a Habitat chapter in Nashville, USA, was made with a three-bedroom home, and we built one with four bedrooms and used only 140 volunteers on the site." The rules provide for construction to commence from an established floor platform. The house is complete when it meets the local building code, and the family can move in.

The project took 14 months to plan. Critical-chain principles were applied using ProChain Software to finalize project schedule. The critical-chain was recalculated 150–200 times and then analyzed to optimize the resulting new sequence of operations. This reiterative process was used progressively to develop the fastest plan.

One of the keys to efficiency was the use of "Laserbilt" prefabricated walls made from 36mm particleboard using technology that had been invented by a company in New Zealand. Another time-saver was the use of a crane that lowered the wooden roof frame (built on adjacent land) onto the four walls.

Once the roof was on the walls, roofing iron was put on. Meanwhile, the wall sheathing was attached to outside walls and windows fitted, with painters almost painting the face of the hammers as sheath nailing was completed. Inside, vinyl was laid first in the utility areas while painters started in the bedrooms. After the vinyl, the bathrooms were fitted and curtains hung. On the outside, while the roofing was being installed, decks and steps were constructed, a front path laid, mailbox and clothesline installed, wooden fence constructed around the perimeter, 3 trees planted, and lawns leveled and seeded.

Postproject assessment revealed that even further time could have been gained. The management rule was to be "One trade(sman) in one room at one time," but enthusiasm took over and people were doing whatever they could wherever they could, especially toward the end. The project manager estimated that if greater discipline had been exercised and if people moved out of the house as soon as they had completed their task, another 15 minutes would have been shaved from the record.

Habitat for Humanity is an international charitable organization that builds simple, affordable houses and sells them on a no-interest, no-profit basis to needy families.

members in Hawaii, who are beginning their workday when the Boston team is about to go home. The Hawaiian team passes their work on to a team in Bangalore, India, who, in turn, pass their work to a team situated in Wiesbaden, Germany. The German team passes its work to the Boston team, and the cycle is repeated. While this tag team approach to project management is limited to only certain kinds of projects, it illustrates the potential existing information technology has for accelerating project completion.

Brainstorming Time Savers.   The quality revolution highlighted the fact that significant improvements do not come from "quality experts" but from people actually doing the work. Project managers should tap into this reservoir of knowledge and experience by holding brainstorming sessions where team members come up with timesaving suggestions. For example, a project manager reported that he was able to shave 3 months off a late development project by implementing his engineers' suggestion that they purchase an existing piece of hardware and perform a few work arounds. Likewise, a film project was able to bypass several activities and enjoy considerable cost savings by purchasing existing footage.

Reducing Project Scope.   Probably the most common response for meeting unattainable deadlines is to reduce or scale back the scope of the project. This invariably leads to a reduction in the functionality of the project. For example, the new car will average only 25 mpg instead of 30 or the software product will have fewer features than originally planned. While scaling back the scope of the project can lead to big savings in both time and money, it may come at a cost of reducing the value of the project. If the car gets lower gas mileage, will it stand up to competitive models? Will customers still want the software minus the features?

The key to reducing a project scope without reducing value is to reassess the true requirements of the project. Often requirements are added under best-case, blue-sky scenarios and represent desirables, but not essentials. Here it is important to talk to the customers and/or project sponsors and explain the situation—you can get it your way but not until February. This may force them to accept an extension or to free up money to expedite the project. If not, then a healthy discussion of what the essential requirements are and what items can be compromised in order to meet the deadline needs to take place. More intense reexamination of requirements may actually improve the value of the project by getting it done more quickly and for a lower cost.

Calculating the savings of reduced project scope begins with the work breakdown structure. Reducing functionality means certain tasks, deliverables, or requirements can be reduced or even eliminated. These tasks need to be found and the schedule adjusted. Focus should be on changes in activities on the critical path.

Phase Project Delivery. In a situation where the entire project cannot be completed by the deadline, it may still be possible to deliver some useful part of it. For example, tenants can move into some floors of a new office building while construction is being completed on the remaining floors, or sections of the freeway can be opened to traffic before the entire freeway is completed. Similarly, software firms will release products that do not meet the original performance specifications, only to add the missing features in subsequent versions. While undesirable, something useful is delivered as soon as possible. As in the case of reducing project scope, care should be exercised that essential requirements are not compromised for the sake of providing something by the deadline.

Compromise Quality. Reducing quality is always an option, but it is rarely acceptable or used. If quality is sacrificed, it may be possible to reduce the time of an activity on the critical path.

What If Cost Reduction, Not Time, Is the Issue?

In today's fast-paced world, there appears to be a greater emphasis on getting things done quickly. Still, organizations are always looking for ways to get things done cheaply. This is especially true for fixed-bid projects, where profit margin is derived from the difference between the bid and actual cost of the project. Every dollar saved is a dollar in your pocket. Sometimes, in order to secure a contract, bids are tight, which puts added pressure on cost containment. In other cases, there are financial incentives tied to cost containment.

Even in situations where cost is transferred to customers, there is pressure to reduce costs. Cost overruns make for unhappy customers and can damage future business opportunities. Budgets can be fixed or cut, and when contingency funds are exhausted, then cost overruns have to be made up with remaining activities.

At first glance there appears to be a direct relationship between getting things done quicker and costing less. This is particularly true for labor-intensive projects where costs are tied to staff hours devoted to the project. However, as discussed earlier, this is not always the case. Shortening project duration may come at the expense of overtime, adding additional personnel, and using more expensive equipment and materials. Conversely, sometimes cost savings can be generated by extending the duration of a project. This may allow for a smaller work force, less skilled (expensive) labor, and even cheaper equipment and materials to be used. Below are some of the more commonly used options for cutting costs.

Reduce Project Scope. Just as scaling back or reducing the scope of the project can gain time, delivering less than what was originally planned also produces significant savings. Again, calculating the savings of a reduced project scope begins with the work breakdown structure. However, since time is not the issue, you do not need to focus on critical activities.

Have Owner Take on More Responsibility.   One way of reducing project costs is identifying tasks that customers can do themselves. Homeowners frequently use this method to reduce costs on home improvement projects. For example, to reduce the cost of a bathroom remodel, a homeowner may agree to paint the room instead of paying the contractor to do it. On IS projects, a customer may agree to take on some of the responsibility for testing equipment or providing in-house training. Naturally, this arrangement is best negotiated before the project begins. Customers are less receptive to this idea if you suddenly spring it on them. An advantage of this method is that, while costs are lowered, the original scope is retained. Clearly this option is limited to areas in which the customer has expertise and the capability to pick up the tasks.

Outsourcing Project Activities or Even the Entire Project.   When estimates exceed budget, it not only makes sense to reexamine the scope but also search for cheaper ways to complete the project. Perhaps instead of relying on internal resources, it would be more cost effective to outsource segments or even the entire project, opening up work to external price competition. Specialized subcontractors often enjoy unique advantages, such as material discounts for large quantities, as well as equipment that not only gets the work done more quickly but also less expensively. They may have lower overhead and labor costs. For example, to reduce costs of software projects, many American firms outsource work to firms operating in India where the salary of a software engineer is one-eighth that of an American software engineer. However, outsourcing means you have less control over the project and will need to have clearly defined deliverables.

Brainstorming Cost Savings Options.   Just as project team members can be a rich source of ideas for accelerating project activities, they can offer tangible ways for reducing project costs. For example, one project manager reported that his team was able to come up with over $75,000 worth of cost saving suggestions without jeopardizing the scope of the project. Project managers should not underestimate the value of simply asking if there is a cheaper, better way.

Summary

Shortening the project duration occurs for many reasons such as imposed duration dates, time-to-market considerations, incentive contracts, key resource needs, high overhead costs, or simply unforeseen delays. These situations are very common in practice and are known as cost/time trade-off decisions. This chapter presented a logical, formal process for assessing the implications of crashing activities in order to shorten project duration. Crashing projects increases the *risk* of being late. How far to reduce the project duration from the normal time toward the optimum depends on the *sensitivity* of the project network. A sensitive network is one that has several critical or near-critical paths. Great care should be taken when shortening sensitive networks to avoid increasing project risks. Conversely, insensitive networks represent opportunities for potentially large project cost savings by eliminating significant overhead costs with little downside risk.

Alternative strategies for reducing project time were discussed within the context of whether or not the project is resource limited. Project acceleration typically comes at a cost of either spending money for more resources or compromising the scope of the project. If the latter is the case, then it is essential that all relevant stakeholders be consulted so that everyone accepts the changes that have to be made. One other key point is the difference in implementing time-reducing activities in the midst of project execution versus incorporating them into the project plan. You typically have far fewer options once the project is underway than before it begins. This is especially true if you want to take advantage of the new scheduling methodologies such as fast tracking and critical-chain. Time spent up front considering alternatives and developing contingency plans will lead to time-savings in the end.

10 MANAGING PROJECT STAKEHOLDERS

As for the best leaders, the people do not notice their existence. The next best, the people honor and praise. The next, the people fear; and the next, the people hate.
Lau-Tzu[1]

One of the keys to being an effective project manager is building cooperative relationships among different groups of people to complete projects. Project success is not just dependent on the performance of the project team. Success or failure often depends on the contributions of top management, functional managers, customers, suppliers, contractors, and others.

We begin this chapter with a brief discussion of the differences between *leading* and *managing* a project. The importance of managing project stakeholders is then covered because managers require a broad influence base to be effective in this area. We discuss different sources of influence, and they are used to describe how project managers build social capital. Special attention is devoted to managing the critical relationship with top management and the importance of leading by example. We end the chapter by identifying personal attributes associated with being an effective project manager. Subsequent chapters will expand on the ideas of managing the project team and working with people outside the organization.

Managing versus Leading

In a perfect world, the project manager would simply implement the project plan and the project would be completed. The project manager would work with others to formulate a schedule, organize a project team, keep track of progress, and announce what needs to be done next, and then everyone would charge along. Of course no one lives in a perfect world, and rarely does everything go according to plan. Project participants get testy; they fail to complement each other; other departments are unable to fulfill their commitments; technical glitches arise; work takes longer than expected. The project manager's job is to get the project back on track. A manager expedites certain activities; figures out ways to solve technical problems; serves as peacemaker when tensions rise; and makes appropriate trade-offs among time, cost, and scope of the project.

However, project managers do more than put out fires and keep the project on track. They also innovate and adapt to ever-changing circumstances. They often have to deviate from what was planned and introduce significant changes in the project scope and schedule to respond to unforeseen threats or opportunities. For example, customers' needs may change, requiring significant design changes midway through the project. Competitors may release new products that dictate switching the time, cost, and scope priorities of the project. Working relationships among project participants may break down, requiring rejuvenating the project team. Ultimately, what was planned or expected in the beginning may be very different from what was accomplished by the end of the project.

Project managers are responsible for integrating assigned resources to complete the project according to plan. At the same time they need to initiate changes in plans and schedules as persistent internal problems make plans unworkable or as unexpected external events require accommodation. In other words, managers want to keep the project going while making necessary adjustments along the way. According to Kotter, these two different activities represent the distinction between management and leadership. *Management* is about coping with complexity, while *leadership* is about coping with change.[2]

Good management brings about order and stability by formulating plans and objectives, designing structures and procedures, monitoring results against plans, and taking corrective action when necessary. Leadership involves recognizing and articulating the need to significantly alter the direction and operation of the project, aligning people to the new direction, and motivating them to work together to overcome hurdles produced by the change and realize new objectives.

Strong leadership, while usually desirable, is not always necessary to successfully complete a project. Well-defined projects that encounter no significant surprises require little leadership, as might be the case in constructing a conventional apartment building in which the project manager simply administrates the project plan. Conversely, the higher the degree of uncertainty encountered on project—whether in terms of changes in project scope, technological stalemates, breakdowns in coordination between people, and so forth—the more leadership is required. For example, strong leadership would be needed for a software development project where the parameters are always changing to meet developments in the industry.

It takes a special person to perform both roles well. Some individuals are great visionaries who are good at exciting people about change. Too often though, these same people lack the discipline or patience to deal with the day-to-day drudgeries of managing. Likewise, there are other individuals who are very well organized and methodical but lack the ability to inspire others. Strong leaders can compensate for their managerial weaknesses by having trusted assistants who oversee and manage the details of the project. A weak leader can likewise complement his or her strengths by having assistants who are good at sensing the need to change and rallying project participants. Still, one of the things that makes good project managers so valuable to an organization is that they have the ability to both manage and lead a project. In doing so they recognize the need to manage project interfaces and build a social network that allows them to find out what needs to be done and obtain the cooperation necessary to achieve it.

Managing Project Stakeholders

First-time project managers are eager to implement their own ideas and manage their people successfully to complete their project. What they soon find out is that project success depends on the cooperation of a wide range of individuals, many of whom do not report to them. For example, during the course of a system integration project, a project manager was surprised by how much time she was spending negotiating and working with vendors, consultants, technical specialists, and other functional managers.

> Instead of working with my people to complete the project, I found myself being constantly pulled and tugged by demands of different groups of people who were not directly involved in the project but had a vested interest in the outcome.

Too often when new project managers do find time to work directly on the project, they adopt a hands-on approach to managing the project. They choose this style not because they are power hungry egomaniacs but because they are eager to achieve results. They quickly become frustrated by how slowly things operate, the number of people that have to be brought on board, and the difficulty of gaining cooperation. Unfortunately, as this frustration builds, the natural temptation is to exert more pressure and get more heavily involved in the project. These project managers quickly earn the reputation of "micromanaging" and begin to lose sight of the real role they play in guiding a project.

Some new managers never break out of this vicious cycle. Others soon realize that authority does not equal influence and that being an effective project manager involves managing a much more complex and expansive set of interfaces than they had previously anticipated. They encounter a web of relationships that requires a much broader spectrum of influence than they felt was necessary or even possible.

For example, a significant project, whether it involves renovating a bridge, creating a new product, or installing a new information system, will likely involve in one way or another working with a number of different groups of stakeholders. First, there is the core group of specialists assigned to complete the project. This group is likely to be supplemented at different times by professionals who work on specific segments of the project. Second, there are the groups of people within the performing organization who are either directly or indirectly involved with the project. The most notable is top management, to whom the project manager is accountable. There are also other project managers, functional managers who provide resources and/or may be responsible for specific segments of the project, and administrative support services such as human resources, finance, etc. Depending on the nature of the project there are a number of different groups outside the organization that influence the success of the project; the most important is the customer for which the project is designed. See Figure 10–1.

Each of these groups of individuals brings different expertise, standards, priorities, and agendas to the project. One of the things that distinguishes project

FIGURE 10–1

Network of Relationships

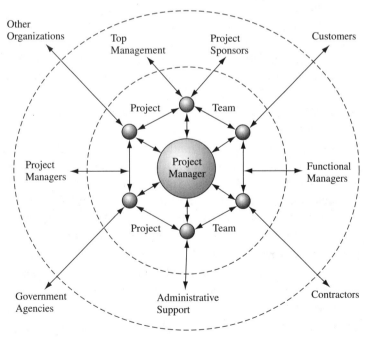

management from regular management is the sheer breadth and complexity of the relationships that need to be managed. To be effective, a project manager must understand how these groups can impact the project and develop methods for managing the dependency. The nature of these dependencies is identified here:

- The **project team** is responsible for completing project work. Most participants want to do a good job, but they are also concerned with their other obligations and how their involvement on the project will contribute to their personal goals and aspirations.
- **Project managers** naturally compete with each other for resources and the support of top management. At the same time they often have to share resources and exchange information.
- **Administrative support** groups such a human resources, information systems, purchasing agents, and maintenance provide valuable support services. At the same time they impose constraints and requirements on the project such as the documentation of expenditures and the timely and accurate delivery of information.
- **Functional managers,** depending on how the project is organized, can play a minor or major role in project success. In matrix arrangements, they may be responsible for assigning project personnel, resolving technical dilemmas, and overseeing the completion of significant segments of the project work. Even in dedicated project teams, the technical input from functional managers may be useful, and acceptance of completed project work is critical to in-house projects. Functional managers want to cooperate up to a point, but only up to a certain point. They are also concerned with preserving their status within the organization and minimizing the disruptions the project may have on their own operations.
- **Top management** approves funding of the project and establishes priorities within the organization. They define success and adjudicate rewards for accomplishments. Significant adjustments in budget, scope, and schedule typically need their approval. They have a natural vested interest in the success of the project, but at the same time have to be responsive to what is best for the entire organization.
- **Project sponsors** championed the project and used their influence to gain approval of the project. Their reputation is tied to the success of the project, and they need to be kept informed of any major developments. They defend the project when it comes under attack and are key project allies.
- **Contractors** may do all the actual work in some cases, with the project team merely coordinating their contributions. In other cases, they are

responsible for ancillary segments of the project scope. Poor work and schedule slips can affect work of the core project team. While contractors' reputations rest with doing good work, they must balance their contributions with their own profit margins and their commitments to other clients.

- **Government agencies** place constraints on project work. Permits need to be secured. Construction work has to be built to code. New drugs have to pass a rigorous battery of U.S. Food and Drug Administration (FDA) tests. Other products have to meet safety standards, for example Occupational Safety and Health Administration (OSHA) standards.

- **Other organizations,** depending on the nature of the project, may directly or indirectly affect the project. For example, suppliers provide necessary resources for completion of the project work. Delays, shortages, and poor quality can bring a project to a standstill. Public interest groups may apply pressure on government agencies. Customers often hire consultants and auditors to protect their interests on a project. The competition may release a new version or add a new feature to a product or service that is being developed that dictates changing the scope of the project.

- **Customers** define the scope of the project, and ultimate project success rests in their satisfaction. Project managers need to be responsive to changing customer needs and requirements and to satisfying customer expectations. Customers are primarily concerned with getting a *good deal* and, as will be elaborated in Chapter 12, this naturally breeds tension with the project team.

These relationships are interdependent in that a project manager's ability to work effectively with one group will affect his or her ability to manage other groups. For example, functional managers are likely to be less cooperative if they perceive that top management's commitment to the project is waning. Conversely, the ability of the project manager to buffer the team from excessive interference from a client is likely to increase his or her standing with the project team.

The project management structure being used will influence the number and degree of external dependencies that will need to be managed. One advantage of creating a dedicated project team is that it reduces dependencies, especially within the organization, because most of the resources are assigned to the project. Conversely, a functional matrix structure increases dependencies, with the result that the project manager is much more reliant upon functional colleagues for work and staff.

The old-fashioned view of managing projects emphasized directing and controlling subordinates; the new perspective emphasizes two areas as the most important aspects of the job:

1. Managing project stakeholders
2. Anticipating change

Project managers need to be able to assuage concerns of customers, sustain support for the project at higher levels of the organization, and quickly identify problems that threaten project work, while at the same time defend the integrity of the project and the interests of the project participants.

Within this web of relationships, the project manager must find out what needs to be done to achieve the goals of the project and build a cooperative network to accomplish it. Project managers must do so without the requisite authority to expect or demand cooperation. This requires sound communication skills, political savvy, and a broad influence base.

Influence As Exchange

To successfully manage a project, a manager must adroitly build a cooperative network among divergent allies. Networks are mutually beneficial alliances that are generally governed by the law of reciprocity.[3] The basic principle is that *one good deed deserves another, and, likewise, one bad deed deserves another.* The primary way to gain cooperation is to provide resources and services for others in exchange for future resources and services. This is the age-old maxim *Quid pro quo ("something for something").* Or in today's vernacular: *You scratch my back, I'll scratch yours.*

Cohen and Bradford[3] described the exchange view of influence as "currencies." If you want to do business in a given country, you have to be prepared to use the appropriate currency, and the exchange rates can change over time as conditions change. Likewise, what is valued by a marketing manager probably is different from what is valued by a veteran project engineer. You are likely to need to use different influence currency to obtain the cooperation of each individual. Although this analogy is a bit of an oversimplification, the key premise holds true that in the long run, "debit" and "credit" accounts must be balanced for cooperative relationships to work.

Table 10–1 presents the commonly traded organizational currencies identified by Cohen and Bradford.

Task-Related Currencies.   This form of influence comes directly from the project manager's ability to contribute to others accomplishing their work. Probably the most significant form of this currency is the ability to respond to subordinates'

TABLE 10–1 Commonly Traded Organizational Currencies

Task-Related Currencies

Resources	Lending or giving money, budget increases, personnel, etc.
Assistance	Helping with existing projects or undertaking unwanted tasks
Cooperation	Giving task support, providing quicker response time, or aiding implementation.
Information	Providing organizational as well as technical knowledge.

Position-Related Currencies

Advancement	Giving a task or assignment that can result in promotion.
Recognition	Acknowledging effort, accomplishments, or abilities.
Visibility	Providing a chance to be known by higher-ups or significant others in the organization.
Network/Contacts	Providing opportunities for linking with others.

Inspiration-Related Currencies

Vision	Being involved in a task that has larger significance for the unit, organization, customer, or society.
Excellence	Having a chance to do important things really well.
Moral/Ethical Correctness	Doing what is "right" by a higher standard than efficiency.

Relationship-Related Currencies

Acceptance/Inclusion	Providing closeness and friendship.
Personal Support	Giving personal and emotional backing.
Understanding	Listening to others' concerns and issues.

Personal-Related Currencies

Challenge/Learning	Sharing tasks that increase skills and abilities.
Ownership/Involvement	Empowering others.
Gratitude	Expressing appreciation.

Adapted from Cohen, A.R., and David L. Bradford, *Influence Without Authority*. New York: John Wiley and Sons, 1990. Reprinted by permission of John Wiley & Sons, Inc.

requests for additional manpower, money, or time to complete a segment of a project. This kind of currency is also evident in sharing resources with another project manager who is in need. At a more personal level it simply may mean providing direct assistance to a colleague in solving a technical problem.

Providing a good word for a colleague's proposal or recommendation is another form of this currency. Because most work of significance is likely to generate some form of opposition, the person who is trying to gain approval for a plan or proposal can be greatly aided by having a "friend in court."

Another form of this currency includes extraordinary effort. For example, fulfilling an emergency request to complete a design document in 2 days instead of the normal 4 days is likely to engender gratitude. Finally, sharing valuable information that would be useful to other managers is another form of this currency.

Position-Related Currencies.   This form of influence stems from the manager's ability to enhance others' positions within their organization. A project manager can do this by giving someone a challenging assignment that can aid his or her advancement by developing skills and enhancing visibility within the organization. Being given a chance to prove yourself generates a strong sense of gratitude. Likewise, sharing the glory and bringing to the attention of higher-ups the efforts and accomplishments of others generates goodwill.

Project managers confide that a key strategy used for gaining the cooperation of professionals in other departments and organizations is figuring out how to make these people look good to their bosses. For example, a project manager was working with a subcontractor whose organization was heavily committed to total quality management (TQM). The project manager made it a point in top-level briefings to point out how quality improvement processes initiated by the contractor contributed to cost control and problem prevention.

Another variation of recognition is enhancing the reputation of others within the firm. "Good press" can pave the way for lots of opportunities while "bad press" can quickly shut a person off and make it difficult to perform. This currency is also evident in helping to preserve someone's reputation by coming to the defense of someone unjustly blamed and making sure the right attributions are made.

Finally, one of the strongest forms of this currency is sharing contacts with other people. Helping individuals expand their own networks by introducing them to key people naturally engenders gratitude. Likewise, tipping a functional manager that he or she should contact Sally X to find out what is really going on in that department or to get a request expedited is likely to engender a sense of indebtedness.

Inspiration-Related Currencies.   Perhaps the most powerful form of influence is based on inspiration. Most sources of inspiration derive from people's burning desire to make a difference and add meaning to their lives. Creating an exciting, bold vision for a project can elicit extraordinary commitment. For example, many of the technological breakthroughs associated with the introduction of the original Macintosh computer were attributed to the feeling that the project members had a chance to change the way people approached computers. A variant form of vision is providing an opportunity to do something really well. Being able to take pride in your work is a significant driving force for many people.

Often the very nature of the project provides a source of inspiration. Discovering a cure for a devastating disease, introducing a new social program that will help those in need, or simply building a bridge that will reduce a major traffic bottleneck can provide opportunities for people to feel good about what they are doing and that they are making a difference. The power of inspiration is that it operates as a magnet—pulling people as opposed to pushing them toward something.

Relationship-Related Currencies. These currencies have more to do with strengthening the relationship with someone than directly accomplishing the project tasks. The essence of this form of influence is friendship. Friendships develop by giving personal and emotional backing. Picking people up when they are feeling down, boosting their confidence, and providing encouragement naturally breed goodwill. Sharing a sense of humor and making difficult times fun is another form of this currency. Likewise, engaging in nonwork-related activities such as sports and family outings are another way relationships are naturally enhanced.

Perhaps the most basic form of this currency is simply listening to other people. Psychologists argue that most people have a strong desire to be understood and that relationships break down because the parties stop listening to each other. Likewise, sharing personal secrets/ambitions and being a wise confidant creates a special bond between individuals.

Personal-Related Currencies. This last form of currency deals with individual needs and an overriding sense of self-esteem. Some argue that self-esteem is a primary psychological need; the extent to which we can help others feel a sense of importance and personal worth will naturally generate goodwill. A project manager can enhance a colleague's sense of worth by sharing tasks that increase skills and abilities, delegating authority over work so others experience ownership, and allowing individuals to feel comfortable stretching their abilities. This form of currency can also be seen in sincere expressions of gratitude for the contributions of others. Care, though, must be exercised in expressing gratitude since it is easily devalued when overused. That is, the first *thank you* is likely to be more valued than the twentieth.

The bottom line is that a project manager will be influential only insofar as he or she can offer something that others value. Furthermore, given the diverse cast of people a project manager is dependent on, it is important that he or she be able to acquire and exercise different influence currencies. The ability to do so will be constrained in part by the nature of the project and how it is organized. For example, a project manager who is in charge of a dedicated team has considerably more to offer team members than a manager who is given the responsibility of coordinating the activities of different professionals across different departments and organizations. In such cases, that manager will probably have to rely more heavily on personal and relational bases of influence to gain the cooperation of others.

Social Network Building

Mapping Dependencies

The first step to building a social network is identifying those on whom the project depends for success. The project manager and his or her key assistants need to ask the following questions:

- Whose cooperation will we need?
- Whose agreement or approval will we need?
- Whose opposition would keep us from accomplishing the project?

Many project managers find it helpful to draw a map of these dependencies. For example, Figure 10–2 contains the dependencies identified by a project

FIGURE 10–2

Dependencies for Financial Software Installation Project

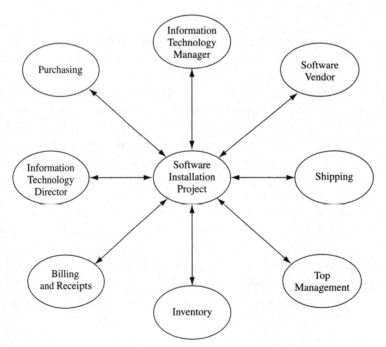

manager who was responsible for installing a new financial software system in her company.

It is always better to overestimate rather than underestimate dependencies. All too often, otherwise talented and successful project managers have been derailed because they were blindsided by someone whose position or power they had not anticipated.

After identifying who you are dependent on, you are ready to "step into their shoes" and see the project from their perspective. To help you do that, ask yourself the following questions:

- What differences exist between myself and the people on whom I depend (goals, values, pressures, working styles, risks)?
- How do these different people view the project (supporters, indifferent, antagonists)?
- What is the current status of my relationship with the people I depend on?
- What sources of influence do I have relative to those on whom I depend?

Once you begin this analysis you can begin to appreciate what others value and what currencies you might have to offer as a basis on which to build a mutually satisfying relationship. Likewise, you begin to realize where potential problems lie—relationships in which you have a current debit or no convertible currency. Furthermore, diagnosing other's points of view as well as the basis for their positions will help you anticipate their reactions and feelings about your decisions and actions. This information is vital for selecting the appropriate influence strategy and tactics and conducting win–win negotiations.

For example, after mapping her dependency network, the project manager who was in charge of installing the software system realized that she was likely to have serious problems with the manager of the receipts department, who would be one of the primary users of the software. She had no previous history of working with this individual but had heard through the grapevine that the manager was upset with the choice of software and that he considered this project to be another unnecessary disruption of his department's operation. Prior to project initiation the project manager arranged to have lunch with the manager, where she sat patiently and listened to his concerns. She invested additional time and attention educating him and his staff about the benefits of the new software. She tried to minimize the disruptions the transition would cause in his department. She altered the implementation schedule to accommodate his preferences as to when the actual software would be installed and the subsequent training would occur. In turn, the receipts manager and his people were much more accepting of the change, and the transition to the new software went more smoothly than anticipated.

Management by Wandering Around (MBWA)

The previous example illustrates the next step in managing stakeholder relationships. Once you have established who the key players are that will determine success, then you initiate contact and begin to build a relationship with those players. Building this relationship requires a management style employees at Hewlett-Packard refer to as "management by wandering around" (MBWA) to reflect that managers spend the majority of their time outside their offices. MBWA is somewhat of a misnomer in that there is a purpose or pattern behind the "wandering." Through face-to-face interactions, project managers are able to stay in touch with what is really going on in the project and build cooperative relationships essential to project success.

Effective project managers initiate contact with key players to keep abreast of developments, anticipate potential problems, provide encouragement, and reinforce the objectives and vision of the project. They are able to intervene to resolve conflicts and prevent stalemates from occurring. In essence, they "manage" the project. By staying in touch with various aspects of the project they become the focal point for information on the project. Participants turn to them to obtain the most current and comprehensive information about the project, which reinforces their central role as project manager.

We have also observed less effective project managers who eschew MBWA and attempt to manage projects from their offices and computer terminals. Such managers proudly announce an open-door policy and encourage others to see them when a problem or an issue comes up. To them no news is good news. What this does is allow their contacts to be determined by the relative aggressiveness of others. Those who take the initiative and seek out the project manager get too high a proportion of the project manager's attention. Those people less readily available (physically removed) or more passive are ignored. This behavior contributes to the adage, "Only the squeaky wheel gets the grease," which produces resentment in those who believe they are more deserving.

While a significant amount of their time is devoted to the project team, effective project managers find the time to regularly interact with more distal stakeholders. They keep in touch with suppliers, vendors, top management, and other functional managers. In doing so they maintain familiarity with different parties, sustain friendships, discover opportunities to do favors, and understand the motives and needs of others. They remind people of commitments and champion the cause of their project. They also shape people's expectations. Through frequent communication they alleviate people's concerns about the project, dispel rumors, warn people of potential problems, and lay the groundwork for dealing with setbacks in a more effective manner.

Unless project managers take the initiative to build a network of supportive relationships, they are likely to see a manager (or other stakeholder) only when there is bad news or when they need a favor (e.g., they don't have the data they promised or the project has slipped behind schedule). Without prior, frequent, easy give-and-take interactions around nondecisive issues, the encounter prompted by the problem is likely to provoke extra tension. The parties are more likely to act defensively, interrupt each other, and lose sight of the common problem.

Experienced project managers build relationships before they need them. They initiate contact with the key stakeholders at times when there are no outstanding issues or problems and therefore no anxieties and suspicions. On these social occasions, they engage in small talk and responsive banter. Astute project managers also seek to make deposits in their relationships with potentially important stakeholders. They are responsive to others' requests for aid, provide supportive counsel, and exchange information. In doing so they are establishing credit in those relationships, which will allow them to deal with more serious problems down the road. When one person views another as pleasant, credible, and helpful based on past contact, he or she is more likely to be responsive to requests for help and less confrontational when problems arise.[4]

Veteran project managers also recognize that personal contact can be motivating. They confer status on the other person by sharing their scarcest resource—their time—with that person. For this to occur there must be a healthy give-and-take interchange. Project managers adapt their interaction pattern to that of the other person. They do so by using the language and jargon of the other party. They don't always dominate the conversation with their own agenda, but frequently listen and respond to the other. Simple questions such as "How are things going?" or "Do you have any questions about the project?" can yield valuable information and establish goodwill at the same time. Inept project managers turn off others by failing to exchange pleasantries and dominating the conversation. The ineffectiveness of these interactions easily can be seen in the stiffness of the body language and the minimal exchange of information. In contrast, when a project manager is able to interact effectively, the interchange is naturally relaxing, and information flows freely. This behavior not only provides satisfaction but also yields better information and insights to the project manager.

Managing Upward Relations

Research consistently points out that project success is strongly affected by the degree to which a project has the support of top management.[5] Such support is reflected in an appropriate budget, responsiveness to unexpected needs, and clearly signally to others in the organization the importance of cooperation. In most organizations priorities are communicated through normal channels. However, companies have found it necessary to take less orthodox approaches to signaling priorities. For example, at Sequent Computer Systems, company president Casey Powell at one critical point handed out buttons. Most of the employees were given green "How can I help?" buttons, but people working on vital projects were given red "Priority" buttons. People with the green buttons were told to do anything to remove obstacles for those with the red buttons. Powell wore a green button. This simple, inexpensive technique clearly communicated project priorities throughout the entire organization.[6]

Visible top management support is not only critical for securing the support of other managers within an organization, but it also is a key factor in the project manager's ability to motivate the project team. Nothing establishes a manager's right to lead more than his or her ability to defend. To win the loyalty of team members, project managers have to be effective advocates. They have to be able to get top management to rescind unreasonable demands, provide additional resources, and recognize the accomplishments of team members.

Perhaps because of the importance of this connection, working relationships with upper management is a common source of consternation on the part of project managers. Comments we have heard from project managers about upper management include the following:

> They don't know how much it sets us back losing Neil to another project.

> I wish they would leave us alone and let us finish the project.

> I would like to see them get this project done with the budget they gave us.

> I just wish they would make up their minds as to what is really important.

While it may seem counterintuitive for a subordinate to "manage" a superior, smart project managers devote considerable time and attention to influencing and garnering the support of top management. To do so project managers have to accept profound differences in perspective and become skilled at the art of persuading superiors.

Many of the tensions that arise between upper management and project managers are a result of differences in perspective.[7] Project managers naturally become absorbed with what is best for their project. To them the most important thing in the world is their project. Upper management has a different set of priorities. They are concerned with what is best for the entire organization. It is only natural for these two interests to conflict. For example, a project manager may lobby intensively for additional personnel only to be turned down because top management believes that the other departments cannot afford a reduction in staff. Although frequent communication can minimize differences, the project manager has to accept the fact that top management inevitably is going to see the world differently.

Once project managers accept that disagreements with superiors are more a question of perspective than substance, they can focus more of their energy on the art of persuading upper management. But before they can persuade superiors, they must first prove loyalty. Loyalty in this context simply means that most of the time project managers have to show that they consistently follow through on requests and adhere to the parameters established by top management without a great deal of grumbling or fuss. Closely linked to loyalty is having credibility, which comes from an established track record of success. Once managers have proven loyalty to upper management, senior management is much more receptive to their challenges and requests.

Project managers have to cultivate strong ties with upper managers who are sponsoring the project. As noted earlier, these are high-ranking officials who championed approval and funding of the project; as such, their reputations are aligned with the project. Sponsors also are the ones who defend the project when it is under attack in the upper circles of management.

Since sponsors' reputations and careers are tied to the success of projects they advocate, it is only natural for them to be anxious about project progress. One common way to relieve anxiety is to get heavily involved in the project, micromanage it, and make sure that it is done right. This typically has the opposite effect and actually interferes with the success of the project. A better way to deal with sponsors' anxiety is to provide them with a steady flow of sufficient information so that sponsors can see what is happening and how things are going. This should allow the sponsors to be more comfortable with empowering the project team to complete the project.

At the same time, project managers should *always* keep such people informed of any problems that may cause embarrassment or disappointment. Project sponsors should be the first to know if costs are beginning to overrun the budget or a technical glitch is threatening to delay the completion of the project.

When negotiating from a subordinate position for additional funds, resources, or extensions, project managers recognize that the timing of a request is critical. Asking for additional budget the day after disappointing third-quarter earnings are reported is going to be much more difficult than making a similar request 4 weeks later. Good project managers pick the optimum time to appeal to top management. They enlist their project sponsors to lobby their cause. They also realize there are limits to top management's accommodations. Here, the Lone Ranger analogy is appropriate—you have only so many silver bullets, so use them wisely.

When giving a status report to superiors, project managers must present the most positive image possible without stretching the truth. They should adapt their communication pattern to that of the superior group, making it a point to use buzzwords and jargon valued by superiors in their presentations. For example, one project manager recognized that top management had a tendency to use sports metaphors to describe business situations, so she framed a recent slip in schedule by admitting that "we lost 5 yards, but we still have two plays to make a first down." Smart project managers learn the language of top management and use it to their advantage.

Finally, a few project managers admit ignoring chains of command. If they are confident that top management will reject an important request and that what they want to do will benefit the project, they do it without asking permission. While acknowledging that this is very risky, they claim that bosses typically won't argue with success.

Leading by Example

A highly visible, interactive management style is not only essential to building and sustaining cooperative relationships, it also allows project managers to utilize their most powerful leadership tool—their own behavior. Often, when faced with uncertainty, people look to others for cues as to how to respond and demonstrate a propensity to mimic the behavior of superiors. A project manager's behavior symbolizes how other people should work on the project. Through her behavior a project manager can influence how others act and respond to a variety of issues related to the project. See *Project Management in Action: Leading at the Edge*[8] for a vivid example of this. To be effective project managers must "walk the talk." Six aspects of leading by example are discussed next (see Figure 10–3).

Priorities.   Actions speak louder than words. Subordinates and others discern project managers' priorities not by what they say but by how they spend their time. If a project manager claims that this project is critical and then devotes more time to other projects, then all his verbal reassurances are likely to fall on deaf ears. Conversely, a project manager who takes the time to observe a critical test instead of simply waiting for a report affirms the importance of the testers and their work. Likewise, the types of questions project managers pose communicate priorities. By repeatedly asking how specific issues relate to satisfying the customer, a project manager can reinforce the importance of customer satisfaction.

Urgency.   Through their actions project managers can convey a sense of urgency, which can permeate project activities. This urgency in part can be conveyed through stringent deadlines, frequent status report meetings, and aggressive solutions for expediting the project. Project managers use these tools like a metronome to pick up the beat of the project. At the same time, such devices will be ineffective if there is not also a corresponding change in the project managers' behavior. If they want others to work faster and solve problems quicker, then they

---

Project Management in Action

Leading at the Edge

In 1914, the intrepid explorer Ernest Shackleton embarked on the *Endurance* with his team of seamen and scientists, intent upon crossing the unexplored Antarctic continent. What happened in the 2 years between their departure and their ultimate incredible rescue rarely has been matched in the annals of survival: a ship crushed by an expanding ice pack . . . a crew stranded on the floes of the frozen Weddell Sea . . . two perilous treks in open boats across a raging Southern Ocean . . . a team marooned on the wild, forlorn Elephant island, stretched the limits of human endurance.

This adventure provided the basis for the book, *Leading at the Edge: Leadership Lessons from the Extraordinary Saga of Shackleton's Antarctic Expedition* by Dennis Perkins.[8] Perkins provides numerous incidents of how Shackleton's personal example influenced the behavior of his beleaguered crew. For example, from the beginning of the trans-Atlantic expedition to its end Shackleton consistently encouraged behavior that emphasized caring and respect:

> After the destruction of the *Endurance* Shackleton heated hot milk for the crew and went from tent to tent with the "life-giving" drink. After the sail to the island of South Georgia, when the exhausted crew had landed, Shackleton took the first watch, which he kept for 3 hours instead of the usual 1.

Crewmembers emulated the caring behaviors that Shackleton modeled. A good example of this occurred during one of most dramatic moments in the *Endurance* saga. The food supply had dwindled to perilously low levels. Less than a week's supply remained, and the tiny ration of seal steak usually served at breakfast was eliminated. The waste meat generally used to feed the dogs was inspected for edible scraps.

Under these wretched conditions, and after a wet sleepless night, an argument broke out among some of the team members. Caught in the middle, one crew member (Greenstreet) spilled his tiny ration of powdered milk and shouted at the biologist (Clark). Alfred Lansing, described what happened next:

> . . . Greenstreet paused to get his breath, and in that instant his anger was spent and he suddenly fell silent. Everyone else in the tent became quiet, too, and looked at Greenstreet, shaggy-haired, bearded, and filthy with blubber soot, holding his empty mug in his hand and looking helplessly down into the snow that had thirstily soaked up his precious milk. The loss was so tragic he seemed almost on the point of weeping. Without speaking, Clark reached out and poured some milk into Greenstreet's mug. Then Worsely, Macklin, and Rickerson and Kerr, Orde-Lees, and finally Blackborrow. They finished in silence.[8]

need to work faster. They need to hasten the pace of their own behavior. They should accelerate the frequency of their interactions, talk and walk more quickly, get to work sooner, and leave work later. By simply increasing the pace of their daily interaction patterns, project managers can reinforce a sense of urgency in others.

Figure 10-3

Leading by Example

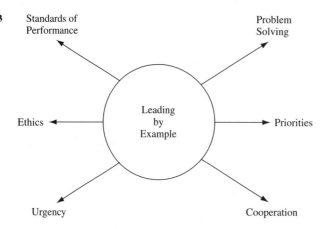

Problem-Solving.   How project managers respond to problems sets the tone for how others tackle problems. If bad news is greeted by verbal attacks, then others will be reluctant to be forthcoming. If the project manager is more concerned with finding out who is to blame instead of how to prevent problems from happening again, then others will tend to cover their tracks and cast the blame elsewhere. If, on the other hand, project managers focus more on how they can turn a problem into an opportunity or what can be learned from a mistake, then others are more likely to adopt a more proactive approach to problem-solving.

Cooperation.   How project managers act toward outsiders influence how team members interact with outsiders. If a project manager makes disparaging remarks about the "idiots" in the Marketing Department, then this often becomes the shared view of the entire team. If project managers set the norm of treating outsiders with respect and being responsive to their needs, then others will more likely follow suit.

Standards of Performance.   Veteran project managers recognize that if they want participants to exceed project expectations then they have to exceed others' expectations of a good project manager. They establish a high standard for project performance through the quality of their daily interactions. They respond quickly to the needs of others, carefully prepare and run crisp meetings, stay on top of all the critical issues, facilitate effective problem solving, and stand firm on important matters.

Ethics.   How others respond to ethical dilemmas that arise in the course of a project will be influenced by how the project manager has responded to similar dilemmas. In many cases, team members base their actions on how they think the project manager would respond. If project managers deliberately distort or with-hold vital information from customers or top management, then they are signaling to others that this kind of behavior is acceptable. Project management invariably creates a variety of ethical dilemmas; this would be an appropriate time to delve into this topic in more detail.

Ethics and Project Management

Questions of ethics have already arisen in previous chapters where we discussed padding cost and time estimations, exaggerating payoffs of project proposals and so forth. Ethical dilemmas involve situations where it is difficult to determine whether conduct is right or wrong. Is it acceptable to falsely assure customers that everything is on track when in reality you are only doing so to prevent them from panicking and making matters worse?

In a survey of project managers, 81 percent reported that they encounter ethical issues in their work. These dilemmas range from being pressured to alter status reports, backdate signatures, or shade documentation to mask the reality of project progress to falsifying cost accounts, compromising safety standards to accelerate progress, and approving shoddy work.[9]

Project management is complicated work, and, as such, ethics invariably involves gray areas of judgment and interpretation. For example, it is difficult to distinguish deliberate falsification of estimates from genuine mistakes, or the willful exaggeration of project payoffs from genuine optimism. Likewise, it becomes problematic to determine whether unfulfilled promises were deliberate deception or an appropriate response to changing circumstances.

To provide greater clarity to business ethics, many companies and professional groups publish a code of conduct. Cynics see these documents as simply window dressing, while advocates argue that they are important, albeit limited, first steps. In practice, personal ethics do not lie in formal statutes but at the intersection of one's work, family, education, profession, religious beliefs, and daily interactions. Most project managers report that they rely on their own private sense of right and wrong, what one project manager called his "internal compass." One common rule of thumb for testing whether a response is ethical is to ask: "Imagine that whatever you did was going to be reported on the front page of your local newspaper. How would you like that? Would you be comfortable?"

Unfortunately, Nazi war crimes have demonstrated the willingness of highly trained professionals to abdicate personal responsibility for horrific actions and to obey the directives of organizational hierarchies. Top management and the culture of an organization play a decisive role in shaping members' beliefs of what is right and wrong. Many organizations encourage ethical transgressions by creating a "win at all costs" mentality. The pressures to succeed obscure consideration of whether the ends justify the means. Other organizations place a premium on "fair play" and command a market position by virtue of being trustworthy and reliable.

Discussing business ethics is like opening Pandora's box. What can be pointed out is that many project managers claim that ethical behavior is its own reward. By following your own internal compass your behavior expresses your personal values. Others argue that ethical behavior is doubly rewarding. Not only are you able to fall asleep at night, but you also develop a sound and admirable reputation. As will be explored in the next section, such a reputation is essential to establishing the trust necessary to exercise influence effectively.

Building Trust: The Key to Exercising Influence

We all know managers who have influence but whom we do not trust; these individuals are often referred to as "political animals" or "jungle fighters." While these individuals are often very successful in the short run, the prevalent sense of mistrust prohibits long-term efficacy. Successful project managers not only need to be influential, they also need to exercise influence in a manner that builds and sustains the trust of others.

The significance of trust cannot be overstated. It can be easily discerned by its absence. Imagine how different a working relationship is when you distrust the other party as opposed to trusting them. When people distrust each other, they often spend inordinate amounts of time and energy attempting to discern hidden agendas and the true meaning of communications, and securing guarantees to promises. They are much more cautious with each other and hesitant to cooperate.

Here is what one functional manager had to say about how he reacted to a project manager he did not trust:

> Whenever I interacted with Jim I found myself stopping and asking myself what is really going on here. When he made a request my initial reaction was "no" until he proved it.

Conversely, trust is the "lubricant" that maintains smooth and efficient interactions. When you are trusted, people are more likely to take your actions and intentions at face value when circumstances are ambiguous. Cohen and Bradford note that with trust, people will be less stringent about whether you are paying back in kind; they will extend you a larger line of credit and be more liberal in your repayment terms.[10] Such flexibility is critical to project managers, especially during times of organizational change and uncertainty, when it is by definition more difficult to establish "fair exchange rates."

For example, here is what a functional manager had to say about how he dealt with a project manager he trusted:

> If Sally said she needed something, no questions were asked. I knew it was important and that I could count on her in a time of need. I accepted what she told me as the truth as she knew it.

Trust is an elusive concept. It is hard to nail down in precise terms why some project managers are trusted and others are not. One popular way to understand trust is to see it as a function of character and competence. Character focuses on personal motives (i.e., does he or she want to do the right thing?) while competence focuses on skills necessary to realize motives (i.e., does he or she know the right things to do?).

Stephen Covey resurrected the significance of character in leadership literature in his best-selling *Seven Habits of Highly Effective People.*[11] Covey criticized popular management literature as focusing too much on shallow human relations skills and manipulative techniques, which he labeled the "personality ethic." He argues that at the core of highly effective people is a "character ethic" that is deeply rooted in personal values and principles such as dignity, service, fairness, the pursuit of truth, and respect.

One of the distinguishing traits of character is consistency. When people are guided by a core set of principles, they are naturally more predictable because their actions are consistent with these principles. Another feature of character is openness. When people have a clear sense of who they are and what they value, they are more receptive to others. This trait provides them with the capacity to empathize and the talent to build consensus among divergent people. Finally, another quality of character is a sense of purpose. Managers with character are driven not only by personal ambitions but also for the common good. Their primary concern is what is best for their organization and the project, not what is best for themselves. This willingness to subordinate personal interests to a higher purpose garners the respect, loyalty, and trust of others.

The significance of character is effectively summarized by the comments made by two team members about two very different project managers.

> At first everyone liked Joe and was excited about the project. But after a while people became suspicious of his motives. He had a tendency to say different things to different people. People began to feel manipulated. He spent too much time with top management. People began to believe that he was only looking out for himself. It was HIS project. When the project began to slip he jumped ship and left someone else holding the bag. I'll never work for that guy again.

> My first impression of Jack was nothing special. He had a quiet, unassuming management style. Over time I learned to respect his judgment and his ability to get people to work together. When you went to him with a problem or a request he always listened carefully. If he couldn't do what you wanted him to do, he would take the time to explain why. When disagreements arose he always thought of what was best

for the project. He treated everyone by the same rules; no one got special treatment. I'd jump at the opportunity to work on a project with him again.

Character alone will not engender trust. We must also have confidence in the competency of the individual.[12] We all know well-intentioned managers whom we like but do not trust. Although we may befriend these managers, we don't like to work with or for them. Competence is reflected at a number of different levels. First, there is task-related knowledge and skills reflected in the ability to answer questions, solve technical problems, and excel in certain kinds of work. Second, there is competence at an interpersonal level demonstrated in being able to listen effectively, communicate clearly, resolve arguments, provide encouragement, and so forth. Finally, there is organizational competence. This includes being able to run effective meetings, set meaningful objectives, reduce inefficiencies, and build a social network. Too often there is a tendency for young engineers and other professionals to place too much value on task or technical competence. They underestimate the significance of organizational skills. Veteran professionals, on the other hand, recognize the importance of management and place a greater value on organizational and interpersonal skills.

One problem new project managers experience is that it takes time to establish a sense of character and competency. Character and competency are often demonstrated when they are tested, such as when a tough call has to be made or when difficult problems have to be solved. Veteran project managers have the advantage of reputation and an established track record of success. Although endorsements from credible sponsors can help a young project manager create a favorable first impression, ultimately he or she will have to demonstrate character and competence during the course of dealings with others in order to gain their trust.

Qualities of an Effective Project Manager

So far this chapter has addressed the importance of building a network of relationships to complete the project based on trust and reciprocity. This section examines the nature of project management work and the personal qualities needed to excel at it.

Project management is, at first glance, a misleading discipline in that there is an inherent logic in the progression from formulating a project scope statement, creating a WBS, developing a network, adding resources, finalizing a plan, and managing milestones. However, when it actually comes to implementing and completing projects, this logic quickly disappears, and project managers encounter a much messier world, filled with inconsistencies and paradoxes. Effective project managers have to be able to deal with the contradictory nature of their work:

Innovate but Maintain Stability.   Project managers have to put out fires, restore order, and get the project back on track. At the same time they need to be innovative and develop new, better ways of doing things. Innovations unravel stable routines and spark new disturbances that have to be dealt with.

See the Big Picture while Getting Your Hands Dirty.   Project managers have to see the big picture and how their project fits within the larger strategy of their firm. There are also times when they must get deeply involved in project work and technology. If they don't worry about the details, who will?

Encourage Individuals but Emphasize the Team.   Project managers have to motivate, cajole, and entice individual performers while at the same time maintain teamwork. They have to be careful that they are considered fair and consistent in their treatment of team members while at the same time treating each member as a special individual.

Hands-Off/Hands-On.   Project managers have to intervene, resolve stalemates, solve technical problems, and insist on different approaches. At the same time they have to recognize when it is appropriate to sit on the sidelines and let other people figure out what to do.

Flexible but Firm.   Project managers have to be adaptable and responsive to events and outcomes that occur on the project. At the same time they have to hold the line at times and tough it out when everyone else wants to give up.

Team versus Organizational Loyalties.   Project managers need to forge a unified project team whose members stimulate one another to extraordinary performance. But at the same time they have to counter the excesses of cohesion and the team's resistance to outside ideas. They have to cultivate loyalties to both the team and the parent organization.

The qualities needed to be a good project manager are summed up in *Project Management in Action: Profile of a Prospective Project Coordinator.*

Managing these and other contradictions requires finesse and balance. Finesse involves the skillful movement back and forth between opposing behavioral patterns.[13] For example, most of the time project managers actively involve others, move by increment, and seek consensus. There are other times when project managers must act as autocrats and take decisive, unilateral action. Balance involves recognizing the danger of extremes and that too much of a good thing invariably becomes harmful. For example, many managers have a tendency to always delegate the most stressful, difficult assignments to their best team members. This habit often breeds resentment among those chosen ("why am I always the one

<u>Project Management in Action</u>

Profile of a Prospective Project Coordinator

Malkin provided this interesting profile based on many years of work in the pharmaceutical industry.[13]

1. Be able to juggle many balls in the air at the same time but know which balls can be dropped when priorities demand it.
2. The consummate separator of the wheat from the chaff but still be able to use the chaff.
3. Able to remain an intelligent, objective, neutral at all times even when you know the limitations of people presenting strategies, i.e., stupid.
4. A person who can talk with kings—and cabbages—and be called a good listener by both.
5. Pesky, persistent but effective, and above all, correct.
6. Able to have both ears to the ground at the same time and never be surprised.
7. At times, possess the discretion of a clam.
8. Able to show favoritism but never be accused of playing favorites.
9. Live without recognition but survive with scorn.
10. Dependable but independent.
11. Able to suffer fools gladly, but take notes.
12. Trusted but not necessarily trusting.

Source: Reprinted from *PMNetwork* with permission of the Project Management Institute, Four Campus Boulevard, Newtown Square, PA 19073-3299, a worldwide organization advancing the state-of-the-art information in project management.

who gets the tough work?") and never allows the weaker members to develop their talents further.

There is no one management style or formula for being an effective project manager. The world of project management is too complicated for formulas. Successful project managers have a knack for adapting styles to specific circumstances of the situation.

So, what should one look for in an effective project manager? Many authors have addressed this question and have generated list after list of skills and attributes associated with being an effective manager.[15] When reviewing these lists, one gets the impression that to be a successful project manager requires someone with superhuman powers. While the authors agree that not everyone has the right stuff to be an effective project manager, there are some core traits and skills that can be developed to successfully perform the job. Nine of these traits are noted below.

Systems Thinker.   Project managers must be able to take a holistic rather than a reductionist approach to projects. Instead of breaking up a project into individual pieces (planning, budget) and managing it by understanding each part, a systems perspective focuses on trying to understand how relevant project factors collectively interact to produce project outcomes. The key to success then becomes managing the interaction between different parts, not the parts themselves.[16]

Personal Integrity.   Before you can lead and manage others, you have to be able to lead and manage yourself. Begin by establishing a firm sense of who you are, what you stand for, and how you should behave. This inner strength provides the buoyancy to endure the ups and downs of the project life cycle and the credibility essential to sustaining the trust of others.

Proactive.   Good project managers take action before it is needed to prevent small problems from escalating into major concerns. They spend the majority of their time working within their sphere of influence to solve problems and not dwelling on things they have little control over.[17] Project managers can't be whiners.

High Tolerance of Stress.   Project management is not for the meek. Deadline pressures technical uncertainties, and dealing with a variety of difficult, even stubborn professionals can generate a great deal of stress. People vary in their tolerance of stress. Physical exercise, a healthy diet, and a supportive homefront are necessary to endure the rigors of project management.

General Business Perspective.   Because the primary role of a project manager is to integrate the contributions of different business and technical disciplines, it is important that a manager have a general grasp of business fundamentals and how the different functional disciplines interact to contribute to a successful business.

Good Communicator.   This one appears on every list and with good reason. Project managers have to be able to communicate with a wide variety of individuals. They not only have to be able to convey their ideas in an easily understandable manner, but they must also be empathic listeners, capable of drawing out the true meaning in what others are trying to say to them.

Effective Time Management.   Time is a manager's scarcest resource. Project managers have to be able to budget their time wisely and quickly adjust their priorities. They need to balance their interactions so no one feels ignored.

Skillful Politician.   Project managers have to be able to deal effectively with a wide range of people and win their support and endorsement of their project. They need to be able to sell the virtues of their project without compromising the truth.

Optimist.   Project managers have to display a can-do attitude. They have to be able to find rays of sunlight in a dismal day and keep people's attention positive. A good sense of humor and a playful attitude are often a project manager's greatest strength.

These nine traits are not all-inclusive. They tend to describe "superstar" project managers.

So how does one develop these traits? Workshops, self-study, and formal education can upgrade one's general business perspective and capacity for systems thinking. Training programs can improve one's communication and political skills. People can also be taught stress- and time-management techniques. However we know of no workshop or magic potion that can transform a pessimist into an optimist or provide a sense of purpose when there is not one. These qualities get at the very soul or being of a person. Optimism, integrity, and even being proactive are not easily developed if there is not already a predisposition to display them.

Summary

To be successful, project managers must build a cooperative network among a divergent set of allies. They begin by identifying who the key stakeholders on a project are, followed by a diagnosis of the nature of the relationships, and the basis for exercising influence. Effective project managers are skilled at acquiring and exercising a wide range of influence. They use this influence and a highly interactive management style to monitor project performance and initiate appropriate changes in project plans and direction. They do so in a manner that generates trust, which is ultimately based on others' perceptions of their character and competence.

Project managers are encouraged to keep in mind the following suggestions:

Build Relationships before You Need Them.   Identify key players and what you can do to help them before you need their assistance. It is always easier to receive a favor after you have granted one. This requires the project manager to see the project in systems terms and to appreciate how it affects other activities and agendas inside and outside the organization. From this perspective they can identify opportunities to do good deeds and garner the support of others.

Be Leery of the Golden Rule.   Many managers boil down managing to this basic premise: "Do unto others as you would wish them to do unto you." While there is a lot of wisdom embedded in this saying, there is one potential danger-ous flaw. Others may not want what you want or need what you need. What is fair to you may not be perceived to be fair by others. Empathy is needed to put yourself in their shoes to understand their specific desires and needs.

Trust Is Sustained through Frequent Face-to-Face Contact. Trust withers through neglect. This is particularly true under conditions of rapid change and un-certainty that naturally engender doubt, suspicion, and even momentary bouts of paranoia. Project managers must maintain frequent contact with key stakeholders to keep abreast of developments, assuage concerns, engage in reality testing, and focus attention on the project. Frequent face-to-face interactions affirm mutual re-spect and trust among others.

Ultimately, exercising influence in an effective and ethical manner begins and ends with how you view the other parties. Do you view them as potential part-ners or obstacles to your goals? If obstacles, then you wield your influence to ma-nipulate and gain compliance and cooperation. If partners, you exercise influence to gain their commitment and support. People who view social network building as building partnerships see every interaction with two goals: resolving the im-mediate problem or concern and improving the working relationship so that next time it will be even more effective. Experienced project managers realize that "what goes around comes around" and try at all cost to avoid antagonizing play-ers for quick success.

11

MANAGING PROJECT TEAMS

Nothing great was ever achieved without enthusiasm
Ralph Waldo Emerson

The magic and power of teams is captured in the term "synergy," which is derived from the Greek word *sunergos*: "working together." There is positive and negative synergy. The essence of positive synergy can be found in the phrase "the whole is greater than the sum of the parts." Conversely, negative synergy occurs when the whole is less than the sum of the parts. Mathematically, these two states can be symbolized by the following equations:

Positive Synergy: $1 + 1 + 1 + 1 + 1 = 10$
Negative Synergy: $1 + 1 + 1 + 1 + 1 = 2$ or even -2

Synergy perhaps can best be seen on a football field, a soccer pitch, or a basketball court. For example, the Chicago Bulls dominated professional basketball during the nineties. Admittedly they had in Michael Jordan, if not the greatest, then one of the best players ever to play the game. Still it wasn't until management found players to complement Jordan's abilities and Jordan himself accepted the fact that he had to play a team game that their reign of championships began. Positive synergy could be seen in how routinely the Bulls executed a fast break, where the combined actions of all five players produced an unchallenged slam dunk, or in their aggressive, denial defense, which stifled the performance of a much taller and more talented opponent. Negative synergy can be seen plainly in cellar dwelling NBA teams where players ignore wide-open teammates to launch wild 3-point shots or when two or three members fail to hustle back on defense leaving a lone teammate to defend a 3-on-1 fast break. Teams that exhibit negative team synergy are often characterized as being underachievers, while champions become synonymous with teams that exhibit positive synergy.

Although less visible than in team sports, positive and negative synergy can also be observed and felt in the daily operations of project teams. Here is a description from one project manager we interviewed:

> Instead of operating as one big team we fractionalized into a series of subgroups. The marketing people stuck together as well as the systems guys. A lot of time was wasted gossiping and complaining about each other. When the project started slipping behind schedule, everyone started covering their tracks and trying to pass the blame on to others. After a while we avoided direct conversation and resorted to e-mail. Management finally pulled the plug and brought in another team to salvage the project. It was one of the worst project management experiences in my life.

This same manager fortunately also was able to recount a more positive experience:

> There was a contagious excitement within the team. Sure we had our share of problems and setbacks, but we dealt with them straight on, and at times were able to do the impossible. We all cared about the project and looked out for each other. At the same time we challenged each other to do better. It was one of the most exciting times in my life.

The following is a set of characteristics commonly associated with high-performing teams that exhibit positive synergy:

1. The team shares a sense of common purpose, and each member is willing to work toward achieving project objectives.
2. The team identifies individual talents and expertise and uses them, depending on the project's needs at any given time. At these times the team willingly accepts the influence and leadership of the members whose skills are relevant to the immediate task.
3. Roles are balanced and shared to facilitate both the accomplishment of tasks and feelings of group cohesion and morale.
4. The team expends energy toward problem solving rather than allowing itself to be drained by interpersonal issues or competitive struggles.
5. Differences of opinion are encouraged and freely expressed.
6. To encourage risk taking and creativity, mistakes are treated as opportunities for learning rather than reasons for punishment.
7. Members set high personal standards of performance and encourage each other to realize the objectives of the project.
8. Members identify with the team and consider it an important source of both professional and personal growth.

High-performing teams become champions, create breakthrough products, exceed customer expectations, and get projects done ahead of schedule and under budget. They are bonded together by mutual interdependency and a common goal or vision. They trust each other and exhibit a high level of cooperation.

The Five-Stage Team Development Model

Just as infants develop in certain ways during their first months of life, many experts argue that groups develop in a predictable manner. One of the most popular models (see Figure 11–1) identifies five stages through which groups develop into effective teams.[1]

Forming. During this initial stage the members get acquainted with each other and understand the scope of the project. They begin to establish ground rules by trying to find out what behaviors are acceptable, with respect both to the project (what role they will play, what performance expectations are) and interpersonal relations (who's really in charge). This stage is completed once members begin to think of themselves as part of a group.

FIGURE 11–1

The Five-Stage Team Development Model

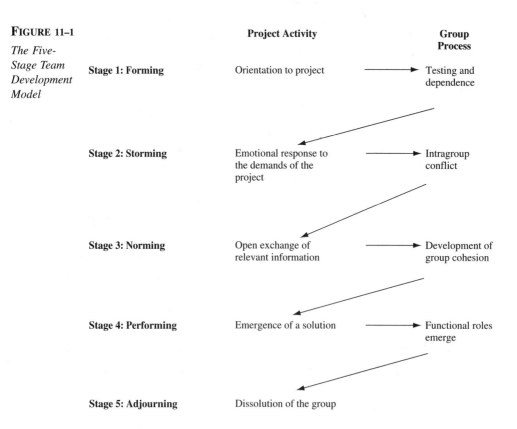

	Project Activity	Group Process
Stage 1: Forming	Orientation to project	Testing and dependence
Stage 2: Storming	Emotional response to the demands of the project	Intragroup conflict
Stage 3: Norming	Open exchange of relevant information	Development of group cohesion
Stage 4: Performing	Emergence of a solution	Functional roles emerge
Stage 5: Adjourning	Dissolution of the group	

Storming. As the name suggests, this stage is marked by a high degree of internal conflict. Members accept that they are part of a project group, but resist the constraints that the project and group put on their individuality. There is conflict over who will control the group and how decisions will be made. As these conflicts are resolved, the project manager's leadership becomes accepted, and the group moves to the next stage.

Norming. The third stage is one in which close relationships develop and the group demonstrates cohesiveness. Feelings of camaraderie and shared responsibility for the project are heightened. The norming phase is complete when the group structure solidifies and the group establishes a common set of expectations about how members should work together.

Performing. The team operating structure at this point is fully functional and accepted. Group energy has moved from getting to know each other and how the group will work together to accomplishing the project goals.

Adjourning. For conventional work groups, performing is the last stage of their development. However, for project teams, there is a completion phase. During this stage, the team prepares for its own disbandment. High performance is no longer a top priority. Instead attention is devoted to wrapping up the project. Responses of members vary in this stage. Some members are upbeat, basking in the project team's accomplishments. Others may be depressed over loss of camaraderie and friendships gained during the project's life.

This model has several implications for those managing project teams. The first is that the project manager needs to devote initial attention to helping the group evolve quickly to the productive fourth phase (performing). The second implication for project managers is that the model provides a framework for the group to understand its own development. Project managers have found it useful to share the model with their teams. It helps members accept the tensions of the storming phase, and it directs their focus to moving to the more productive phases. The final implication is that it stresses the importance of the norming phase, which contributes significantly to the level of productivity experienced during the performing phase. Project managers, as we shall see, have to take an active role in shaping group norms that will contribute to ultimate project success.

Situational Factors Affecting Team Development

Experience and research indicate that high-performing project teams are much more likely to develop under the following conditions:[2]

- There are 10 or fewer members per team.
- Members volunteer to serve on the project team.
- Members serve on the project from beginning to end.
- Members are assigned to the project full-time.

- Members are part of an organization culture that fosters cooperation and trust.
- All relevant functional areas are represented on the team.
- The project involves a compelling objective.
- Members are located within conversational distance of each other.

In reality, it is rare that a project manager is assigned a project that meets all of these conditions. For example, many projects' requirements dictate the active involvement of more than 10 members and may consist of a complex set of interlocking teams comprising more than 100 professionals. In many organizations, functional managers or central staff offices assign project members with little input from the project manager. To optimize resource utilization, team member involvement may be part time, and/or participants may move in and out of the project team on an as-needed basis. In the case of ad hoc committees, no member of the team works full time on the project. In many corporations, an NIH (not invented here) culture exists that discourages collaboration across functional boundaries. Team members often report to different managers, and, in some cases, the project manager will have no direct input over performance appraisals and advancement opportunities of team members. Key functional areas may not be represented during the entire duration of the project but may only be involved in a sequential manner. Not all projects have a compelling objective. It can be hard to get members excited about mundane projects such as a simple product extension or a conventional apartment complex. Finally, team members often are scattered across different corporate offices and buildings or, in the case of a virtual project, across the entire globe.

It is important for project managers and team members to recognize the situational constraints they are operating under and do the best they can. It would be naive to believe that every project team has the same potential to evolve into a high-performing team. Under less than ideal conditions, it may be a struggle just to meet project objectives. Ingenuity, discipline, and sensitivity to team dynamics are essential to maximizing the performance of a project team.

Building a High-Performing Project Team

Project managers play a key role in developing high-performing project teams. They recruit members, conduct meetings, establish a team identity, create a common sense of purpose or shared vision, orchestrate decision making, create and manage a reward system that encourages teamwork, lead team-building sessions, and resolve conflicts that emerge within the team (see Figure 11–2). Project managers take advantage of situational factors that naturally contribute to team development while improvising around those factors that inhibit team development.

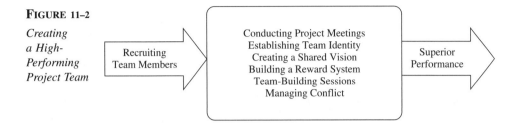

FIGURE 11–2

*Creating
a High-
Performing
Project Team*

Recruiting
Team Members

Conducting Project Meetings
Establishing Team Identity
Creating a Shared Vision
Building a Reward System
Team-Building Sessions
Managing Conflict

Superior
Performance

In doing so they exhibit a highly interactive management style that exemplifies teamwork and, as discussed in the Chapter 10, manage the interface between the team and the rest of the organization.

Recruiting Project Members

The process of selecting and recruiting project members will vary across organizations. Two important factors affecting recruitment are the importance of the project and the management structure being used to complete the project. Often for high-priority projects that are critical to the future of the organization, the project manager will be given virtual carte blanche to select whomever he or she deems necessary. For less-significant projects, the project manager will have to persuade personnel from other areas within the organization to join the team. In many matrix structures, the functional manager controls who is assigned to the project; the project manager will have to work with the functional manager to obtain necessary personnel. Even in a project team where members are selected and assigned full-time to the project, the project manager has to be sensitive to the needs of others. There is no better way to create enemies within an organization than to be perceived as robbing other departments of essential personnel.

Experienced project managers stress the importance of asking for volunteers. However, this desirable step oftentimes is outside the manager's control. Still, the value of having team members volunteer for the project as opposed to being assigned cannot be overlooked. Agreeing to work on the project is the first step toward building personal commitment to the project. Such commitment will be essential to maintain motivation when the project hits hard times and extra effort is required.

When selecting and recruiting team members, project managers naturally look for individuals with the necessary experience, knowledge, and technical skills critical for project completion. At the same time, there are less obvious considerations that need to be factored into the recruitment process:[3]

Problem-Solving Ability.   If the project is complex and fuzzy, then a manager wants people who are good at working under uncertainty and have strong problem-identification and problem-solving skills. These same people are likely to be bored and less productive working on straightforward projects that go by the book.

Availability.   Sometimes the people who are most available are not the ones wanted for the team. Conversely, if members recruited are already overcommitted, they may not be able to offer much.

Technological Expertise.   Managers should be wary of people who know too much about a specific technology. They may be technology buffs who like to study but have a hard time settling down and doing the work. See *Project Management in Action: Managing Martians* for advice on managing technology experts.

Credibility.   The credibility of the project is enhanced by the reputation of the people involved in the project. Recruiting a sufficient number of "winners" lends confidence to the project.

Political Connections.   To begin to establish a cooperative relationship with a significant, but potentially uncooperative stakeholder group, managers would be wise to recruit individuals who already have a good working relationship with that group. This is particularly true for projects operating in a matrix environment in which a significant portion of the work will be under the domain of a specific functional department and not the core project team.

Ambition, Initiative, and Energy.   These qualities can make up for a lot of shortcomings in other areas and should not be underestimated.

After reviewing needed skills, the manager should try to find out through the corporate grapevine who is good, who is available, and who might want to work on the project. Some organizations may allow direct interviews. Once key people are recruited, it is wise to have them involved in the interviewing and recruiting process of other team members. Often a manager will have to expend political capital to get highly prized people assigned to the project.

In matrix environments, the project manager will have to request appointments with functional managers to discuss project requirements for staffing. The following documents should be available at these discussions: an overall project scope statement, endorsements of top management, and a description of the tasks and general schedule that pertains to the people from their departments. Managers need to be precise as to what attributes they are seeking and why they are important. Good negotiation skills are necessary at this meeting. Functional managers should be encouraged to suggest names of people within their departments as candidates.

Project Management in Action

Managing Martians

Donna Shirley's 35-year career as an aerospace engineer reached a pinnacle in July 1997 when Sojourner—the solar-powered, self-guided, microwave-oven-sized rover—was seen exploring the Martian landscape in Pathfinder's spectacular images from the surface of the red planet. The event marked a milestone in space exploration—no vehicle had ever before roamed the surface of another planet. Shirley, a manager at the Jet Propulsion Laboratory's Mars Exploration Program, headed the mostly male team that designed and built Sojourner. In her insightful memoir, *Managing Martians*, she makes the following observation about managing creative teams:

> When you are managing really brilliant, creative people, at some point you find it's impossible to command or control them because you can't understand what they are doing. Once they have gone beyond your ability to understand them, you have a choice to make as a manager. You can limit them and the project by your intelligence, which I think is the wrong way to do it. Or you can trust them and use your management skills to keep them focused on the goal.

A lot of bad managers get threatened when their "subordinates" know more than they do. They either hire people who are inferior to them so they can always feel in control or they bottleneck people who know something they don't so they can maintain control. The whole project suffers from the manager's insecurities.

From Shirley, Donna, and Morton, Danelle. *Managing Martians.* New York: Broadway Books, 1998, pp. 88–89.

If the project manager is asked to suggest names it might be wise to say, "Well, I would really like Pegi Young, but I know how critical her work is. How about Billy Talbot?" If the conversation goes this way, the project manager may be able to cut a deal then and there and will want to be sure to put the agreement in writing immediately after the meeting as a memorandum of understanding.

If, on the other hand, the functional manager balks at the suggestions and the meeting is not progressing, the project manager should adroitly terminate the conversation with an understanding that the matter will be discussed again in a few days. This technique demonstrates persistence and a desire to do what it takes to resolve the issue. Ultimately, of course, the project manager will have to settle on the best offer. Managers should exercise care not to reveal how different members of the team were selected. The project might be crippled at the start if members know they were fourth or fifth choices.

Conducting Project Meetings

The First Project Team Meeting

The *project kick-off meeting is critical* to the early functioning of the project team. According to one veteran project manager:

> The first team meeting sets the tone for how the team will work together. If it is disorganized, or becomes bogged down with little sense of closure, then this can often become a self-fulfilling prophecy for subsequent group work. On the other hand, if it is crisply run, focusing on real issues and concerns in an honest and straightforward manner, members come away excited about being part of the project team.

Typically there are three objectives project managers try to achieve during the first meeting of the project team.

1. The first is to provide an overview of the project, including the scope and objectives, the general schedule, method, and procedures.
2. The second is to begin to address some of the interpersonal concerns captured in the team development model: who the other team members are, why we are here, how does each person fit in, what are we doing, and why?
3. The third and most important objective is to begin to model how the team is going to work together to complete the project.

The project manager must recognize that first impressions are important; his or her behavior will be carefully monitored and interpreted by team members. This meeting should serve as an exemplary role model for subsequent meetings and reflect the leader's style.

The meeting itself comes in a variety of shapes and forms. It is not uncommon in major projects for the kick-off meeting to involve 1 or 2 days, often at a remote site away from interruptions. This retreat provides sufficient time to make preliminary introductions, to begin to establish ground rules, and to define the structure of the project. One advantage of offsite kick-off meetings is that they provide ample opportunity for informal interaction among members during breaks, meals, and evening activities; such informal interactions are critical to forming relationships.

However, many organizations do not have the luxury of holding elaborate retreats. In other cases the scope of project and level of involvement of different participants does not warrant such an investment of time. In these cases, the key operating principle should be KISS (keep it simple stupid!) Too often when constrained by time, project managers try to accomplish too much during the first meeting; in doing so, issues do not get fully resolved and members come away with an information headache. Managers must remember that there are limits to how much information any one individual can absorb and that there will be opportunities in future meetings to establish ground rules and procedural matters. The primary goal is to run a productive meeting, and objectives should be realistic given the time available. If the meeting is only 1 hour, then the project manager should simply review the scope of the project, discuss how the team was formed, and provide an opportunity for members to introduce themselves.

Establishing Ground Rules

Whether as part of an elaborate first meeting or during follow-up meetings, the project manager quickly must begin to establish operational ground rules for how the team will work together. These ground rules involve not only organizational and procedural issues but also normative issues on how the members will interact with each other. Although specific procedures will vary across organizations and projects, some of the major issues that need to be addressed include the following:

Planning Decisions
- How will the project plan be developed?
- What tools will be used to support the project?
- Will a specific project management software package be used? If so, which one?
- Who will document the planning information?
- Who in addition to the team will be working on the plan?
- What are the specific roles and responsibilities of the participants?
- Who needs to be informed of decisions? How will they be kept informed?
- What are the relative importance of cost, time, and performance?
- What are the deliverables of the project planning process?
- What format is appropriate for each deliverable?
- Who will approve and sign off at the completion of each deliverable?
- Who receives each deliverable?

Tracking Decisions
- How will progress be assessed?
- At what level of detail will the project be tracked?
- How will team members get data from each other?
- How often will they get this data?
- Who will generate and distribute reports?

- Who needs to be kept informed about project progress and how will they be informed?
- What content and format is appropriate for each audience?
- Meetings
  - Where will meetings be located?
  - What kind of meetings will be held?
  - Who will run these meetings?
  - How will agendas be produced?
  - How will information be recorded?

Managing Change Decisions

- How will changes be instituted?
- Who will have change approval authority?
- How will plan changes be documented and evaluated?

Relationship Decisions

- What department or organizations will the team need to interact with during the project?
- What are the roles and responsibilities of each organization (reviewer, approver, creator, user)?
- How will all involved parties be kept informed of deliverables, schedule dates, expectations, etc.?
- How will the team members communicate among themselves?
- What information will and won't be exchanged?

Checklists like this are only a guide; items should be added or deleted as needed. Many of these procedures already will have been established by precedent and will only have to be reviewed briefly. For example, Microsoft Project or Primavera may be the standard software tool for planning and tracking. Likewise, a specific firm is likely to have an established format for reporting status information. How to deal with other issues will have to be determined by the project team. When appropriate, the project manager should actively solicit input from the project team members and draw upon their experience and preferred work habits. This process also contributes to their buying into the operational decisions. Decisions should be recorded and circulated to all members.

During the course of establishing these operational procedures, the project manager, through word and deed, should begin working with members to establish the norms for team interaction. Researchers have identified several norms associated with high performance teams:[4]

- There are no sacred cows: members should feel free to raise any relevant issues.
- We do what it takes to get the job done.
- Confidentiality is maintained; no information is shared outside the team unless all agree to it.
- It is acceptable to be in trouble but it is not acceptable to surprise others. We tell others immediately when deadlines or milestones will not be reached.
- There is zero tolerance for bullying your way through a problem or an issue.
- We agree to disagree, but when a decision has been made, regardless of personal feelings, we get behind it 100 percent.
- We respect outsiders, and do not flaunt our position on the project team.
- Hard work does not get in the way of having fun.

In many cases, some of these norms already may be established as part of the pervasive culture of the organization (see *Project Management in Action: Software Development Teams at Microsoft*). In other cases, as pointed out in Chapter 10, such norms are not part of the dominant culture. The project manager will have to work hard at developing constructive norms.

One way of making norms more tangible is by creating a project team charter that goes beyond the scope statement of the project and states in explicit terms the norms and values of the team. This charter should be a collaborative effort on the part of the core team. Project managers can lead by proposing certain tenets, but they need to be open to suggestions from the team. Once there is general agreement as to the rules of conduct, each member signs the final document to symbolize commitment to the principles it contains. Unfortunately, in some cases this becomes a meaningless ritual because the charter is signed and filed away, never to be discussed again. To have a lasting effect, the charter has to be a legitimate part of the project monitoring system. Just as the team reviews progress toward project objectives, the team assesses the extent to which members are adhering to the principles in the charter.

Project managers play a major role in establishing team norms through personal example. If they freely admit mistakes and share what they have learned from them, other team members will begin to do the same. At the same time, project managers need to intervene when they believe such norms are being violated. They should talk to offenders privately and clearly state their expectations. The amazing thing about groups is that once a group is cohesive, with well-established norms, the members will police themselves so that the manager doesn't have to be the heavy. For example, one project manager confided that his team had a

Software Development Teams at Microsoft

Microsoft Corporation is the leading computer software company in the world. Microsoft's success stems in part from its use of teams of software developers to create and refine new products. No matter how big the project—even a complex one such as the development of the successful Windows 2000 operating system—the project is broken down into small parts that can be handled by teams of about 12 developers. The segment of the project each team is assigned is further subdivided so that each developer is assigned a specific part of the project to work on. Developers with greater experience are given more responsibilities than new members of the team, but the entire team knows that project success depends on the sum of their individual inputs.

Team members provide considerable support for each other. It is not uncommon to see two team members hunched over a computer screen trying to solve a problem. Team members can also be stern critics if a team member fails to perform at an acceptable level.

Developers are granted considerable autonomy in performing their work. At the same time, behavior at Microsoft is governed by a shared work culture that almost everyone follows. One set of informal rules governs the basic issue of working hours. Developers are free to adopt whatever work schedule suits them. If a developer has a sudden insight at midnight, it is not unusual for people to work until dawn. Likewise, if a developer's child is sick, the developer can stay home to take care of the child, and do make-up work at some other time. Along with these "rules" on flexible working hours, almost all developers abide by another norm: They put in the hours necessary to get a job done, even if it requires staying up all night to work on a particularly difficult part of a program.[5]

practice of having a small beanbag on the table at every meeting. If any one member felt that a colleague was spouting hot air or shading the truth, he or she was obligated to toss the beanbag at the speaker.

Managing Subsequent Project Meetings

The project kick-off meeting is one of several kinds of meetings required to manage a project. Other meetings include status report meetings, problem-solving meetings, and audit meetings. Issues unique to these meetings will be discussed in subsequent chapters. For now, here are some general guidelines for running effective meetings.

- Start meetings on time regardless of whether everyone is present.
- Prepare and distribute an agenda prior to the meeting.

- Identify an adjournment time.
- Periodically take time to review how effective previous meetings have been.
- Solicit recommendations and implement changes.
- Assign record keeping.
- Review the agenda before beginning, and tentatively allocate time for each item.
- Prioritize issues so that adjustments can be made given time constraints.
- Encourage active participation of all members by asking questions instead of making statements.
- Summarize decisions and review assignments for the next meeting.
- Prepare and distribute a summary of the meeting to the appropriate people.
- Recognize accomplishments and positive behavior.

Meetings are often considered an anathema to productivity, but this does not have to be the case. The most common complaint is that meetings last too long. Establishing an agenda and adjournment time helps participants budget discussion time and provides a basis for expediting the proceedings. Recordkeeping can be an unwelcome, tedious task. Utilizing laptop computers to record decisions and information in real time can facilitate the communication process. Careful preparation and consistent application of these guidelines can make meetings a vital part of projects.

Establishing a Team Identity

One of the challenges project managers often face in building a team is the lack of full-time involvement of team members. Specialists work on different phases of the project and spend the majority of their time and energy elsewhere. They are often members of multiple teams, each competing for their time and allegiance. Project expert David Frame points out that for many of these specialists a specific project is an abstraction; as a consequence their level of motivation suffers. Project managers need to try to make the project team as tangible as possible to the participants by developing a unique team identity to which participants can become emotionally attached.[6] Team meetings, common location of team members, team names, and team rituals are common vehicles for doing so.

Effective Use of Meetings. Periodic project team meetings provide an important forum for communicating project information. A less obvious function of project meetings is to help establish a concrete team identity. During project meetings, members see that they are not working alone. They are part of a larger project team, and project success depends on the collective efforts of all the team members. Timely gatherings of all the project participants help define team membership and reinforce a collective identity.

Common Location of Team Members.   The most obvious way to make the project team tangible is to have members work together in a common space. This is not always possible in matrix environments where involvement is part-time and members are working on other projects and activities. A worthwhile substitute for a common location is the creation of a project office, sometimes referred to as the project war room or clubhouse. Such rooms are the common meeting place and contain the most significant project documentation. Frequently, their walls are covered with Gantt charts, cost graphs, and other output associated with project planning and control. These rooms serve as a tangible sign of project effort.

Creating a Project Team Name.   Developing a team name such as the "A-Team" or "Casey's Crusaders" is a common device for making a team more tangible. Frequently an associated team logo is also created. Again the project manager should rely on the collective ingenuity of the team to come up with the appropriate name and logo. Such symbols then can be affixed to stationery, T-shirts, coffee mugs, etc., to help signify team membership.

Team Rituals.   Just as corporate rituals help establish the unique identity of a firm, similar symbolic actions at the project level can contribute to a unique team subculture. For example, on one project members were given ties with stripes that corresponded to the number of milestones on the project. After reaching each milestone, members would gather and cut the next stripe off their ties to signify progress.[7] Likewise, Katz reports it was common practice on Digital Equipment's alpha chip design team to recognize people who found a bug in the design by giving them a phosphorescent toy roach. The bigger the bug that was discovered, the bigger the toy roach received.[8] Such rituals help set project work apart from mainstream operations and reinforce a special status.

Creating a Shared Vision

Unlike project scope statements (which include specific cost, completion dates, and performance requirements), a vision involves the less-tangible aspects of project performance. It refers to an image a project team holds in common about how the project will look at completion, how they will work together, and or how customers will accept the project. At its simplest level, a shared vision is the answer to the question, "What do we want to create?" Not everyone will have the same vision, but the images will be similar. Visions come in a variety of shapes and forms; they can be captured in a slogan or a symbol or can be written as a formal vision statement.

What a vision does is more important than what it is. A vision inspires members to give their best effort. Moreover, a shared vision unites professionals with different backgrounds and agendas to a common aspiration. It helps motivate members to subordinate their individual agendas and do what is best for the project. As psychologist Robert Fritz puts it, "In the presence of greatness, pettiness disappears."[9] Visions also provide focus and help communicate less-tangible priorities, helping members make appropriate judgment calls. Finally, a shared vision for a project fosters commitment to the long term and discourages expedient responses that collectively dilute the quality of the project.

Visions can be surprisingly simple. For example, the vision for a new car could be expressed as a "pocket rocket." Compare this vision with the more traditional product description—a sports car in the mid-price range. The "pocket rocket" vision provides a much clearer picture of what the final product should be. Design engineers immediately understand that the car will be both small and fast, and that it should be quick at the getaway, nimble in the turns, and very fast in the straightaways. Obviously, many details would have to be worked out, but the vision would help establish a common framework for making decisions.[10]

There appear to be four essential qualities of an effective vision (see Figure 11–3).

1. First, it must be able to communicate its essential qualities. A vision is worthless if it resides only in someone's head.

2. Second, it has to make strategic sense, given the objectives, constraints, resources, and opportunities inherent within the project. Visions have to be challenging but also realistic. For example, members of a task force directed at overhauling the curriculum at the College of Business at a state university are likely to roll their eyes if the dean announces that the vision

FIGURE 11–3

Requirements for an Effective Project Vision

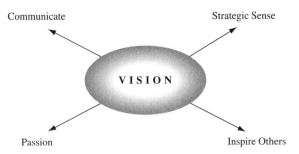

Communicate   Strategic Sense

VISION

Passion   Inspire Others

is to design a curriculum to compete with the business schools at Harvard and Stanford. Conversely, developing the best undergraduate business program in that state may be a realistic vision for the task force.

3. Third, the project manager has to believe in the vision. Passion is required to inspire others!

4. Finally, the vision should be a source of inspiration to others.

Once a project manager accepts the importance of building a shared vision, the next question is how to get a vision for a particular project. First, project managers don't create visions. They act as catalysts and midwives for the formation of a shared vision for a project team. In many cases visions are inherent in the scope and objectives of the project. People naturally get excited about being the first ones to bring a new technology to the market or solve a problem that is threatening their organization. Even with mundane projects, there are often ample opportunities for establishing a compelling vision. One way is to talk to various people involved in the project and find out early on what gets them excited about the project. For some it may be doing a better job than on the last project or the satisfaction in the eyes of the customers when the project is over. Many visions evolve reactively in response to competition. For example, the Kodak team responsible for developing the single-use FunSaver camera was driven by the vision of beating a similar effort by Fuji to the market.[11]

Some experts advocate engaging in formal vision building meetings. These meetings generally involve several steps, beginning with members identifying different aspects of the project and generating ideal scenarios for each aspect. For example, on a construction project the scenarios may include *"no accidents," "no lawsuits," "winning a prize,"* or *"how we are going to spend our bonus for completing the project ahead of schedule."* The group reviews and chooses the scenarios that are most appealing and translates them into vision statements for the project. The next step is to identify strategies for achieving the vision statements. For example, if one of the vision statements is "no lawsuits," members will identify how they will have to work with the owner and subcontractors to avoid litigation. Next, members volunteer to be the keeper of the flame for each statement. The vision, strategies, and the name of the responsible team member are published and distributed to relevant stakeholders.

In more cases than not, shared visions emerge informally. Project managers collect information about what excites participants about the project. They test bits of their working vision in their conversations with team members to gauge the level of excitement the early ideas elicit in others. To some extent they engage in basic market research. They seize opportunities to galvanize the team, such as a disparaging remark by an executive that the project will never get done on time or the threat of a competing firm launching a similar project. Consensus in the beginning is not essential. What is essential is a core group of at least one third of the project team that is genuinely committed to the vision. They will provide the critical mass to draw others aboard. Once the language has been formulated to communicate the vision, then the statement needs to be a staple part of every working agenda, and the project manager should be prepared to deliver a "stump" speech at a moment's notice. When problems or disagreements emerge, all responses should be consistent with the vision.

Much has been written about visions and leadership. Critics argue that vision is a glorified substitute for shared goals. Others argue that it is one of the things that separates leaders from managers. The key is discovering what excites people about a project, articulating this source of excitement in an appealing manner, and finally protecting and nurturing this source of excitement throughout the duration of the project. For a good example, see *Project Management in Action: "Rat Fax" Galvanizes ELITE Team at Newspaper.*

Managing Project Reward Systems

Project managers are responsible for managing the reward system that encourages team performance and extra effort. One advantage they have is that often project work is inherently satisfying, whether it is manifested in an inspiring vision or simple sense of accomplishment. Projects provide participants with a change in scenery, a chance to learn new skills, and an opportunity to break out of their departmental cocoon. Another inherent reward is what was referred to in *The Soul of the New Machine*[12] as "pinball"; project success typically gives team members an option to play another exciting game.

Still, many projects are underappreciated, are boring, interfere with other more significant priorities, and are considered an extra burden. In some of these cases, the biggest reward is finishing the project so that team members can go back to what they really enjoy doing and what will yield the biggest personal payoffs. Unfortunately, when this attitude is the primary incentive, project quality is likely to suffer. In these circumstances, external rewards play a more important role in motivating team performance.

Most project managers we talk to advocate the use of group rewards. Because most project work is a collaborative effort, it only makes sense that the reward system would encourage teamwork. Recognizing individual members regardless of their accomplishments can distract from team unity. Project work is highly interdependent so it can become problematic to distinguish who truly deserves additional credit. Cash bonuses and incentives need to be linked to project

---

Project Management in Action

"Rat Track Fax" Galvanizes ELITE Team at Newspaper

Knight-Ridder's *Tallahassee Democrat*, like many American newspapers in the late 1980s, was struggling to survive in the face of declining revenues. Fred Mott, the general manager of the *Democrat*, was convinced that the key to the newspaper's future was to become more customer focused. Despite his best efforts, little progress was being made toward becoming a customer-driven newspaper. One area that was particularly problematic was advertising, where lost revenues due to errors could be as high as $10,000 a month.

Fred Mott created a team of 12 of his best workers from all parts of the newspaper. They became known as the ELITE team because their mission was to "ELIminate The Errors." At first the team spent a lot of time pointing fingers at each other rather than coming to grips with the error problems at the newspaper. A turning point came when one member produced what became known as "the rat tracks fax" and told the story behind it. It turns out a sloppily prepared ad arrived through a fax machine looking like "a rat had run across the page." Yet the ad passed through the hands of seven employees and probably would have been printed if it had not been totally unreadable. The introduction of this fax broke the ice, and the team started to admit that everyone—not everyone else—was at fault. Then, recalls one member, "We had some pretty hard discussions. And there were tears at those meetings."

The emotional responses galvanized the group to the task at hand and bonded them to one another. The ELITE team looked carefully at the entire process by which an ad was sold, created, printed, and billed. When the process was examined, the team discovered patterns of errors, most of which could be attributed to bad communication, time pressures, and poor attitude. They made a series of recommendations that completely transformed the ad process at the *Democrat*. Under ELITE's leadership, advertising accuracy rose sharply and stayed above 99 percent. Lost revenues from errors dropped to near zero. Surveys showed a huge positive swing in advertiser satisfaction.

The impact of ELITE, however, went beyond numbers. The ELITE team's own brand of responsiveness to customer satisfaction spread to other parts of the newspaper. In effect this team of mostly front line workers spearheaded a cultural transformation at the newspaper that emphasized a premium on customer service.[13]

---

priorities. It makes no sense to reward a team for completing their work early if controlling cost was the number one priority.

One of the limitations of lump-sum cash bonuses is that all too often they are consumed by the household budget to pay the dentist or mechanic. To have more value, rewards need to have lasting significance. Many companies convert cash into vacation rewards, sometimes with corresponding time off. For example, one firm rewarded a project team for getting the job done ahead of schedule with a 4-day, all expenses paid trip to Disney World for the members and their families. That vacation will be remembered for years, and it also rewards spouses and children who, in a sense, also contributed to the project success. Likewise, other firms have been known to give members home computers and entertainment centers. Wise project managers negotiate a discretionary budget so that they can reward teams surpassing milestones with gift certificates to popular restaurants or tickets to sporting events. Impromptu pizza parties and barbecues are also used to celebrate key accomplishments.

Sometimes project managers have to use negative reinforcement to motivate project performance. For example, Ritti recounts the story of one project manager who was in charge of the construction of a new, state-of-the-art manufacturing plant.[14] His project team was working with a number of different contracting firms. The project was slipping behind schedule, mostly because of a lack of cooperation among the different players. The project manager did not have direct authority over many key people, especially the contractors from the other companies. He did, however, have the freedom to convene meetings at his convenience. So the project manager instituted daily 6:00 AM "coordination meetings" that the principals were required to attend. The meetings continued for about 2 weeks until the project got back on schedule. At that time the project manager announced that the next meeting was canceled, and no further *sunrise* meetings were needed.

While project managers tend to focus on group rewards, there are times when they need to reward individual performance. This is done not only to compensate extraordinary effort but also to signal to the others what exemplary behavior is. Experienced project managers recognize the need to develop an informal reward system that is independent of the formal one prescribed by the company. Managers are adroit at utilizing different influence currencies (see Chapter 10) to create a favorable bank account in the minds of project participants. More specifically, among the rewards they use to motivate and recognize individual contributions are the following:

Letters of Commendation. While project managers may not have responsibility for their team members' performance appraisals, they can write letters commending their project performance. These letters can be sent to supervisors to be placed in team members' personnel files.

Public Recognition for Outstanding Work. Superlative workers should be publicly recognized for their efforts. Some project managers begin each status review meeting with a brief mention of project workers who have exceeded their project goals.

Job Assignments.   Good project managers recognize that, while they may not have much budgetary authority, they do have substantial control over who does what, with whom, when, and where. Good work should be rewarded with desirable job assignments. Managers should be aware of member preferences and, when appropriate, accommodate them.

Flexibility.   Being willing to make exceptions to rules, if done judiciously, can be a powerful reward. Allowing members to work at home when a child is sick or excusing a minor discretion, can engender long-lasting loyalty.

We reiterate that individual rewards should be used judiciously, and the primary emphasis should be on group incentives. Nothing can undermine the cohesiveness of a team more than members beginning to feel that others are getting special treatment or that they are being treated unfairly. Camaraderie and collaboration can quickly vanish only to be replaced by bickering and obsessive preoccupation with group politics. Such distractions can absorb a tremendous amount of energy that otherwise would be directed toward completing the project. Individual rewards typically should be used only when everyone in the team recognizes that a member is deserving of special recognition.

Managing the Decision-Making Process

Most decisions on a project do not require a formal team meeting to discuss alternatives and determine solutions. Instead decisions are made in real time as part of the daily interaction patterns between project managers, stakeholders, and team members. For example, as a result of a routine "how's it going?" question, a project manager discovers that a mechanical engineer is having problems meeting the performance criteria for a prototype she is responsible for building within the imposed budget. The project manager goes down the hallway to talk to the designers, explains the problem, and asks what if anything can be done. The designers distinguish which criteria are essential and which ones they think can be compromised. The project manager then checks with the marketing group to make sure the modifications are acceptable. They agree with all but two of the modifications. The project manager goes back to the mechanical engineer and asks whether the proposed changes would help solve the problem. The engineer agrees. Before authorizing the changes, the project manager calls the project sponsor, reviews the events, and gets the sponsor to sign off on the changes. This is an example of how, by practicing MBWA, project managers consult team members, solicit ideas, determine optimum solutions, and create a sense of involvement that builds trust and commitment to decisions.

Still, projects encounter problems and decisions that require the collective involvement of all core team members as well as relevant stakeholders. Group decision making should be used when it will improve the quality of important decisions. This is often the case with complex problems that require the input of a variety of different specialists. Group decision making should also be used when strong commitment to the decision is needed and there is a low probability of acceptance if only one person makes the decision. Participation is used to reduce resistance and secure support for the decision. Group decision making would be called for with controversial problems that have a major impact on project activities or when trust is low within the project team. Guidelines for managing group decision making are provided below.

Facilitating Group Decision Making

Project managers play a pivotal role in guiding the group decision-making process. They must remind themselves that their job is not to make a decision but to facilitate the discussion within the group so that the team reaches a consensus on the best possible solution. Consensus within this context does not mean that everyone supports the decision 100 percent, but that they all agree what the best solution is under the circumstances. Facilitating group decision making essentially involves four major steps. Each step is briefly described below with suggestions for how to manage the process:[15]

1. Problem identification. The project manager needs to be careful not to state the problem in terms of choices (e.g., should we do X or Y?). Rather the project manager should identify the underlying problem to which these alternatives (and probably others) are potential solutions. This allows group members to generate alternatives, not just choose among them. One useful way of defining problems is to consider the gap between where a project is (that is, the present state) and where it should be (the desired state). For example, the project may be 4 days behind schedule or the prototype weighs 2 pounds more than the specifications. Whether the gap is small or large, the purpose is to eliminate it. The task of the group is to find one or more courses of action that will the change the existing state into the desired one.

If you detect defensive posturing during the problem identification discussion, then it may be wise to postpone the problem-solving step if possible. This allows for emotions to subside and members to gain a fresh perspective on the issues involved.

2. Generating alternatives. Once there is general agreement as to the nature of the problem, then the next step is to generate alternative solutions. If the problem requires creativity, then brainstorming is commonly recommended. Have the team generate a list of possible solutions on a flipchart or blackboard. Make sure you establish a moratorium on criticizing or evaluating ideas. Encourage the team to "piggyback" on other's ideas by extending them or combining them into a new idea. The object is to create as many alternatives as possible no matter how outlandish. Some project managers report that for really tough problems they have found it beneficial to conduct such sessions away from the normal work environment; the change in scenery stimulates creativity.

3. Reaching a decision. The next step is to evaluate and assess the merits of alternative solutions. During this phase it is useful to have a set of criteria for evaluating the merits of different solutions. In many cases the project manager can draw on the priorities for the project and have the group assess each alternative in terms of its impact on cost, schedule, and performance as well as reducing the problem gap. For example, if time is critical, then the solution that solves the problem as quickly as possible would be chosen.

During the course of the discussion the project manager attempts to build consensus among the group. This can be a complicated process. Project managers need to provide periodic summaries to help the group keep track of its progress. They need to guarantee that everyone has an opportunity to share opinions and that no individual or group dominates the conversation. It may be useful to bring a 2-minute timer to regulate the use of airtime. When conflicts occur, managers need to apply some of the ideas and techniques discussed in the next section.

Project managers then need to engage in consensus testing to determine which points the group agrees on and which are still sources of contention. Be careful not to interpret silence as agreement, and confirm agreement by asking questions. Ultimately, through thoughtful interaction, the team reaches a "meeting of the minds" as to what solution is best for the project.

4. Follow-up. Once the decision has been made and implemented, it is important for the team to find the time to evaluate the effectiveness of the decision. If the decision failed to provide the anticipated solution, then the reasons why should be explored and the lessons learned added to the collective memory bank of the project team.

Managing Conflict within the Project Team

Disagreements and conflicts naturally emerge within a project team during the life of the project. Participants will disagree over priorities, allocation of resources, the quality of specific work, solutions to discovered problems, and so forth. Some conflicts support the goals of the group and improve project performance. For example, two members may be locked in a debate over a design trade-off decision involving different features of a product. They argue that their preferred feature is what the customer wants. This disagreement may force them to talk to or get more information from the customer, with the result that they realize neither feature is highly valued, but instead the customer wants something else. On the other hand, conflicts can also hinder group performance. Initial disagreements can escalate into heated arguments with both parties storming out of the room and refusing to work together.

The line between functional and dysfunctional conflict is neither clear nor precise. In one team, members may exchange a diatribe of four-letter expletives and eventually resolve their differences. Yet in another project team, such behavior would create irreconcilable divisions and would prohibit the parties from working together productively again. The distinguishing criterion is how the conflict affects project performance, not how individuals feel. Members can be upset and dissatisfied with the interchange, but as long as the disagreement furthers the objectives of the project, then the conflict is functional. Project managers should recognize that conflict is an inevitable and even a desirable part of project work; the key is to encourage functional conflict and manage dysfunctional conflict.

Encouraging Functional Conflict

A shared vision can transcend the incongruities of a project and establish a common purpose to channel debate in a constructive manner. Without shared goals there is no common ground for working out differences. In the previous example involving the design trade-off decision, when both parties agreed that the primary goal was to satisfy the customer, then there was a basis for more objectively resolving the dispute. Therefore, agreeing in advance which priority is most important—cost, schedule, or scope—can help a project team decide what response is most appropriate.

Sometimes it's not the presence of conflict, but the absence of conflict that is the problem. Members may be reluctant to voice objections because of compressed time pressures, self-doubt, or the desire to preserve team harmony. This hesitation robs the team of useful information that might lead to better solutions and the avoidance of critical mistakes. Project managers need to encourage healthy dissent in order to improve problem solving and innovation. They can demonstrate this process by asking tough questions and challenging the rationale behind recommendations. They can also orchestrate healthy conflict by bringing people with different points of view to critical meetings.

Project managers can legitimize dissent within the team by designating someone to play the role of devil's advocate or by asking the group to take 15 minutes to come up with all the reasons the team should not pursue a course of action. Functional conflict plays a critical role in obtaining a deeper understanding of the issues and coming up with the best decisions possible.

One of the most important things project managers can do is model an appropriate response when someone disagrees or challenges their ideas. They need to avoid acting defensively and instead encourage critical debate. They should exhibit effective listening skills and summarize the key issues before responding. They should check to see if others agree with the opposing point of view. Finally, project managers should value and protect dissenters. Organizations have a tendency to create too many yes-men, and the emperor needs to be told when he doesn't have any clothes on.

Managing Dysfunctional Conflict

Managing dysfunctional conflict is a much more challenging task than encouraging functional conflict. First, dysfunctional conflict is hard to clearly identify. A manager might have two highly talented professionals who hate each other's guts, but in the heat of competition they produce meritorious results. Is this a pleasant situation? No. Is it functional? Yes, as long as it contributes to project performance. Conversely, sometimes functional conflict degenerates into dysfunctional conflict. This change occurs when technical disagreements evolve into irrational personality clashes or when failure to resolve an issue causes unnecessary delays in critical project work.

The second major difficulty managers face is that there is often no easy solution to dysfunctional conflict. Project managers have to decide among a number of different strategies to manage it. We offer five possibilities:

Mediate the Conflict.   You can intervene and try to negotiate a resolution by using reasoning and persuasion, suggesting alternatives, and the like. One of the keys is trying to find common ground. In some cases you can make the argument that the win-lose interchange has escalated to the point that it has become lose-lose for everyone and now is the time to make concessions.

Arbitrate the Conflict.   You can impose a solution to the conflict after listening to each party. The goal is not to decide who wins but rather to have the project win. In doing so it is important to seek a solution that allows each party to save face; otherwise the decision may provide only momentary relief. One project manager admits that she has had great success using a King Solomon approach to resolving conflict. She confided she announces a solution that neither party will like and gives the opponents 2 hours to come up with a better solution they can both agree on.

Control the Conflict.   Reducing the intensity of the conflict by smoothing over differences or interjecting humor is an effective strategy. If feelings are escalating, you can adjourn the interaction and hope cooler heads will prevail the next day. If the conflict continues to escalate, you may need to rearrange project assignments, if possible, so that two parties don't have to work together.

Accept the Conflict.   In some cases the conflict will outlive the life of the project and, although a distraction, it is something you can live with.

Eliminate the Conflict.   Sometimes the conflict has escalated to the point that it is no longer tolerable. In this case you remove the members involved from the project. If there is a clear villain then only he or she should be removed. If, as is often the case, two parties are at fault, then it is wise, if possible, to eliminate both individuals. Their removal gives a clear signal to the others on the team that this kind of behavior is unacceptable.

In summary, project managers establish the foundation for functional conflict by establishing clear roles and responsibilities, developing common goals or a shared vision, and using group incentives that reward collaboration. Project managers have to be adroit at reading body language to identify unspoken disagreement. They also have to keep in touch with what is going on in a project to identify small problems that might escalate into big conflicts. Well-timed humor and redirecting the focus to what is best for the project can alleviate the interpersonal tensions that are likely to flare up on a project team.

Team-Building Sessions

Sometimes during the course of a long project, the project manager recognizes that the work processes of the team could be improved with a formal team-building session. A team-building session is particularly appropriate if the manager senses that the team is approaching a transition point in its development. The goal of a team-building session is to improve the project team's effectiveness through better management of project demands and group processes. The team takes an inward look at its own performance, behavior, and culture for the purpose of eliminating dysfunctional behaviors and strengthening functional ones. It critiques its performance, analyzes its way of doing things, and attempts to develop strategies to improve its operation.

The best approach to a team-building session is to bring in an outside facilitator to run the session. This can be an external consultant or an internal staff specialist. The advantages of using an outside facilitator are that it brings a more objective perspective to the table, it frees the project manager to be part of the process, and it provides a specialist trained in group dynamics. Also, if the facilitator is collecting information prior to the session, team members may be more candid and open to the facilitator than they would be to the project manager.

One caveat about using outside facilitators is that too often managers resort to this as a method for dealing with a problem that they have been unable or unwilling to handle themselves. The marching order to the consultant is "fix my team for me." What the managers fail to recognize is that one of the keys to fixing the team is improving the working relationship between themselves and the team. For such sessions to be effective, project managers have to be willing to have their own role scrutinized and be receptive to changing their own behavior and work habits based on the comments and suggestions of the project team.

Facilitators use a wide variety of team-building techniques to elevate team performance. Here is a brief description of one of the more common approaches:

- The first step is to gather information and make a preliminary diagnosis of team performance. Whether through individual interviews or in a group forum, the facilitator asks general questions about the project team performance, for example, What obstacles are getting in the way of the team being able to perform better? The facilitator then summarizes the information in terms of themes.

- Next, the facilitator presents the themes to the project team. When everyone understands the themes, the group ranks them in two ways: (1) in terms of their importance to the team, and (2) in terms of the extent the team has ownership of them. The second dimension is critical. Ownership refers to whether the team has direct influence over the issue. For example, a team probably has little influence over delivery of contracted supplies, but they do control how quickly they inform each other of sudden changes in plans. If the group becomes preoccupied with issues outside their control, the meeting can quickly evolve into a demoralizing gripe session. Therefore, the most important issues that the team has direct control over become the subjects of the agenda.

- During the course of the meeting, lots of interpersonal and group process information is generated, and that is examined too. Thus, the group, with the help of the facilitator, works on two sets of items: the agenda items and the items that emerge from the interaction of the participants. This is where the expertise of the facilitator becomes critical for identifying interaction patterns and their implications for team performance. As the group discusses the important problems, they begin to develop alternatives for action. The team-building session concludes by deciding on specific action steps for remedying problems and setting target dates for *who will do what, when.* These assignments can be reviewed at project status meetings or at a special follow-up session.

It has become fashionable to link team-building activities with outdoor experiences. The outdoor experience, whether it is whitewater rafting down the Rogue

River in Oregon or rock climbing in Colorado, places group members in a variety of physically challenging situations that must be mastered through teamwork, not individual effort. By having to work together to overcome difficult obstacles, team members are supposed to experience increased self-confidence, more respect for one another's capabilities, and a greater commitment to teamwork. No empirical data are available to support such exotic endeavors other than the enthusiastic support of the participants. Such activities are likely to provide an intense common experience that may accelerate the social development of the team. Such an investment of time and money communicates the importance of teamwork and is considered by some a perk for being on the project. At the same time, unless the lessons from these experiences can be immediately transferred to actual project work, their significance is likely to vanish.

Managing Virtual Project Teams

Building a high-performing project team among a mixture of part-time and full-time members is a challenging task. Imagine how much more challenging it would be to build a team when members cannot engage in face-to-face interactions. Such would be the case for a virtual project team in which the team members are geographically situated so that they seldom, if ever, meet face-to-face as a team. For example, Hewlett-Packard's integrated circuit business headquarters and a portion of its R&D facilities are located in Palo Alto, California; the two wafer fabrication operations are located in Corvallis, Oregon, and Fort Collins, Colorado; and the packaging assembly process is primarily in Singapore and Korea. It is not uncommon for professionals at each of these locations to be involved in the same project. When team members are spread across different time zones and continents, the opportunity for direct communication is severely limited and the associated costs of both face-to-face and electronic communication increase dramatically. Electronic communication such as the Internet, e-mail, and teleconferencing takes on much more importance in virtual projects because this is the primary means of communication.

The two biggest challenges involved in managing a virtual project team are:

1. Developing trust
2. Developing effective patterns of communication

Developing Trust

Trust is crucial to virtual project management. Unlike traditional team work, where members can see whether someone has done what he or she has promised, virtual team members depend on the word of distant members. At the same time, it can be difficult to trust someone whom you may have met only one or two times or not at all. Likewise, geographical separation prohibits informal social interactions that are often essential to building trust and camaraderie among team members. As one virtual team member put it, "You can't have a beer together over the Internet."

So how can a project manager facilitate the development of trust within a virtual team?

- First, if it is impossible to hold a face-to-face meeting in the beginning, you need to orchestrate the exchange of social information. A good way to do this is to set aside some time during the initial electronic interchange to introduce each team member and encourage them to share some personal background with the team.
- Second, set clear roles for each team member. Ideally, specific tasks should be assigned to each member so that they can make an immediate contribution to the project.
- Third, set up a communication grid so that project reports and technical information, as well as jokes, logos, and mottos, can be freely shared electronically. Most project software can be linked directly to the Internet, and project Web sites can evolve into an electronic clubhouse for the project members.
- Finally, consistently display enthusiasm and an action orientation in all messages in hopes that your spirit will spread to other team members.

Developing Effective Patterns of Communication

The second major challenge for managing a virtual project team is to establish effective patterns of communication. E-mail and faxes are great for communicating facts but not the feelings behind the facts; nor do they allow for real-time communication. Conference calls and project chat rooms can help, but they also have their limitations. Videoconferencing is a significant improvement over nonvisual electronic forms of communication. Still it is a very expensive medium, and real-time interaction is available only on the most advanced and expensive systems. Even with the best system, managers have to overcome the problem of time zone differences and cultural nuances. Here are some tips for alleviating communication problems and enhancing the performance of virtual teams.

1. Include face-to-face time if at all possible. Hold an initial meeting for all team members so they can meet each other and socialize. Hold subsequent meetings at key junctures in the project. These meetings will help establish ties among team members and facilitate effective problem solving.

2. Keep team members informed on how the overall project is going. Use shareware or develop a central access point such as either a Web site or local area network (LAN) account to provide members with updated project schedules. Team members need to know where they fit in the big picture.

3. Don't let team members vanish. Virtual teams often experience problems getting in touch with each other. Use an Internet scheduling software to store member's calendars.

4. Establish a code of conduct to avoid delays. Team members need to agree not only on what, when, and how information will be shared but also on how and when they will respond to it. Develop a priority system to distinguish messages that require immediate response from those with longer time frames.

5. Establish clear norms and protocols for discovering assumptions and conflicts. Since most communication is nonvisual, you cannot watch body language and facial expressions to develop a sense of what is going on. Instead, you will need to probe deeper when communicating to force members to explain their viewpoints, actions, and concerns more clearly; then you must double-check comprehension.

To a large extent managing a virtual project team is no different from managing a regular project team. The key is working within the constraints of the situation to develop effective ways for team members to interact and combine their talents to complete the project.

Project Team Pitfalls

High-performance project teams can produce dramatic results. However, like any good thing, there is a dark side to project teams that managers need to be aware of. We referred to this phenomenon as "projectitis" in Chapter 3. In this section we examine in more detail some of the pathologies that high-performance project teams can succumb to and highlight what project managers can do to reduce the likelihood of these problems occurring.

Groupthink

Janis first identified *groupthink* as a factor that influenced the misguided 1961 Bay of Pigs invasion of Cuba.[16] His term refers to the tendency of members in highly cohesive groups to lose their critical evaluative capabilities. This malady appears when pressures for conformity are combined with an illusion of invincibility to suspend critical discussion of decisions. As a result, decisions are made quickly with little consideration of alternatives; often the practice leads to fiascoes that, after the fact, appear totally improbable. Some of the symptoms of groupthink include the following:

Illusion of invulnerability. The team feels invincible. It is marked by a high degree of esprit de corps, an implicit faith in its own wisdom, and an inordinate optimism that allows group members to feel complacent about the quality of their decisions.

Whitewash of critical thinking. The group members discuss only a few solutions, ignoring alternatives; they fail to examine the adverse consequences that could follow their preferred course of action; and they too quickly dismiss any alternatives that on the surface appear to be unsatisfactory.

Negative stereotypes of outsiders. *Good guy, bad guy* stereotypes emerge in which the group considers any outsiders who oppose their decisions as the bad guys, who are perceived as incompetent and malicious and whose points are unworthy of serious consideration.

Direct pressure. When a team member does speak out or question the direction in which the team is headed, direct pressure is applied to the dissenter. He or she is reminded that speed is important and that the aim is agreement not argument.

Bureaucratic Bypass Syndrome

Project teams are often licensed to get things done without having to go through normal protocols of the parent organization. Bypassing bureaucratic channels is appealing and invigorating. However, if bypassing becomes a way of life, it results in the rejection of bureaucratic policies and procedures, which provide the glue for the overall organization. A team that operates outside the organization may alienate other workers who are constrained by the norms and procedures of the organization; eventually, these outside bureaucrats will find ways to put up roadblocks and thwart the project team.[17]

Entrepreneurs Disease

Project teams can be intoxicating in the same way that start-up ventures are. Such intoxication is exciting and contributes greatly to the success of the team. But abuse can occur as the team makes decisions based on what is best for the project instead of on what's best for the parent organization. The team becomes myopic in its focus and often views the constraints imposed by the parent organization as something to overcome. When this attitude occurs on developmental projects, the team members, enthralled with their accomplishments, sometimes quit the parent organization and start their own business. While starting a new venture may be good for the project team, it does little for the parent organization that sponsored and financed the development work.

Team Spirit Becomes Team Infatuation

High-performing project teams can be a tremendous source of personal satisfaction. The excitement, chaos, and joy generated by working on a challenging project can be an invigorating experience. Leavitt and Lipman-Blumen even go so far as to say that team members behave like people in love.[18] They become infatuated with the challenge of the project and the talent around them. This total preoccupation with the project and the project team, while contributing greatly to the remarkable success of the project, can leave in its wake a string of broken professional and personal relationships that contribute to burnout and disorientation upon completion of the project.

Going Native

Going native is a phrase first used by the British Foreign Service during colonial times to describe agents who assumed the customs, values, and prerogatives of their foreign country assignment. They did so to the point that they were no longer representing the best interests of the British Empire but rather those of the natives. This same phenomenon can occur within project teams working abroad or in those who become closely identified with their customers. In essence, the customer's interests take precedent over the parent organization's interests. This change in viewpoint can lead to excessive scope creep and open defiance of corporate policy and interests.

Dealing with these maladies is problematic because, in most cases, they are a distortion of a good thing, rather than a simple evil. Awareness is the first step for prevention. The next step is to take preemptive action to reduce the likelihood of these pitfalls occurring. For example, managers can reduce the isolation of the project team by creating work-related connections outside the project team. These interactions naturally occur in a matrix environment where members work on multiple projects and maintain ties to their home department.

Likewise, the isolation of dedicated project teams can be reduced by the timely involvement of external specialists. In either case, the active involvement of relevant members of the parent organization at project status meetings can help maintain the link between the project and the rest of the organization. If the team appears to be suffering from groupthink, then the project manager can encourage functional conflict by playing the devil's advocate to encourage dissent. Finally, formal team-building sessions may reveal dysfunctional norms and refocus the attention of the team on project objectives.

Overcoming Barriers to Performance

Earlier we discussed situational factors that contribute to the development of a high-performing project team. We also stated that it is rare that a project has all of these factors going for it and that project managers have to improvise and do the best they can with the cards they were dealt. Now that the essential elements for managing a project teams have been discussed it is appropriate to discuss some of the strategies that can be used to overcome these barriers.

- **There are more than 10 members per team.** Break the team into smaller subgroups around deliverables or objectives. At the same time create an inner project council of less than 10 members that represent the subgroups.
- **Members did not volunteer to serve on the project team.** This can be a tough one to overcome if most of the members really do not want to be on the project. A lot depends on the perceived importance of the project and pay-offs individuals believe they will receive as a result of project success. See *Project Management in Action: Managing Low-Priority Projects* for tips on overcoming this barrier. The key again is building commitment to the project when it does not exist naturally.
- **Members do not serve on the project from beginning to end.** Insist on having a representative core group that serves from beginning to end. Keep part-timers abreast of developments and document the history of the project so that newcomers can get up to speed quickly.
- **Members are not assigned to the project full-time.** Again insist on having a core group work full-time on the project. Work out in advance the rules for sharing team members with other relevant managers. Here it is critical that top management clearly establish priorities. Try as best you can to create a situation where team members work on the project until they achieve closure on the tasks at hand. Avoid splitting tasks as much as possible. Work on establishing a team identity so that when part-timers do work on the project they feel they are part of something special. Try to arrange it so that all members can enjoy milestone celebrations.
- **Members are part of an organization culture that fosters mistrust and internal competition.** Select people as best you can that do not subscribe to these norms and values. Work hard at establishing a counterculture within the team that cherishes openness and cooperation. Lead by example and celebrate that "we" are doing things the right way.
- **Not all relevant functional areas are represented on the team.** Keep appropriate functional areas abreast of project developments. Involve them at key junctures in the project where their interests are at stake and their input is critical. This can be done formally by inviting them to pivotal meetings or informally through MBWA.
- **The project does not involve a compelling objective.** Again some of the tips in the *Managing Low-Priority Projects* are relevant here. Make

Project Management in Action

Managing Low-Priority Projects

So far the discussion of team building has been directed primarily to significant projects that command the attention and involvement of assigned members. But what about projects that have low priority for team members: the perfunctory task forces that members begrudgingly join? The committee work people get assigned to do? The part-time projects that pull members away from the critical work they would rather be doing? Projects that cause members to question privately why they are doing this?

There is no magic wand available that can be used to transform mildly interested, part-time project teams into high-performance teams. We interviewed several project managers about such project scenarios. They all agreed that these can be very difficult and frustrating assignments and that there are limits to what is possible. Still, they offered tips and advice for making the best of the situation. Most of these tips focus on building commitment to the project when it does not exist naturally.

One project manager advocated orchestrating a large "time" investment up front on such projects, either in the form of a lengthy meeting or a significant early assignment. He viewed this as a form of down payment that members would forfeit if they didn't carry the project to completion.

Others emphasize interjecting as much fun into activities as possible. Here, the rituals discussed under building team identity come into play. People become committed because they enjoy working together on the project. One project manager even confided that the perfect attendance at her project meetings was due primarily to the quality of the donuts she provided.

Another strategy is to make the benefits of the project as real to the team members as possible. One project manager escalated commitment to a mandated accidents prevention task force by bringing accident victims to a project meeting. Another project manager brought the high-ranking project sponsor to recharge the team by reinforcing the importance of the project to the company.

Most project managers emphasized the importance of building a strong personal relationship with each of the team members. When this connection occurs, members work hard not so much because they really care about the project but because they don't want to let the project manager down. Although not couched in influence currency terms, these managers talked about getting to know each member, sharing contacts, offering encouragement, and extending a helping hand when needed.

Finally, all project managers cautioned that nothing should be taken for granted on low-priority projects. They recommend reminding people about meetings and bringing extra copies of materials to meetings for those who have forgotten them or can't find them. Project managers should remain in frequent contact with team members and remind them of their assignments. One manager summed it up best when he said, "Sometimes it all boils down to just being a good nag."

the outcome of the project tangible whether by demonstrating the "pain" the problem you are trying to solve is causing or the benefit people will experience when the project is successfully completed. Work on establishing an internal vision for the team in terms of how they work together (i.e., having fun or being the best).

- **Members are not located within conversational distance of each other.** Bring members together at key junctures in the project, especially at the kick-off meeting. Try to recruit people who have worked together before. Utilize visual telecommunication systems as much as possible.

In most cases these strategies will not eliminate the barrier but rather dampen the effect it has on team development. The project manager's behavior plays a key role in turning around a tough situation. We are constantly amazed at how much genuine enthusiasm can help rally people around a project.

Summary

Project managers often must work under less than ideal conditions to develop a cohesive team committed to working together and completing the project to the best of their abilities. They have to recruit personnel from other departments and manage the temporary involvement of team members. They have to bring strangers together and quickly establish a set of operational procedures that unite their efforts and contributions. They have to be skilled at managing meetings so that the meetings do not become a burden but rather a vehicle for progress. Project managers need to forge a team identity and a shared vision that command the attention and allegiance of participants. They need to use group incentives to encourage teamwork while recognizing when it is appropriate to single out individuals for special recognition. Project managers have to encourage functional conflict that contributes to superior solutions while being on guard against dysfunctional conflict that can break a team apart. In doing these things, they have to be careful not to do too good a job and avoid the pitfalls of excessive group cohesion.

While agendas, charters, visions, rewards, and so forth are important tools and techniques, it has been emphasized both in this chapter and in Chapter 10 that the most important tool a project manager has to build an effective project team is his or her own behavior. Just as the founding members of an organization shape the culture of the organization, the project manager shapes and influences the internal culture of the project team. A positive example can define how team members respond to changes, how they handle new tasks, and how they relate to one another and the rest of the organization. There is no easy way to lead by example. It requires personal conviction, discipline, sensitivity to team dynamics, and a constant awareness of how personal actions are perceived by others.

12

MANAGING PROJECTS ACROSS ORGANIZATIONS

. . . being a good partner has become a key corporate asset. I call it a company's collaborative advantage. In the global economy, a well-developed ability to create and sustain fruitful collaborations gives companies a significant competitive leg up.
Rosabeth Moss Kanter[1]

It is rare in today's downsized world to find significant projects that are being completed totally in-house. Outsourcing or contracting significant segments of project work to other companies is commonplace. For example, nine states attempting to unify the accounting of all their state agencies did not have the internal resources to implement such a large project. Hence, project teams were formed consisting of personnel from software, hardware, and accounting firms to implement the projects. Small high-tech firms outsource research to determine what features customers value in new products they are developing. Even industry giants such as Microsoft and Intel commonly hire independent firms to test new products they are developing.

Contracting project work has long been the norm in the construction industry, where firms hire general contractors, who in turn, hire and manage cadres of subcontractors to create new buildings and structures. For example, the Chunnel project, which created a transportation tunnel between France and England, involved more than 250 organizations. Contracting is not limited to large projects. For example, an insurance company worked with an outside contractor to develop an answering service that directs customers to specific departments and employees. And the production of this book was outsourced by its publisher to a production service. The trend for the future suggests that more and more projects will involve working with people from different organizations.

In this chapter we will extend the previous two chapters' discussion of building and managing relations by focusing specifically on issues surrounding working with people from other organizations to complete a project. The term *partnering* is used to describe this process. Partnering is a process for transforming contractual arrangements into a cohesive, collaborative team that deals with issues and problems encountered in implementing projects to meet a customer's need. First, we review the genesis of project partnering and its major assumptions. This introduction is followed by a general description of the partnering process and the barriers to collaboration. The focus then shifts to the art of negotiating that is at the heart of effective partnering. Negotiating skills and techniques for resolving disagreements and reaching optimal solutions are then presented. The chapter closes with a brief note on managing customer relations. In addition, an appendix on contract management is included to suggest some differences in the nature of partnering arrangements—given a particular type of contract.

The Genesis of Project Partnering

The term *partnering*, as it relates to projects, emerged during the 1980s in the construction industry. During this period a study conducted by the Construction Industry Institute concluded that "the U.S. construction industry is ill."[2] The report went on to document the general decline in productivity over the past 2 decades. Delays in construction were common and expensive, and litigation related to design and construction was rising at an exponential rate. As one building contractor put it, "The only people making money in construction are the lawyers."

The industry response was to test the concept of "partnering" with a few adventurous owners and construction firms. The intent was to keep the formal contract intact but change the way the owner and construction firms interact during project implementation. A variety of definitions of partnering are found in the literature. Two of the more popular ones are noted here:

> Partnering is a long-term commitment between two or more organizations for the purpose of achieving specific business objectives by maximizing the effectiveness of each participant's resources. This requires changing traditional relationships to a shared culture without regard to organizational boundaries. The relationship is based upon trust, dedication to common goals, and an understanding of each other's individual expectations and values. Expected benefits include improved efficiency and cost effectiveness, increased opportunity for innovation, and the continuous improvement of quality products and services.[3]

> Project partnering is a method of transforming contractual relationships into a cohesive, cooperative project team with a single set of goals and established procedures for resolving disputes in a timely manner.[4]

Partnering is more than a set of goals and procedures; it is a state of mind, a philosophy on how to conduct business with other organizations. Partnering represents a commitment from all the participants working on a project to respect, trust, and collaborate. Today, partnering is used across all industries because it makes good business sense.

Partnering is based on the assumption that the traditional adversarial relationship between owner and contractor is ineffective and self-defeating. The basis for this adversarial posturing centers on the inherent conflict between the cost to the owner and the profit to the contractor. This is essentially a zero-sum game in which one party's gain is the other party's loss. The apparent conflict of interest predisposes owners and contractors to be suspicious of the motives and actions of each other. For the owners, this suspicion manifests itself by oppressively monitoring the contractor's performance, challenging each and every request to make an adjustment in plans or budget, and forcing compliance by withholding funds. Contractors respond by exploiting loopholes in the contract, withholding or manipulating information, or taking advantage of the owner's ignorance to inflate cost estimates and charging for unnecessary work.

Suspicion and mistrust prevent effective problem solving. Mistakes and problems are often hidden. When they surface, a game of "hot potato" is played as to who is responsible for correcting them. When conflicts emerge they are often deferred up the hierarchy. This creates costly delays as well as, at times, questionable responses because upper management is often too removed from the situation to make an effective decision. Many disputes end up in court as each side realizes that the only way to protect its interests is through litigation. To some extent litigation becomes a self-fulfilling prophecy. Managers spend almost as much time doing the work as they do preparing a case. The tragedy is that often small problems mushroom into major obstacles because problems were not resolved at inception.

Partnering naturally emerged as people began to realize that the traditional win–lose adversarial relationship between owner and contractor degenerates into a costly lose–lose situation for all the parties. Furthermore, partnering assumes that the parties share sufficient common goals to warrant a more collaborative relationship. For example, both contractors and owners want projects completed on time and safely. Neither party wants rework. Both parties would prefer to avoid costly litigation. Each party would like to reduce costs while at the same time improving quality.

The existence of common goals, the prohibitive costs of the adversarial approach, and the benefits that can be shared provide an opportunity for transforming a competitive situation into a more collaborative relationship. The differences between the traditional approach and the partnering approach to managing contracted relationships are summarized in Table 12–1.[5]

TABLE 12–1   **Key Practices in Partnering Relationships versus Traditional Practices**

Key Practices in Partnering Relationships	*Traditional Practices*
Mutual trust forms the basis for working relationships.	Suspicion and distrust; each party is wary of the motives for actions by the other.
Shared goals and objectives ensure common direction.	Each party's goals and objectives, while similar, are geared to what is best for them.
Joint project team exists with high level of interaction.	Independent project teams; teams are spatially separated with managed interactions.
Open communications avoids misdirection and bolsters effective working relationships.	Communications are structured and guarded.
Long-term commitment provides the opportunity to attain continuous improvement.	Single project contracting is the norm.
Objective critique is geared to candid of performance.	Objectivity is limited due to fear of assessment reprisal and lack of continuous improvement opportunity.
Access to each other's organization resources occurs.	Access is limited with structured procedures and self-preservation taking priority over total optimization.
Total company involvement requires commitment from CEO to team members.	Involvement is normally limited to project level personnel.
Integration of administrative systems equipment occurs.	Duplication and/or translation occurs with attendant costs and delays.
Risk shared jointly among the partners which encourages innovation and continuous improvement.	Risk is transferred to the other party.

Major benefits can be enjoyed when partnering arrangements extend across multiple projects and are long term. For example Bechtl, Inc. began a partnering arrangement with Union Carbide in 1988 to provide engineering, procurement, and construction services for all major projects involving Union Carbide's chemical and plastics group. Among the many advantages for establishing a long-term partnership are the following:[6]

- **Reduced administrative costs.** The costs associated with bidding and selecting a contractor are eliminated. Contract administration costs are reduced as partners become knowledgeable of their counterpart's legal concerns.

- **More efficient utilization of resources.** Contractors have a known forecast of work while owners are able to concentrate their workforce on core businesses and avoid the demanding swings of project support.

- **Improved communication.** As partners gain experience with each other, they develop a common language and perspective, which reduces misunderstanding and enhances collaboration.

- **Improved innovation.** The partners are able to discuss innovation and associated risks in a more open manner and share risks and rewards fairly.
- **Improved performance.** Over time partners become more familiar with each other's standards and expectations and are able to apply lessons learned from previous projects to current projects.

Partnering requires more than a simple handshake. Partnering typically entails a considerable up-front investment in time and resources to forge a common team identity among participants from different organizations, and the creation of mechanisms designed to sustain and expand collaboration over the course of the project.

The actual partnering process can take many shapes and forms, depending on the nature of the project and contract, the number of organizations involved, and their prior experience working together. Still, our research suggests that there are several core elements associated with most first-time partnering endeavors.[7] These elements are summarized in Figure 12–1.

Project Management in Action

The Kodak Orion Project[8]

An excellent example of multinational companies employing partnering on a project is the Orion Project: Kodak, Fuji, Canon, Minolta, and Nikon joined forces to create a new camera technology. This project developed a new film cassette that drops into a camera without threading or adjusting. The cassette can also be used for storing negatives, rather than having loose negatives as is currently the case. No one firm had the total competency or resources to develop the new technology, and moreover, be sure others in the industry would adopt the technology. Research strongly suggested customers would readily accept and use the new technology. Hence the benefits provided a compelling reason for major players in the industry to develop a strong bond because of the shared vision of a new photo system that would be truly exciting and would have a major impact on company performance and the photo industry.

The partnering arrangement did not just happen. Partners were selected by their belief in a shared vision, ability to pursue separate goals and still support and contribute to the partnership, and skills that complement each other. The companies worked cooperatively and voluntarily shared progress reports. The number of partners was restricted to five. Top management support was persistent and visible. All partners were able to develop their own products using the new technology platform, and they launched them on the agreed date of April 22, 1996.

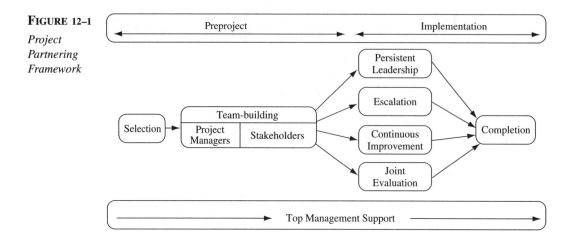

FIGURE 12–1

Project Partnering Framework

Preproject Activities: Setting the Stage for Successful Partnering

Selecting a Partner

Ideally contractors and even owners are selected based on an established track record of partnering on previous projects. Owners select only contractors with an interest and expertise in partnering. Likewise, contractors screen potential work according to the owner's commitment to partnering principles. In some cases partnering provisions are explicitly stated in an advertised "invitation for bid" (IFB) and are a formal part of the contract. In other cases, the decision to pursue a partnering approach is made after the contract is awarded.

In either case, the first step is to get the commitment of the top management of all the firms involved to use the partnering process. For example, in the case of one public works contract, the owner arranged a meeting with the general contractor. At this meeting the owner congratulated the contractor for winning the contract and expressed a desire to manage the project according to partnering principles. The owner described in detail how this partnership would work and the benefits each would enjoy. The owner was careful to frame the proposal as an invitation and indicated that the contractor was free to choose whether to try partnering. Partnering will not work unless all sides freely commit themselves to it. Intimidation, shallow inducements, or half-hearted commitments on the part of either party will lead to failure.

Team-Building: The Project Managers

Once top management from the major parties agree to try partnering, the next step is to begin to build a collaborative relationship among the key people from each organization who will actually be responsible for managing the project. This typically involves the lead representatives or project managers from the different organizations. For experienced managers, this may simply involve meeting to review mutual objectives and outline the implementation of the partnering process. For less-experienced managers this may involve more elaborate activities. For example, one CEO who regularly oversees capital projects in excess of $50 million insists on sending the top managers from the respective organizations to a week-long leadership conference high in the Rocky Mountains. There participants are exposed to principles of teamwork and effective communication. The training not only reinforces collaborative concepts but more importantly accelerates the evolution of relationships from strangers to partners. Not only do they attend the conference together, they are also required to be roommates. The CEO reports that after 1 week his project manager knows whether or not he can work with the other parties. If they cannot, then new managers are assigned or, under extreme circumstances, the project is canceled.

Team Building: The Stakeholders

Once the principal managers establish a personal commitment to partnering, the next step is to expand this commitment to the other key managers and specialists who will be working together on the project. Team-building workshops are held prior to starting the project. All the key players from the different firms, e.g., engineers, architects, lawyers, specialists, and other staff, attend the workshops. In many cases, firms find it useful to hire an outside consultant to design and facilitate the sessions. Such a consultant is typically well-versed in interorganizational team building and can provide an impartial perspective. In other cases, the project managers jointly design and lead the sessions.

The length and design of the team-building sessions will depend on the experience, commitment, and skill level of the participants. For example, one project, in which the owner and the contractors were relatively inexperienced but committed to partnering, utilized a 3-day workshop. The first day was devoted to ice-breaking activities and establishing the rationale behind partnering. The conceptual foundation was supported by exercises and mini-lectures on teamwork, synergy, win–win, and constructive feedback. The second day began by examining the problems and barriers that have prevented collaboration in the past. Representatives from the different organizations were separated and each asked the following:

- What actions do the other groups engage in that create problems for us?
- What actions do we engage in that we think create problems for them?
- What recommendations would we make to improve the situation?

The groups shared their responses and asked questions on points needing clarification. Participants noted agreements and disparities in the lists and identified specific problems.

Once problem areas were noted, each group was assigned the task of identifying its specific interests and goals for the project. Groups shared goals and devoted special attention to establishing common goals. Recognizing shared goals is critical for transforming the different groups into a cohesive team.

Members from the different organizations were put into smaller mixed groups composed of their counterparts from the other organizations. For example, all of the lawyers were put in one group. These groups were assigned specific problems germane to their area of responsibility and asked to work out a recommended solution for each problem. The second day concluded with each group reporting their solutions to the entire group for review and agreement.

The final day of the workshop was devoted to consolidating the efforts of the previous day into a series of agreements and procedures to guide the partnering process. The session culminated with the creation of a project charter signed by all of the participants. This charter states their common goals for the projects as well as the procedures that will be used to achieve these goals (see Figure 12–2 for an example of the first page of a project charter).

FIGURE 12–2

Partnering Charter

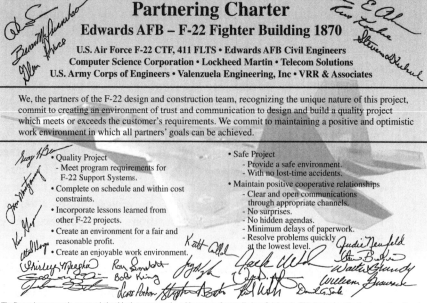

Partnering Charter

Edwards AFB – F-22 Fighter Building 1870

U.S. Air Force F-22 CTF, 411 FLTS • Edwards AFB Civil Engineers
Computer Science Corporation • Lockheed Martin • Telecom Solutions
U.S. Army Corps of Engineers • Valenzuela Engineering, Inc • VRR & Associates

We, the partners of the F-22 design and construction team, recognizing the unique nature of this project, commit to creating an environment of trust and communication to design and build a quality project which meets or exceeds the customer's requirements. We commit to maintaining a positive and optimistic work environment in which all partners' goals can be achieved.

• Quality Project
  - Meet program requirements for F-22 Support Systems.
• Complete on schedule and within cost constraints.
• Incorporate lessons learned from other F-22 projects.
• Create an environment for a fair and reasonable profit.
• Create an enjoyable work environment.

• Safe Project
  - Provide a safe environment.
  - With no lost-time accidents.
• Maintain positive cooperative relationships
  - Clear and open communications through appropriate channels.
  - No surprises.
  - No hidden agendas.
  - Minimum delays of paperwork.
  - Resolve problems quickly at the lowest level.

The Partnering concept is a team relationship that promotes the achievement of mutually beneficial goals. This Partnering Charter does not create any legally enforceable rights or duties. Any changes to the contracts must be made by the contracting officers under the terms of the written contracts.

It is imperative to carefully set the stage for successful project implementation. Too often managers become preoccupied with the plans and technical challenges of the project and assume that people issues will work themselves out over time. Partnering recognizes that people issues are as important if not more important than technical issues. After all, who solves technical problems? Partnering accepts that one of the major barriers to effective collaboration is that participants come from different organizational cultures with different standards, habits, and priorities. The team-building sessions provide an opportunity for people to discuss differences and similarities and to begin to build a relationship with their counterparts before the project starts. At best, a common team culture begins to emerge that is based on successfully completing the project. At worst, participants develop a shared understanding so that cultural differences can coexist while jointly achieving the common objectives of the project.

Project Implementation: Sustaining Collaborative Relationships

One of the objectives of the team-building sessions is to establish a "we" as opposed to an "us and them" attitude toward the project. Some companies reinforce this point by having the management teams from the different organizations work at the same location. Our experience tells us that colocation is critical and well worth the added expense and inconvenience. A second objective of the sessions is to establish in advance mechanisms designed to ensure that this collaborative spirit is able to withstand the problems and setbacks that invariably will occur on the project. These mechanisms require the unwavering, consistent, and fanatical support of senior management. Among the most significant mechanisms are problem resolution, continuous improvement, joint evaluation, and persistent leadership.

Problem Resolution

Escalation is the primary control mechanism for dealing with and resolving problems. The basic principle is that problems should be resolved at the lowest level within a set time limit (i.e., 24 hours), or they are "escalated" to the next level of management. If so, the principals have the same time limit to resolve the problem, or it gets passed on to the next higher level. "No action" is not an option. Nor can one participant force concessions from the other by simply delaying the decision. There is no shame in pushing significant problems up the hierarchy; at the same time, managers should be quick to point out those problems or questions that subordinates should have been able to resolve on their own.

Continuous Improvement

Partnering assumes that continuous improvement is a joint effort to eliminate waste and pursue opportunities for cost savings. Risks as well as benefits are shared 50/50 between the principals with the owner adhering to a fast-track review to withstand the problems and setbacks that will invariably occur in the project approval process. *Project Management in Action: Incentive System for a Partnering Project* shows an alternative arrangement from a project involving two partners and an owner.

Joint Evaluation

Joint evaluation means that all involved parties meet on a regular basis to review and evaluate the partnering process. Specific criteria such as teamwork and timely

---

Project Management in Action

Incentive System for a Partnering Project

The project was a high-technology oil drilling ship for the North Sea. The ship would be capable of finding a selected location within less than 1 meter and hold the location for drilling. The project included the owner and two major partners. Early, precontract meetings indicated all three were interested in the benefits partnering could offer. All three wanted to complete the project on time, within budget, and meet specifications.

After several meetings, the owner and partners agreed to a simple incentive system to encourage continuous improvement during project implementation. The crux of the system centered on sharing *proportionally* any savings in total project cost or in cost overruns. The proportions for the project were determined by the money value (NKr) each controlled—the owner, 33 percent, and 22 percent, and 45 percent respectively for the partners.

This exhibit (Figure 12–3) explains the numbers and process to all stakeholders.

Three cost levels were agreed upon: *not to exceed cost, most likely cost,* and *target cost.* Getting to these agreed costs was sticky, but the team did it.

Everyone came out a winner! The project was on time, under target cost, and met specifications and expectations. Success can be attributed to primarily three factors:

1. The incentive system forced the owner to join the effort.
2. Sharing was proportional to cost responsibility.
3. The three project teams were housed in one location. Responsibility for project implementation, control, and improvements was charged to the merged project team.

The project manager suggests that the last factor of merging the three independent teams seems to be a key that significantly increases the chances of success.

FIGURE 12–3

*Incentive
System for
Ship Contract*

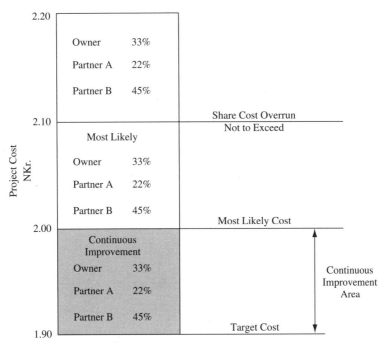

problem resolution are evaluated. This provides a forum for identifying problems not only with the project but also with working relationships so that they can be resolved quickly and appropriately. Joint evaluation usually includes a periodic survey. Comparing survey responses period by period identifies areas of improvement and potential problems. See Figure 12–4 for a partial example of a survey.

Persistent Leadership

Project managers and their subordinates must "walk the talk" and consistently display a collaborative as opposed to confrontational response to problem solving. This is especially true early in the project, where mutual trust will be tested by how the partners respond to the first disagreements or setbacks that emerge. Likewise, the project managers have to reward those within their own organization who adhere to the principles of partnering as well as admonish those who resort to more adversarial practices. Finally, when it is time to celebrate a significant milestone, no matter who is responsible, all parties should gather to celebrate the success. This reinforces a common identity.

FIGURE 12–4

*Sample
Partnering
Evaluation
Survey*

EVALUATING PARTNERING PROCESS: Attitudes, teamwork, process. (Answers are collected separately from owner and contractor participants. They are then compared, aggregated, and shared with the project team.

1. Communications between the owner/contractor personnel are

1	2	3	4	5

Difficult,   Easy, open,
guarded   up front

2. Top management support of partnering process is

1	2	3	4	5

Not evident or   Obvious and
inconsistent   consistent

3. Problems, issues, or concerns are

1	2	3	4	5

Ignored   Attacked
                                                                                                    promptly

4. Cooperation between owner and contractor personnel is

1	2	3	4	5

Cool, detached,   Genuine,
unresponsive,   unreserved,
removed   complete

5. Responses to problems, issues, or concerns frequently become

1	2	3	4	5

Personal issues   Treated as
                                                                                                    project problems

Project Completion: Celebrating Success

Once the project is completed, management jointly needs to review accomplishments as well as disappointments and derive lessons to be applied to future projects. This formal review of project execution is typically accompanied by a more festive celebration (picnic or banquet) involving all the participants. Top management takes advantage of this social function to recognize special contributions. Such a festivity provides a sense of closure and reaffirms the collaborative nature of the project.

Why Project Partnering Efforts Succeed or Fail

Since organizations continue to downsize and concentrate on their core competencies, the use of outside sources to assist or implement projects will continue to increase. The trend for the future suggests there will be an even greater need for partnering (see *Project Management in Action: Competing Against Giants* for another example of partnering). Although the results achieved from successful partnering can be phenomenal, we have noticed three areas that lead to the breakdown of the partnering arrangement and an additional area that is frequently overlooked.

Lax Senior Management. The first and most significant problem is with senior management—the owner and contractor. The owner and contractor must have compelling reasons to make the partnering relationship work. Although most

---

Project Management in Action

Competing against Giants[9]

SATT Control (SC) is a Swedish electronics firm that sells electronic products and control systems world-wide. It has 550 employees in Sweden and about the same number abroad. So how does SC successfully bid against such electronic giants as ABB, Siemens, and Hewlett Packard on major contracts for equipment that the company has never sold before? In the words of Hedberg and his coauthors, SC does so by acting as *system integrator*. In this role SC recruits a contracting syndicate by preparing a system description and dividing the system into various subsystems with each potential partner bidding for a part of the system. SC's ability to describe the system and divide it into subsystems that can be outsourced are two of its core competencies.

Another core competence at SC is project management. After the company has received an order for a project, one of its first actions is to work with the customer to develop clear specification of functions. While time consuming, this process is critical to success. The first step is to specify what the system is supposed to do, before deciding how it is to be done. This is commonly referred to as designing system architecture. It is crucial that the specifications are correct at the outset otherwise errors reappear all down the line. SC works hard at developing a common agreement among all the partners as to what the basic concept of the project is.

SC is also adroit at establishing a collaborative atmosphere among all the partners. The key is instilling a sense of "what is good for you is good for me." This comes from a history of treating partners with mutual respect and drafting contracts that share and not isolate risks.

partnering arrangements start out with good intentions, when senior management fails to keep on top of the project and partnership, the seeds for failure are planted. The breakdown typically begins with a problem that needs resolution. A minor problem is escalated instead of being solved at the first level. Team members are hesitant to accept risk. The owner and contractor fail to return the problem to the first level where it should have been solved. Soon all problems are escalated and the relationship deteriorates as both sides hurl accusations and begin defensive posturing. Senior management must give clear signals that team members are empowered and encouraged to make decisions at the lowest possible level. The same problem occurs when senior management fails to resolve an escalated problem within the time limit set. Senior management is not leading the way. Senior management support of the partnering process cannot be ad hoc; leadership and commitment must be 100 percent and constant. Partnering will be successful only if senior management works at it!

Cultural Differences.   A second major reason partnering arrangements break down is the failure to deal adequately with cultural differences among the contributing organizations. Differences in management styles, terminology, operating procedures, and perspectives of time can result in culture shock that frustrates the development and maintenance of good rapport between the participants. The key is to try to merge these cultural differences into a common team culture that is based on successfully completing the project. This process begins with the team-building sessions but must be a priority throughout the project. Much of the material on developing a high-performing team discussed in Chapter 11 must be applied. Each organization also must be careful to select and place savvy professionals in key positions who are adept at forging relationships with people who do not necessarily share the same priorities, time orientation, or work habits.

Lack of a Formal Evaluation Procedure.   A third reason for a partnering relationship to deteriorate is the absence of a formal evaluation procedure. We estimate that fewer than 20 percent of partnering projects have a formal, effective procedure for evaluating the partnering process. Without regular evaluation, problems and deterioration of the process will not be recognized until it is too late to correct things. Regardless of the procedure used (questionnaires, interviews by outsiders, weekly evaluation meetings), it should regularly identify problems and opportunities at the operating level. The "partnering report card" measures team performance and encourages team accountability. In addition, the evaluation should measure and track the overall state of the partnering relationship. The latter measures if the relationship is improving or degenerating.

Continuous Improvement.   Finally, there is one opportunity that most partnering arrangements fail to exploit as fully as they should—continuous improvement. Many partnering projects give lip service to continuous improvement, but that is the extent of it. In the words of one owner, "I expect that of any hired software contractor." The key, for those who have been successful, is setting up an incentive program to encourage a contractor to seek improvements and innovation as the project is implemented. These procedures need to be set up *before* the project begins. In essence there is little incentive for a contractor to strive for improvements, except for repeat business and reputation. All of the risk of innovation failure is on the contractor. An approach known as the "50/50 percent split" appears to work well and has resulted in saving millions of dollars across a variety of projects—e.g., R&D, construction, time to market. This procedure has the owner and contractor share the costs (risk) for any innovation and share rewards on a 50/50 basis.

Partnering is a conscious effort on the part of management to form collaborative relationships with personnel from different organizations to complete a project. For partnering to work, the individuals involved need to be effective negotiators capable of merging interests and discovering solutions to problems that contribute to the ultimate success of the project and the partnership.

The Art of Negotiating

Effective negotiating is critical to successful partnering. All it takes is one key discussion to break down to unravel a partnering arrangement. At the same time, negotiating is pervasive through all aspects of project management work. Project managers must negotiate support and funding from top management. They must negotiate staff and technical input from functional managers. They must coordinate with other project managers and negotiate project priorities and commitments. They must negotiate within their project team to determine assignments, deadlines, standards, and priorities. Project managers must negotiate price and standards with vendors and suppliers. A firm understanding of the negotiating process, skills, and tactics is essential to project success.

Many people approach negotiating as if it is a competitive contest. Each negotiator is out to win as much as he or she can for his or her side. Success is measured by how much is gained compared with the other party. While this may be applicable when negotiating the sale of a house, it is not true for project management. *Project management is not a contest.* First, the people working on the project, whether they represent different companies or departments within the same organization, are not enemies or competitors but rather allies or colleagues. They have formed a temporary alliance to complete a project. For this alliance to work requires a certain degree of trust, cooperation, and honesty. Second, although the parties within this alliance may have different priorities and standards, they are bound by the success of the project. If conflicts escalate to the point where negotiations break down and the project comes to a halt, then everyone loses.

Third, unlike bartering with a street vendor, the people involved in project work have to continue to work together. Therefore, it behooves them to resolve disagreements in a way that contributes to the long-term effectiveness of their working relationship. Finally, as pointed out in the Chapter 11, conflict on a project is good. When dealt with effectively, it can lead to innovation, better decisions, and more creative problem-solving.

Successful project managers accept this noncompetitive view of negotiation and realize that negotiation is essentially a two-part process.[10] The first part deals with reaching an agreement; the second part is the implementation of that agreement. It is the implementation phase, not the agreement itself, that determines the success of negotiations. All too often, managers reach an agreement with someone only to find out later that the person failed to do what he or she agreed to do or that the actual response fell far short of expectations. Experienced project managers recognize that implementation is based on satisfaction not only with the outcome but also with the process by which the agreement was reached. If someone feels they have been bullied or tricked into doing something, this feeling will invariably be reflected by halfhearted compliance and passive resistance.

Veteran project managers do the best they can to merge individual interests with what is best for the project and come up with effective solutions to problems. Fisher and Ury from the Harvard Negotiation Project champion an approach to negotiating that embodies these goals.[11] It emphasizes developing win–win solutions while protecting yourself against those who would take advantage of your forthrightness. Their approach is called *Principle Negotiation* and is based on four key points, to which we have added a fifth–"Establish rapport before you negotiate."

Principle Negotiation
1. Separate the people from the problem.
2. Establish rapport before you negotiate.
3. Focus on interests not positions.
4. Invent options for mutual gain.
5. When possible use objective criteria.

Separate the People from the Problem

Too often personal relations become entangled with the substantive issues under consideration. Instead of attacking the problem, people attack each other. Once people feel attacked or threatened, their energy naturally goes to defending themselves not to solving the problem. The key, then, is to focus on the problem—not the other person—during the negotiation. Avoid personalizing the negotiation and framing the negotiation as a contest. Instead, try to keep the focus on the problem to be resolved. In Fisher and Ury's words: *Be hard on the problem, soft on the people.*

By keeping the focus on the issues, not personalities, negotiators are better able to let the other person blow off steam. On important problems it is not uncommon for people to become upset, frustrated, and angry. However, one angry attack produces an angry counterattack, and the discussion quickly escalates into a heated argument, an emotional chain reaction. In some cases a person uses anger as a means of intimidating and forcing concessions because the other person wishes to preserve the relationship. When people become emotional, negotiators should keep a cool head and remember the old German proverb, "Let anger fly out the window." In other words, in the face of an emotional outburst, imagine opening a window and letting the heat of the anger out the window.[12] Avoid taking things personally, and redirect personal attacks back to the question at hand. Don't react to the emotional outburst, but try to find the issues that triggered it. Skilled negotiators keep their cool in stressful times and, at the same time, build a bond with others by empathizing and acknowledging common sources of frustration and anger.

Establish Rapport before You Negotiate

While it is important to separate the person from the problem during actual negotiations, it is beneficial to have a friendly rapport with the other person prior to negotiating. Friendly rapport is consistent with the social network tenet (introduced in Chapter 9) of building a relationship before you need it. Psychologist Robert Cialdini refers to this as the "liking rule." As he puts it, "We most prefer to say yes to the requests of someone we know and like."[13]

You can reduce the likelihood of misunderstandings and getting off on the wrong foot by having a history of interacting in a friendly, responsive manner with the other person. If, in the past, the relationship has been marked by healthy give and take in which both parties have demonstrated a willingness to accommodate the interests of each other, then neither individual is likely to adopt an immediate win–lose perspective. Furthermore, a positive relationship adds a common interest beyond the specific points of contention. Not only do both parties want to reach an agreement that suits their individual interests, but they also want to do so in a manner that preserves their relationship. Each is therefore more likely to seek solutions that are mutually beneficial. Conversely, if the relationship has been dominated by one individual who takes more than he or she gives, then the resentment and mistrust that have been slowly building over time will naturally spill into the immediate interaction.

It is not always possible to build a reservoir of goodwill prior to negotiating. In many cases, the situation dictates working with people you have never met.

Although not ideal, you can still practice the principle. Here a little bit of schmoozing can go a long way in creating a more receptive mood for bargaining. Instead of jumping right into the problem, spend a little time talking about something you have in common with the other party like family, traffic, or the weather. For example, if you notice a daughter's high school graduation picture proudly displayed on a bookshelf, make some innocent inquiries about what school she graduated from and what she is doing now. Be willing to share similar information about your family. This establishes that you both share something important that will help develop mutual trust.

Focus on Interests Not Positions

Negotiations often stall when people focus on positions:

I'm willing to pay $10,000. No, it will cost $15,000.

I need it done by Monday. That's impossible, we can't have it ready until Wednesday.

While such interchanges are common during preliminary discussions, managers must prevent this initial posturing from becoming polarized. When such positions are stated, attacked, and then defended, each party figuratively begins to draw a line they will not cross. This line creates a win–lose scenario where someone has to lose by crossing the line in order to reach an agreement. As such, the negotiations can become a war of wills, with concessions being seen as a loss of face.

The key is to focus on the interests behind your positions (what you are trying to achieve) and separate these goals from your ego as best you can. Not only should you be driven by your interests, but you should try to identify the interests of the other party. Ask why it will cost so much or why it can't be done by Monday. At the same time, make your own interests come alive. Don't just say that it is critical that it be done by Monday; explain what will happen if it isn't done by Monday.

Sometimes when the true interests of both parties are revealed, there is no basis for conflict. Take, for example, the Monday versus Wednesday argument. This argument could apply to a scenario involving a project manager and the production manager of a small, local firm that was contracted to produce prototypes of a new generation of computer mouse. The project manager needs the prototypes on Monday to demonstrate to a users' focus group. The production manager said it would be impossible. The project manager said this would be embarrassing because Marketing had spent a lot of time and effort setting up this demonstration. The production manager again denied the request and added that he already had to schedule overtime to meet the Wednesday delivery date. However, when the project manager revealed that the purpose of the focus group was to gauge consumers' reactions to the color and shape of the new devices, not the finished product, the conflict disappeared. The production manager told the project manager that she could pick up the samples today if she wanted because production had an excess supply of shells.

When focusing on interests, it is important to keep in mind one of the habits of effective interpersonal communication *Seek first to understand, then to be understood*. This involves what Covey calls empathetic listening, which allows a person to fully understand other people's frames of reference—not only what they are saying but also how they feel.[14] Covey asserts that people have an inherent need to be understood. He goes on to observe that satisfied needs do not motivate human behavior, only unsatisfied needs do. People try to go to sleep when they are tired not when they are rested. The key point is that until the other party believes they are being understood, they will expend time and energy trying to bring about that understanding. They will repeat their points and reformulate their arguments. If, on the other hand, you satisfy this need by seeking first to understand, then the other party is free to understand your interests and focus directly on the issues at hand. Seeking to understand requires discipline and compassion. Instead of responding to the other person by asserting your agenda, you need to respond by summarizing both the facts and feelings behind what the other person has said and checking the accuracy of comprehension.

Invent Options for Mutual Gain

Once the individuals involved have identified their interests, then they can explore options for mutual gain. This is not easy. Stressful negotiations inhibit creativity and free exchange. What is required is collaborative brainstorming in which people work together to solve the problem in a way that will lead to a win–win scenario. The key to brainstorming is separating the inventing from the deciding. Begin by taking 15 minutes to generate as many options as possible. No matter how outlandish any option is, it should not be subject to criticism or immediate rejection. People should feed off the ideas of others to generate new ideas. When all the possible options are exhausted, then sort through the ideas that were generated to focus on those with the greatest possibilities.

Clarifying interests and exploring mutual options creates the opportunity for dovetailing interests. Identifying options means one person identifies options that are of low cost to him or her but of high interest to the other party. This is only possible if each party knows what the other's needs are. For example, in negotiating price with a parts supplier, a project manager learned from the discussion that the supplier was in a cash flow squeeze after purchasing a very expensive fabrication machine. Needed cash was the primary reason the supplier had taken such a rigid position on price. During the brainstorming session, one of the options presented was to prepay for the order instead of the usual payment on delivery arrangement. Both parties seized on this option and reached an amicable agreement in which the project manager would pay the supplier for the entire job in advance in exchange for a faster turnaround time and a significant price reduction. Such opportunities for win–win agreements are often overlooked because the participants become fixated on solving their problems and not on opportunities to solve the other person's problems.

When Possible, Use Objective Criteria

Most established industries and professions have developed standards and rules to help deal with common areas of dispute. Both buyers and sellers rely on the *Blue Book* to establish price parameters for a used car. The construction industry has building codes and fair practice policies to resolve proof of quality and safe work procedures. The legal profession uses precedents to adjudicate claims of wrongdoing.

Whenever possible, you should insist on using external, objective criteria to settle disagreements. For example, a disagreement arose between a regional airline and the independent accounting team entrusted with preparing the annual financial statement. The airline had made a significant investment by leasing several used airplanes from a larger airline. The dispute involved whether this lease should be classified as an operating or capital lease. This was important to the airline because if the purchase was classified as an operating lease, the associated debt would not have to be recorded in the financial statement. However, if the purchase was classified as a capital lease, then the debt would be factored into the financial statement and the debt/equity ratio would be much less attractive to stockholders and would-be investors. The two parties resolved this dispute by deferring to formulas established by the Financial Accounting Standards Board. As it turns out the accounting team was correct, but, by deferring to objective standards, they were able to deflect the disappointment of the airline managers away from accounting team and preserve a professional relationship with that firm.

Dealing with Unreasonable People

Most people working on projects realize that in the long run it is beneficial to work toward mutually satisfying solutions. Still, occasionally you encounter someone who has a dominant win–lose attitude about life and will be difficult to deal with. Fisher and Ury recommend that you use negotiation jujitsu when dealing with such a person. That is, when the other person begins to push, don't push back. As in the martial arts, avoid pitting your strengths against the person's directly; instead use your skill to step aside and turn their strength to your ends. When someone adamantly sets forth a position, neither reject it nor accept it. Treat it as a possible option and then look for the interests behind it. Instead of defending your ideas, invite criticism and advice. Ask the person why it's a bad idea to discover the underlying interest.

Those who use negotiation jujitsu rely on two primary weapons. First they ask questions instead of making statements. Questions allow for interests to surface and do not provide the opponent with something to attack. The second weapon is silence. If the other person makes an unreasonable proposal or attacks you personally, just sit there and don't say a word. Wait for the other party to break the stalemate by answering your question or coming up with a new suggestion.

The best defense against unreasonable, win–lose negotiators is having what Fisher and Ury call a strong BATNA (best alternative to a negotiated agreement). They point out that people try to reach an agreement to produce something better than the result of not negotiating. What those results would be (BATNA) is the true benchmark for determining whether you should accept an agreement. A strong BATNA gives you the power to walk away and say, "No deal unless we work toward a win–win scenario."

Your BATNA reflects how dependent you are on the other party. If you are negotiating price and delivery dates and can choose from a number of reputable suppliers, then you have a strong BATNA. If on the other had, there is only one vendor who can supply you with specific, critical material on time, then you have a weak BATNA. Under these circumstances you may be forced to concede to the vendor's demands. At the same time, you should begin to explore ways of increasing your BATNA for future negotiations. This can be done by reducing your dependency on that supplier. Begin to find substitutable material or negotiate better lead times with other vendors.

Negotiating is an art. There are many intangibles involved in practicing this art. This section has reviewed some time-tested principles of effective negotiating based on the ground-breaking work of Fisher and Ury. Given the significance of negotiating, we encourage you to read their book as well as others on negotiating.[15] Likewise, attending training workshops can provide an opportunity to practice these skills. Furthermore you should take advantage of day-to-day interactions to your sharpen negotiating acumen.

A Note on Managing Customer Relations

In Chapter 4 we emphasized that ultimate success is not determined by whether the project is completed on time, within budget, or according to specifications, but whether the customer is satisfied with what has been accomplished. Customer satisfaction is the bottom line. In today's competitive world where information flows freely, reputation is essential to long-term success. As advocates of the total quality revolution are quick to point out, there is about an 8:1 ratio between the communication of customer dissatisfaction and satisfaction. This means that for every satisfied customer who shares his or her satisfaction regarding a particular product or service with another person, a dissatisfied customer is likely to share his or her dissatisfaction with 8 other people.[14] Bad news travels faster and farther than good news. Project managers need to cultivate positive working relations with clients in order to ensure success and preserve their reputations.

Customer satisfaction is a complex phenomenon. One simple but useful way of viewing customer satisfaction is in terms of met expectations.[15] According to this model customer satisfaction is a function of the extent to which perceived performance (or outcome) exceeds expectations. Mathematically, this relationship can be represented as the ratio between perceived performance and expected performance (see Figure 12–5). When performance falls short of expectations (ratio less than 1), the customer is dissatisfied. If the performance matches expectations (ratio equals 1), the customer is satisfied. If the performance exceeds expectations (ratio is greater than 1), the customer is very satisfied or even delighted.

High customer satisfaction is the goal of most projects. However, profitability is another major concern. Exceeding expectations typically entails additional costs. For example, completing a construction project 2 weeks ahead of schedule may involve significant overtime expenses. Likewise, exceeding reliability requirements for a new electronic component may involve considerably more design and debugging effort. Under most circumstances, the most profitable arrangement occurs when the customer's expectations are only slightly exceeded. Returning to the mathematical model, with all other things being equal, one should strive for a satisfaction ratio of 1.05 not 1.5!

The met expectations model of customer satisfaction highlights the point that whether a client is dissatisfied or delighted with a project is not based on hard facts and objective data but on perceptions and expectations. For example, a customer may be dissatisfied with a project that was completed ahead of schedule and under budget if he thought the work was poor quality and that his fears and concerns were not adequately addressed by the project team. Conversely, a customer may be very satisfied with a project that was over budget and behind

FIGURE 12–5

The Met-Expectations Model of Customer Satisfaction

$$\underset{\text{Dissatisfied}}{0.90} = \frac{\text{Perceived Performance}}{\text{Expected Performance}} = \underset{\substack{\text{Very} \\ \text{Satisfied}}}{1.10}$$

schedule if she felt the project team protected her interests and did the best job possible under adverse circumstances.

Project managers must be skilled at managing customer expectations and perceptions. Too often they deal with these expectations after the fact when they try to alleviate a client's dissatisfaction by carefully explaining why the project cost more or took longer than planned. A more proactive approach is to begin to shape the proper expectations up front and accept that this is an on-going process throughout the life of a project. Project managers need to direct their attention to both the customer's base expectations, the standard by which perceived performance will be evaluated, and the customer's perceptions of actual performance. The ultimate goal is to educate clients so that they can make a valid judgment as to project performance as well as reduce chances for misunderstandings that can lead to disappointment and dissatisfaction.

Managing customer expectations begins during the preliminary project approval phase of negotiations. It is important to avoid the temptation to oversell the virtues of a project to win approval because this may create unrealistic expectations that may be too difficult, if not impossible, to achieve. At the same time, project proponents have been known to lower customer expectations by underselling projects. If the estimated completion time is 10 to 12 weeks, they will promise to have the project completed within 12 to 14 weeks, therefore increasing the chances of exceeding customer expectations by getting the project completed early.

Once the project is authorized, the project manager and team need to work closely with the client organization to develop a well-defined project scope statement that clearly states the objectives, parameters, and limits of the project work. The project scope statement is essential to establishing customer expectations regarding the project. It is critical that all parties are in agreement as to what is to be accomplished and that everyone is reading as best they can from the same page. It is also important to share significant risks that might disrupt project execution. Customers do not like surprises, and if they are aware in advance of potential problems they are much more likely to be accepting of the consequences.

Once the project is initiated it is important to keep customers abreast of project progress. The days when you would simply take orders from customers and tell them to return when the project is done are over. More and more organizations and their project managers are treating their customers as de facto members of the project team and are actively involving them in key aspects of project work. They consult with customers on important technical decisions to ensure that solutions are consistent with customer needs. Project managers need to keep customers informed of project developments so that customers can make adjustments in their own plans. When circumstances dictate changing the scope or priorities of the project, project managers need to be quick to spell out as best they can the implications of these changes to the customers so that they can make an informed choice. Active customer involvement allows customers to adjust their expectations naturally in accordance with the decisions and events that transpire on a project, while, at same time, the customer's presence keeps the project team focused on the customer's objectives for the project.

Active customer involvement also provides a firmer basis for assessing project performance. The customer not only sees the results of the project but also acquires glimpses of the effort and actions that produced those results. Naturally project managers want to make sure these glimpses reflect favorably on their project teams, so they exercise extra care that customer interactions are handled in a competent and professional manner. In some respects, customer perceptions of performance are shaped more by how well the project team deals with adversity than by actual performance. Project managers can impress customers with how diligently they deal with unexpected problems and setbacks. Likewise, industry analysts have noted that customer dissatisfaction can be transformed into customer satisfaction by quickly correcting mistakes and being extremely responsive to customer concerns.

Managing customer relations on a project is a broad topic; we have only highlighted some of the central issues involved. This brief segment concludes with two pieces of advice passed on by veteran project managers:

Speak with one voice. Nothing erodes confidence in a project more than for a customer to receive conflicting messages from different project members. The project manager should remind team members of this fact and work with them to ensure that appropriate information is shared with customers.

Speak the language of the customer. Too often project members respond to customer inquiries with technical jargon that exceeds the customer's vocabulary. Project managers and members need to describe problems, trade-offs, and solutions in ways that the customer can understand.

Summary

More and more companies are seeking cooperative arrangements with each other to compete in today's business world. Project partnering represents a proactive response to many of the challenges associated with working with people from different organizations. Before the project is started, significant time and effort are invested up front to build relationships among stakeholders and develop agreed upon procedures and provisions for dealing with problems and opportunities before they happen. These procedures typically include joint assessments of how well the partnering arrangement is working, escalation guidelines for resolving disputes in a timely and effective manner, and provisions for process improvement and risk sharing. Persistent leadership is required to make partnering work. Project managers must "walk the talk" and consistently display a collaborative response to problems. Similarly, top management must consistently and visibly champion the principles of openness, trust, and teamwork.

Partnering is not limited to contracted relationships. More and more companies are applying the partnering approach to managing internal projects involving different subsidiaries and departments. For example, in a large high-tech firm a team made up of 49 individuals from multiple disciplines used partnering to establish a more cohesive, cooperative relationship to implement their section of a project. There is a definite increase in the use of partnering within many firms' teams on large projects.

Effective negotiating skills are essential to making partnering work. People need to resolve differences at the lowest level possible in order to keep the project on track. Veteran project managers realize that negotiating is not a competitive game and work toward collaborative solutions to problems. They do so by separating people from the problem, focusing on interests and not positions, inventing options for mutual gain, and relying on objective criteria whenever possible to resolve disagreements. They also recognize the importance of developing a strong BATNA, which provides them with the leverage necessary to seek collaborative solutions.

Customer satisfaction is the litmus test for project success. Project managers need to take a proactive approach to managing customer expectations and perceptions. They need to actively involve customers in key decisions and keep them abreast of important developments. Active customer involvement keeps the project team focused on the objectives of the project and reduces misunderstandings and dissatisfaction.

APPENDIX 12A
CONTRACT MANAGEMENT

Because most interorganizational work on projects is contractual in nature, this appendix discusses the different kinds of contracts that are used, their strengths and weaknesses, and how contracts shape the motives and expectations of different participants.

A contract is a formal agreement between two parties wherein one party (the contractor) obligates itself to perform a service and the other party (the client) obligates itself to do something in return, usually in the form of a payment to the contractor. For example, an insurance firm contracted with a consulting firm to reprogram segments of its information system to conform to year 2000 standards.

A contract is more than just an agreement between parties. A contract is a codification of the private law, which governs the relationship between the parties to it.

It defines the responsibilities, spells out the conditions of operation, defines the rights of the parties in relationship to each other, and grants remedies to a party if the other party breaches its obligations. A contract attempts to spell out in specific terms the transactional obligations of the parties involved as well as contingencies associated with the execution of the contract. An ambiguous or inconsistent contract is difficult to understand and enforce.

There are essentially two different kinds of contracts. The first is the "fixed-price" contract in which a price is agreed upon in advance and remains fixed as long as there are no changes to scope or provisions of the agreement. The second is a "cost plus" contract in which the contractor is reimbursed for some or all of the expenses incurred during the performance of the contract. Unlike the fixed-price contract, the final price is not known until the project is completed. Within these two types of contracts, several variations exist.[1]

Fixed-Price Contracts

Under a fixed-price (FP) or "lump sum" agreement, the contractor agrees to perform all work specified in the contract at a fixed price. Clients are able to get a minimum price by putting out the contract to competitive bid. Advertising an invitation for bid (IFB) that lists customer requirements usually results in low bids.[2] Prospective contractors can obtain IFB notices through various channels. In the case of large business organizations and government agencies, potential contractors can request to be included on the bidder's list in the area of interest. In other cases, IFBs can be found by scanning appropriate industry media such as newspapers, trade journals, and the *Commerce Business Daily*. In many cases, the owner can put restrictions on potential bidders, such as requiring that they be ISO 9000 certified.

With fixed-price bids, the contractor has to be very careful in estimating target cost and completion schedule because once agreed upon, the price cannot be adjusted. If the contractor overestimates the target cost in the bidding stage, they may lose the contract to a lower-priced competitor; if the estimate it too low, they may win the job but make little or no profit.

Fixed-price contracts are preferred by both owners and contractors when the scope of the project is well defined with predictable costs and low implementation risks. Such might be the case for producing parts or components to specifications, executing training programs,

or orchestrating a banquet. With fixed price-contracts, clients do not have to be concerned with project costs and can focus on monitoring work progress and performance specifications. Likewise, contractors prefer fixed-price contracts because the client is less likely to request changes or additions to the contract. Fewer potential changes reduce project uncertainty and allows the contractors to more efficiently manage their resources across multiple projects.

The disadvantage of a fixed-price contract for owners is that it is more difficult and more costly to prepare. To be effective, design specifications need to be spelled out in sufficient detail to leave little doubt as to what is to be achieved. Because the contractor's profit is determined by the difference between the bid and the actual costs, there is some incentive for contractors to use cheaper quality materials, perform marginal workmanship, or extend the completion date to reduce costs. The client can counteract these by stipulating rigid end-item specifications and completion date and by supervising work. In many cases, the client will hire a consultant who is an expert in the field to oversee the contractor's work and protect the client's interest.

The primary disadvantage of a fixed-price contract for contractors is that they run the risk of underestimating. If the project gets into serious trouble, cost overruns may make the project unprofitable, and in some cases may lead to bankruptcy. To keep this from happening, contractors have to invest significant time and money to ensure that their estimates are accurate.

Contracts with long lead times such as construction and production projects may include escalation provisions that protect the contractor against external cost increases in materials, labor rates, or overhead expenses. For example, the price may be tied to an inflation index, so it can be adjusted for sudden increases in labor and material prices, or it may be redetermined, as costs become known. A variety of redetermination contracts are used: some establish a ceiling price for a contract and permit only downward adjustments, others permit upward and downward adjustments; some establish one readjustment period at the end of the project, others use more than one period. Redetermination contracts are appropriate where engineering and design efforts are difficult to estimate or when final price cannot be estimated for lack of accurate cost data.

While, in principle, redetermination contracts are used to make appropriate adjustments in cost uncertainties,

---

Project Management in Action

Can Partnering Work in the Public Sector?

Many question whether partnering arrangements can work on public works projects such as renovating a segment of a highway or building a new public school. Contracts for these projects tend to be mandated by law to be awarded on a competitive, low-bid basis. As a result, the government agencies do not get to screen potential contractors as to experience and willingness to work as partners. Critics also argue that the binding nature of the low-bid contractual arrangement prevents the necessary flexibility to work out optimal solutions when unexpected problems arise. Another drawback is that sustained business, which is one of the major incentives for adhering to partnering principles, is seldom possible because each contract must be awarded under open competition.

Despite these handicaps, the U.S. Army Corps of Engineers has been quite successful in creating partnering arrangements with contractors who were awarded contracts on a competitive, low-bid basis. For example, the Portland, Oregon, District of the Corps successfully partnered the completion of a $330 million Bonneville Lock project. Using a partnering process very similar to what is described in this chapter, the project was completed 3 months ahead of schedule, obtained more than $1.8 million in value engineering savings, and encountered no litigation. Likewise, Weston and Gibson compared the performance of 16 partnered Corp projects with 28 nonpartnered projects and reported that the partnered projects achieved superior cost savings.[3] Col. Charles Cowan, who managed the Bonneville Lock project, said that while team building, joint evaluations, and the other partnering components were all important, the key to success was that the parties involved realized that partnering was a much more enjoyable way to work together.

---

they are prone to abuse. A contractor may win an initial low bid contract, initiate the contracted work, and then "discover" that the costs are much higher than expected. The contractor can take advantage of redetermination provisions and a client's ignorance to justify increasing the actual cost of the contract. The contract evolves into a "costs-plus" kind of a contract.

To alleviate some of the disadvantages of a fixed-price contract while maintaining some certainty as to final cost, many fixed-price contracts contain incentive clauses designed to motivate contractors to reduce costs and improve efficiency. For example, a contractor negotiates to perform the work for a target price based on target cost and a target profit. A maximum price and maximum

profit are also established. If the total cost ends up being less than the target cost, the contractor makes a higher profit up to the profit maximum. If there is a cost overrun, the contractor absorbs some of the overrun until a profit floor is reached.

Profit is determined according to a formula based on a cost-sharing ratio (CSR). A CSR of 75/25, for example, indicates that for every dollar spent above target costs, the client pays 75 cents and the contractor pays 25 cents. This provision motivates contractors to keep costs low since they pay 25 cents on every dollar spent above the expected cost and earn 25 cents more on every dollar saved below the expected cost. Fixed price-incentive contracts tend to be used for long-duration projects with fairly predictable cost estimates. The key is being able to negotiate a reasonable target cost estimate. Unscrupulous contractors have been known to take advantage of the ignorance of the client to negotiate an unrealistically high target cost and use performance incentives to achieve excessive profits.

Cost-Plus Contracts

Under a cost-plus contract the contractor is reimbursed for all direct allowable costs (materials, labor, travel) plus an additional fee to cover overhead and profit. This fee is negotiated in advance and usually involves a percentage of the total costs. On small projects this kind of contract comes under the rubric "time and materials" contract in which the client agrees to reimburse the contractor for labor cost and materials. Labor costs are based on an hourly or daily rate, which includes direct and indirect costs as well as profit. The contractor is responsible for documenting labor and materials costs.

Unlike fixed-contracts, cost plus contracts put the burden of risk on the client. The contract does not indicate what the project is going to cost until the end of the project. Contractors are supposed to make the best effort to fulfill the specific technical requirements of the contract but cannot be held liable, in spite of their best efforts, if the work is not produced within the estimated cost and time frame. These contracts are often criticized because there is little formal incentive for the contractors to control costs or finish on time because they get paid the same fee regardless of the final cost. The major factor motivating contractors to control costs and schedule is the effect overruns have on their reputation and their ability to secure future business. The government has curtailed use of cost-plus contracts in favor of incentive contracts in response to abuse by contractors.

The inherent weakness of cost-plus contracts has been compensated for by a variety of incentive clauses directed at providing incentives to contractors to control costs, maintain performance, and avoid schedule overruns. Contractors are reimbursed for costs, but instead of the fee being fixed, it is based on an incentive formula and subject to additional provisions. This is very similar to fixed-price incentive contracts but instead of being based on a target cost, the fee is based on actual cost, using a cost-sharing formula.

Most contracts are concerned with the negotiated cost of the project. However, given the importance of speed and timing in today's business world, more and more contracts involve clauses concerning completion dates. To some extent schedule incentives provide some cost control measures because schedule slippage typically but not always involves cost overruns. Schedule incentives/penalties are stipulated depending upon the significance of time to completion for the owner. For example, the contract involving the construction of a new baseball stadium is likely to contain stiff penalties if the stadium is not ready for opening day of the season. Conversely, time-constrained projects in which the number one priority is getting the project completed as soon as possible are likely to include attractive incentives for completing the project early. For example, a software firm that is anxious to get a new product to market may offer a testing firm a sizable bonus for each day the tests are completed ahead of schedule.

Contract Change Control System

A contract change control system defines the process by which the contract may be modified. It includes the paperwork, tracking systems, dispute resolution procedures, and approval levels necessary for authorizing changes. There are a number of reasons a contract may need to be changed. Clients may wish to alter the original design or scope of the project once the project is initiated. This is quite common as the project moves from concept to reality. For example, an owner may wish to add windows after inspecting the partially completed home site. Market changes may dictate adding new features or increasing the performance requirements of equipment. Declining financial resources may dictate that the owner cut back on the scope of the project. The contractor may initiate changes in the contract in response to unforeseen legitimate problems. A building contractor may need to renegotiate the contract in the face of excessive groundwater or the lack of availability of specified materials. In some cases, external forces may dictate contract changes, such as a need to comply with new safety standards mandated by the federal government.

There need to be formal, agreed-upon procedures for initiating changes in the original contract. Contract change orders are subject to abuse. Contractors sometimes take advantage of owners' ignorance to inflate the costs of changes to recoup profit lost from a low bid. Conversely, owners have been known to "get back" at contractors by delaying approval of contract changes, thus delaying project work and increasing the costs to the contractor. All parties need to agree upon the rules and procedures for initiating and making changes in the original terms of the contract in advance.

Contract Management in Perspective

Contract management is not an exact science. For decades, the federal government has been trying to develop a more effective contract administration system. Despite their best efforts, abuses are repeatedly exposed in the news media. The situation is similar to trying to take a wrinkle out of an Oriental rug. Efforts to eliminate a wrinkle in one part of the rug invariably create a wrinkle in another part. Likewise, each new revision in government procurement procedures appears to generate a new loophole that can be exploited. There is no perfect contract management system. Given the inherent uncertainty involved in most project work, no contract can handle all the issues that emerge. Formal contracts cannot replace or eliminate the need to develop effective working relationships between the parties involved that are based on mutual goals, trust, and cooperation. For this reason, the earlier discussion of project partnering and effective negotiating is very important.

13 MONITORING PROJECT PERFORMANCE

How does a project get 1 year late?
. . . One day at a time.
Frederick P. Brooks[1]

Evaluation and control are part of every project manager's job. Control by "wandering around" and/or "involvement" can overcome most problems in small projects. However, in larger projects informal control is difficult, and formal control is a necessity. To evaluate and control projects, a single information system is required. The system must measure project progress and performance against the original project plan of schedule, budget, and quality requirements.

We suggest using an earned value evaluation and control system. A short description of the steps required to develop one is presented below. The description of the steps is followed by the details of an integrated project information system used by practicing project managers.

The Project Control Process

Project control is not performed well in most organizations. It is one of the most neglected areas of project management. Control holds people accountable, allows for traceability, and keeps focus. Control has negative connotations for many and frequently is resisted. When you hear the following phrases, the speakers are resisting control:

- The system stifles flexibility.
- The system gets in the way of completing the project.

- The system takes too much effort for the return.
- The data are too old to be of use.
- Numbers can't tell us what is really happening.

Budget control is a particularly troublesome area in some industries. Favorite excuses of project managers in manufacturing firms are "accounting is not interested in managing projects per se," and "the project software is not compatible with the accounting system," so control may be almost ignored. Construction companies frequently are an exception; their accounting systems are set up for job-costing of tasks, labor, and materials. Their format is similar to that of project management software and may require only a simple coding system to integrate project management software with the accounting software.

Most people who work in an environment in which the control system is effective cannot imagine how to manage without one. They are able to perceive the benefits individually as well as for the organization as a whole. In essence, those who minimize the importance of control are passing up a great opportunity to be effective managers and give their organization a competitive edge.

Any system for monitoring project performance should provide the project manager and stakeholders with the ability to answer questions such as:

- What is the current status of the project in terms of schedule and cost?
- How much will it cost to complete the project?
- When will the project be completed?
- Are there potential problems that need to be addressed now?
- What, who, and where are the causes for cost or schedule overruns?
- What did we get for the dollars spent?
- If there is a cost overrun midway in the project, can we forecast the overrun at completion?
- Can potential problems be identified before it is too late to correct them?

A system called earned value (EV) facilitates answers to these questions. Of course, the validity of any monitoring system depends on data that are accurate and reliable. The usefulness of the EV system depends on data from the work breakdown structure—resources, time and cost estimates, and a time-phased budget for each task—and new estimates of percent complete that are realistic and as accurate as possible.

Basically, measuring and evaluating project performance requires a control process that includes the following four steps:

1. Setting a baseline plan.
2. Measuring progress and performance.

3. Comparing plan against actual.
4. Taking action.

Each of the control steps is described below.

Step 1: Setting a Baseline Plan.   The baseline plan provides the elements for measuring performance. The baseline is derived primarily from the work breakdown structure (WBS) database. The WBS defines the work in discrete work packages that are tied to deliverables and organization units. In addition, each work package defines the work, duration, and budget. From the WBS, the project network schedule is used to time-phase all work, resources, and budgets into a baseline plan.

Step 2: Measuring Progress and Performance.   Time and budgets are quantitative measures of performance that readily fit into the integrated information system. Qualitative measures such as meeting customer technical specifications and product function are most frequently determined by on-site inspection or actual use. This chapter is limited to quantitative measures of time and budget. Measurement of time performance is relatively easy and obvious; i.e., is the critical path early, on schedule, or late? Is the slack of near-critical paths decreasing to cause new critical activities? Are milestones being achieved on time? Measuring performance against budget (e.g., money, units in place, labor hours) is more difficult and is *not* simply a case of comparing actual versus budget. Earned value is necessary to provide a realistic estimate of performance against a time-phased budget. Earned value will be defined as the budgeted cost of the work performed (BCWP).

Step 3: Comparing Plan against Actual.   Because plans seldom materialize as expected, it becomes imperative to measure deviations from plan to determine if action is necessary. Periodic monitoring and measuring the status of the project allow for comparisons of actual versus expected plans. It is critical that the timing of status reports be frequent enough to allow for early detection of variations from plan and early corrections of causes. Usually status reports should take place every 1 to 4 weeks to be useful and allow for proactive correction.

Step 4: Taking Action.   If deviations from plans are significant, corrective action will be needed to bring the project back in line with the original or revised plan. In some cases, conditions or scope can change, which, in turn, will require a change in the baseline plan to recognize new information.

In the remainder of this chapter, we will discuss performance and monitoring systems for controlling time and cost performance. Time performance and monitoring are discussed first, then an integrated project cost/schedule or EV system.

Monitoring Time Performance

One of the major goals of progress reporting is to catch any schedule delays as early as possible to determine if corrective action is necessary. Fortunately, monitoring schedule performance is relatively easy. The project network schedule, derived from the WBS/OBS, serves as the baseline to compare against actual performance. Gantt charts and control charts are the typical tools used for communicating project schedule status. As suggested in Chapter 4, we believe the Gantt chart is the most understandable. This kind of chart is commonly referred to as a tracking Gantt chart. Adding actual and revised time estimates to the Gantt chart gives a quick overview of project status on the report date.

Gantt and control charts serve well as a means for tracking and trending schedule performance. Their visual format makes them favorite tools for communicating project schedule status—especially to top management who prefer less detail.

Figure 13–1 presents a baseline and an updated Gantt chart for a software project. The bars represent activity durations. In the tracking Gantt chart, the solid

FIGURE 13–1

Baseline Gantt Chart

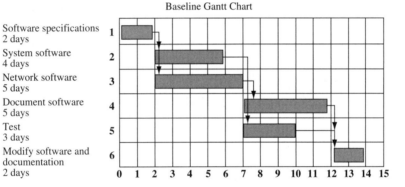

Baseline Gantt Chart

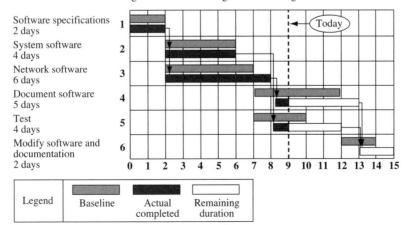

Tracking Gantt Chart Showing Status—Through Period 8

bars below the original baseline bar represent the actual start and work completed to date. For example, the actual start time for activity 3 (network software) is day 2-3; the actual finish time is day 7-8; the actual duration is 6 time units, rather than the 5 days scheduled in the baseline. Activities in process show the actual start time until the present; the extended bar represents the remaining expected duration (see activities 4 and 5). The remaining expected durations for activities 4, 5, and 6 are shown with the vertical clear bars. Note that activity 2 now has slack of 2 days, which is represented by the horizontal line. Activity 6, which has not started, shows a revised estimated actual start on day 13-14 and the finish time (15); This is a project delay of 1 day, which was caused by the extended duration of 1 day for activity 3 (network software). Observe that this 1 day delay of activity 3 caused the start activities 4, 5, and 6 to be delayed 1 day.

Note how activities can have durations that differ from the original schedule, as in activities 3 and 5. Either the activity is complete and the actual is known, or new information suggests the estimate of time be revised and reflected in the status report. In activity 5 the revised duration is expected to be 4 time units, which is 1 day longer than the baseline schedule.

The control chart is another tool used to monitor past project schedule performance and current performance and to estimate future schedule trends. Figure 13–2 is a project control chart. The chart is used to plot the difference between the scheduled time on the critical path at the report date with the actual point on the critical path. Although Figure 13–2 shows the project was behind early in the project, the plot suggests corrective action brought the project back on track. If the trend is sustained, the project will come in ahead of schedule. Because the activity scheduled times represent average durations, four observations trending in one direction indicate there is a very high probability that there is an identifiable cause. The cause should be located and action taken if necessary.

FIGURE 13–2

*Project
Schedule
Control
Chart*

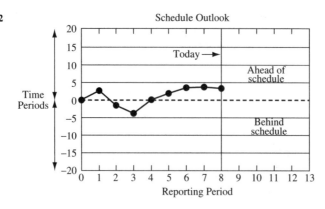

Control charts are also frequently used to monitor progress toward milestones. Milestones are significant project events that mark major accomplishments. To be effective, milestones need to be concrete, specific, measurable events. Milestones—for example, "product testing complete"—must be easily identifiable by all project stakeholders. From a strictly scheduling point of view, the completion of critical burst activities and the start of critical merge activities are good candidates for milestones. Control charts very similar to the example shown in Figure 13–2 are often used to record and communicate project progress toward a milestone.

Schedule slippage of 1 day seldom receives a great deal of attention. However, 1 day here and another there soon add up to large delay problems. It is well known that once work gets behind, it has a tendency to stay behind because it is difficult to make up. Examples of causes of schedule slippage are unreliable time estimates, minor redesign, scope creep, and unavailable resources. Using slack early in a path may create a problem for someone responsible for a later activity; flexibility and potential opportunities are reduced. For these reasons, having frequent and clearly defined monitoring points for work packages can significantly improve the chances of catching schedule slippage early. Early detection reduces the chance of small delays growing to large ones and thereby reducing opportunities for corrective action to get back on schedule. See *Project Management in Action: Status Reports at Microsoft* for a look at how Bill Gates monitors project performance.

Recall from Chapter 8, the critical-chain (C-C) method uses buffers to monitor project time performance. Figure 13–3 shows a project buffer tool. Remember that a project buffer is used to insulate the project against delays along the critical chain. For monitoring purposes, this buffer is typically divided into three zones. As the buffer begins to decrease and moves into the second zone, alarms are set off to seek corrective action.[2] To be truly effective, buffer management requires comparing buffer usage with actual progress on the project. For example, if the project is 75 percent complete and you have only used 50 percent of the project buffer, then the project is in pretty good shape. Conversely, if the project is only 25 percent complete and 50 percent of the buffer has already been used, you are in trouble and corrective action is needed. A method for estimating percentage complete is described later in this chapter.

An Integrated Cost/Schedule System

In the 1960s, the U.S. Department of Defense (DOD) was concerned with cost overruns and a lack of consistency among contractors. This concern served as a major motivation for the DOD to search for a system to track schedule and cost in large project contracts.[3] The system they developed brings discipline to the

---
Project Management in Action

Status Reports at Microsoft*

At Microsoft each software product has a corresponding project status report. Project teams send these reports each month to Bill Gates and other top executives as well as to the managers of all related projects. The status reports are brief and have a standard format. Gates can read most of them quickly and still spot potential project delays or changes he does not want. He especially looks for schedule slips, cutting too many product features, or the need to change a specification. Gates usually responds to the relevant managers or developers directly by electronic mail. Status reports are an important mechanism for communicating between top management and projects. As Gates explains:

> I get all of the status reports. Right now there might be a hundred active projects . . . [The status reports] contain the schedule, including milestones dates, and any change in spec, and any comments about 'Hey we can't hire enough people,' or 'Jeez, if this OLE (Object Linking and Embedding) 2 Mac release isn't done, we're just going to have to totally slip' . . . They know [their report] goes up to all the people who manage all the other groups that they have dependencies with. So if they don't raise it in the status report and then 2 months later they say something, that's a breakdown in communication . . . The internal group is totally copied on those things, so it's sort of the consensus of the group.

---
*Michael A. Cusumano, *Microsoft Secrets,* New York: The Free Press, 1995, pp. 28–29.

FIGURE 13–3

Project Control—Buffer Management

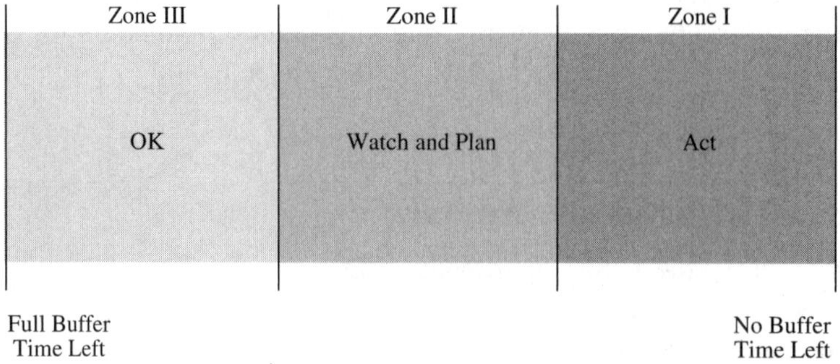

Zone III	Zone II	Zone I
OK	Watch and Plan	Act

Full Buffer Time Left   No Buffer Time Left

process of measuring project progress by keeping track of schedules and budgets against time. The private sector was quick to recognize the worth of the system as a totally integrated project management system. It is probably safe to say that project managers in every major country are using some form of the system developed by the DOD. It is not limited to construction or contracts. The system is being used on internal projects in the manufacturing, pharmaceutical, and high-tech industries. For example, organizations such as EDS, NCR, Levi Strauss, Tektronics, and Disney have used the systems to track projects. The basic framework of the system is withstanding the test of time. Most project management software includes the original framework; many systems have added industry-specific variations to more precisely track progress and costs. This chapter presents the generic core of an integrated cost/schedule information system. Carefully note that the system depends on a well-developed plan and schedule similar to those presented in Chapters 4 and 8.

The Earned Value System

The system developed by the DOD came to be called the earned value system. Earned value (EV) is a method for measuring project cost and schedule performance. It compares the timing and amount of work that was planned with what was actually accomplished.

The Need for an Earned Value System

Systems that only compare actuals against budget fail to measure what work was actually accomplished for the money spent. Such systems fail to include the *time* variable as part of the equation. An example of a hypothetical project will demonstrate the need for using earned value. Imagine a high-tech firm implementing an R&D project. The original plan calls for completion of the project in 10 months at a cost of exactly $200,000 per month for a total cost of $2.0 million. After 5 months, top management wishes to assess the status of the project. The following information is available:

- Actual costs for the first 5 months are $1.3 million.
- Planned costs for the first 5 months are $1.0 million.

Management might draw the conclusion that the project has a $300,000 cost overrun. This could be a correct conclusion, but it may not be. It is possible the project work is way ahead of schedule and the $300,000 represents payments to labor working ahead of schedule. It is also possible that there is both a cost overrun and the project is behind schedule. These data do not tell the full story.

Using the same high-tech example with another set of outcome data, we again see the data are inadequate to draw accurate conclusions 5 months into the project:

- Actual costs for the first 5 months are $800,000.
- Planned costs for the first 5 months are $1.0 million.

These data can lead to the conclusion the project is costing less than expected by $200,000. Is this true? If the project is behind schedule, the $200,000 may represent planned work that has not started. It is possible the project is behind schedule and also over in cost.

From the data in these two examples, it is easy to understand why real-world systems using only actual and planned costs can mislead management and customers in evaluating project progress and performance. This cost variance (budget-to-actual) alone is inadequate. It does not measure how much work was accomplished for the money spent. Earned value overcomes the problems described by keeping track of schedules and budgets against time.

Outline for an Earned Value System

Following five careful steps ensures that the cost/schedule system is integrated. These steps are outlined below. Steps 1, 2, and 3 are accomplished in the planning stage and occur simultaneously. Steps 4 and 5 are accomplished sequentially during the execution stage of the project.

1. **Define the work using a work breakdown structure (WBS).** This step involves developing documents that include the following information:
   a. Scope
   b. Work packages
   c. Deliverables
   d. Organization units
   e. Resources
   f. Budgets for each work package
2. **Develop work and resource schedules.**
   a. Time-phase work packages into a network
   b. Schedule resources to activities
3. **Develop a time-phased budget using work packages included in an activity.** The cumulative values of these budgets will become the baseline and will be called the budgeted cost of the work scheduled (BCWS). The sum should equal the budgeted amounts for all the work packages in the cost accounts.
4. **At the work package level, collect the actual costs for the work performed.** These costs will be called the actual cost of the work

performed (ACWP). Collect the budgeted values for the work actually accomplished. These will be called earned value or budgeted cost of the work performed (BCWP).

5. **Compute the schedule variance (SV = BCWP–BCWS) and cost variance (CV = BCWP–ACWP).** Prepare hierarchical status reports for each level of management—from work package manager to customer or project manager. The reports should also include project rollups by organization unit and deliverables. In addition, actual time performance should be checked against the project network schedule.

Figure 13–4 shows a schematic overview of the integrated information system, which includes the techniques and systems presented in earlier chapters. Those of you who have tenaciously labored through the early chapters can relax! Steps 1 and 2 are already carefully developed.

Developing Project Baselines

The baseline (BCWS) serves as an anchor point for measuring performance. The baseline is a concrete document and commitment; it is the planned cost and expected schedule against which actual cost and schedule performance are measured. It can also serve as a basis for developing cash flows and awarding progress payments. Developing the project baseline is properly part of the planning process. The baseline is included in this chapter because it is the major input to the

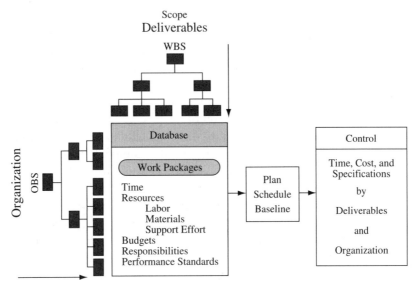

FIGURE 13-4

Project Management Information System Overview

FIGURE 13–5

*Baseline
Data
Relations*

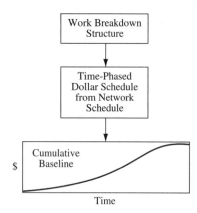

cost/schedule system to be described. The building blocks or data for development of the baseline have already been set in place. Placing work packages in the activities of the network essentially assigns start times for those work packages; it also *time-phases the budgets* that are tied to the work packages. These time-phased budgets are added along a project timeline to create the project baseline. The cumulative sum of all these time-phased budgets should equal the sum of all the work packages found in the cost accounts. Figure 13–5 depicts the relationship of the data used to create the baseline.

What Costs Are Included in Baselines?

The baseline (BCWS) is the sum of the cost accounts, and each cost account is the sum of the work packages in the cost account. Three costs are typically included in baselines—labor and equipment, materials, and level of effort (LOE) (see Chapter 3 for a more detailed discussion). Because LOE costs are very different, it is common to have separate cost accounts for each type to compute variances.[4]

Level of effort work packages represent time-related activities. These activities, such as administrative support, computer support, legal, public relations, etc., exist for a segment or the duration of the project. The ability to control LOE costs is minimal, which is the reason they are typically included in indirect project overhead costs. LOE costs can also be tied to hammock activities that cover a segment of a project. When LOE costs are also tied to work packages that have no measurable outputs, their costs are usually budgeted as a rate per unit of time (e.g., $200 per day). LOE work packages should represent a very small portion of project costs (1–10 percent). There are a few rare circumstances that warrant high LOE costs. For example, the cost of having a crew on site on the Alaskan pipeline exceeds the direct cost of their actual work. This cost of providing housing, food, and 10 days leave for every 23 days of work was counted as LOE cost and exceeded the 10 percent level. The nuclear industry faces a similar situation with crews working in "hot spots." After workers are exposed to a fixed number of REMs (Roentgen equivalent in man), they are required to stop working until the number decreases to a safe level. During this waiting period, the individuals are paid; this waiting cost is considered an LOE cost. These examples are extreme and under normal circumstances should be minimized as much as possible.

Most work packages should be discrete, of short time span, and be measurable. Usually the major costs are labor, machines, and/or materials. If materials are a significant portion of the cost of work packages, they can be budgeted in separate work packages and cost accounts.[5]

Placing Costs in Baselines Using Percent Complete

Percent complete is the work horse for developing the baseline and monitoring project progress. In the planning stage, monitoring points, which represent percent complete, are identified, and someone familiar with a task or activity will break the task into distinct segments that can be used for monitoring. Each segment is assigned a time and cost that are placed in the project baseline exactly as they are expected to be earned. As each checkpoint is completed, the cumulative percent complete increases until the whole segment is finished. The best method for assigning costs to the baseline under the percent complete rule is to establish frequent checkpoints to avoid large time gaps when measuring progress—a rule of thumb is at least once a week. When measuring percent complete in the monitoring phase of the project, it is common to limit the amount earned to 80 percent until the work package is 100 percent complete.

In practice, at lower levels, percent complete does not have to be expressed in monetary units. You will find many metrics such as labor hours, lines of code, drawings completed, cubic yards of concrete in place, prototypes complete, etc. However, in most cases these metrics are ultimately converted to monetary units (dollars, yen, pesos, guilders, marks, pounds, etc.) as they are integrated for examination in summary reports.

Methods of Variance Analysis

Generally the method for measuring accomplishments centers on two key computations:

1. Comparing earned value with the expected schedule value
2. Comparing earned value with the actual costs

These comparisons can be made at the project level or down to the cost account level. Project status can be determined for the latest period or all periods to date, and estimated to the end of the project.

To the uninitiated, the terms used in practice appear horrendous and intimidating. However, once a few basic terms are understood, the intimidation evaporates rapidly.

Glossary of Terms

BCWS	Budgeted cost of the work scheduled. A cost estimate of the resources scheduled in a time-phased cumulative baseline.
BCWP	Budgeted cost of the work performed. The earned value or original budgeted cost for work actually completed.
ACWP	Actual cost of the work completed. The sum of the costs incurred in accomplishing work.
SV	Schedule variance (**BCWP − BCWS**).
CV	Cost variance (**BCWP − ACWP**).
BAC	Budgeted cost at completion. The total budgeted cost of the baseline or project cost accounts.
EAC	Estimated costs at completion. Includes costs to date plus *revised* estimated costs for the work remaining.
FAC	Computed forecasted costs at completion (uses a formula).
VAC	Variance at completion. (**BAC − EAC** or **BAC − FAC**). Indicates expected actual over or underrun at completion.

Assessing the current status of a project using the earned value cost/schedule system requires three data elements—BCWS, BCWP, and ACWP. From these data the schedule variance (SV) and cost variance (CV) are computed for each reporting period, as shown in the glossary. *A positive variance indicates a desirable condition, while a negative variance suggests problems or changes that have taken place.*

Cost variance tells us if the work accomplished costs more or less than was planned at any point over the life of the project. If labor, equipment, and materials have not been separated, cost variance should be reviewed carefully to isolate the cause to either labor, equipment, or materials—or some combination.

Schedule variance presents an overall assessment of *all* work packages in the project scheduled to date. It is important to note schedule variance contains *no* critical path information. Schedule variance measures progress in dollars rather than time units. Therefore, it is unlikely any translation of dollars to time will yield accurate information telling if any milestone or critical path is early, on time, or late (even if the project occurs exactly as planned). *The only accurate method for determining the true time progress of the project is to compare the project network schedule against the actual network schedule to measure if the project is on time* (see Figure 13–2). However, schedule variance is very useful in assessing the direction all the work in the project is taking—after 20 percent or more of the project has been completed.

Figure 13–6 presents a sample cost/schedule graph with variances identified for a project at the current status report date. Note the graph also focuses on what remains to be accomplished and any favorable or unfavorable trends. The "today" label marks the report date (time period 25) of where the project has been and where it is going. Because our system is hierarchical, graphs of the same form can be developed for different levels of management. The top line to date represents the actual costs (ACWP) incurred for the project work to date. The middle line is the baseline (BCWS) and ends at the scheduled project duration (45). The bottom line is the budgeted value of the work actually completed to date (BCWP) or the earned value. The dashed line extending the actual costs from the report date to the new estimated completion date represents revised estimates of *expected* actual costs; that is, additional information suggests the costs at completion of the project will be different from what was planned. Note that the project duration has been extended and the variance at completion (VAC) is negative (BAC − EAC).

Another interpretation of the graph uses percentages. At the end of period 25, 75 percent of the work was scheduled to be accomplished. At the end of period 25, the value of the work accomplished is 50 percent. The actual cost of the work completed to date is $340, or 85 percent of the total project budget. The graph suggests the project will have about a 12 percent cost overrun and be 5 time units

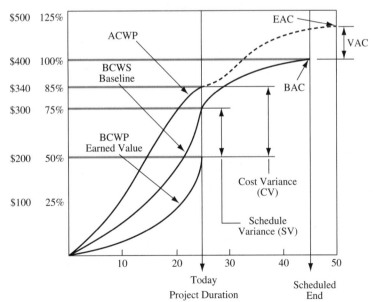

FIGURE 13–6

Cost/Schedule Graph

FIGURE 13–7

Earned Value Scenarios

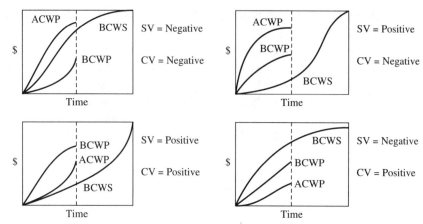

late. The current status of the project shows the cost variance (CV) to be over budget by $140 (BCWP − ACWP = 200 − 340 = −140). The schedule variance (SV) is negative $100 (BCWP − BCWS = 200 − 300 = −100), which suggests the project is behind schedule. Before moving into an example, consult Figure 13–7 to observe typical outcomes of cost/schedule graphs found in practice.

Developing a Status Report: A Hypothetical Example

Assumptions

Working through an example demonstrates how the baseline serves as the anchor from which the project can be monitored using earned value techniques. Because the process becomes geometrically complex with the adding of project detail, some simplifying assumptions are made in the example to demonstrate the process more easily:

1. Assume each cost account has only one work package and each cost account will be represented as an activity on the network.
2. The project network early start times will serve as the basis for assigning the baseline values. Baseline values will be assigned linearly, for the purposes of this example. (*Note:* In practice costs can be assigned any way that is consistent with actual expected conditions.)
3. From the moment work on an activity begins, some actual costs will be incurred each period until the activity is completed.

Baseline Development

Figure 13–8 presents a simple work breakdown structure (WBS/OBS) for our example. There are three deliverables (X, Y, Z), and four departments (A, B, C, D) are responsible. The total for all the cost accounts is $147.

Figure 13–9 depicts the project network with the ES, LS, EF, LF, and slack times. This network information is used to time-phase the project baseline.

FIGURE 13–8

Example of Work Breakdown Structure

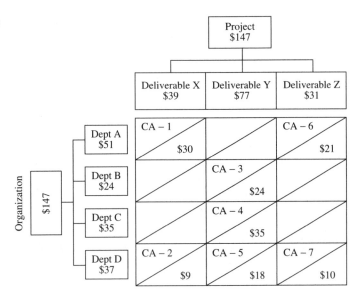

FIGURE 13–9

Example of Project Network

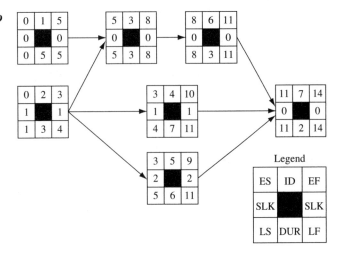

FIGURE
13–10

*Project
Baseline
Budget
Needs*

Schedule Information						Baseline Budget Needs														
ACT/WP	Dur	ES	LF	Slack	Total BCWS	Time Period														
						0	1	2	3	4	5	6	7	8	9	10	11	12	13	14
1	5	0	5	0	30		6	6	6	6	6									
2	3	0	4	1	9		3	3	3											
3	3	5	8	0	24							8	8	8						
4	7	3	11	1	35					5	5	5	5	5	5	5				
5	6	3	11	2	18					3	3	3	3	3	3					
6	3	8	11	0	21										7	7	7			
7	2	11	13	0	10													5	5	
Total BCWS by Period							9	9	9	14	14	16	16	16	15	12	7	5	5	
Cumulative BCWS by Period							9	18	27	41	55	71	87	103	118	130	137	142	147	

Figure 13–10 presents a worksheet with the baseline developed using the percent complete rule. Remember, in practice this rule should be used "exactly" as managers plan to monitor and measure schedule and cost performance.

Figure 13–10 also shows the placement of the time-phased costs. They are dispersed linearly for purposes of demonstration. For example, activity 4, which has an ES of 3 and a duration of 7, has the expected expenditure of $5 for each period of its duration. These assignments of dollars to time periods form the baseline for measuring task and project performance as the project is implemented.

Developing the Project Status Report

A status report is analogous to a snapshot of a project at a specific point in time. The status report uses earned value to measure schedule and cost performance. Measuring earned value begins at the work package or activity level. Work packages are in one of three conditions on a report date:

1. Not yet started
2. Finished
3. In-process or partially complete

Earned values for the first two conditions present no difficulties. Work packages that are not yet started earn 0 percent of the BCWS (budget). Packages that are completed earn 100 percent of their BCWS (budget). In-process activities require the observed actual percent complete to be collected to compute earned value and to measure schedule and cost performance. Working through an example will illustrate the process of completing a status report.

Figure 13–11 presents a worksheet for developing a status report at the end of period 6-7. The following information has been gathered for the status report:

1. Activities 1 and 2 are complete.
2. Activities 3, 4, and 5 are in process.
   a. Activity 3 now has a duration of 4 time units.
   b. Activity 5 now has a duration of 7 time units.
3. Activities 3, 4, 5, and 6 have revised cost estimates to complete.
4. Activity 3 is 50 percent complete in budget dollars.
5. Activity 4 is 80 percent complete in budget dollars.
6. Activity 5 is 66.7 percent complete in budget dollars.
7. Activities 6 and 7 are not yet started and will be late.

In Figure 13–11 the actual costs (ACWP) for each activity and each period have been collected; they are in the shaded section for each period. For example, the actual cost for activity 2 in periods 0-3 are 6, 4, and 10 respectively. Also, revised estimates have been gathered from the field and built into the status report to estimate cost at completion (EAC). Often these revised estimates of expected costs differ from the original planned budget in terms of timing and money amounts. For example, Activity 3 now has an expected duration of 4 time units

FIGURE 13–11

Updated Status Report

Status End of Period 7	Act/ WP	Dur	Total BCWS	Actual and Earned Value by Period (0–7)							ACWP / BCWP	Revised Cost Estimate to Complete (8–15)								EAC
				1	2	3	4	5	6	7		8	9	10	11	12	13	14	15	
Finished (ACWP)	1	5	30	7	6	7	8	7			35									35
Finished (BCWP)				6	6	6	6	6			30									
Finished (ACWP)	2	3	9	6	4	10					20									20
Finished (BCWP)				3	3	3					9									
50% Complete (ACWP)	3	4/3	24						9	8	17	5	8							30
50% Complete (BCWP)									6	6	12									
80% Complete (ACWP)	4	7	35				7	6	6	8	27	5	5	5						42
80% Complete (BCWP)							7	7	7	7	28									
66.7% Complete (ACWP)	5	7/6	18				3	6	3	3	15	3	3	3						24
66.7% Complete (BCWP)							3	3	3	3	12									
Not Started	6	3	21											8	8	8				24
Not Started	7	2	10														5	5		10
ACWP Totals				13	10	17	18	19	18	19		13	16	16	8	8	5	5		
Cumulative ACWP Total				10	23	40	58	77	95	114		127	143	159	167	175	180	185		185
BCWP Totals				9	9	9	16	16	16	16	Cost Variance = BCWP − ACWP = 91 − 114 = (−$23)									
Cumulative BCWP Total				9	18	27	43	53	69	91	Schedule Variance = BCWP − BCWS = 91 − 87 = (+$4)									

and expected costs of 30. Activity 3 is 50 percent complete in 2 time periods, but it still has 2 time periods remaining with additional costs expected in periods 7-8 (5) and 8-9 (8).

The ACWP and BCWP totals for each period are shown. The cumulative values for each period to date are recorded below the period totals. The cumulative ACWP to the status report date is \$114; the cumulative BCWP to date is \$91. Given these cumulative values, the cost variance (CV = BCWP − ACWP) is negative −\$23 (91 − 114 = −23). The project to date *appears* to be in an unfavorable cost situation. The schedule variance (SV = BCWP − BCWS) is positive \$4 (91 − 87 = +4). The BCWS is found in the baseline. (See Figure 13–10; the BCWS at the status report date (6-7) is \$87.) This positive schedule variance is not telling the full story. A careful look at activity 3 and the network tells us the activity will require 4 time units to complete, rather than 3 planned time units. Also, activity 5 is now expected to require 7 actual time units rather than 6. *Remember, SV is in dollars and is not an accurate measure of time;* however, it is a fairly good indicator of the status of the whole project (after 20 percent completed) in terms of being ahead or behind schedule. Only the project network and actual work schedule can give an accurate assessment of schedule performance down to the work package level.

Figure 13–12 presents a cost/schedule graph derived from the worksheet. This graph represents the data found in Figures 13–10 and 13–11. A glance at the graph suggests that, at the end of period 6, project cost performance looks unfavorable. The expected performance for the remainder of the project should give the customer and project manager some concern. The graph shows the project will be

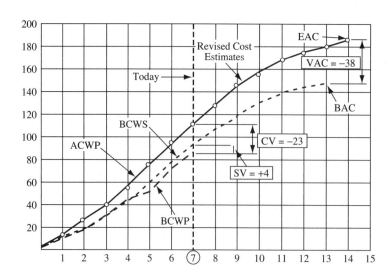

FIGURE 13–12

Cost/Schedule Graph

1 period late and have a cost overrun of -$38. Although schedule performance to date is positive, a clearer picture of schedule progress would be given in a bar chart similar to Figure 13–2.

Given the revised cost estimates and schedules, the finished project will not come in on time or on budget unless corrective action can alter future trends. The project duration is estimated to finish in time period 14 rather than 13. The variance at completion (VAC = BAC − EAC = 147 − 185) is a cost overrun of −$38. See Figure 13–13 for the project cost summary chart.

The project cost summary report is similar in form to the outputs of some computer software programs. Note the data through period 7 represent the cost variance of −$23 (91 − 114 = −23). The variance at completion (VAC) is −$38 (147 − 185 = −38). At this checkpoint we anticipate the project to be $38 over budget at completion.

Figure 13–14 shows an oversimplified project cost rollup at the end of period 6-7. The rollup is by deliverables and organization units. The cost variance does not look favorable at this halfway point; only department C has a positive

FIGURE 13–13

Project Cost Summary Report

	COST SUMMARY REPORT To Date					
	Work Performed to Date			**Total Cost at Completion**		
Activity/ WP	Earned Budget Value (BCWP)	Actual Cost (ACWP)	Cost Over/ Under Run	Original Cost Budget (BCWS)	Latest Expected Actual (EAC)	Cost Over/ Under Run
1	30	35	−5	30	35	−5
2	9	20	−11	9	20	−11
3	12	17	−5	24	30	−6
4	28	27	+1	35	42	−7
5	12	15	−3	18	24	−6
6				21	24	−3
7				10	10	0
Total	91	114	−23	147	185	−38

FIGURE

13–14

*Example
Project
Cost Rollup
Variance*

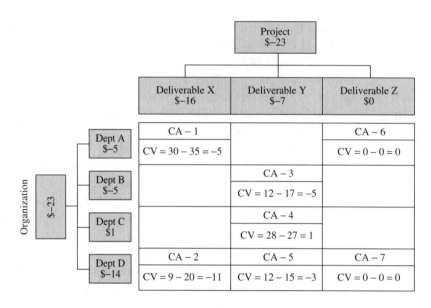

variance. Departments A and D have negative variances and the revised estimates suggest departments A and D probably will not improve. In more complex projects the cross tabs of cost accounts by deliverables and organization units can be very revealing and even more profound than in our simple example.

Other Earned Value Rules

Although the percent complete is the basic rule for earned value, two additional rules are sometimes used to reduce date collection and handling costs. These simplifying rules are the 50/50 rule and 0/100 percent rule (100 percent when complete). These two rules can dramatically reduce the overhead costs of collecting detailed data and processing paperwork. They are typically used for tasks of short duration and those that have small costs, relative to other tasks. These rules are described more fully as follows:

0/100 Percent Rule. This rule assumes credit is earned for having performed the work once it is completed. Hence, 100 percent of the budget is earned when the work package is completed. This rule is used for work packages having very short durations. This rule can also be useful when the task requires purchase and installation of equipment, where the equipment cost is the major cost.

50/50 Rule. This approach allows 50 percent of the value of the work package budget to be earned when it is started and 50 percent to be earned when the package is completed. This rule is popular for work packages of short duration and small total costs.

These rules are assigned by project planners/managers familiar with the work. The rules are used to integrate the baseline budget plan with monitoring performance over the life of the project. The placing of the 0/100 and 50/50 rules in the baseline is not shown here.[5]

Indexes

Indexes are typically used at the cost account level and above. In practice, the database is also used to develop indexes that allow the project manager and customer to view progress from several angles. An index of 1.00 (100 percent) indicates progress is as planned. An index greater than 1.00 shows progress is better than expected. An index less than 1.00 suggests progress is poorer than planned and deserves attention.

Performance Indexes

There are two indexes of performance efficiency. These indexes are illustrated using our example above. The first index measures *cost* efficiency of the work accomplished to date:

$$Cost\ Performance\ Index\ (CPI) = BCWP/ACWP = 91/114 = .80$$

The CPI of $.80 shows that $.80 worth of work planned to date has been completed for each $1.00 actually spent—an unfavorable situation indeed. The CPI is the most accepted and used index. It has been tested over time and found to be the most accurate, reliable, and stable.[6]

The second index is a measure of *scheduling* efficiency to date:

$$Scheduling\ Performance\ Index\ (SPI) = BCWP/BCWS = 91/87 = 104.6$$

The schedule index indicates about $1.05 worth of work has been accomplished for each $1.00 worth of scheduled work to date. Table 13–1 presents the interpretation of the indexes.

Percent Complete Index

These next indexes compare the to-date progress to the end of the project. The implications underlying use of these indexes are that conditions will not change, no improvement or new action will be taken, and the information in the database is accurate. The first index looks at percent complete in terms of budget amounts:

$$Percent\ Complete\ Index\ (PCI - B) = BCWP/BAC = 91/147 = .62\ (62\%)$$

TABLE 13–1   Interpretation of Indexes

Index	Cost (CPI)	Schedule (SPI)
> 1.00	Under cost	Ahead of schedule
= 1.00	On cost	On schedule
< 1.00	Over cost	Behind schedule

This PCI indicates the work accomplished represents 62 percent of the total budgeted (BAC) dollars to date. Observe that this calculation does not include actual costs incurred. Because actual dollars spent do not guarantee project progress, this index is favored by many project managers when there is a high level of confidence in the original budget estimates. Figure 13–15 shows the indexes plotted for our example project through period 6-7. This figure is another example of graphs used in practice.

The second index views percent complete in terms of actual dollars spent to accomplish the work to date and the actual expected dollars for the completed project (EAC). The application of this view is written as

$$\text{Percent Complete Index (PCI - C)} = \text{ACWP/EAC} = 114/185 = .62$$

This percent complete indicates 62 percent of the project is completed, when viewed from the actual dollars spent to complete the work to date and the revised actual expected costs to complete the project. Some managers favor this index because it includes actual and revised estimates that include newer, more complete information.

These two views of percent complete present different views of the "real" percent complete and frequently differ in practice. Management must be careful to use all input sources to have a full grasp of the progress of the project. (*Note*: This index was not plotted in Figure 13–14. The new figures for EAC would be derived each period by estimators in the field.)

Technical Performance Measurement

Measuring technical performance is as important as measuring schedule and cost performance, even if its measurement does not fit the earned value format. Although technical performance is often assumed, the opposite can be true. The ramifications of poor technical performance frequently are more profound—something works or it doesn't, if technical specifications are not adhered to. Assessing technical performance of a system, facility, or product is often accomplished by examining the documents found in the scope statement and/or work package documentation. These documents should specify criteria and tolerance

FIGURE
13–15

*Project
Indexes*

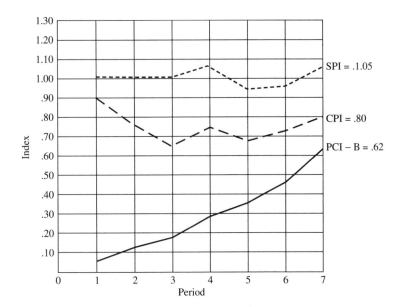

limits against which performance can be measured. It is very difficult to specify how to collect and measure technical performance because it depends on the nature of the project. Sometimes technical performance is dependent on surrogate measures that are directly related to technical performance—e.g., errors per line of code. In rare cases, measuring technical performance may come down to expert opinion or a group assessment. Suffice it to say, measuring technical performance must be done. Project mangers need to be creative in finding ways to control this very important area.

Software for Project Cost/Schedule Systems

Software developers have created sophisticated schedule/cost systems for projects that track and report budget, actual, earned, committed, and index values. These values can be labor hours, materials, and/or dollars. This information supports cost and schedule progress, performance measurements, and cash flow management. Recall from Chapter 4 that budget, actual, and committed dollars usually run in different time frames (see Figure 3–6). A typical computer-generated status report includes the following information:

1. Revised costs at completion (EAC)
2. New forecast costs at completion (FAC)
3. Actual paid this period (ACWP)

4. Total paid to date (ACWP)

5. Schedule variance (BCWP/BCWS) by cost account and WBS and OBS

6. Cost variance (BCWP/ACWP) by cost account and WBS and OBS

7. Indexes—cost, schedule, total percent complete (BCWP, BCWS, ACWP, BAC, EAC)

8. Paid and unpaid commitments

The variety of software packages, with their features and constant updating, is too extensive for inclusion in this text. Software developers and vendors have done a super job of providing software to meet the information needs of most project managers. Differences among software in the past decade have centered on improving "friendliness" and output that is clear and easy to understand. Anyone who understands the concepts and tools presented in Chapters 4 through 8 and Chapter 13 should have little trouble understanding the output of any of the popular, top-10 project management software packages. (Caveat: A few software packages reverse the variance signs. That is, a negative cost or schedule variance is considered desirable; you may have to adapt to this variation, depending on the software used.)

Forecasting Final Project Cost

Early questions raised by management are: Are we on budget? What will the final project cost be? If the project is small or moderate in size, and a good look-ahead system for revising cost estimates exists, the EAC procedure suggested earlier in the chapter is probably adequate to estimate final costs. However, if the project is a large one, revised cost estimates far into the future are less reliable or nonexistent. One method that has gained acceptance and proven to be accurate and reliable in forecasting final project costs uses the CPI performance index (CPI = BCWP/ACWP). The equation for this model is below:

$$\text{ETC} = \frac{\text{work remaining}}{\text{CPI}} = \frac{\text{BAC} - \text{BCWP}}{\text{BCWP/ACWP}}$$

$$\text{FAC} = \text{ETC} + \text{ACWP}$$

where: ETC = remaining forecasted cost to complete.

CPI = cumulative cost performance index to date.

BCWP = cumulative budgeted cost of work completed to date.

ACWP = cumulative actual cost of work completed to date.

BAC = total budget of the baseline.

FAC is the forecasted total cost at completion.

For example, if we assume the following information is available, the forecast cost at completion (FAC) is computed as follows:

Total baseline budget (BAC) for the project	$ 5,000
Cumulative earned value (BCWP) to date	$ 1,600
Cumulative actual cost (ACWP) to date	$ 2,000

$$\mathbf{FAC} = \frac{\$5,000 - \$1,600}{\$1,600/\$2,000} + \$2,000 = \frac{\$3,400}{.8} + \$2,000 = \$4,250 + \$2,000$$

$$= \$ 6,250$$

The final project cost forecast is $ 6,250. Research data[7] indicate that on large projects that are more than 20 percent complete, the model performs well with an error of less than 10 percent. This model can also be used for WBS and OBS cost accounts that have been started to forecast remaining and total costs. It is important to note that this model assumes conditions will not change, the cost database is reliable, BCWP and ACWP are cumulative, and past project progress is representative of future progress. This objective forecast represents a good starting point or benchmark that management can use to compare other forecasts that include other conditions and subjective judgments.

A summary report is shown in the *Project Management in Action: Trojan Decommissioning Project.*

Project Management in Action

Trojan Decommissioning Project

Portland General Electric Company has been charged with decommissioning the Trojan Nuclear Plant. This is a long and complex project extending over 2 decades. The first segment of the project of moving the used reactors to a storage location is complete and was awarded the Project of the Year, 2000, by the Project Management Institute (PMI). The remainder of the project—decontamination of the remaining structures and waste—is ongoing.

Figure 13–16 shows their earned value status report through December, 2000. This report measures schedule and cost performance for monitoring the project and forecasts next year's expected costs (TDF). The report also serves as a basis for funding for rate filings with the Public Utilities Commission.

The SPI (0.88) suggests the project schedule is falling behind. Resolving issues with a major vendor and solutions for technical problems should solve these delay problems. The CPI (1.14) for the project is positive. Some of this good cost performance is attributed to partnering and incentive arrangements with vendors and labor unions.

FIGURE 13-16

Decommissioning Cumulative Costs

Cost/Budget Performance (BCWS and TDF) — Decommissioning Cumulative Costs — Nominal Year Dollars

Portland General Electric Co.—Trojan Nuclear Plant Report Run: 23-Jan-01 8:13 AM Report Number: DECT005 Page: 1 of 1

Description	Dec-2000			Year-to-Date			YTD Variance BCP-ACP	2000 BCWS	2000 TDF	CPI BCP/ACP	SPI BCP/TDF
	BCWS	BCWP	ACWP	BCWS	BCWP	ACWP					
ISFSI	193,014	162,573	162,579	3,655,677	3,586,411	3,263,995	322,416	3,655,877	4,346,754	1.10	0.83
RVAIR	0	0	0	0	0	399	(399)	0	0	0.00	0.00
Equip Removal-AB/FB	79,053	79,649	73,899	497,197	504,975	308,461	196,514	497,197	479,534	1.64	1.05
Equip Removal-Other	0	0	0	0	(36,822)	519	(37,341)	0	0	0.00	0.00
Embed Piping-AB/FB	3,884	0	2,118	532,275	540,232	515,235	24,997	532,275	763,579	1.05	0.71
Embed Piping-Other	0	0	3,439	175,401	210,875	79,235	131,640	175,401	195,405	2.66	1.08
Surface Decon-AB/FB	29,935	23,274	21,466	1,266,665	1,293,315	1,171,712	121,603	1,266,665	1,453,029	1.10	0.90
Surface Decon-Other	2,875	2	11,005	308,085	199,853	251,266	(51,413)	308,085	141,183	0.80	1.24
Surface Decon-Containment	680,502	435,657	474,427	5,271,689	4,950,528	4,823,338	127,190	5,271,689	4,693,551	1.03	0.96
Radwaste Disposal	884,873	453,032	(28,675)	10,680,116	8,276,616	10,807,916	(2,531,300)	10,680,116	10,645,292	0.77	0.78
Final Survey	58,238	57,985	27,091	780,990	780,990	700,942	80,048	780,990	1,568,600	1.11	0.50
Non-Radiological Areas	92,537	91,956	58,538	2,471,281	2,376,123	834,643	1,541,480	2,471,281	3,579,292	2.85	0.66
Staffing	714,806	714,509	466,658	9,947,775	9,947,775	8,241,383	1,706,392	9,947,775	9,772,793	1.21	1.02
ISFSI-Long Term Ops	85,026	85,026	19,173	2,004,398	2,004,398	337,206	1,667,192	2,004,398	2,707,316	5.94	0.74
Labor Loadings	258,289	258,289	240,229	3,216,194	3,216,194	2,755,604	460,590	3,216,194	3,216,194	1.17	1.00
Material Loadings	17,910	17,910	(95,128)	211,454	211,454	136,973	74,481	211,454	211,454	1.54	1.00
Corporate Governance	153,689	226,499	226,621	1,814,523	1,814,523	1,814,620	3	1,814,523	2,277,711	1.00	0.80
Undistributable Costs	431,840	401,720	242,724	5,541,679	5,575,679	4,007,732	1,567,947	5,541,679	5,455,764	1.39	1.02
Total Decommissioning	3,686,481	3,008,081	1,906,064	48,375,399	45,453,119	40,051,079	5,402,040	48,375,399	51,507,451	1.13	0.87
Total (less ISFSI and RVAIR)	3,493,467	2,845,508	1,743,485	44,719,720	41,866,710	36,786,680	5,080,024	44,719,720	47,160,700	1.14	0.88

Other Control Issues

The Costs and Problems of Data Acquisition

There can be issues surrounding resistance to data collection of percent complete for earned value systems. So pseudo-percent complete systems have been developed.[8] *Project Management in Action: A Pseudo-Percent Complete Approach* captures some of the frequently seen issues of data collection. Such pseudo-percent complete approaches appear to work well in multiproject environments that include several small and medium-sized projects. Assuming a 1-week reporting period, take care to develop work packages with a duration of about 1 week long so problems are identified quickly. For large projects, there is no substitute for

---

Project Management in Action

A Pseudo-Percent Complete Approach

A consultant for the U.S. Forest Service suggested the use of earned value to monitor the more than 50 timber sale projects taking place concurrently in the district. As projects were completed, new ones were started. Earned value was tried for approximately 9 months. After a 9-month trial, the process was to be reviewed by a task force. The task force concluded the earned value system provided good information for monitoring and forecasting project progress; however, the costs and problems of collecting timely percent complete data were unacceptable because there were no funds available to collect such data.

The level of detail dilemma was discussed, but no suggestions satisfied the problem. The discussion recognized that too little data fail to offer good control, while excessive reporting requires paperwork and people, which are costly. The task force concluded progress and performance could be measured using a pseudo-version of percent complete while not giving up much accuracy for the total project. This modified approach to percent complete required that very large work packages (about 3 to 5 percent of all work packages in a project) be divided into smaller work packages for closer control and identification of problems sooner. It was decided work packages of about a week's duration would be ideal. The pseudo-version required only a telephone call and "yes/no" answers to the following questions to assign percent complete:

Has work on the work package started?	No = 0 percent
Working on the package?	Yes = 50 percent
Is the work package completed?	Yes = 100 percent

Data for the pseudo-earned value, percent complete system was collected for all 50-plus projects by an intern working fewer than 8 hours each week.

using a percent complete system that depends on data collected through observation at clearly defined monitoring points.

Baseline Changes

Changes during the life cycle of projects are inevitable. Some changes can be beneficial to project outcomes; changes having a negative impact are the ones we wish to avoid. Careful project definition can minimize the need for changes. The price for poor project definition can be changes that result in cost overruns, late schedules, low morale, and loss of control. Change comes from external sources or from within. Externally, for example, the customer may request changes that were not included in the original scope statement and that will require significant changes to the project and thus to the baseline. Or the government may render requirements that were not a part of the original plan and that require a revision of the project scope. Internally, stakeholders may identify unforeseen problems or improvements that change the scope of the project. In rare cases scope changes can come from several sources. For example, the Denver International Airport automatic baggage handling system was an afterthought supported by several project stakeholders that included the Denver city government, consultants, and at least one airline customer. The additional $2 billion in costs were staggering, and the airport opening was delayed 16 months. If this automatic baggage scope change had been in the original plan, costs would have been only a fraction of the overrun costs, and delays would have been reduced significantly.

Generally, project managers should resist baseline changes. Baseline changes should be allowed only if it can be proven the project will fail without the change or the project will be improved significantly with the change. This statement is an exaggeration, but it sets the tone for approaching baseline changes. In the field, if the change results in a significant impact on the project and requires a scope change, the baseline should be changed. The impact of the change on the scope and baseline should be accepted and signed off by the project customer. Figure 13–17 depicts the cost impact of a scope change on the baseline at a point in time—"today." Line A represents a scope change that results in an increase in cost. Line B represents a scope change that decreases cost. Quickly recording scope changes to the baseline keeps the computed earned values valid. Failure to do so results in misleading cost and schedule variances.

Be careful to avoid using baseline changes to disguise poor performance on past or current work. A common signal of this type of baseline change is a constantly revised baseline that seems to match results. Practitioners call this a "rubber baseline" because it stretches to match results. Most changes will not result in serious scope changes and should be absorbed as positive or negative variances. Retroactive changes for work already accomplished should not be allowed. Transfer of money

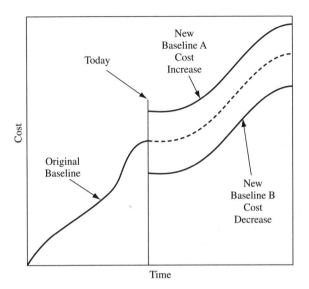

FIGURE 13–17

Scope Changes to a Baseline

among cost accounts should not be allowed after the work is completed. Unforeseen changes can be handled through the contingency reserve. The project manager typically makes this decision. In some large projects, a partnering "change review team," made up of members of the project and customer teams, makes all decisions on project changes.

Contingency Reserve

Plans seldom materialize in every detail as estimated. Because perfect planning doesn't exist, some contingency funds should be agreed upon before the project commences to cover the unexpected. The size of the management reserve should be related to the uncertainty and risk of schedule and cost estimate inaccuracies. For example, if the project represents little that is new to the project team, the management reserve might be 1 to 2 percent of the total cost of the project. Conversely, if the project represents something that is new to all team members, the reserve might be 5 to 20 percent of the total cost. A rule of thumb used by a construction management firm centers around the percent of design complete when the project begins. For example, if 30 percent of design is completed when the project begins, a management reserve of 25 percent is included as a hedge against uncertainty; if 60 percent of design is complete, the reserve is 15 percent; if design is 95 percent complete, a 10 percent reserve is included. Contingency reserve funds represent flexibility for the project manager so he or she can move the project forward.

Contingency reserve is not a free lunch for all who come. Reserve funds should be released by the project manager only on a formal and documented basis. *Budget reserve* contingency funds are not for scope changes. Scope changes are covered by *management reserve* funds. Chapter 7 provides a detailed description of budget and management contingency funds. The trend today is to allow all stakeholders to know the size of the contingency reserve (even subcontractors). This approach is built on trust, openness, and the self-discipline of the project stakeholders who are focused on one set of goals.

Scope Creep

Large changes in scope are easily identified. It is the "minor refinements" that eventually build to be major scope changes that can cause problems. These small refinements are known in the field as *scope creep*. For example, the customer of a software developer requested small changes in the development of a custom accounting software package. After several minor refinements, it became apparent the changes represented a significant enlargement of the original project scope. The result was an unhappy customer and a development firm that lost money and reputation.

Although scope changes are usually viewed negatively, there are situations when scope changes result in positive rewards. Scope changes can represent significant opportunities. In product development environments, adding a small feature to a product can result in a huge competitive advantage. A small change in production process may get the product to market 1 month early or reduce product cost.

Scope creep is common early in projects—especially in new-product development projects.[9] New technology, poor design assumptions, customer requirements for additional features etc., all manifest pressures for scope changes. Frequently these changes are small and go unnoticed until time delays or cost overruns are observed. Scope creep affects the organization, project team, and project suppliers. Scope changes alter the organization's cash flow requirements in the form of fewer or additional resources, which may also impact other projects. Frequent changes eventually wear down team motivation and cohesiveness. Clear team goals are altered, become less focused, and cease being the focal point for team action. Starting over again is annoying and demoralizing to the project team because it disrupts project rhythm and lowers productivity. Project suppliers resent frequent changes because they represent higher costs and have the same effect on their team as on the project team.

Because scope creep is inevitable, controlling it is imperative! The key to managing scope creep is change control.[10] (Chapter 5 discusses the process. See Figure 7–8 to review the key variables to document in project changes.) First, the original baseline must be well defined and agreed upon with the project customer. Before the project begins, it is imperative that clear procedures be in place for authorizing and documenting scope changes made by either the customer or project team. All changes should be cleared with the project manager. If a scope change is necessary, the impact on the baseline should be clearly documented—for example, cost, time, dependencies, specifications, responsibilities, etc. Finally, the scope change must be quickly added to the original baseline to reflect the change in budget and schedule; these changes and their impacts need to be communicated to all project stakeholders.

Summary

The best information system does not ensure good control. Control requires the project manager to *use* information to steer the project through rough waters. Gantt (bar) charts are useful for monitoring time performance. The earned value system allows the manager to have a positive influence on cost and schedule in a timely manner. The ability to influence cost decreases with time; therefore, timely reports identifying adverse cost trends can greatly assist the project manager in getting back on budget and schedule. The integrated cost/schedule model provides the project manager and other stakeholders with a snapshot of the current and future status of the project. The benefits of the earned value model are as follow:

1. Measures accomplishments against plan and deliverables
2. Provides a method for tracking directly to a problem workpackage and organization unit responsible and accountable
3. Alerts all stakeholders to early identification of problems and allows for quick, proactive corrective action
4. Improves communication because all stakeholders are using the same database
5. Keeps customer informed of progress and encourages customer confidence that the money spent is resulting in the expected progress

Today, the continuing trend toward industry consolidation has forced organizations to create and manage portfolios of projects. Monitoring performance of all the individual projects in the portfolio has resulted in the adoption of cost/schedule earned value systems. Such systems facilitate consistency and bring discipline to the process of monitoring progress of all the projects in the portfolio. In large organizations the process is managed by the project office.

14

PROJECT AUDIT
AND CLOSURE

Those who cannot remember the past are condemned to relive it.
George Santayana 1863–1952

Mistakes are made; the unexpected happens; conditions change. In organizations that have several projects going on concurrently, it is prudent to have periodic reality checks. Current and recently completed projects and their role in the organization's future should be assessed. The postproject audit includes three major tasks:

1. Evaluate the project: Did the project deliver the expected benefits to all stakeholders? Was the project managed well? Was the customer satisfied?
2. Assess what was done wrong and what contributed to successes.
3. Identify changes to improve the delivery of future projects.

The project audit and report are instruments for supporting continuous improvement and total quality management.

Unfortunately, it is estimated that about 90 percent of all projects are not seriously reviewed or audited. The most common reason given is "we're too busy to stop and assess how well we manage projects." This is a big mistake. Without reflective assessment, valuable lessons learned are forgotten and mistakes are repeated. Sadly, those projects that are audited tend to be major failures or disasters. This is another big mistake. We tend to learn only what *not* to do from failures, not what *to* do. By examining both successes and failures, best practices can be incorporated into the project management system of an organization.

We have observed that when projects are seriously audited, they appear to be done by extremely well-managed organizations that are leaders in their fields. These organizations are vigorously committed to continuous improvement and exhibit characteristics synonymous with the highest level of the project maturity model—optimizing.

In this chapter, we begin by discussing different kinds of project audits as well as the audit process. Issues related to project closure are addressed next. We conclude the chapter by discussing the evaluation of team and individual performance on a project.

Project Audits

Project audits are more than the status reports described in Chapter 13, which check on project performance. Status reports are analogous to viewing the project through a telescope. Audits are analogous to viewing the project through field glasses—a wide-angle view of the project in its bigger organizational environment. Project audits do use performance measures and forecast data, but they are more inclusive. The goals of a project audit are to:

- Review why the project was selected.
- Reassess the project's role in the organization's priorities.
- Check on the organization culture to ensure it facilitates the type of project being implemented.
- Assess whether the project team is functioning well and is appropriately staffed.
- Check on external factors that might change where the project is heading or its importance—for example, technology, government laws, competing products.
- Review all factors relevant to the project and managing future projects.

Project audits can be performed while a project is in process and after a project is completed. There are only a few minor differences between these audits.

In-process Project Audits.   Project audits early in projects allow for corrective changes if they are needed on the audited project or others in progress. In-process project audits concentrate on project progress and performance and check if conditions have changed. For example, have priorities changed? Is the project mission still relevant? In rare cases, the audit report may recommend closure of a project that is in process.

Postproject Audits.   These audits tend to include more detail and depth than in-process project audits. Project audits of completed projects emphasize improving the management of future projects. These audits are more long-term oriented than in-process audits. Postproject audits do check on project performance, but the audit represents a broader view of the project's role in the organization; for example, were the strategic benefits claimed actually delivered?

Audit Depth and Detail

The depth and detail of the project audit depend on many factors. Some are listed below.

Organization size
Project importance
Project type
Project risk
Project size
Project problems

Because audits cost time and money, they should include no more time or resources than are necessary and sufficient. Early in-process project audits tend to be perfunctory unless serious problems or concerns are identified. Clearly, in this latter situation the audit is carried out in more detail. Because in-process project audits can be worrisome and destructive to the project team, take care to protect project team morale. The audit should be carried out quickly and the report should be as positive and constructive as possible. Postproject audits are more detailed and inclusive and contain more project team input.

In summary, plan the audit and limit the time of the audit. For example, in postproject audits, for all but very large projects, a 1-week limit is a good benchmark. Beyond this time, the marginal return of additional information diminishes quickly. Small projects may require only 1 or 2 days and one or two people to conduct an audit.

The priority team functions well in selecting projects and monitoring performance—cost and time. However, reviewing and evaluating projects and the process of managing projects is usually delegated to independent audit groups.[1] Each audit group is charged with evaluating and reviewing *all* factors relevant to the project and to managing future projects. The outcome of the project audit is a report.

The Project Audit Process

Initiation and Staffing

How the audit process is initiated depends primarily on organization size and project size. Every effort should be made to make the project audit a normal process rather than a surprise notice.

In small organizations and projects where face-to-face contact at all levels is prevalent, an audit may be informal in the form of a staff meeting. But even in these environments, the content of the formal project audit should be documented with notes made of the lessons learned. In medium-sized organizations that have several projects occurring simultaneously, initiation can come from a formal project review group, come from the project priority team, or be automatic. For example, in the latter case, all projects are audited at specific stages in the project life cycle—perhaps when a project is 10 to 20 percent complete in time or money, 50 percent complete, and after completion. The automatic process works well because it removes the perceptions that a project has been singled out for evaluation and that someone might be on a witch hunt. For large projects, the audit may be planned for major milestones.

There are rare circumstances that require an unplanned project audit, but they should be few and far between. For example, in a project that involved the development of a very large computer accounting system for multiple locations, one major consulting firm (of many) gave notice of withdrawal from the project, with no apparent reason. The project customer became alarmed that perhaps there was a serious fundamental problem in the project that caused the large consulting firm to drop out. A project audit identified the problem: members of a small consulting firm were sexually harrassing members of the larger consulting firm. The small consulting firm engagement was terminated and replaced with a firm of similar expertise. The larger firm agreed to remain with the project. Other circumstances, internal and external to the project, can cause an unplanned audit—for example, large cost or time overruns, change in project managers, or cover-ups. Regardless, unplanned audits should be avoided except in unusual circumstances.

A major tenet of the project audit is that the outcome must represent an independent, outside view of the project. Maintaining independence and an objective view is difficult, given that audits are frequently viewed as negative by project stakeholders. Careers and reputations can be tarnished even in organizations that tolerate mistakes. In less forgiving organizations, mistakes can lead to termination or exile to less significant regions of an organization. Of course, if the result of an audit is favorable, careers and reputations can be enhanced. Given that project audits are susceptible to internal politics, some organizations rely on outside consulting firms to conduct the audits. Regardless, it is imperative the audit leader possess the following characteristics:

1. No direct involvement or direct interest in the project.
2. Respect (perceived as impartial and fair) of senior management and other project stakeholders.
3. Willingness to listen.
4. Independence and authority to report audit results without fear of recriminations from special interests.
5. Perceived as having the best interests of the organization in mind when making decisions.
6. Broad-based experience in the organization or industry.

Other audit members should have similar characteristics even if they are selected for their special expertise. Some project team members will need to be included in the audit evaluation. Postproject audits have a stronger representation of project team members than in-process project audits because of the slightly different orientation. The concern that team members will come to the audit with strong biases is usually overstated. In general, project team members are genuinely interested in improving the future project management process; they make every attempt to be objective.

Information and Data Collection and Analysis

The traditional content model for a project audit presents two perspectives. The first is to evaluate the project from the view of the organization. The second perspective represents the project team's evaluative view. The organization perspective is developed by a small group primarily made up of persons not having a direct interest in the project. The project team perspective is developed by a group composed primarily of team members along with persons independent of the project to ensure the evaluation is objective.

Each organization and project is unique. Therefore, many factors need to be considered. For example, the industry, project size, newness of technology, and project experience can influence the nature of the audit. However, information and data are gathered to answer questions similar to those suggested next.

Organization View

1. Was the organization culture supportive and correct for this type of project? Why? Why not?
2. Was senior management's support adequate?

3. Did the project accomplish its intended purpose?
    a. Is there a clear link to organization strategy and objectives?
    b. Does the priority system reflect importance to the future of the organization?
    c. Has the environment (internal or external) changed the need for the project's completion (if project is still in process)?
4. Were the risks for the project appropriately identified and assessed? Were contingency plans used? Were they realistic? Have risk events occurred that have an impact greater than anticipated?
5. Were the right people and talents assigned to this project?
6. If the project was completed, have staff been fairly assigned to new projects?
7. What does evaluation from outside contractors suggest?
8. Were the project start-up and hand-off successful? Why? Is the customer satisfied?

Project Team View

1. Were the project planning and control systems appropriate for this type of project? Should all similar size and type projects use these systems? Why or why not?
2. Did the project conform to plan? Is the project over or under budget and schedule? Why?
3. Were interfaces with project stakeholders adequate and effective?
4. If the project is completed, has the staff been fairly assigned to new projects?
5. Did the team have adequate access to organization resources—people, budget, support groups, equipment? Were there resource conflicts with other ongoing projects? Was the team managed well?
6. What does evaluation from outside contractors suggest?

The audit group should not be limited to these questions.[2] The audit group should include other questions related to their organization and project type—e.g., research and development, marketing, information systems, construction, facilities. The generic questions above, although overlapping, represent a good starting point and will go a long way toward identifying project problem and success patterns. *Project Management in Action: Operation Eagle Claw* illustrates an audit of a military action.

Guidelines for Conducting a Project Audit

The following guidelines should improve chances for a successful audit:

1. First and foremost, the philosophy must be that the project audit is not a witch hunt.

Project Management in Action

Operation Eagle Claw

On November 4, 1979, a mob in Iran stormed the U.S. Embassy and took 52 Americans hostage. After 6 months of failed negotiation, the decision was made to execute Operation Eagle Claw, a joint military effort to free the U.S. hostages.

The plan called for eight Navy RH-53D helicopters to fly 600 miles to a remote site in Iran, code named Desert One. Under the cover of darkness, the helicopters would be refueled by KC-130 tanker planes. The helicopters would then fly the assault force to a spot near the outskirts of Tehran where they would meet up with special agents already in the country. The agents would lead them to a safe house to await the assault on the embassy the next night. Upon rescuing the hostages, the assault team would escort the hostages to a nearby air field that had been secured by a second attack team where they would be flown to safety.

What actually happened was far different from what was planned.

The helicopter pilots were ordered to fly at or below 200 feet to avoid radar. This caused them to run into "haboobs" or dust storms. Two helicopters malfunctioned and turned back. The remainder battled the dust storms and arrived at Desert One an hour late. The rescue attempt was dealt its final blow when it was discovered that a third helicopter had a hydraulic leak and was inoperable. Only five aircraft were serviceable and six were needed, so the mission was aborted.

Things got worse, though, when one of the helicopters moved into position to refuel and collided with a KC-130 plane. Both aircraft burst into flames. All told, eight soldiers died and dozens were injured. The Iranians scattered the hostages around the country afterward, making any further rescue attempts impossible.

The Armed Services routinely conduct audits of every exercise and operation. Given the gravity of the situation, a special six-member commission was appointed by the Joint Chiefs of Staff to investigate the failed operation. They discovered a number of issues that contributed to the failure. One issue was the selection of air crew. Navy and Marine pilots with little experience in long-range overland navigation or refueling were selected though more than 100 qualified Air Force pilots were available. Another issue was the lack of a comprehensive mission rehearsal program. From the beginning, training was not conducted in a truly joint manner; it was compartmentalized by service and held in scattered locations across the United States. The limited rehearsals that were conducted assessed only portions of the total mission. Also at issue was the number of helicopters used. The commission concluded that 10 and perhaps 12 helicopters should have been launched to guarantee the minimum six required for completion of the mission. Finally, the hopscotch method of ground refueling was criticized. If the planners had chosen to use en-route air fueling, the entire Desert One scenario could have been avoided. The final report of the commission contained several important recommendations designed to prevent such a tragedy from occurring again.[3]

2. Comments about individuals or groups participating in the project are no-nos. Keep to project issues, not what happened or by whom.

3. Audit activities should be intensely sensitive to human emotions and reactions. The inherent threat to those being evaluated should be reduced as much as possible.

4. Accuracy of data should be verifiable or noted as subjective, judgmental, or hearsay.

5. Senior management should announce support for the project audit and see that the audit group has access to all information, project participants, and (in most cases) project customer.

6. The attitude toward a project audit and its aftermath depend on the *modus operandi* of the audit leadership and group. The objective is not to prosecute. The objective is to learn and conserve valuable organization resources where mistakes have been made. Friendliness, empathy, and objectivity encourage cooperation and reduce anxiety.

7. The audit should be completed as quickly as is reasonable.

8. The audit leader should be given access to senior management above the project manager.

The Audit Report

General Requirements

The major goal of the audit report is to improve the way future projects are managed. Succinctly, the report attempts to capture needed changes and lessons learned from a current or finished project. The report serves as a training instrument for managers of future projects.

Audit reports need to be tailored to the specific project and organization environment. Nevertheless, a generic format for all audits facilitates development of an audit database and a common outline for those who prepare audit reports and the managers who read and act on their content. A very general outline common to those found in practice is as follows:

1. Classification of project
2. Analysis of information gathered
3. Recommendations
4. Lessons learned
5. Appendix

Classification.   Each project audit is categorized because there are differences in the way projects are managed and handled in an organization. A prospective project manager of a software coding project will have little interest in the construction of a clean room or recycling of inkjet reservoirs for printers. A prospective project manager of a small project will not be as interested in a computer project planning and control system as a project manager who is going to manage a very large project. The classification of projects by characteristics allows prospective readers and project managers to be selective in the use of the report content. Typical classification categories include the following:

- Project type—e.g., development, marketing, systems, construction
- Size—monetary
- Number of staff
- Technology level—low, medium, high, new
- Strategic or support

Other classifications relevant to the organization should be included.

Analysis.   The analysis section includes succinct, factual review statements of the project. For example:

- Project mission and objectives
- Procedures and systems used
- Organization resources used

Recommendations.   Usually audit recommendations represent major corrective actions that should take place. However, it is equally important to recommend positive successes that should be continued and used in future projects. Postproject audits may be the place to give credit to the project team for an outstanding contribution.

Lessons Learned.   These do not have to be in the form of recommendations. Lessons learned serve as reminders of mistakes easily avoided and actions easily taken to ensure success. In practice, new project teams reviewing audits of past projects similar to the one they are about to start have found audit reports very useful. Team members will frequently remark later, "The recommendations were good, but the 'lessons learned' section really helped us avoid many pitfalls and made our project implementation smoother." In the *Project Management in Action: Lessons Learned: Bell Canada Business Transformation Project*, the project involved a business transformation process of bringing more than 500 independent projects under one generic project management process umbrella. This

Lessons Learned: Bell Canada
Business Transformation Project

The following are the "lessons learned" by Bell Canada in its postproject audit of its Business Transformation Project:

- Managing the team's expectations of the planning process was crucial. Team members needed to understand that frustrations, "surprises," and recycling were a normal part of planning. Planning is hard work, and more effort spent in planning would improve the success factor.

- The teams were often scattered along functional lines rather than organized from a project perspective. This made reporting and identifying roles and responsibilities very difficult for the project manager. Project team structure was also challenged by the geography, cross-functional membership, and two organizations (Bell Canada and Bell Sygma) playing equal roles. The understanding and use of organization structure played a key role in the planning and implementation of the project.

- The level of coaching required by the project manager once the project plan was completed was more than anticipated. Understanding and using the processes for day-by-day project management were challenging once team members returned to their work environments.

- Not all consultants hired were successful. Initially feedback from the project team was the biggest factor in determining the consultant's effectiveness. This was a mistake. The team was too dependent on the consultant's knowledge and could not judge the value. Subsequently, the senior consultant or a member of another team accompanied all new consultants for the first few days.

- The primary hiring skills for consultants were (1) project management skills, (2) proven and recent experience in managing IT projects, and (3) facilitation skills. It turned out that if facilitation skills were lacking, it did not matter how strong the first two skill sets were—the consultant could not succeed.

- There is a fine line between what *must* be done and what *should* be done in these situations. It was a struggle to maintain a pragmatic, minimalist approach in applying project management with novice teams, especially without supporting infrastructure in place. Even with the short-term process that was established, we had to pull back on some of the initial requirements (structure of the WBS, postplanning review, and uninterrupted planning). In many cases the consultants' desire to "do it right" often had to give way to "getting it done."

- Some of the business transformation projects would have not been approved had there been proper planning in the first phase of the project. Knowing the true cost of development and implementation could have resulted in a nonviable business case from a financial perspective.[4]

project was especially challenging because most managers had little project management experience. The lessons learned demonstrate some of the difficulties and insights gained by the implementation team trying to integrate project management into the culture of the organization.

Appendix. The appendix may include backup data or details of analysis that would allow others to follow up if they wished. It should not be a dumping ground, or used for filler; only critical pertinent information should be attached.

Finally, it is good to keep a small summary booklet of "major lessons learned." Give references to archived audit reports if additional information is desired. This process may appear a bit formal, but people use these summaries and archives when they are available—more frequently than most would believe.

Project Audits: The Bigger Picture

Individual audits or postproject reviews can yield valuable lessons that team members can apply to future project work. When done on a consistent basis across all significant projects, audits can lead to significant improvements in the processes and techniques organizations use to complete projects. This is the sign of an organization that has reached the "optimizing" phase of the project maturity model. This phase is characterized by systematic analysis of common causes of variation in project performance. Such analyses can lead to incremental improvements in the conduct of project management such as the institutionalization of common scope and reporting templates or risk assessment checklists. Audits can also lead to major changes in how projects are managed. For example, the result of series of postproject audits in one organization revealed teams were "throwing their part of the project over the fence" to the next team in the sequence with little or no coordination. To alleviate this problem management mandated that projects be organized to include a member of the receiving team on the team passing the project on, so problems could be identified and corrected before passing to the next team.

Robert Graham and Randall Englund in their book, *Creating an Environment for Successful Projects* provide a number of examples of how Hewlett-Packard (HP) has improved project management performance through systematic project reviews.[5] For example, one review team identified 150 issues that had to be resolved to complete a major project. The team classified each issue as high, medium, and low complexity and determined on average how long it took to resolve issues at each level of complexity. The complexity scheme was applied to a subsequent project with the averages used with bottom-up estimates to come up with a more accurate schedule. A related study revealed that HP engineers were not good at separating technical issues from organizational ones. Technical issues, within this context, had clearly definable solutions based on objective criteria while organizational issues had no clear-cut solution and typically involved trade-offs between project criteria. Further analysis revealed that no clear process existed for making a decision based on trade-offs, nor did the engineers have the perspective or skills to solve these organizational issues. This lead to the creation of a program to train engineering leaders in project management and the establishment of a process for escalating organizational issues promptly to appropriate levels in management. See *Project Management in Action: Hewlett-Packard's Project Management Initiative* for more information on HP's efforts to improve project management.

More and more organizations that are committed to project management excellence are using project audits as a vehicle for studying and improving their

---

Project Management in Action

Hewlett-Packard's Project Management Initiative

In 1989 Hewlett-Packard (HP) launched a corporate-wide project management initiative. HP's senior management recognized that time-to-market was increasingly important as a competitive weapon and that the company needed to get the right products to market quickly and effectively. The initiative provided the following:

- Conceptual frameworks for project management
- Curriculum for project manager development
- Internal consulting services
- Forums for developing best practices
- Depository of best project management practices
- Upper management conferences
- Help in project manager selection and development
- A central information source for project managers entering new areas
- Formation of a project management council

The project management council was given the broad charge of improving project management techniques at HP. Members consisted of veteran project managers as well as representatives from major organizations throughout HP. The council reviews and prioritizes project plans such as new training modules, certification, benchmarking, and sponsorship. They also review early drafts of internal project management related publications and assist in post-project review.[6]

capacity to manage projects. They are investing time and energy in benchmarking and developing performance metrics so they can assess the efficacy of their project management system.

Project Closure

Every project comes to an end, eventually. On some projects the end may not be as clear as would be hoped. Although the scope statement may define a clear ending for a project, the actual ending may or may not correspond. Fortunately, a majority of projects are blessed with a well-defined ending. Regular project audits and a priority team will identify those projects that should have endings different from those planned.

Conditions for Project Closure

Normal.   The most common circumstance for project closure is simply a completed project. In the case of turnkey projects, such as building a new manufacturing facility or creating a customized information system, the finish is marked by transferring ownership to the customer. For many development projects, the end involves handing off the final design to production and the creation of a new product or service line. For other internal projects, such as system upgrades or creation of new inventory control systems, the end occurs when the output is incorporated into going operations. Although in the case of all of these projects some modifications in scope, cost, and time may have occurred during implementation, the projects are completed near plan.

Premature.   For a few projects, the project may be completed early with some parts of the project eliminated. For example, in a new product development project, a marketing manager may insist on production models before testing:

> Give the new product to me now, the way it is. Early entry into the market will mean big profits! I know we can sell a bizzillion of these. If we don't do it now, the opportunity is lost!

The pressure is on to finish the project and send it to production. Before succumbing to this form of pressure, the implications and risks associated with this decision should be carefully reviewed and assessed by senior management and all stakeholders. Too frequently, the benefits are illusory, are dangerous, and carry large risks. Why have the original project scope and objectives changed? If early project closure occurs, it should have the support of all project stakeholders. This decision should be left to the audit group, project priority team, or senior management.

Perpetual. Some projects never seem to end.[7] That is, the project appears to develop a life of its own. Although these projects are plagued with delays, they are viewed as desirable when they finally are completed. The major characteristic of this kind of project is constant "add-ons." The owner or others continuously require more small changes that will improve the project outcome—product or service. These changes typically represent extras perceived as being part of the original project intent. Examples are adding features to software, product design, systems, or construction projects. Constant add-on changes suggest a poorly conceived project scope. More care in up-front definition of the project scope and limitations will reduce the add-on phenomenon.

At some point the project manager or audit group needs to call the project design locked to bring closure. Although these projects are exhibiting scope, cost, and schedule creep, facing the fact that the project should be brought to an end is not an easy chore. Project managers or audit/priority groups have several alternatives. They can redefine the project end or scope to force closure. They can limit budget or resources. They can set a time limit. All alternatives should be designed to bring the project to an end as quickly as possible to limit additional costs and still gain the positive benefits of a completed project. The audit group should recommend methods for bringing closure to this type of project. Failed projects are usually easy to identify and easy for an audit group to close down. However, every effort should be made to communicate the technical reasons for termination of the project; project participants should not be left with an embarrassing stigma of working on a project that failed.

Failed Project. In rare circumstances projects simply fail—for a variety of reasons. For example, developing a prototype of a new technology product may show the original concept to be unworkable. Or in the development of a new pharmaceutical drug, the project may need to be abandoned because side effects of the drug are deemed unacceptable.

Changed Priority. The priority team continuously revises project selection priorities to reflect changes in organizational direction. Normally these changes are small over a period of time, but periodically major shifts in an organization require dramatic shifts in priorities. In this transition period, projects in process may need to be altered or cancelled. Thus, a project may start with a high priority but see its rank erode or crash during its project life cycle as conditions change. For example, a computer game company found their major competitor placed a 64-bit, 3-D game on the market while their product development projects still centered on 32-bit games. From that moment on, 32-bit game projects were considered obsolete and met sudden death.

In some cases the original importance of the project was misjudged; in some the needs have changed. In other situations implementation of the project is impractical or impossible. Because the audit group and priority team are periodically reviewing a project, the changed perception of the project's role (priority) in the total scheme of things becomes apparent quickly. If the project no longer contributes significantly to organization strategy, the audit group or priority team needs to recommend the project be terminated. In many termination situations, these projects are integrated into related projects or routine daily operations.

Termination of "changed priority" projects is no easy task. The project team's perception may be that the project priority is still high in relation to other projects. Egos and, in some cases perhaps, jobs are on the line. Individuals or teams feel success is just over the horizon. Giving up is tantamount to failure. Normally, rewards are given for staying with a project when the chips are down, for not giving up. Such emotional issues make project termination difficult.

There is little advantage to placing blame on individuals. Other modes should be used to "justify" early project closure or to identify a project problem—for example, customer needs or tastes have changed, technology is ahead of this project, or competition has a better, more advanced product or service. These examples are external to the organization and perceived as beyond anyone's control. Another approach that weakens close team loyalty is changing team members or the project manager. This approach tends to minimize team commitment and makes closing the project easier, but it should only be used as a last resort. Minimizing embarrassment should be a primary goal for a project review group closing down an unfinished project.

Signals for Continuing or Early Project Closure

Those who are preparing to join a project audit group for the first time would find it rewarding to read a few studies that identify barriers to project success and the antithesis, factors that contribute to success. Knowledge of these factors will suggest areas to review in an audit. These factors signal where problems or success patterns might exist. In rare cases their existence may signal problems and the need for an in-process project to be terminated early.

A number of studies have examined this area.[8] There is surprising conformity among these studies. For example, all of these studies (and others) rank poor project definition (scope) as a major barrier to project success. There is no evidence these factors have changed over the years, although some differences in relative importance have been noted in different industries. Table 14–1 presents the barriers identified by 1,654 participating project managers in a survey by Gobeli and Larson.[9]

The signals noted in Table 14–1 can be useful to audit groups in their preliminary review of in-process projects or even in postproject audits.

TABLE 14-1 Barriers to Project Success

Activity	Barrier	Incidence (%)
Planning	Unclear definition	50
	Poor decision making	28
	Bad information	12
	Changes	11
Scheduling	Tight schedule	42
	Not meeting schedule	38
	Not managing schedule	20
Organizing	Lack of responsibility or accountability	54
	Weak project manager	41
	Top management interference	5
Staffing	Inadequate personnel	52
	Incompetent project manager	29
	Project member turnover	14
	Poor staffing process	5
Directing	Poor coordination	34
	Poor communication	24
	Poor leadership	21
	Low commitment	21
Controlling	Poor follow-up	39
	Poor monitoring	38
	No control system	13
	No recognition of problems	10

The Closure Decision

For an incomplete project, the decision to continue or close down the project is fundamentally an organizational resource allocation decision. Should the organization commit additional resources to complete the project and realize the project objectives? This is a complex decision. The rationale for closing or proceeding is often based on many cost factors that are primarily subjective and judgmental. Thus, care needs to be taken to avoid inferences concerning groups or individuals. The audit report needs to focus on organizational goals, changing conditions, and changing priorities requiring reallocation of scarce organizational resources.

When the audit group or priority team suggests closure, the announcement may need to come from a CEO position if the effect is large or if key egos are involved. But, in most cases, the closure decision is left to the audit group or priority team. Prior to announcement of closure, a plan for future assignment of the project team members should be in place.

Project Closure Process

As the project nears the end of its life cycle, people and equipment are directed to other activities or projects. Carefully managing the closure phase is as important as any other phase of the project. The major challenges for the project manager and team members are over. Getting the project manager and team members to wrap up the odds and ends of closing down the project is sometimes difficult. For example, accounting for equipment and completing final reports are perceived as boring by project professionals who are action-oriented individuals. They are looking forward to new opportunities and challenges. The major activities found in project terminations are developing a plan, staffing, communicating the plan, and implementing the plan.

The typical close-out plan includes answers to questions similar to these:

- What tasks are required to close the project?
- Who will be responsible for these tasks?
- When will closure begin and end?
- How will the project be delivered?

Staffing usually is not a significant issue if the termination is not a sudden hatchet job. If the project suddenly is canceled early, it may be judicious to seek someone other than the project manager to close out the project. In successful, completed projects, the project manager is the likely choice for closing down the project. In this case it is best to have the project manager's next assignment known; this will serve as an inducement to terminate the project as quickly as possible and move on to new challenges.

Communicating the termination plan and schedule early allows the project team to (1) accept the psychological fact the project will end and (2) prepare to move on. The ideal scenario is to have the team member's next assignment ready when the termination is announced. Conversely, a major dilemma in the termination phase is that project participants are looking forward to future projects or other opportunities. The project manager's challenge is to keep the project team focused on the project activities and delivery to the customer until the project is complete. Project managers need to be careful to maintain their enthusiasm for completing the project and hold people accountable to deadlines, which are prone to slip during the waning stages of the project.

Implementing the close-down plan includes several wrap-up activities. Many organizations develop lengthy lists for closing projects as they gain experience. These are very helpful and ensure nothing is overlooked.[10] Implementing close down includes the following five major activities:

1. Getting delivery acceptance from the customer.
2. Shutting down resources and releasing to new uses.
3. Reassigning project team members.

4. Closing accounts and seeing that all bills are paid.

5. Evaluating the project team, project team members, and the project manager.

Figure 14–1 depicts a partial close-down checklist for the Euro conversion for a space company.

Orchestrating the closure of a project can be a difficult task and a challenge to the manager's leadership ability. Implementing closure usually takes place in

FIGURE 14–1

Example of a Closedown Checklist

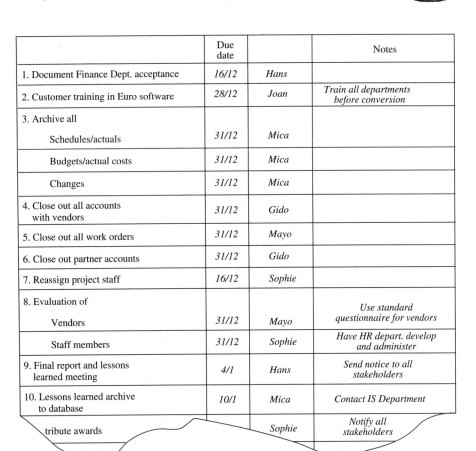

European Space Launch, AG

PROJECT CLOSURE CHECKLIST

Project ____Euro Conversion____   Customer ____Finance Department____

Project manager ____Hans Krammer____   Completion date ____12 December 98____

	Due date		Notes
1. Document Finance Dept. acceptance	*16/12*	*Hans*	
2. Customer training in Euro software	*28/12*	*Joan*	*Train all departments before conversion*
3. Archive all			
Schedules/actuals	*31/12*	*Mica*	
Budgets/actual costs	*31/12*	*Mica*	
Changes	*31/12*	*Mica*	
4. Close out all accounts with vendors	*31/12*	*Gido*	
5. Close out all work orders	*31/12*	*Mayo*	
6. Close out partner accounts	*31/12*	*Gido*	
7. Reassign project staff	*16/12*	*Sophie*	
8. Evaluation of			
Vendors	*31/12*	*Mayo*	*Use standard questionnaire for vendors*
Staff members	*31/12*	*Sophie*	*Have HR depart. develop and administer*
9. Final report and lessons learned meeting	*4/1*	*Hans*	*Send notice to all stakeholders*
10. Lessons learned archive to database	*10/1*	*Mica*	*Contact IS Department*
tribute awards		*Sophie*	*Notify all stakeholders*

an emotionally charged web of happiness from successful completion of the project and sadness that newly forged friendships are now being severed as individuals go their separate ways. It is customary in organizations to arrange a celebration of the completion of the project. This could range from an informal pizza party after work to a more formal banquet including speeches and awards or certificates of recognition for participants. Such a festivity provides a sense of closure and emotional release for the participants as they bid farewell to each other. For less successful projects, this ending can take the form of a ceremonial wake; even though the atmosphere may be less than festive, such an event can also provide a sense of closure and help people move on with their lives.

Team, Team Member, and Project Manager Evaluations

Auditing includes performance evaluations of the project team, individual team members, and the project manager. Evaluation of performance is essential to encourage changes in behavior, to support individual career development, and to support continuous improvement through organization learning. Evaluation implies measurement against specific criteria. Experience corroborates that before commencement of the project, the stage must be set so all expectations, standards, supportive organization culture, and constraints are in place; if not, the effectiveness of the evaluation process will suffer.

In a macrosense the evidence today suggests that performance evaluation in each of these realms is not done well. The major reasons cited by practitioners are twofold:

1. Evaluations of individuals are still left to supervisors of the team member's home department.
2. Typical measures of team performance center on time, cost, and specifications.

Most organizations do not go beyond these measures, although they are important and critical. Organizations should consider evaluating the team-building process, effectiveness of group decision and problem-solving processes, group cohesion, trust among team members, and quality of information exchanged. Addressing evaluation of teams, team members, and project managers is extremely complex and project dependent. The discussion that follows touches on some of the major issues and approaches found in practice.

Team Evaluation

Before an auditing of the project team can be effective and useful, a minimum core of conditions needs to be in place before the project begins. Some conditions are listed here in the form of questions:

1. Do standards for measuring performance exist? (You can't manage what you can't measure.) Are the goals clear for the team and individuals? Challenging? Attainable? Lead to positive consequences?

2. Are individual and team responsibilities and performance standards known by all team members?

3. Are team rewards adequate? Do they send a clear signal that senior management believes the synergy of teams is important?

4. Is a clear career path for successful project managers in place?

5. Does the team have discretionary authority to manage short term difficulties?

6. Is there a relatively high level of trust emanating from the organization culture?

7. Team evaluation should go beyond time, cost, and specifications. Are there criteria beyond the triple-threat criteria? The "characteristics of high-performance teams" from Chapter 11 can easily be adapted as measurements of team effectiveness.

These "in-place conditions" will support any evaluation approach for teams and their members.

In practice the actual team evaluation process takes many forms—especially when evaluation goes beyond time, budget, and specifications. The typical mechanism for evaluation of teams is a survey administered by a consultant, a staff member from the human resources department, or through computer e-mail. The survey is normally restricted to team members, but, in some cases, other project stakeholders interacting with the team may be included in the survey. When the results are tabulated, the team meets with senior management, and the results are reviewed. An example of a partial survey is found in Table 14–2.

This session is comparable to the team-building sessions described in Chapter 11 except that the focus is on using the survey results to assess the development of the team, its strengths and weaknesses, and the lessons that can be applied to future project work. The results of team evaluation surveys are helpful in changing behavior, stressing the importance of supporting the team approach, and continuous improvement.

Individual Team Member and Project Manager Evaluation

Team evaluation is crucial, but at some point a project manager is likely to be asked to evaluate the performance of individual members. Such an evaluation typically will be required as part of the closure process and will then be incorporated in the annual performance appraisal system of the organization. These evaluations constitute a major element of an individual's personnel file and often form the

---

TABLE 14–2   Team Evaluation and Feedback Survey

Using the scale below, assess each statement.

	Disagree				Agree
1. The team shared a sense of common purpose, and each member was willing to work toward achieving project objectives.	1	2	3	4	5
2. Respect was shown for other points of view. Differences of opinion were encouraged and freely expressed.	1	2	3	4	5
3. All interaction among team members occurred in a comfortable, supportive atmosphere.	1	2	3	4	5

---

basis for making decisions about promotions, future job assignments, merit pay increases, and other rewards.

Organizations vary in the extent to which project managers are actively involved in performing the appraisal process. In organizations where projects are managed within a functional organization or functional matrix, the individual's area manager, not the project manager, is responsible for assessing performance. The area manager may solicit the project manager's opinion of the individual's performance on a specific project; this will be factored into the individual's overall performance. In a balanced matrix, the project manager and the area manager jointly evaluate an individual's performance. In project matrix and project organizations in which the lion's share of the individual's work is project related, the project manager is responsible for appraising individual performance. One new process that appears to be gaining wider acceptance is the multirater appraisal or the "360° feedback," which involves soliciting feedback concerning team members' performance from all the people their work affects. This would include not only project and area managers, but also peers, subordinates, and even customers.

Performance appraisals generally fulfill two important functions. The first is developmental in nature; the focus is on identifying individual strengths and weaknesses and developing action plans for improving performance. The second is evaluative and involves assessing how well the person has performed in order to determine salary or merit adjustments. These two functions are not compatible. Employees, in their eagerness to find out how much pay they will receive tend to tune out constructive feedback on how they can improve their performance. Likewise, managers tend to be more concerned with justifying their decision than engaging in a meaningful discussion on how the employee can improve his or her performance. It is difficult to be both a coach and a judge. As a result, several experts on performance appraisal systems recommend that organizations separate performance reviews (which focus on individual improvement) and pay reviews (which allocate the distribution of rewards).[11] In some matrix organizations, project managers conduct the performance reviews, while area managers are responsible for pay reviews. In other cases, performance reviews are part of the project closure process, and pay reviews are the primary objective of the annual performance appraisal. Other organizations avoid this dilemma by allocating only group rewards for project work. The remaining discussion is directed at reviews designed to improve performance because pay reviews are often outside the jurisdiction of the project manager.

Performance Reviews

Organizations employ a wide range of methods to review individual performance on a project. In general, all review methods of individual performance center on the technical and social skills brought to the project and team. Some organizations simply rely on an informal discussion between the project manager and the project member. Other organizations require project managers to submit written essays that describe and assess an individual's performance on a project. Many organizations use rating scales similar to the team evaluation survey in which the project manager rates the individual according to a certain scale (e.g., from 1 to 5) on a number of relevant performance dimensions (e.g., teamwork, customer relations). Some organizations augment these rating schemes with behaviorally anchored descriptions of what constitutes a 1 rating, a 2 rating, and so forth. Each method has its strengths and weaknesses and, unfortunately, in many organizations the appraisal systems were designed to support mainstream operations and not unique project work. The bottom line is that project managers have to use the performance review system mandated by their organization as best they can.

Regardless of the method, the project manager needs to sit down with each team member and discuss his or her performance. Below are some general tips for conducting performance reviews:

- Always begin the process by asking the individual to evaluate his or her own performance. First, this approach may yield valuable information that you were not aware of. Second, the approach may provide an early warning for situations in which there is disparity in assessments. Finally, this method reduces the judgmental nature of the discussion.
- Avoid drawing comparisons with other team members; instead, assess the individual in terms of established standards and expectations.

Comparisons tend to undermine cohesion and divert attention from what the individual needs to do to improve performance.

- When you have to be critical, focus the criticism on specific examples of behavior rather than on the individual personally. Describe in specific terms how the behavior affected the project.

- Be consistent and fair in your treatment of all team members. Nothing breeds resentment more than if individuals feel that they are being held to a different standard than are other project members.

- Treat the review as only one point in an on-going process. Use it to reach an agreement as to how the individual can improve his or her performance.

Managers and subordinates often dread a formal performance review. Neither side feels comfortable with the evaluative nature of the discussion and the potential for misunderstanding and hurt feelings. Much of this anxiety can be alleviated if the project manager is doing his or her job well. Project managers should be giving team members feedback throughout the project so that individual team members have a pretty good idea how well they have performed and how the manager feels before the formal meeting.

While in many cases the same process that is applied to reviewing the performance of team members is applied to evaluating the project manager, many organizations augment this process, given the importance of the position to their organization. This is where conducting the 360° review is becoming more popular. (See *Project Management in Action: 360° Feedback.*) In project-driven organizations, directors or vice presidents of project management will be responsible for collecting information on a specific project manager from customers, vendors, team members, peers, and other managers. This approach has tremendous promise for developing more effective project managers.

Summary

Project audits enhance individual and organizational change and improvement. In this chapter processes for conducting project audits and developing the report were examined. Project closures and the importance of conducting team and individual evaluations were also reviewed. Key points of the chapter include the following:

- It is better to have automatic times or points when audits will take place. Avoid surprises.

- Audits of projects (especially those in process) need to be conducted carefully and with sensitivity to human reactions. The audit should focus on issues, problems, and successes and avoid references to groups or individuals.

Project Management in Action

360° Feedback

More and more companies are discarding the traditional superior–subordinate performance feedback process and replacing it with 360° feedback systems. The 360° feedback approach gathers behavioral observations from many sources within the organization and includes employee self-assessment. The individual completes the same structured evaluation process that superiors, project team members, peers and, in many cases, external customers use to evaluate performance. Survey questionnaires, augmented by a few open-ended questions, typically are used to gather information.

Summary results are compared against organizational strategies, values, and business objectives. The feedback is communicated to the individual with the assistance of the company's human resources department or an outside consultant. The technique is used by a growing number of firms including General Electric, AT&T, Mobil Oil, Nabisco, Hewlett-Packard, and Warner-Lambert.

The objective of the 360° process is to identify areas for individual improvement. When anonymous feedback solicited from others is compared with the individual's self-evaluations, the individual may form a more realistic picture of strengths and weaknesses. This may prompt behavioral change if the weaknesses identified were previously unknown to the individual. Such appears to be the case for Jerry Wallace, an up-and-coming manager at General Motors. "The strongest message I got was that I need to delegate more," he says, "I thought I'd been doing it. But I need to do it more and sooner. My people are saying, 'Turn me loose.'

Many firms obtain feedback from internal and external project customers. For example, a client may evaluate a project manager or member of the project team according to, "How effectively does the individual get things done without creating unnecessary adversarial relationships?" Incorporating customer feedback in the evaluation process underscores collaboration and the importance of client expectations in determining project success.

William J. Miller, a program director at Du Pont, helped install a 360° feedback system for 80 scientists and support people. "A high or low score didn't predict a scientist's ability to invent Teflon," says Miller. "But what feedback did was really improve the ability of people to work in teams. Their regard for others and behaviors that were damaging and self centered are what changed."[12]

- The audit is best staffed with individuals independent of the project.
- Audit reports need to be used and accessible. Audits support an organizational culture that vigorously promotes continuous improvement and organization learning.
- Project closures should be planned and orderly regardless of the type of closure.

- Certain core conditions should be in place to support team and individual evaluation.
- Both individual and team evaluations should be conducted, and performance reviews should be separated from pay or merit reviews.

Competitive conditions appear to be forcing more organizations to adopt continuous improvement and organization learning. Regular use of project audits has yielded dramatic improvements in the way projects are managed. As more members of these organizations are learning from project mistakes and what is contributing to project successes, the process of managing projects is continuously improving in their respective organizations. This is the mark of organizations that have evolved to highest level of project management execution. The major instrument for implementing this philosophy is the project audit and report.

15

PROJECT MANAGEMENT: THE FUTURE

The best way to predict the future is to create it
Peter Drucker

Before we look toward the future we need to look at the past. The Great Wall of China, pyramids of Egypt, Roman aqueducts, printing press, steam engine, and airplane are living testaments of project management. However, it was not until the end of World War II that the discipline of project management began to emerge as a profession. Returning veterans applied planning skills and logistic techniques, which were critical to victory, to industrial projects. During the sixties and seventies critical-path-based network planning techniques were developed for building complex vehicles and products such as submarines and spacecraft. The introduction of microcomputers in the eighties made computerized planning and control tools available for all kinds of projects and organizations. Project management received wide acclaim as a platform for developing new products and services. The nineties saw an expansion of project management into mainstream business. Project planning and control methods still dominant the discipline, but the human side to managing projects has taken on greater importance.

The scope of project management has expanded to touch every fiber of the organization. As more organizations found themselves managing more and more projects, some effort to centralize these efforts was inevitable. Today, we see a major emphasis on the development of an integrated project management process that focuses all effort toward the organization strategic plan, development of an organization culture that supports a multiproject environment, and mastery of *both* interpersonal skills and project management tools and techniques and necessary to manage a project to successful completion.

In the new millennium project management appears to be ideally positioned to meet many of the challenges confronting business enterprises. We begin this chapter by briefly reviewing major forces that are contributing to the growth and importance of project management. The project management maturity model is reintroduced to describe how organizations will evolve to respond to these forces. Since the premise is that project management has a bright future, it is appropriate to conclude with some suggestions on how to pursue a career in project management.

Emergence of Project-Driven Organizations

Assessing the future process of managing projects requires identifying the forces of change. (Some of these forces were mentioned in Chapter 1.) These megaforces are typically beyond the control of individual managers or organizations; they represent changes in the basic fabric of society—sweeping across all nations.

The compression of the *product life cycle* is perhaps the most prodigious force driving changes in the process of managing projects. Only 50 years ago the average life cycle of all products was in the neighborhood of 15–20 years. Today, business executives estimate the life cycle to be close to 3 years for all products. Managers in high-technology firms estimate the life cycle to be closer to 6 months. Clearly, the velocity of new product development has increased geometrically. Each new product is a new project!

Another megaforce closely linked with the product life cycle is the *knowledge/technology* explosion. It is a popular belief that more knowledge has been created in the past 2 or 3 decades than in the history of the human race. Although these numbers are difficult to verify, the magnitude is obvious to all. Today 33 percent of GNP comes from new knowledge products. This explosion is best exemplified by two projects that will be completed this decade that will help unlock the secrets of outer and inner space: see *Project Management in Action: The International Space Station (ISS) Project* and *Project Management in Action: The Human Genome Project.*

Speed is a critical competitive advantage for most firms. Product life cycle and competition have made "time-to-market" a challenge for project teams. Getting closer to the customers and their needs is the first priority in selecting projects. Short life cycles increase the number of projects an organization can handle simultaneously. It is not unusual for organizations to have more than 100 projects occurring simultaneously. Resource shortages and conflicts can be rampant in this environment. How will time-to-market be reconciled with resources? These outcomes have created problems that will alter the way projects are selected and managed. Improved knowledge and technology support innovation. Innovation results in new projects!

Project Management in Action

The International Space Station (ISS) Project

By 2006 the space station assembly hopes to be complete and functional 220 miles above the earth at a cost of more than $40 billion. The station will cover an area of approximately two football fields and have a housing unit the size of a jumbo jet. This space station will conduct research concerning human life and the production of products in space. The complexity of the space station and the coordination required among 16 partner nations is daunting.

Russia launched the first piece of the space station on November 20, 1998. This module provides power for future assembly operations. On December 3 of the same year the United States launched the first space component hub, which serves as the connector for other pieces of the station. This hub also serves as housing for up to seven astronauts. In total it is planned that 34 space deliveries will transport more than 900,000 pounds of materials needed to assemble the completed station. It is estimated that more than 144 two-person space walks and 800 hours of construction will be needed to assemble the station.

The project has had a bumpy ride to date, and more problems are expected before the project is complete. The project is billions of dollars over budget; the total cost could reach $96 billion. The collapse of the Russian economy has caused delays on their development of a major module of the station. Financial support has been needed to get the Russian effort back on track. Redesign has been continual because of the multiple needs of the partners of the 16 nations; these changes have resulted in costly delays. Some of the risks have been underestimated, and reassessment has suggested failures along the way are inevitable—delivery vehicles blowing up, docking problems, even someone killed during construction. There have been calls to "pull the plug" on the project. Nevertheless, the project moves forward.

The ESA (European Space Agency) is coordinating several ISS projects linked to the development of an ATV (Automatic Transfer Vehicle—not related to all-terrain vehicles) that will supply 9 tons of cargo and fuel to the space station. These projects, which include countries and companies from France, Germany, Russia, and Italy, will take place in their respective countries under the guidance of ESA. DaimlerChrysler will produce the estimated 15 ATVs scheduled for delivery between 2003 and 2013. Standard penalty clauses for late delivery are in place. Incentive provisions for continuous improvement of mission success and payload mass are included in this multination endeavor.[1]

Problems are deemed surmountable and plans to complete the assembly by 2006 are in place. It is expected that the world-class laboratory will lead to discoveries that will touch the lives of everyone. Perhaps the lessons learned will be as valuable as the discoveries.

Project Management in Action

The Human Genome Project

Begun in 1990, the Human Genome Project (HGP) is a 15-year, $3 billion effort coordinated by the U.S. Department of Energy and the National Institutes of Health. The project goals are the following:

- Identify all the approximate 30,000 genes in human DNA.
- Determine the sequences of the 3 billion chemical base pairs that make up human DNA.
- Store this information in databases.
- Improve tools for data analysis.
- Transfer related technologies to the private sector.
- Address the ethical, legal, and social issues that may arise from the project.

The project involves the active partnership of medical, government, and business communities. All total more than 43 different institutes, medical schools, pharmaceutical firms, and research centers are involved in completing the project.

In June 2000, HGP leaders announced that the rough draft of the human genome had been completed 1 year ahead of schedule. The draft sequence will provide a scaffold of sequence across about 90 percent of the human genome. Remaining gaps will be closed and accuracy improved over the following 3 years to achieve a complete high-quality DNA reference sequence by 2003, 2 years early than originally planned.

The completion of the human DNA sequence in 2003 will coincide with the fiftieth anniversary of Watson and Crick's description of the fundamental structure of DNA. Current and potential applications of genome research address international needs in molecular medicine, waste control and environmental cleanup, biotechnology, energy sources, and risk assessment. The analytical power arising from the reference DNA sequences of entire genomes and other genomic resources is anticipated to jump start what has been predicted to be the "biology century."[2]

Global competition touches every part of our world. No country or product is immune from this turbulent force. Surviving and being successful in the savage competition witnessed today intensifies the need for sustained innovation and process improvements. Organizations that are best at innovations and process improvements win. These activities represent projects!

These forces as well as others are not only increasing sheer number of projects but also making project management the dominant vehicle for business growth and survival in the future. Perhaps noted project management expert Paul Dinsmore sums it up best when he predicts that in the future " . . . companies will perceive themselves not as hierarchical, functional organizations, but as fast-tracking entrepreneurial enterprises, made up of a 'portfolio of projects'—ever-changing and ever-renewable—all of which need to be done faster, cheaper, better."[3]

Dinsmore is describing what was referred to in Chapter 1 as the emergence of project-driven organizations. Such organizations will integrate strategy, project selection, culture, and processes consistently on all projects. Project-driven organizations will use projects as the major instrument to accomplish the organization vision, goals, and strategies. The linkages between organization direction, strategy, and projects will be well defined. Project driven organizations will very carefully select a prioritized portfolio of projects that clearly guide the organization toward its ever-changing needs. These organizations emphasize cooperation, enhance group performance, and enhance continuous improvement and renewal. Stakeholder skill requirements will shift from technical skills to a razor-sharp understanding and use of business skills and processes. Project-driven organizations provide the environment for quickly adapting to change and the uncertainties of the volatile environment in which they must survive.

Project Management Maturity Model

As projects become the focal point of business, organizations will naturally adapt and evolve to support more effective project management. Project management maturity models have been developed to capture this transition. The term *maturity model* was coined in the late 1980s from a research study by the U.S. government and the Software Engineering Institute (SEI) at Carnegie-Mellon University. (See their Web site at http://www.sei.cmu.edu/activities/sema/profile.html.) The government wanted a tool that would predict success of contractors developing software. The outcome of this research was the capability maturity model (CMM). The model focuses on guiding and assessing organizations in implementing concrete best practices of managing software development projects.

Today organizations in a variety of different industries use some form of a maturity model to assess their progress in implementing the best practices in their industry. It is important to understand that the model does not ensure success; it only serves as a measuring stick and an indicator of progress.

Many versions of the model exist. Typically, these models are divided into a continuum of growth levels such as the one introduced in Chapter 1: Initial, Repeatable, Defined, Managed, and Optimized. Figure 15–1 presents our version that borrows liberally from other models.[4] What we have tried to do is focus less on a process and more on the state an organization has evolved to in managing projects.

FIGURE 15–1

*Project
Management
Maturity
Model*

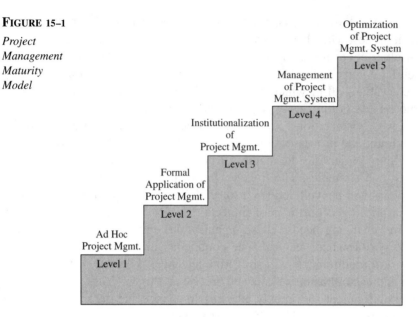

Level 1: Ad Hoc Project Management.   No consistent project management process is in place. How a project is managed depends upon the individuals involved. Characteristics of this level include:

- No formal project selection system exists—a project is done because people decide to do it or because a high-ranking manager orders it done.
- Unpredictable—how any one project is managed varies by individual.
- No investment in project management training.
- Working on projects is a struggle because it goes against the grain of established policies and procedures.

Level 2: Formal Application of Project Management.   The organization applies established project management procedures and techniques. This level is often marked by tension between project managers and line managers who need to redefine their roles. Features of this level include:

- Standard approaches to managing projects including scope statements, WBS, and activity lists.
- Quality emphasis is on the product or outcome of the project and is inspected instead of built in.
- Organization moving in direction of stronger matrix with project managers and line managers working out their respective roles.

- Growing recognition of need for cost control not just scope and time management.
- No formal project priority system is established.
- Limited training in project management.

Level 3: Institutionalization of Project Management.   The establishment of organization-wide project management system tailored to specific needs of the organization with the flexibility to adapt the process to unique characteristics of the project. Characteristics of this level include:

- Established process for managing projects is evident by planning templates, status report systems, and checklists for each stage of project life cycle.
- Formal criteria are used to select projects.
- Project management is integrated with quality management and concurrent engineering.
- The organization is moving toward a team-based reward system to recognize project execution.
- Risk assessment derived from WBS, technical analyses, and customer input.
- Expanded training in project management.
- Time-phased budgets are used to measure and monitor performance based on earned value analysis.
- A specific change control system for requirements, cost, and schedule is developed for each project and a work authorization system is in place.
- Project audits tend to be performed only when a project fails.

Level 4: Management of Project Management System.   The organization develops a system for managing multiple projects that are aligned with strategic goals of the organization. Characteristics of this level include:

- Portfolio project management is practiced; projects are selected based on resource capacity and contribution to strategic goals.
- Project priority system is established.
- Project work is integrated with ongoing operations.
- Quality improvement initiatives are designed to improve both the quality of the project management process and the quality of specific products and services.
- Benchmarking is used to identify opportunities for improvement.
- Project Management Office or Center of Excellence is established.

- Project audits are performed on all significant projects, and lessons learned are recorded and used on subsequent projects.
- An integrative information system is established for tracking resource usage and performance of all significant projects.

Level 5: Optimization of Project Management System. The focus is on continuous improvement through incremental advancements of existing practices and by innovations using new technologies and methods. Features include:

- Project management information system is fine-tuned—specific and aggregate information is provided to different stakeholders.
- Informal culture that values improvement, not policies and procedures, drives the organization.
- Greater flexibility in adapting project management process to demands of a specific project.

Progress from one level to the next will not occur over night. It usually takes 6 to 18 years for an organization to evolve into a project-driven organization. Why does it take so long? One reason is simply organizational inertia. It is difficult for complex social organizations to institute significant changes while at the same time maintaining business efficacy. "How do we find time to change when we are so busy just keeping our heads above water?"

A second reason is resistance to change. For many managers the shift from a hierarchical, functional organization to a flatter, project-driven organization represents a loss in power, authority, and prestige. People with power do not like to lose it, and they often use their power to preserve their status and position. Case in point, one of the authors was invited by a Fortune 500 firm to present the results of a research program to its management team. The research strongly supported the use of a project matrix structure to develop new products and was critical of the functional matrix. After presenting the findings he was bombarded with questions from managers on the right side of room that doubted the validity and interpretation of the findings. From the left side came favorable questions and comments. Soon a verbal free-for-all erupted between the managers on the two sides of the room. As it turns out, all project managers were sitting on the left side of the room, while all of the functional managers were sitting on the right side.

Another reason why the changes will not necessarily occur quickly is the lack of strong top-management support. Most of today's CEOs have very little formal project management experience. They achieved their success by working their way up a functional hierarchy. Embracing project management as a core activity will require a paradigm shift in how executives view their organizations. This pattern will change as project managers ascend to the ranks of top management.

Finally, you cannot leapfrog past any one level. Just as a child can not avoid the trials and tribulations of being a teenager by adopting all the lessons learned by his or her parents, people within the organization have to work through the unique challenges and problems of each level to get the next level. Learning of this magnitude naturally takes time and can not be avoided by quick fixes or simple remedies.

Many organizations will struggle to adapt their project management systems; the driving forces for change will not dissipate. Those organizations that successfully ride the winds of change and accelerate the institutionalization of a project-driven organization will have a competitive advantage in the twenty-first century.

Career Paths in Project Management

There is no set career path for becoming a project manager. Career avenues vary from industry to industry, organization to organization, and from profession to profession. What can be said is that advancement occurs incrementally. You don't graduate and simply become a project manager. As in other careers you have to work your way up to the position. For example, in project-based organizations such as construction firms you may begin by working on several projects as an assistant engineer, then take an assignment as a project analyst. From there you are promoted to principal engineer, advance to assistant project manager, assume the role of project manager over a small project, and then continue to bigger, riskier projects. In other organizations project management careers run parallel with functional advancement with many crossovers. For example, at Intel an MIS specialist might start a career as a designer, then take an assignment as a project specialist, later work as a project manager, and then return to a functional position as head of a department or a product manager.

Other people find that their project management responsibilities expand as they move up the organization's hierarchy. For example, a former marketing student began her career as an assistant buyer for a large retail company. She then became area sales manager at a specific store and became involved on a part-time basis in a series of projects acting as a facilitator of focus groups. She was promoted to buyer and eventually became a store manager. In her current position she coordinates a variety of projects ranging from improving the sales acumen of her sales force to altering the physical layout of the store. Although the title of project manager does not appear in her job description, more than 50 percent of her work involves managing projects.

One aspect of project managing that is unique is the temporary nature of assignments. With line appointments, promotions are for the most part permanent and there is a natural, hierarchical progression to positions with greater authority and responsibility. In the example of the former marketing student described above, she progressed from assistant buyer to sales manager to buyer to store manager. Only under very unusual circumstances would she regress to being a buyer. Conversely, tenure is rarely granted to project managers. Once the project is completed, the manager may return to his or her previous department, even at a lesser position. Or, depending upon the projects available, he or she may be assigned to manage a more or less significant project. Future work is dependent upon what projects are available at the time the individual is available and how well the last project went. A promising career can be derailed by one unsuccessful project.

Advancing Your Career in Project Management

Many of you are already established in the field of project management. For those less experienced who are considering pursuing a career in project management, first find out what specific project job opportunities exist in your company. You should talk to people in project management positions and find out how they got to where they are and what advice they can give you. Since career paths, as noted earlier, vary from organization to organization, you need to be attuned to the unique pathways within your company. For example, retail companies naturally assign marketing managers to projects. Conversely, high-tech firms like Motorola and Ericsson prefer engineers as project managers and generally require that they have at least 5 years experience working on projects.

Once you have concluded that you wish to pursue a career in project management, you need to share your aspirations with your immediate superior. Your superior can champion your ambitions, sanction additional training in project management, and assign immediate work that will contribute to your project skill base.

Most project managers have never received formal training in project management. They mastered the job through on-the-job training, buttressed by occasional workshops or on specific project topics such as project scheduling or negotiating contracts. It wasn't until recently that universities started offering courses on project management outside of the Schools of Engineering; to date there are only a handful of degree programs in project management. Regardless of your level of training you will likely need to supplement your education. Many large companies have in-house training programs on project management. For example, Hewlett Packard has more than 32 training modules in its project management curriculum, which is organized around five levels of experience: project team, new project manager, project manager, experienced project manager, and manager of project managers. As noted in *Project Management in Action: Harvesting Project Leaders,* many companies combine classroom instruction with on-the-job training.

For those companies that cannot provide in-house training there are many training and consulting firms that offer seminars and workshops on project management

Project Management in Action

Harvesting Project Leaders

Executives "don't have a clue about how to grow project managers," says Gopal Kapur, president of the Center for Project Management, a consulting agency in San Ramon, California. "Project managers do not grow on trees. You have to understand the process of gardening before you can grow something." Kapur advocates that corporations develop internal programs to develop project managers.

The Federal Reserve Bank of St. Louis has had such a program for more than a year and it's helped the bank grow 45 new project managers. It combines hands-on work in medium- to low-risk projects with classroom training. A new project manager is guided by a veteran leader who acts as a coach or mentor. Gary Arnold, manager of learning and development services, calls that a very critical piece of the program. The coach/mentor can offer advice based on experience.

Typically, Arnold says, project manager wannabes are sent to the classroom for a few days before they apply some skills. But the Federal Reserve Bank found that the opposite works better and starts them off in the trenches. This way they experience firsthand the need to master key project management tools and concepts.[5]

in a variety of locations. For example, Table 15–1 outlines the courses offered by ESI International, a major provider of project management training.

Continuing education should not be restricted to project management. It is important to continue to develop your people skills by reading and going to workshops on team management, negotiation, conflict resolution, and personal development (see *Project Management in Action: Works Well with Others*). Likewise, many technical professionals return to universities to complete an MBA or take night classes in management to expand their general business background.

Many professionals find it beneficial to join the Project Management Institute (PMI).[6] Membership entitles you to subscriptions to PMI publications including the academic *Project Management Journal* and the *PM Network*, a trade magazine. PMI sponsors workshops and national forums on project management. When you join PMI you also become a member of one of the more than 200 local chapters across North America. These chapters meet on a monthly basis and provide project managers with opportunities to network and learn from each other. In addition, PMI, as part of its effort to advance the profession, certifies mastery of project manager competency through a formal examination that covers the entire body of knowledge of project management. Passing the exam and being certified

---

TABLE 15–1   Training Courses in Project Management

Core Project Management Courses:

Managing Projects in Organizations
Project Leadership and Communications
Quality for Project Managers
Scheduling and Cost Control
Risk Management
Contracting for Project Managers
Project Management Applications

Specialized Project Management Courses:

Financial Management for Project Managers
Business Process Analysis, Innovation, & Redesign
Aligning Project Management with Corporate Strategy
Cost Estimation Process Management

Global Business Management Courses:

International Project Management
International Contracting
Managing Across Cultures

Information Technology Project Management Courses:

Software Project Management
Managing IT Projects
Software Risk Management
Managing Software Quality
Project Leadership and Communications
Scheduling and Cost Control
Software Testing
Telecommunications Principles for Project Managers
Systems Integration Project Management
Project Management Applications in
Information Technology

Negotiation and New Business Development Courses:

Negotiation Skills for Project Managers
Negotiation of Commercial Contracts
Winning New Business
Federal Contracting Basics

Course for Experienced Project Managers:

Rapid Assessment & Recovery of Troubled Projects
Requirements Management
Risk Management: Perspectives, Tools & Techniques
Managing e-Business Projects
Establishing the Project Management Office

---

* SOURCE: ESI international 2001 Program (www.esi-intl.com).

as a "Project Management Professional" is a clearly visible way to signal your competence and interest.

As you accumulate knowledge and techniques you need to apply them to your immediate job situation. Most people's jobs entail some form of projects, whether it is realizing a mandated objective or simply figuring out ways to improve the quality of performance. Gantt charts, scope statements, responsibility matrices, risk assessments, and other project management tools can be used to plan and implement these endeavors.

It may also be wise to look outside the workplace for opportunities to develop project management skills. Active involvement in your local community can provide numerous opportunities to manage projects. Organizing a local soccer tournament, managing a charitable fundraising event, or coordinating the renovation of the neighborhood park can allow you to practice project management. Furthermore, given the volunteer nature of most of these projects they can provide

Project Management in Action

Works Well With Others

The phrase "works well with others" has long been a staple on grade school report cards; now, in the IT world, it's the No. 1 criteria for management candidates. In a nationwide survey conducted in 1999, 27 percent of chief information officers (CIOs) cited strong interpersonal skills as the single most important quality for reaching management levels. Advanced technical skills came in second, receiving 23 percent of the response.

The project was sponsored by RHI Consulting, which provides information technology professionals on a project basis. An independent research firm was hired by to administer the survey. More than 1,400 CIOs responded to the questionnaire.

Survey respondents were also asked, "In 2005, how frequently will employees in your IT department work on project-based teams with members of other departments throughout the company?"

Their responses:		
	Very frequently	57 percent
	Somewhat frequently	26 percent
	Somewhat infrequently	10 percent
	Very infrequently	6 percent
	Never	1 percent

Greg Scileppi, RHI Consulting's executive director, recommends that IT professionals develop their interpersonal skills. "The predominance of project teams has created a corresponding need for strong communication and team-player abilities. Technical staff put these skills to test daily as they work with employees at all levels to create and implement IT solutions ranging for simple troubleshooting to corporate Web initiatives and system-wide upgrades."[7]

you with an excellent training ground to sharpen your ability to exercise influence without formal authority.

Regardless of how competent and worthy you are, your project management skills must be visible to others for them to be recognized. Even in a subordinate position you can take advantage of project review meetings to demonstrate to your bosses and peers that you have the necessary skills for project planning and control.

Many project managers' careers began by volunteering for task forces and small projects. Ideally you should select task forces and projects that allow you access to higher-ups and other departments within your organization, providing you with opportunities to develop contacts. This was certainly true for a former student of ours named Bob who escaped the bowels of a large corporation by volunteering to lead the organization's annual United Way campaign. While an important cause, directing the United Way campaign was generally given to someone who was considered expendable. This was true for Bob whose career had hit a dead end. Bob took advantage of the United Way task force to show off his project management skills. Through recruiting key participants, establishing a shared vision, scheduling milestones, and contagious enthusiasm the campaign was a resounding success, shattering previous records. Bob's efforts caught the eye of top management and he was rewarded with more project work. He is currently one of most sought-after project managers at his corporation.

In pursuing your ambition you should continually be on the lookout for a mentor. Most fast-track managers acknowledge that mentors played a significant role in their advancement. Mentors are typically superiors who take a special interest in you and your career. They use their clout to champion your ambitions and act as a personal coach, teaching you "the ropes to skip and the ropes to know." They also share their social network and defend you when you are under attack. This special treatment does not come without a price. Mentors typically require fervent loyalty and superior performance; after all, the mentor's reputation rests on your performance. How do you find a mentor? Most people say it just happens. But it doesn't happen to everyone. Mentors typically seek A+ workers, not C workers, and you must make your abilities known to others.[8]

Many organizations have instituted formal mentoring programs in which experienced project managers are assigned to promising young managers. Although the relationship may not evolve to the personal level experienced with an informal mentor, designated mentors play a very similar role in coaching and championing one's professional progress. You should take advantage of this opportunity to learn as much as you can from these seasoned veterans.

Since much of project work will be temporary and contractual in nature, it is important to develop contacts that may lead to future work. Attending professional meetings, trade fairs, and training workshops provide good opportunities to network and develop social connections that could precipitate project assignments. These social and professional networks can provide a safety net for project work in this time of downsizing and lay-offs.

Ultimately your goal is to accumulate a portfolio of project management experiences that broaden your skill base and reputation. Early on you should choose, when possible, projects with the greatest learning opportunities. Pick projects more for the quality of the people working on them than for the scope of the projects. There is no better way to learn how to be an effective project manager than by watching one at work. Keep a diary of your observations and review and refine lessons learned. Later, as your confidence and competency grow, you should try to get involved in projects that will enhance your reputation within the firm. Remember the comments about customer satisfaction. You want to exceed your superiors' expectations. Avoid run-of-the-mill projects or assignments. Seek high-profile projects that have some risks and tangible payoffs. At the same time, be careful to be involved in projects commensurate with your abilities.

Finally, despite your efforts you may find that you are not making satisfactory progress toward your career goals. If this is your appraisal, you may wish to seriously consider moving to a different company or even a different industry that will provide more project management opportunities. Hopefully you have managed to accumulate sufficient project management experience to aid in your job search. One advantage of project work over general management is that it is typically easier to highlight and sell your accomplishments. Instead of simply listing tenure in certain positions, a project manager can highlight the accomplishments of specific projects.

Summary

The twenty-first century should be the Golden Age for project management. Not only will there be an increased demand for project management skills and know-how, but organizations will evolve and change to support more effective project management. Instead of trying to get projects done despite everything else, the organization's culture, structure, reward system, and administrative systems will be reengineered to support successful project management. Mastery of the process of managing projects will be critical to business growth and survival. The project manager of the new millennium will be a business person with responsibilities that encompass the total organization. The past 30 years have seen the transition from a technically oriented project manager to one skilled in all aspects of business. Worldwide competition will direct projects toward technology transfer, infrastructure, consumer goods, environment/ecological, defense, and fundamental needs. The project-driven organization will recognize the project manager as an agent of change and from their ranks select the senior managers of tomorrow.

Ten years from now career paths in project management should be more clearly defined. Until then people wishing to pursue a career in project management should take advantage of the transition and improvise within the constraints of their situation to develop their project management skills. They should volunteer to work on task forces, take advantage of training opportunities, and apply project management tools and techniques to their work. They should signal to their superiors their interest in project management and garner project assignments. Over time they should accumulate a portfolio of project management experiences that establishes their skill base and reputation as someone who gets things done quickly and done right.

Conclusions

By reading this book you have been exposed to the major elements of the process of managing projects. We offer three suggestions for applying these ideas and techniques to real project situations:

- First, maintain a sense of the big picture. Engage regularly in what some have called "helicopter management"—which means expand your perspective beyond immediate concerns and assess how the project fits in the larger scheme of things. Project managers need to constantly assess how the project fulfills the mission and strategy of the firm, how the project is impacting the rest of the organization, whether the expectations of stakeholders are changing, and what key project interfaces have to be managed.

- The second suggestion is to remember that successful project management is essentially a balancing act. Project managers need to balance the soft (people) side of project management with the hard (technical) side, the demands of top management with the needs of team members, short-term gain with long-term need, and so forth.

- Finally, remember that the most important project management tool is your behavior. Your positive example can shape how others respond to the project and interact with each other. Do not underestimate the power of genuine enthusiasm.

NOTES

Preface

1. Stewart, Thomas A., "The Corporate Jungle Spawns a New Species: The Project Manager," *Fortune,* September 1996, pp. 14–15.
2. Wysocki, Bernard, "Flying Solo: High-Tech Nomads Write New Program for Future of Work," *The Wall Street Journal,* August 19, 1996, p. 1.
3. Stewart.

Chapter 1

1. Cleland, David I., "The Age of Project Management," *Project Management Journal,* 12 (1), pp. 19–24.
2. Baker, Stephen, "The Best Wireless Phone on the Market," *BusinessWeek,* August 10, 1998, p. 60.
3. Kerzner, Harold, *Applied Project Management,* New York: John Wiley & Sons, 2000, p. 221.
4. Standish Group, "Most programming projects are late," http://www.standishgroup.com/chaos.html.
5. Carnegie Mellon University and Software Engineering Institute, "Capability Maturity Model—Integrated Systems/Software Engineering," version 0.2b, September 1999.
6. See Rosenstock, Christian, et al, "Maturity Model Implementation and Use: A Case Study," *Proceedings of The Project Management Institute Annual Seminars & Symposium* (September 7–16, 2000), Newtown Square, PA, pp. 273–278. and Fincher, Anita and Levin, Ginger, "Project Management Maturity Model," *Proceedings of the 28th Annual PMI Symposium,* 1997, Newtown Square, PA, pp. 1028–1035.

Chapter 2

1. Pearce, John A., II, and David, Fred, "Corporate Mission Statements: The Bottom Line," *Academy of Management Executive*, 1 (2) (1987), pp. 109–113.
2. Doran, George T., "There's A Smart Way To Write Management Goals and Objectives," *Management Review,* (November, 1981), pp. 35–36.
3. Schmeidawind, J., "Kodak Joins Fuji, Others for Project," *USA Today* (March 1992), p. B1.
4. This is an excellent article describing the implementation gap and how it is measured. Floyd, Steven W., and Wooldridge, Bill, "Managing Strategic Consensus: The Foundation of Effective Implementation," *Academy of Management Executive*, 6 (4) (1992), pp. 27–39.
5. Beard, Donald W., and Dess, Gregory G., "Corporate Business Strategy, Business Level Strategy, and Firm Performance," *Academy of Management Journal*, 24 (4) (December 1981), pp. 663–688.
6. Booz-Allen & Hamilton Inc., "Making Strategy Work: The Challenge for the 1990s," (1990).
7. Fusco, Joseph C., "Better Policies Provide the Key to Implementing Project Management," *Project Management Journal,*"28 (3) (1997), pp. 38–41.
8. Kanter, Rosebeth M., *Men and Women of the Corporation,* New York: Basic Books, 1977, pp. 176–181.
9. Gobeli, David, and Redeluis, William, "Managing Innovation: Lessons Learned from the Cardiac-Pacing Industry," *Sloan Management Review*, (Summer 1985), pp. 29–43.
10. Kharbanda, O. P., and Pinto, Jeffrey K., *What Made Gertie Gallop: Learning from Project Failures,* New York: Van Nostrand Reinhold, 1996, pp. 106–111, 263–283.
11. Chillous, Sandra E., "Project Prioritization—Why Not Do It," *PM Network* (March 1994), pp. 41–42.
12. Wheelwright, Steven C., and Clark, Kim B., "Creating Project Plans to Focus Product Development," *Harvard Business Review* (March-April, 1992), pp. 70–82.
13. Johnson, Roy E., "Scrap Capital Project Evaluations," *Chief Financial Officer,* (May 1998), p. 14. Also see July 1998, pp. 6–7 for responses.
14. For other variations in screening and priority systems, see Wheelright and Clark, (note 12) and Kepner, Charles H., and Tregoe, Benjamin B., *The New Rational Manager,* Princeton, NJ: Princeton Research Press, 1981, pp. 87–88.
15. Kepner, Charles H., and Tregoe, Benjamin B., *The New Rational Manager*, Princeton, N.J.: Princeton Research Press, 1981, pp. 87–88.
16. Matheson, David, and Matheson, Jim, *The Smart Organization*, Cambridge, Mass.: Harvard Business School Press 1998, pp. 203–209.
17. Kaplan, Robert S., and Norton, David P., "Putting the Balanced Scorecard to Work" (September-October 1993); "The Balanced Scorecard—Measures That Drive Performance" (January-February, 1992); and "Using the Balanced Scorecard as a Strategic Management System" (January-February 1996), *Harvard Business Review on Measuring Corporate Performance.*
18. Stewart, Wendy E., "Balanced Scorecard For Projects," *Project Management Journal*, 32 (1) (March 2001), pp. 41–42.

Chapter 3

1. Kerzner, Harold, *Applied Project Management: Best Practices on Implementation*, New York: John Wiley & Sons, 2000, p. 213.
2. The discussions of the advantages and disadvantages of different project management structures are based in part on Stuckenbruck, Linn C., *Implementation of Project Management,* Upper Darby, PA: Project Management Institute, 1981; Youker, Robert, "Organizational Alternatives for Project Management," *Project Management Quarterly* 8 (March 1977), pp. 24–33; Verma, Vijay K., *Organizing Projects for Success: The Human Aspects of Project Management,* Newtown Square, PA: Project Management Institute, 1995; Gobeli, David H., Larson, David, and Larson, Erik, "Relative Effectiveness of Different Project Management Structure," *Project Management Journal*, 18 (2) (June 1987), pp. 81–85.
3. Carlton, Jim, *Apple: The Inside Story of Intrigue, Egomania, and Business Blunders,* New York: Random House, 1997, pp. 13–14.
4. Sculley, John, *Odyssey: Pepsi to Apple . . . A Journey of Adventure, Ideas, and the Future,* New York: Harper & Row, 1987, pp. 270–279.
5. Larson, Erik, and Gobeli, David H., "Project Management Structures: Is There a Common Language?" *Project Management Journal*, 16 (2) (June 1985), pp. 40–44; Smith, Preston G., and Reinertsen, Donald G., *Developing Products in Half the Time,* New York: Van Nostrand Reinhold, 1995; Bowen, Kent H., Clark, Kim B., Holloway, Charles A., and Wheelwright, Steven C., *The Perpetual Enterprise Machine*, New York: Oxford University Press, 1994.
6. Larson, Erik, and Gobeli, David H., "Matrix Management: Contradictions and Insights," *California Management Review*, 29 (4) (Summer 1987), pp. 126–137.
7. Hobbs, B., and Ménard, P., "Organizational Choices for Project Management," in Dinsmore, Paul (ed.), *The AMA Handbook of Project Management,* New York: AMACOM, 1993.
8. Gradante, William, and Gardner, Donald, "Managing Projects from the Future, not from the Past," *Proceedings of the 29th Annual Project Management Institute 1998 Seminars & Symposium,* Newtown Square, PA: Project Management Institute, 1998, pp. 289–294; Block, Thomas R., and Frame, J. Davidson, *The Project Office–A Key to Managing Projects Effectively,* Menlo Park, CA: Crisp Publications, 1998.
9. Bowen, Kent H., Clark, Kim B., Holloway, Charles A., and Wheelwright, Steven C., *The Perpetual Enterprise Machine,* New York: Oxford University Press, 1994, pp. 154–156.
10. See Davies, Stanley M. and Lawrence, Paul R., *Matrix*, Reading, MA: Addison-Wesley, 1977; Kerzner, Harold, *In Search of Excellence in Project Management,* New York: Von Nostrand Reinhold, 1997; Graham, Robert J., and Englund, Randall L., *Creating an Environment for Successful Projects: The Quest to Manage Project Management,* San Francisco: Jossey-Bass, 1997.
11. Deal, Terrance E., and Kennedy, Anthony A., *Corporate Cultures: The Rites and Rituals of Corporate Life,* Reading, MA: Addison-Wesley, 1982; Trice, Harrison M., and Beyer, Janice M., *The Culture of Organizations,* Englewood Cliffs, NJ: Prentice-Hall, 1993.

12. Hofstede, Gert B., Neuijen, D. D., Ohayv, D. D., and Sanders D., "Measuring Organizational Culture: A Qualitative and Quantitative Study Across Twenty Cases," *Administrative Science Quarterly* (June 1990), pp. 286–316; O'Reilly, Charles A., Chatman, J., and Caldwell, D. F., "People and Organizational Culture: A Profile Comparison Approach to Assessing Person-Organization Fit," *Academy of Management Journal*, 34 (3) (September 1991), pp. 487–516; Schein, Edgar, *Organizational Culture and Leadership: A Dynamic View,* San Francisco, Ca: Jossey-Bass, 1985.
13. Roberts, P., "The Empire Strikes Back," *Fast Company*, Issue 22 (February–March) 1999.
14. Barboza, D., "Monsanto Visionary in a Cubicle," *New York Times*, March 3, 1999, p. C1.
15. Elmes, Michael, and Wilemon, David, "Organizational Culture and Project Leader Effectiveness," *Project Management Journal*, 19 (4) (September 1989), pp. 54–63.
16. Collins, James C., and Porras, Jerry I., *Built to Last: The Successful Habits of Visionary Companies,* New York: Harper Collins, 1994, pp. 150–158.
17. "Through the Mill," *The Economist* 33 (7880) (September 10, 1994, p. 76: McWilliams, G,. "Crunch Time at DEC." *BusinessWeek*, no. 3264 9 May 4, 1992), pp. 30–33.
18. Bowen, et al., Ibid, 1994, p. 274.
19. Preston, et al., Ibid, 1995, p. 149–150.

Chapter 4

1. Allen, Roger E., and Allen, Stephen D., *Winnie-the-Pooh on Success,* New York: Penguin, 1977, p. 10.
2. Smithand, M.A., and Tucker, R. L., "Early Project Problem—Assessment of Impact and Cause," *1984 Proceedings*, Newtown Square, PA: Project Management Institute, 1984, p. 226.
3. Pinto, Jeffrey K., and Slevin, Dennis P., "Critical Success Factors Across the Project Life Cycle," *Project Management Journal*, vol. 19, (3) (June 1988), p. 72.
4. Ashley, David B., et al., "Determinants of Construction Project Success," *Project Management Journal,* vol. 18, (2) (June 1987), p. 72.
5. Posner, Barry Z., "What It Takes To Be a Good Project Manager," *Project Management Journal,* vol. 18, (1) (March 1987), p. 52.
6. Gobeli, David, and Larson, Erik, "Barriers Affecting Project Success," in R. Brunies and P. Ménard, (eds.), *Measuring Success,* Newtown Square, PA: Project Management Institute, 1986, pp. 22–29.
7. Tate, Karen, and Hendrix, Karen, "Chartering IT Projects," *Proceedings, 30th Annual Project Management Institute,* Philadelphia, 1999, CD.
8. Eager, David, "Aussie Project Management: The Sidney 2000 Olympic Games," *PM Network*, vol. 12, (9) (September 1998), pp. 63–66.

Chapter 5

1. Kharbanda, O. P., and Pinto, Jeffrey K., *What Made Gertie Gallop: Learning from Project Failures*, New York: Van Nostrand Reinhold, 1996, p. 73.

2. Jones, Casper, *Applied Software Measurement*, New York: McGraw-Hill, 1991, p. 11.

3. See Hamburger, David, "Three Perceptions of Project Cost—Cost Is More Than A Four-Letter Word" for a more detailed discussion. *Project Management Journal*, 17 (3), (June 1986), pp. 51–58.

4. Boehm, B.W., "Understanding and Controlling Software Costs," *IEEE Transactions on Software Engineering*, SE 14 (10), (1988), pp. 1462–75; Dreger, J.B., *Function Point Analysis*, New York: Prentice Hall, 1989; Low, Jeffery R., Barnes, G.C., and Barnes, M., "A Comparison of Function Point Counting Techniques," *IEEE Transactions on Software Engineering*, SE 19 (5), (1993), pp. 529–32; McLeod, G., and Smith, D., *Managing Information Technology Projects*, Cambridge, MA: Course Technology, 1996; Pressman, R. S., *Software Engineering: A Practitioner's Approach*, 4th ed., New York: McGraw Hill, 1997; Symons, C.R., "Function Point Analysis: Difficulties and Improvements," *IEEE Transactions on Software Engineering*, 14 (1), (1988), pp. 2–11.

Chapter 6

1. Turtle, Quentin C., *Improving Concurrent Project Management*, Englewood Cliffs, NJ: Prentice Hall, 1994.

Chapter 7

1. Adapted from *Project Management Body of Knowledge*, Newtown Square, PA: Project Management Institute, 1994, p. 6.

2. *The Orlando Sentinel*, "Math Mistake Proved Fatal to Mars Orbiter," November 23, 1999.

3. Kepner, Charles H., and Tregoe, Benjamin B., *The New Rational Manager*, Kepner-Tregoe, Inc, 1981.

4. Carr, Marvin J., Konda, Suresh L., Monarch, Ira, Ulrich, F. Carol, and Walker, Clay F. "Taxonomy-Based Risk Identification," Technical Report CMU/SEI-93-TR-6, Pittsburgh, PA: Software Engineering Institute, Carnegie Mellon University, 1993.

5. Graves, Roger, "Qualitative Risk Assessment," *PM Network*, 14 (10), October 2000, pp. 61–66.

6. Kangari, Roozbeh, and Boyer, LeRoy T., "Risk Management By Expert Systems," *Project Management Journal*, XX, (1) (1989), pp. 40–47.

7. Pritchard, Carl L., "Advanced Risk—How Big is Your Crystal Ball?" *Proceedings of the 31st Annual Project Management Institute 2000 Seminars and Symposium*, Houston, Texas, 2000: CD, pp. 933–936.

8. Schuler, John R., "Decision Analysis in Projects Monte Carlo Simulation." *PM Network*, VIII, (1), (January 1994), pp. 30–36; Hulett, David T., "Project Schedule Risk

Assessment," *Project Management Journal*, XXVI, (1) 1995, pp. 21–31; Gray, Clifford F., and Reiman, Robert, "PERT Simulation: A Dynamic Approach to the PERT Technique," *Journal of Systems Management,* March 1969, pp. 18-23.

9. *New York Times Sunday Magazine*, March 19, 2000; *Seattle Times,* March 27, 2000, Web site.

10. Krakauer, Jon, *Into Thin Air*, New York: Doubleday, 1997, p. 190; Coburn, Broughton, *Everest: Mountain Without Mercy*, New York: National Geographic Society, 1997, p. 190.

11. Levine, Harvey A., "Risk Management For Dummies: Managing Schedule, Cost and Technical Risk, and Contingency," *PM Network*, IX, (10), (October 1995), pp. 31–33.

12. Smith, Preston G., and Reinertsen, Donald G., *Developing Products in Half The Time*, New York: Van Nostrand Reinhold, 1995, pp. 218–219.

13. Smith, Preston G., and Reinertsen, Donald G., *Developing Products in Half The Time*, Van Nostrand Reinhold, NY, 1995, pp. 219–220.

14. Baker, Bud and Menon, Raj, "Politics and Project Performance: The Fourth Dimension of Project Management," *PM Network*, IX (11), (November 1995), 16–21.

15. Hamburger, David H., "The Project Manager: Risk Taker and Contingency Planner," *Project Management Journal*, XXI, (4), (1990), pp. 11–16.

Chapter 8

1. Burgess, A.R., and Kellebrew, J.B., "Variations in Activity Level on Cyclical Arrow Diagrams," *Journal of Industrial Engineering,* 13 (March–April, 1962), pp. 76–83; J Wiest, D., "A Heuristic Model for Scheduling Large Projects with Limited Resources," *Management Science*, 18 (February 1967), pp. B359–77; and Woodworth, Bruce M., and Willie, C. J., "A Heuristic Algorithm for Resource Leveling in Multiproject, Multisource Scheduling," *Decision Sciences*, 7 (July, 1975), pp. 525–40.

2. Arrow, Kenneth J., and Hurowicz, L. *Studies in Resource Allocation Processes,* New York: Cambridge University Press, 1977; Charnes, A., and Cooper, W.W., "A Network Interpretation and Direct Subdual Algorithm for Critical Path Scheduling," *Journal of Industrial Engineering* (July–August 1962); Talbot, B. F., and Patterson, J.H., "Optimal Methods for Scheduling Under Resource Constraints," *Project Management Journal* (December 1979); and Woodworth, Bruce M., and Shanahan, Sean, "Identifying The Critical Sequence In A Resource Constrained Project," *International Journal of Project Management*, 6, (2), (1988), pp. 89–96.

3. Fendly, L.G., "Towards The Development of a Complete Multiproject Scheduling System," *Journal of Industrial Engineering*, 19 (October 1968), pp. 505–15; and Pascoe, T.L., "Heuristic Methods for Allocating Resources," unpublished Ph.D. Dissertation, United Kingdom: University of Cambridge, 1965.

4. For a complete and interesting discussion of the theory of constraints see Goldratt, Eliyahu, *Critical-Chain,* Great Barrington, MA: North River Press, 1997. See also Newbold, Robert C., "Leveraging Project Resources: Tools for the Next Century," *Proceedings of 28th Annual Project Management Institute, 1997 Seminars and Symposium,* Newtown Square, PA: Project Management Institute, 1997, pp. 417–21; Noreen,

Eric, Smith, Debra, and Mackey, James, *The Theory of Constraints and Its Implication for Management Accounting,* Barrington, MA: North River Press, 1995; and Leach, Lawrence P., "Critical-Chain Project Management," *Proceedings of 29th Annual Project Management Institute, 1998 Seminars and Symposium,* Newtown Square, PA: Project Management Institute, 1998, pp. 1239–1244.

5. Cited in materials developed by Eliyahu Goldratt Institute, New Haven, CT, for a workshop entitled, "Project Management: The TOC Way," 1998.

6. Zalmanson, Edna, "Reader Feedback," *PM Network,* 15 (1), (January 2001), p. 4.

7. Wilkins, Tammo T., "Critical Path, or Chain, or Both?" *PM Network*, 14, (7). (July 2000), pp. 68–74.

8. Mitchel, Russ, "How to Manage Geeks," *Fast Company*, June 1999, pp. 175–180.

Chapter 9

1. Baxter, Jerry B., "Responding to the Northridge Earthquake," *PM Network* (November, 1994), pp. 13–22.

2. Lerner, Mathew, "Outsourcing in Bio-Technology Picks Up Speed," *Chemical Market Reporter*, 251, (14), p. 17.

3. Brooks Jr., Frederick P., *The Mythical Man-Month: Essays on Software Engineering Anniversary Edition,* Reading, MA: Addison-Wesley Longman, Inc., 1994, pp. 15–26.

4. Vroom, V. H., *Work and Motivation,* (New York: Wiley & Sons, 1964).

5. Abdel-Hamid, T., and Madnick, S., *Software Project Dynamics: An Integrated Approach,* Englewood Cliffs, N.J.: Prentice Hall, 1991.

6. Sources: "A 4 Bedroom House in 3 Hours, 44 Minutes & 59 Seconds," Avraham Y. Goldratt Institute, www.goldratt.com. "Fastest House in the World," Habitat for Humanity International, www.habitat.org.

Chapter 10

1. Lau-Tzu, *Tao Te Ching*, 515 B.C.

2. Kotter, John P., "What Leaders Really Do," *Harvard Business Review,* 68 (3), (May-June 1990), pp. 103–111.

3. Cohen, A.R., and Bradford, David L. *Influence Without Authority,* New York: John Wiley and Sons, 1990.

4. This discussion is based on Sayles, Leonard R., *Leadership: Managing in Real Organizations,* New York: McGraw-Hill, 1989, pp. 70–78.

5. See for example: Pinto, Jeffrey L., and Sleven, D. P., "Critical Success Factors in Successful Project Implementation," *IEEE Transactions in Engineering Management,* 34 (1) 1987, pp. 22–27; Pinto, Jeffrey L., and Samuel K., Mantel, "The Causes of Project Failure," *IEEE Transactions in Engineering Management,* 37 (4), (1990), pp. 269–276.

6. Kouzes, James M., and Posner, Barry Z., *The Leadership Challenge.* San Francisco: Jossey-Bass, 1987.

7. This discussion of managing upward relations is based on Sayles, Leonard R., 1989, Ibid., pp. 136–145; Graham, Robert J., and Englund, Randall L., *Creating an Environment for Successful Projects,* San Francisco: Jossey-Bass, 1997, p. 136.

8. Adapted from Perkins, Dennis N. T., *Leading at the Edge: Leadership Lessons from the Extraordinary Saga of Shackleton's Antarctica Expedition,* New York: AMACOM press, 2000, p. 94–95 and Lansing, Alfred, *Endurance: Shackleton's Incredible Voyage* New York: Carroll & Graf, 1998, p. 127.

9. This discussion of project management and ethics is based on: Cabanis, Jeannette, "A Question of Ethics: The Issues Project Managers Face and How They Resolve Them." *PMNetwork,* December 1996, pp. 19–24. Badaracco Jr., J. L., and Webb, A.P., "Business Ethics: A View from the Trenches," *California Management Review,* 37 (2), (Winter 1995), pp. 8–28. Robb, David J., "Ethics in Project Management: Issues, Practice, and Motive," *PMNetwork,* December 1996, pp. 13–18.

10. Cohen, A. R., and Bradford, David L., 1990, Ibid.

11. Covey, Stephen R. *The Seven Habits of Highly Effective People,* New York: Simon & Schuster, 1989.

12. See Kanter, Rosabeth M., "Power Failure in Management Circuits," *Harvard Business Review,* (July-August 1979), pp. 65–75. Posner, Barry Z., and Kouzes, John R. Kouzes, Ibid., 1993.

13. Sayles, Leonard R., Ibid, 1989, pp. 296.

14. Cited in Englehart, John E., and Malkin, Martin F., "From the Laboratory to the Pharmacy: Therapeutic Drug Development at Merck Sharp & Dohme Research Laboratories," *PMNetwork,* 3 (6), (August, 1989), pp. 11–28.

15. For examples of lists of characteristics of effective project managers see Posner, Barry Z., "What It Takes to Be an Effective Project Manager," *Project Management Journal,* (March 1987), pp. 51–55. Shenhar, Aaron J., and Nofziner, Brian, "A New Model for Training Project Managers," *Proceedings of the 28th Annual Project Management Institute Symposium,* Chicago, Illinois, (September 29–October 1, 1997), pp. 301–306; Shtub, Avraham, Bard, Jonathan F., and Globerson, Shlomo, *Project Management: Engineering, Technology, and Implementation,* Englewood Cliffs, NJ: Prentice-Hall, 1994; Wysocki, Robert K., Beck, Robert, and Crane, David B., *Effective Project Management,* New York: John Wiley & Sons, 1995.

16. For a practical elaboration of what it means to be a systems thinker see Senge, Peter M., *The Fifth Discipline,* New York: Doubleday, 1990.

17. For a more extensive discussion of the habit of being proactive see Covey, Ibid., 1989, pp. 65–94.

Chapter 11

1. Tuchman, B. W., "Developmental Sequence of Small Groups," *Psychological Bulletin* 63, 1965, pp. 384–399; Tuchman, B. W., and Jensen, M.C., "Stages of Small Group Development Revisited," *Group and Organizational Studies,* 2, (1977), pp. 419–427.

2. Homans, George C., *Social Behavior: Its Elementary Forms*, New York: Harcourt Brace Jovanovich, 1961; Sherif, M., *Group Conflict and Cooperation: Their Social Psychology*, Chicago: Aldine Publishing Co., 1967; Seta, J. J., Paulus, P.B., and Schkade, J., "Effects of Group Size and Proximity under Cooperative and Competitive Conditions" *Journal of Personality and Social Psychology*, 98 (2), (1976), pp. 47–53; Zander, A., *Making Groups Effective*, San Francisco: Jossey-Bass, 1982; Smith, G. Preston and Reinertsen, Donald G. *Developing Products in Half the Time.* New York: Van Nostrand Reinhold, 1995.

3. These considerations are based in part on Lientz, Bennet P., and Rea, Kathryn P., *Project Management for the 21st Century*, San Diego: Academic Press, 1995, pp. 118–119.

4. Morton, Shirley, Donna, and Danelle. *Managing Martians.* New York: Broadway Books.

5. Rebello, K., "Inside Microsoft," *Business Week*, July 15, 1996, pp. 56–67; Filipczak, B., "Beyond the Gates of Microsoft," *Training*, September 1992, pp. 37–44.

6. Katzenbach, Jon R., and Smith, Douglas K., "The Discipline of Teams," *Harvard Business Review*, 71 (2), (March/April 1993), pp. 111–121; Bolman, Lee G., and Deal, Terrence E., "What Makes a Team Work?" *Organizational Dynamics*, 21 (2), (Autumn 1992), pp. 34–45; Katz, Ralph, "How a Team at Digital Equipment Designed the 'Alpha' Chip," *The Human Side of Managing Technological Innovation*, ed. Ralph Katz, New York: Oxford Press, 1997, pp. 137–148.

7. Frame, J. D., *Managing Projects in Organizations*, San Francisco: Jossey-Bass, 1995, pp. 101–103.

8. This anecdote was provided by Dr. Frances Hartman, University of Calgary, Alberta.

9. Katzenbach, Jon R., and Smith, Douglas K., *The Wisdom of Teams*, Boston: Harvard Business School Press, 1993, pp. 67–72.

10. Quoted in Senge, Peter M, *The Fifth Discipline*, New York: Doubleday, 1990, p. 209.

11. Bowen, Kent H., Clark, Kim B., Holloway, Charles A., and Wheelwright, Steven C., *The Perpetual Enterprise Machine*, New York: Oxford Press, 1994, p. 72.

12. Kidder, Tracy, *The Soul of the New Machine*, New York: Avon Books, 1981, pp. 221–232.

13. Katz, Ralph, "How a Team at Digital Equipment Designed the 'Alpha' Chip," *The Human Side of Managing Technological Innovation.* ed. Ralph Katz, New York: Oxford Press, 1997, pp. 137–148.

14. Ritti, Richard R., *The Ropes to Skip and the Ropes to Know: Studies in Organizational Behavior*, 5th ed., New York: Wiley, pp. 89–90.

15. This discussion is based on N.R.F. Maier's classic research: Maier, N.R.F., *Problem Solving Discussion and Conferences*, New York: McGraw-Hill, 1963; Maier, N.R.F., *Problem Solving and Creativity in Individuals and Groups*, Belmont, CA: Brooks-Cole, 1970.

16. Janis, Irving L., *Groupthink*, Boston: Houghton Mifflin, 1982, p. 36.

17. This section is based in part on Johansen, Robert, Sibbet, David, Benson, Suzyn, Martin, Alexia, Mittman, Robert, and Saffo, Paul,. *Leading Business Teams: How Teams*

Can Use Technology and Group Process Tools to Enhance Performance, Reading, MA: Addison-Wesley, 1991, pp. 93–98.

18. Leavitt, Harold J., and Lipman-Blumen, Jean, "Hot Groups," *Harvard Business Review,* 73 (1995), pp. 109–116.

Chapter 12

1. Kanter, Rosabeth M., "Collaborative Advantage: The Art of Alliances." *Harvard Business Review*, 72, (4), (July–August 1994), p. 96.

2. Referenced in DiDonato, S. Leonard., "Contract Disputes: Alternatives for Dispute Resolution (Part 1)," *PM Network,* (May 1993), pp. 19–23.

3. Construction Industry Institute, "In Search of Partnering Excellence," *Special Report 17-1*, July 1991, p. 2.

4. Cowan, Charles, Gray, Clifford, and Larson, Erik, "Project Partnering." *Project Management Journal* 24, (4), (December 1992), p. 5. Note: A significant portion of the material on partnering implementation is drawn from this article.

5. Construction Industry Institute, op. cit., pp. 8–10.

6. Cowan, et al., op cit., p. 6; Construction Industry Institute, op. cit. p. 5.

7. Authors, research on project partnering includes: Cowan, op. cit.; Larson, Erik, "Project Partnering: Results of a Study of 280 Construction Projects," *Journal of Management Engineering (ASCE)* 11, (2), pp. 30–35; Larson, Erik, and Gray, Clifford, "Project Partnering in the Construction Industry: The Wave of the Future," *National Productivity Review*, Winter 1994/95, pp. 15–24; Larson, Erik, "Partnering on Construction Projects: A Study of the Relationship between Partnering Activities and Project Success," *IEEE Transactions in Engineering Management*, 44, (2), (May 1997), pp. 188–195; Larson, Erik, and Drexler, John A., "Barriers to Project Partnering: Report from the Firing Line," *Project Management Journal*, 28, (1), (March 1997), pp. 46–52.

8. For a more detailed description see Adams, Chris E., "Industrial Cooperation in a Competitive Environment—The Story of the Advanced Photo System," *Proceedings of 28th Annual Project Management Institute 1997 Seminars and Symposium,* pp. 907–912.; Adams, Chris, "A Kodak Moment," *PM Network*, 12, (1), (1998), pp. 21–28. The Orion project was named Project Of the Year by the Project Management Institute.

9. Hedberg, Bo, Dahlgren, Goran, Hansson, Jorgen, and Olve, Nils-Goran, *Virtual Organizations and Beyond*, New York: John Wiley & Sons, 1997, pp. 82–84.

10. Kezsbom, Deborah S., Schilling, Donald L., and Edward, Katherine A., *Dynamic Project Management*, New York: Wiley, 1989, p. 255.

11. The majority of this segment on negotiating is based on Fisher, Roger, and Ury, William, *Getting to Yes: Negotiating Agreement Without Giving In*, 2 ed, New York: Penguin Books, 1991.

12. This parable was referenced in Quinn, Robert E., Faerman, Sue R., Thompson, Michael P., and McGrath, Michael R., *Becoming a Master Manager: A Competency Framework*. New York: Wiley, 1990, p. 290.

13. Cialdini, Robert H., *Influence: The Psychology of Persuasion*, New York: Morrow, 1993, pp. 167–207.
14. For a more in-depth discussion of this habit see: Covey, Stephen R., *The Seven Habits of Highly Effective People*, New York: Simon and Schuster: 1990, pp. 235–260.
15. Other books on negotiating we would recommend include: Economy, Peter, *Business Negotiating Basics*, Burr Ridge, IL, 1994; Shell, G. Richard, *Bargaining for Advantage*, New York: Penguin, 1999; Fisher, Roger, and Brown, Scott Brown, *Getting Together: Building a Relationship that Gets to Yes*, Boston: Houghton Mifflin Co., 1988; Cohen, Herb, *You Can Negotiate Anything*, Secaucus, NJ: Lyle Stuart, Inc, 1980.

Appendix 12A

1. For more detailed information on contract management see: Martin, M., Teagarden, C., and Lambreth, C., *Contract Administration for the Project Manager*, Upper Darby, PA: Project Management Institute, 1983; Cavendish, P., and Martin, M., *Negotiating and Contracting for Project Management*, Upper Darby, PA: Project Management Institute, 1982; Downey, J., Gilbert, R., and Gilbert, P., *Successful Interior Projects Through Effective Contract Documents*, New York: R. S. Means, 1995; Cohen, Cary, *Effective Contract Administration*, New York: Amacom Books, 1996.
2. It is beyond the scope of this book to discuss submitting proposals and bids. For information on these subjects see: Fraser, J., *Professional Project Proposals*, New York: Gower, 1995; Barakat, R., "Writing to Win New Business," *PM Network*, November, 1991; Beveridge, Jim M., and Velton, J. I., *Creating Superior Proposals*, Talent, OR: J. M. Beveridge Associates, 1978.
3. Weston, D. C., and Gibson, G. E., "Partnering-Project Performance in U.S. Army Corps of Engineers," *Journal of Management Engineering,* ASCE, 9 (4), (1993), pp. 410–425.

Chapter 13

1. Brooks, Frederick P., The *Mythical Man-Month*, Reading, MA.: Addison Wesley, anniversary ed., 1997, p. 153.
2. For a complete and interesting discussion of the theory of constraints see Goldratt, Eliyahu, *Critical Chain,* Great Barrington, MA, North River Press, 1997. See also Newbold, Robert C., "Leveraging Project Resources: Tools for the Next Century," *Proceedings of 28th Annual Project Management Institute 1997 Seminars and Symposium,* Newtown Square, PA: Project Management Institute. 1997), pp. 417–21; Noreen, Eric, Smith, Debra, and Mackey, James, *The Theory of Constraints and Its Implication for Management Accounting,* Great Barrington, MA: North River Press, 1995; Leach, Lawrence P., "Critical Chain Project Management," *Proceedings of 29th Annual Project Management Institute, 1998, Seminars and Symposium,* Newtown Square, PA: Project Management Institute, 1998, pp. 1239–1244.
3. There are many publications on the system. A good discussion is found in *Cost/ Schedule Control Systems Criteria: Joint Implementation Guide,* Departments of the

Air Force, the Army, the Navy, and the Defense Logistics Agency, Washington, D.C.: U.S. Department of Defense, 1987. See also *Performance Measurement for Selected Acquisition*, Department of Defense Instruction no. 500.2, part 11, section B, attachment 2, Washington, D.C.: U.S. Department of Defense, 1991.

4. Quentin, Fleming W., and Koppelman, Joel M., "The Earned Value Concept: Back to Basics," *PM Network*, 8, (1), (January 1994), pp. 27–29. See also Quentin, Fleming W., and Koppelman, Joel M., "Forecasting the Final Cost and Schedule Results," *PM Network,* 10, (1), (January 1996), pp. 13–19: and Quentin, Fleming W., and Koppelman, Joel M., "The Earned Value Body of Knowledge," *PM Network*, 11, (5), (May 1996), pp. 11–15.

5. Gray, Clifford, and Larson, Erik, *Project Management: The Managerial Process,* Boston, MA: McGraw-Hill 2000, pp. 408–409.

6. Quentin and Koppelman, op.cit.

7. Ibid.

8. Brandon, Jr., Daniel M., "Implementing Earned Value Easily and Effectively," *Project Management Journal*, 29, (2), (June 1998), pp. 11–18.

9. Keifer, S. Craig, "Scope Creep . . . Not Necessarily a Bad Thing," *PM Network* 10, (5), (May 1996), pp. 33–35.

10. Ibid.

Chapter 14

1. For a discussion of separating the audit group from the project priority team see Balachandra, R., and Raelin, A. J., "How To Decide When To Abandon A Project," *Research Management*, 23 (4), (July 1980), pp. 24–29.

2. For an extensive list and another view see Buell, C.K., "When to Terminate a Research and Development Project," *Research Management,* 10 (4), (July 1987), pp. 275–284.

3. Giangreco, D. M., and Griswold, Terry A*., Delta: America's Elite Counterterrorist Force*, New York: Motorbooks International, 1992.

4. Daw, Catherine, and Sills, Suzanne, "Kick-Starting Project Management for a $1.7B Transformation Program in Bell Canada," *Proceedings of 28ᵗʰ Annual Project Management Institute 1997 Seminars and Symposium,* Newtown Square, PA: PMI, 1997 p. 728.

5. Graham, Robert J., and Englund, Randall L., *Creating an Environment for Successful Projects: The Quest to Manage Project Management*, San Francisco: Jossey-Bass Inc., 1997, pp. 175–223.

6. Graham and Randall op. cit. pp. 203–223.

7. Staw, Berry M., and Ross, Jerry, "Knowing When to Pull The Plug," *Harvard Business Review*, (March-April 1987), pp. 68–74.

8. Ashley, David B., Lurie, Clive S., and Jaselskis, Edward J., "Determinants of Construction Project Success." *Project Management Journal*, 18 (2), (June, 1987), p. 72; Pinto, Jefferey K., and Slevin, Dennis P., "Critical Success Factors Across The Project Life Cycle," *Project Management Journal*, 19 (3), (June 1988), p. 72; Gobeli, David

B., and Larson, Erik, "Barriers Affecting Project Success." In *1986 Proceedings Project Management Institute: Measuring Success*, Upper Darby, PA: Project Management Institute, 1986, pp. 22–29.

9. Gobeli and Larson op. cit.
10. For a detailed termination checklist see Archibald, Russell D., *Managing High-Technology Programs and Projects*. New York: John Wiley & Sons, 1992, pp. 364–370.
11. See for example, Romanoff, K. E., "The Ten Commandments of Performance Management." *Personnel*, 66 (1), (1989), pp. 24–26; Latham, Gary P., and Wexley, K. N., *Increasing Productivity through Performance Appraisal*. 2nd ed., Reading, MA.: Addison-Wesley, 1994; Myere, H. H., Kay, E. A., and French Jr., J.R.P., "Split Role in Performance Appraisal," *Harvard Business Review*, 43, (1965), pp. 123–129.
12. Adapted from O'Reilly, Brian, "360 Degree Feedback Can Change Your Life," *Fortune*, (October, 17, 1994), pp. 93–100. Hoffman, Robert, "Ten Reasons You Should Be Using 360 Degree Feedback," *HRMagazine*, (April 1995), 82–85.

Chapter 15

1. Taverna, Michael A., "Europe Advances ATV Development for ISS," *Aviation Week and Space Technology*, (November 30, 1998), p. 29.
2. Source: ⟨www.ornl.gov/TechResources/Human_Genome/home.html⟩.
3. Dinsmore, Paul C., "Toward a Corporate Project Management Culture: Fast Tracking into the Future," *Proceedings of the Project Management Institute 28th Annual Seminars & Symposium*, 1997, p. 450.
4. Carnegie Mellon University and Software Engineering Institute, "Capability Maturity Model—Integrated Systems/Software Engineering," version 0.2b, September 1999; Ficher, Anita, and Levin, Ginger, "Project Management Maturity Model," *Proceedings of the Project Management Institute 28th* Annual Seminars & Symposium, Chicago, Ill, October 1, 1997, pp. 1028–1035; Kerzner, Harold, *Strategic Planning for Project Management using a Project Management Maturity Model*, New York: John Wiley & Sons, 2001.
5. Saia, Rick, "Harvesting Project Leaders," *Computerworld* 31, (29), (July 21, 1997), p. 1.
6. You can contact PMI at Project Management Institute, 130 South State Road; Upper Darby, PA 19082 or at their Web site ⟨www.pmi.org⟩.
7. Cited by Nellenbach, Joanita M., "People Skills Top Technical Knowledge, CIO Insists," *PMNetwork*, (August, 1999), pp. 7–8.
8. For some useful advice on how to find a mentor see Mackay, Harvey, *Dig Your Well Before You're Thirsty*, New York: Doubleday, 1997.

GLOSSARY

activity Task(s) of the project that consumes time while people/equipment either work or wait.

activity duration Estimate of time (hours, days, weeks, months, etc.) necessary to complete a project task.

actual cost of the work performed (ACWP) Actual cost of the work performed in a given time period. The sum of the costs incurred in accomplishing work.

AOA Activity-on-arrow method for drawing project networks. The activity is shown as an arrow.

AON Activity-on-node method for drawing project networks. The activity is on the node (rectangle).

backward pass The method used to compute the late start and finish times for each activity in the project network.

balanced matrix A matrix structure in which the project manager and functional managers share roughly equal authority over the project. The project manager decides what needs to be done; functional managers are concerned with how it will be accomplished.

balanced scorecard method Model that measures the long-run results of major program activities in four areas—customer, internal, innovation and learning, and financial.

bar chart A graphic presentation of project activities depicted as a time-scaled bar line (also called a Gantt chart).

baseline A concrete document and commitment; it represents the first real plan with cost, schedule, and resource allocation. The planned cost and schedule performance are used to measure actual cost and schedule performance. Serves as an anchor point for measuring performance.

brainstorming Generating as many ideas/solutions as possible without critical judgment.

budget at completion (BAC) Budgeted cost at completion. The total budgeted cost of the baseline or project cost accounts.

budgeted cost of the work performed (BCWP) The value for completed work measured in terms of the planned budget for the work. The earned value or original budgeted cost for work actually completed.

budget reserve Reserves set up to cover identified risks that may occur and influence baseline tasks or costs. These reserves are typically controlled by the project manager and the project team. See *management reserve.*

burst activity An activity that has more than one activity immediately following it.

change management system A defined process for authorizing and documenting changes in the scope of a project.

chart of accounts A hierarchical numbering system used to identify tasks, deliverables, and organizational responsibility in the work breakdown structure.

concurrent engineering or simultaneous engineering Cross-functional teamwork in new-product development projects that provides product design, quality engineering, and manufacturing process engineering all at the same time.

consensus decision making Reaching a decision that all involved parties basically agree with and support.

contingency plan A plan that covers possible identified project risks that may materialize over the life of the project.

contingency reserves Usually an amount of money or time set aside to cover identified and unforeseen project risks.

contract A formal agreement between two parties wherein one party (the contractor) obligates itself to perform a service and the other party (the client) obligates itself to do something in return, usually in the form of a payment to the contractor.

cost account A control point of one or more work packages used to plan, schedule, and control the project. The sum of all the project cost accounts represents the total cost of the project.

cost performance index (CPI) The ratio of budgeted costs to actual costs (BCWP/ACWP).

cost-plus contract A contract in which the contractor is reimbursed for all direct allowable costs (materials, labor, travel) plus an additional fee to cover overhead and profit.

cost variance (CV) The difference between BCWP and ACWP (CV = BCWP − ACWP). Tells if the work accomplished cost more or less than was planned at any point over the life of the project.

crash point The most a project activity time can realistically be compressed with the resources available to the organization.

crash time The shortest time an activity can be completed (assuming a reasonable level of resources).

critical path The longest activity path(s) through the network. The critical path can be distinguished by identifying the collection of activities that all have the same minimum slack.

critical path method (CPM) A scheduling method based on the estimates of time required to complete activities on the critical path. The method computes early, late, and slack times for each activity in the network. It

establishes a planned project duration, if one is not imposed on the project.

culture shock A natural psychological disorientation that most people suffer when they move to a culture different from their own.

dedicated project team An organizational structure in which all of the resources needed to accomplish a project are assigned full-time to the project.

direct costs Costs that are clearly charged to a specific work package—usually labor, materials, or equipment.

dummy activity An activity that does not consume time; it is represented on the AOA network as a dashed line. A dummy activity is used to ensure a unique identification number for parallel activities and used to maintain dependencies among activities on the project network.

duration (DUR) The time needed to complete an activity, a path, or a project.

dysfunctional conflict Disagreement that does not improve project performance.

early finish The earliest an activity can finish if all its preceding activities are finished by their early finish times (EF = ES + DUR).

early start The earliest an activity can start. It is the largest early finish of all its immediate predecessors (ES = EF − DUR).

enterprise project management (EPM) Centralized selection and management of a portfolio of projects to ensure the allocation of resources to projects are directed and balanced toward the strategic focus of the organization.

escalation A control mechanism for resolving problems in which people at the lowest appropriate level attempt to resolve a problem within a set time limit or the problem is "escalated" to the next level of management.

estimated cost at completion (EAC) The sum of actual costs to date plus revised estimated costs for the work remaining in the WBS.

event A point in time when an activity(s) is started or completed. It does not consume time.

Failure Mode and Effects Analysis (FEMA) Each potential risk is assessed in terms of severity of impact, probability of the event occurring, and ease of detection.

fast-tracking Accelerating project completion typically by re-arranging the network schedule and using start-to-start lags.

fixed-price or "lump-sum" contract A contract in which the contractor agrees to perform all the work specified in the contract at a predetermined, fixed price.

float See *slack*.

forecast at completion (FAC) The forecasted cost at completion—using forecast equation.

forward pass The method for determining the early start and finish times for each activity in the project network.

free slack The maximum amount of time an activity can be delayed from its early start (ES) without affecting the early start (ES) of any activity immediately following it.

functional conflict Disagreement that contributes to the objectives of the project.

functional matrix A matrix structure in which functional managers have primary control over project activities and the project manager coordinates project work.

functional organization A hierarchical organizational structure in which departments represent individual disciplines such as engineering, marketing, purchasing.

Gantt chart See *bar chart*.

going native Adopting the customs, values, and prerogatives of a foreign culture.

Golden Rule Do unto others as you would wish them to do unto you.

groupthink A tendency of members in highly cohesive groups to lose their critical evaluative capabilities.

hammock activity A special-purpose, aggregate activity that identifies the use of fixed resources or costs over a segment of the project—e.g., a consultant. Derives its duration from the time span between other activities.

implementation gap The lack of consensus between the goals set by top management and those independently set by lower levels of management. This lack of consensus leads to confusion and poor allocation of organization resources.

infrastructure Basic services (i.e., communication, transportation, power) needed to support project completion.

insensitive network A network in which the critical path is likely to remain stable during the life of the project.

lag The amount of time between the end of one activity and the start of another. A duration assigned to the activity dependency. The minimum amount of time a dependent activity must be delayed to begin or end.

lag relationship The relationship between the start and/or finish of a project activity and the start and/or finish of another activity. The most common lag relationships are (1) finish-to-start, (2) finish-to-finish, (3) start-to-start, and (4) start-to-finish.

late finish The latest an activity can finish and not delay a following activity (LF = LS + DUR).

late start The latest an activity can start and not delay a following activity. It is the largest late finish (LF) of all activities immediately preceding it (LS = LF − DUR).

law of reciprocity People are obligated to grant a favor comparable to the one they received.

level of effort (LOE) Work packages that represent time-related activities. These activities, such as administrative support, computer support, legal, public relations, etc. exist for a segment or the duration of the project. LOE work packages have no measurable outputs.

macro and micro estimating Macro estimates are top-down, rough estimates that use surrogates to estimate project time and cost and are used to determine project selection or go-ahead decisions. Bottom-up micro estimates are detailed estimates of work packages usually made by those who most familiar with the task.

management by wandering around (MBWA) A management style in which managers spend majority of their time outside their offices interacting with key people.

management reserve A percentage of the total project budget reserved for contingencies. The fund exists to cover unforeseen, new problems—not unnecessary over-runs. The reserve is designed to reduce the risk of project delays. Management reserves are typically controlled by the project owner or project manager. See *budget reserve.*

matrix Any organizational structure in which the project manager shares responsibility with the functional managers for assigning priorities and for directing the work of individuals assigned to the project.

mentor Typically a more experienced manager who acts as a personal coach and champions a person's ambitions.

merge activity An activity that has more than one activity immediately preceding it.

met expectations model Customer satisfaction is a function of the extent to which perceived performance exceeds expectations.

milestone An event that represents significant, identifiable accomplishment toward the project's completion.

mitigating risk Action taken to either reduce the likelihood that a risk will occur and/or the impact the risk will have on the project.

Monte Carlo simulation A method of simulating project activity durations using probabilities. The method identifies the percentage of times activities and paths are critical over thousands of simulations.

negative reinforcement A motivational technique in which negative stimuli are removed once desired behavior is exhibited.

net present value (NPV) A minimum desired rate of return discount (e.g., 15 percent) is used to compute present value of all future cash inflows and outflows.

network A logic diagram arranged in a prescribed format (e.g., AOA or AON) consisting of activities, sequences, interrelationships, and dependencies.

network sensitivity The likelihood that the critical path will change on a project.

objective An end you seek to create or acquire. Should be specific, measurable, realistic, assignable, and include a time frame for accomplishment.

organizational culture A system of shared norms, beliefs, values, and assumptions held by an organization's members.

organizational politics Actions by individuals or groups of individuals to acquire, develop, and use power and other resources to obtain preferred outcomes when there is uncertainty or disagreement over choices.

organization breakdown structure (OBS) A structure used to assign responsibility for work packages.

parallel activity One or more activities that can be carried on concurrently or simultaneously.

partnering See *project partnering.*

path A sequence of connected activities.

payback method The time it takes to pay back the project investment (Investment/net annual savings). The method does not consider the time value of money or the life of the investment.

precedence diagram method A method used to construct a project network that uses nodes (e.g., a rectangle) to represent activities and connecting arrows to indicate dependencies.

principle of negotiation A process of negotiation that aims to achieve win/win results.

priority system The process used to select projects. The system uses selected criteria for evaluating and selecting projects that are strongly linked to higher level strategies and objectives.

priority team The group (sometimes the project office) responsible for selecting, overseeing, and updating project priority selection criteria.

project A complex, nonroutine, one-time effort to create a product or service limited by time, budget, and specifications.

project interfaces The intersections between a project and other groups of people both within and outside the organization.

projectitis A social phenomenon in which project members exhibit inappropriately intense loyalty to the project.

projectized organization An organizational structure in which core work is accomplished by project teams.

project kick-off meeting Typically the first meeting of the project team.

project life cycle The stages found in all projects—definition, planning, execution, and delivery.

project management The application of knowledge, skills, tools, and techniques to project activities to meet the project requirements.

project management office (PMO) A centralized unit within an organization or department that oversees and improves the management of projects.

project manager The individual responsible for managing a project.

project matrix A matrix structure in which the project manager has primary control over project activities and functional managers support project work.

project partnering A nonbinding method of transforming contractual relationships into a cohesive, cooperative project team with a single set of goals and established procedures for resolving disputes in a timely manner.

project portfolio Group of projects that have been selected for implementation balanced by project type, risk, and ranking by selected criteria.

project sponsor Typically a high-ranking manager who champions and supports a project.

project vision An image of what the project will accomplish.

positive synergy A characteristic of high-performing teams in which group performance is greater than the sum of individual contributions.

ratio (parametric) methods Uses the ratio of past actual costs for similar work to estimate the cost for a potential project. This macro method of forecasting cost does not provide a sound basis for project cost control since it does not recognize differences among projects.

resource Any person, groups, skill, equipment or material used to accomplish a task, work package, or activity.

resource-constrained project A project that assumes resources are limited (fixed) and therefore time is variable.

responsibility matrix A matrix whose intersection point shows the relationship between an activity (work package) and the person/group responsible for its completion.

risk The chance that an undesirable project event will occur and the consequences of all its possible outcomes.

"sacred cow" A project that is a favorite of a powerful management figure who is usually the champion for the project.

schedule performance index (SPI) The ratio of the work performed to work scheduled (BCWP/BCWS).

schedule variance (SV) The difference between the planned dollar value of the work actually completed and the value of the work scheduled to be completed at a given point in time ($SV = BCWP - BCWS$). Schedule variance contains no critical path information.

scope statement A definition of the end result or mission of a project. Scope statements typically includes project objectives, deliverables, milestones, specifications, and limits and exclusions.

slack Time an activity can be delayed before it becomes critical.

splitting A scheduling technique in which work is interrupted on one activity and the resource is assigned to another activity for a period of time, then reassigned to work on the original activity.

stakeholder Individuals and organizations that are actively involved in the project, or whose interests may be positively or negatively affected as a result of project execution or completion. They may also exert influence over the project and its results.

systems thinking A holistic approach to viewing problems that emphasizes understanding the interactions among different problem factors.

task See *activity*.

team-building A process designed to improve the performance of a team.

360-degree feedback A multirater appraisal system based on performance information that is gathered from multiple sources (superiors, peers, subordinates, customers).

time-constrained project A project that assumes time is fixed and, if resources are needed, they will be added.

Total slack The amount of time an activity can be delayed and not affect the project duration ($TS = LS - ES$ or $LF - EF$).

variance at completion (VAC) Indicates expected actual cost over- or underrun at completion (VAC = BAC − EAC).

virtual organization An alliance of several organizations created for the purpose of creating products and services for customers.

virtual project team Spatially separated project team whose members are unable to communicate face to face. Communication is usually by electronic means.

work breakdown structure (WBS) A hierarchical method that successively subdivides the work of the project into smaller detail.

ACRONYMS

ACWP	Actual cost of work performed		**KISS**	Keep it simple, stupid
AOA	Activity on arrow		**LF**	Late finish
AON	Activity on node		**LS**	Late start
BAC	Budget at completion		**MBWA**	Management by wandering around
BCWP	Budgeted cost of work performed		**NIH**	Not invented here
BCWS	Budgeted cost of work scheduled		**NPV**	Net present value
C-C	Critical-chain approach to project planning and management		**OBS**	Organization breakdown structure
CPI	Cost performance index		**PCI**	Percent complete index
CPM	Critical path method		**PCI-B**	Percent complete index—budget costs
CV	Cost variance		**PCI-C**	Percent complete index—actual costs
DU	Duration		**PDM**	Precedence diagram method
EAC	Estimate at completion (with revised cost estimates)		**PERT**	Project evaluation review technique
			PMO	Project management office
EF	Early finish		**PV**	Price variance
EPM	Enterprise project management		**RM**	Responsibility matrix
ES	Early start		**SPI**	Schedule performance index
ETC	Estimate to complete		**SV**	Schedule variance
EV	Earned value		**TF**	Total float
FAC	Forecast at completion (formula)		**UV**	Usage variance
FF	Free float		**VAC**	Variance at completion
IFB	Invitation to bid		**WBS**	Work breakdown structure

Project Management Equations

$$(PCI - B) = \frac{BCWP}{BAC}$$

$$CV = BCWP - ACWP$$

$$CPI = \frac{BCWP}{ACWP}$$

$$FAC = \frac{(BAC - BCWP)}{\left(\dfrac{BCWP}{ACWP}\right)} + ACWP$$

$$(PCI - C) = \frac{ACWP}{EAC} \text{ or } \frac{ACWP}{FAC}$$

$$SV = BCWP - BCWS$$

$$SPI = \frac{BCWP}{BCWS}$$

$$VAC = BAC - FAC \text{ or } BAC - EAC$$

INDEX

Page numbers in *italics* denote figures; those followed by "t" denote tables.

About the Authors

Clifford Gray, D.B.A., is professor emeritus of management at Oregon State University. The president of Project Management International, Inc., since 1977, Dr. Gray has published dozens of articles on operations and project management and taught numerous popular executive development seminars and workshops.

Erik Larson, Ph.D., is a professor and chairman of the Department of Management, Marketing, and International Business at Oregon State University's College of Business. A published author and recognized authority on matrix management, product development, and project partnering, Dr. Larson teaches executive, graduate, and undergraduate courses on project management, organizational behavior, and leadership.